MW01037774

THE WAR ON DRUGS

The War on Drugs

A History

Edited by
David Farber

NEW YORK UNIVERSITY PRESS
New York

NEW YORK UNIVERSITY PRESS
New York
www.nyupress.org

References to Internet websites (URLs) were accurate at the time of writing. Neither the author nor New York University Press is responsible for URLs that may have expired or changed since the manuscript was prepared.

Library of Congress Cataloging-in-Publication Data
Names: Farber, David R., editor.
Title: The war on drugs : a history / edited by David Farber.
Description: New York : New York University Press, [2021] | Includes
    bibliographical references.
Identifiers: LCCN 2021009013 | ISBN 9781479811359 (hardback) |
    ISBN 9781479811366 (paperback) | ISBN 9781479811427 (ebook) |
    ISBN 9781479811397 (ebook other)
Subjects: LCSH: Drug control—United States—History. | Drug traffic—
    United States—History. | Drug abuse—Government
    policy—United States—History.
Classification: LCC HV5825 .W3812777 2021 | DDC 364.1/770973—dc23
LC record available at https://lccn.loc.gov/2021009013

New York University Press books are printed on acid-free paper, and their binding materials are chosen for strength and durability. We strive to use environmentally responsible suppliers and materials to the greatest extent possible in publishing our books.

Manufactured in the United States of America

10 9 8 7 6 5 4 3 2 1

Also available as an ebook

CONTENTS

PART V: THE ALTERNATIVE TO WAR

Introduction

DAVID FARBER

Over the past fifty years, the United States government has spent over a trillion dollars fighting a "War on Drugs." This massive budgetary expenditure and concomitant commitment to a fiercely punitive treatment of illegal drug users and sellers represents a major inflection point in Americans' much longer campaign against the distribution and use of cocaine, cannabis, heroin, and a number of other targeted intoxicants. As this collection demonstrates, the scope, strategy, and tactics of that extraordinarily costly and punitive war have changed over time.

One near-constant, however, has been drug warriors' relentless effort to criminalize people who sell or use illegal drugs. In recent years, about 1.5 million people have been arrested annually on drug charges—and most of these arrests involve cannabis. Nearly five hundred thousand Americans are currently incarcerated for drug offenses. Exactly which Americans authorities have chosen to imprison on drug charges is another piece of the story this collection offers. Suffice it to say here that Black Americans are almost six times more likely than white Americans to have been incarcerated on drug charges, even as white and Black Americans use drugs at about the same rate. Currently, the federal government expends well over $9 million every day, or well over $3 billion a year, to lock up drug offenders; states and localities, combined, pay far more.[1]

Today, in part as a response to those human and financial costs, Americans are fast losing their faith that a "War on Drugs" is fair, moral, or sensible, let alone winnable. Recent surveys show that only about one in ten Americans believe that anyone should go to jail for possessing a small amount of marijuana. During the 2020 election campaign, erstwhile drug warrior extraordinaire President Joe Biden went further, arguing, "No one should be incarcerated for drug use [of any kind]." He insisted that education, prevention, and redemption—not incarceration—should govern American drug policy.[2]

At least one recent survey of American public opinion indicates that Biden's position has become a majoritarian one in the US. Fifty-five percent of those surveyed said that *all* drug offenses should be treated not as felonies but simply as civil offenses. In the words of the survey, such offenses "would be treated like minor traffic violations rather than crimes."[3] That newfound perspective, as this collection indicates, has been hard won, and it has yet to change fundamental aspects of the punitive drug regime that has long reigned in the US.

Even though the War on Drugs has lost a great deal of popular support, the "sunk costs" of the war continue to drive it forward. People increasingly worry about the financial and human cost of prisons larded with convicted non-violent drug offenders, but prison guard unions, police unions and fraternal organizations, private contractors, and other economic interests fight to keep the drug offender–to–prison pipeline flowing. And after fifty years of successful drug-dependent state building, fiefdoms of drug-fighting agencies and organizations at every level of government insist on the continued need to maintain their institutional prerogatives, power, and funding.[4] Pharmaceutical industries, as well as political careers, have been built on the logic of a punitive War on Drugs.[5] A great many voters, while increasingly uncomfortable with this fifty-year-long war are—rightfully—anxious about what could and should replace it. These factors, and more, have made fundamental, let alone equitable, change in American drug policy an extraordinary political challenge.

In this collection, we examine how and why so many fought so hard to criminalize the use and sale of such a great variety of drugs. We also draw attention to those who fought both the logic and the punitive practices of the War on Drugs. Writing in this seemingly transformational moment, we also ponder what might replace this war. Should the model Americans use to regulate "white market" drugs expand to include currently illegal "black market" drugs?[6] Could public health approaches further ameliorate drug addiction? Should legalization extend beyond cannabis to other drugs, such as cocaine and hallucinogenics? Ending the punitive War on Drugs, almost all reformers would agree, demands more than simply "saying yes" to all currently illegal drugs.

When President Richard Nixon launched the modern War on Drugs in 1971, few Americans believed that cannabis, let alone so-called "hard" drugs, should be legal or even "decriminalized" in the US. In 1969, 84 percent of Americans said they believed anyone caught with even the smallest amount of marijuana should go to jail. Users and dealers of "hard" drugs, Americans believed, demanded even greater punishment.[7] Just thirty years ago, in the midst of the crack cocaine scourge, then-*Senator* Joe Biden followed the public's conventional wisdom. He was one of America's most outspoken drug war "hawks," calling for more arrests, more convictions, and more prison time for drug dealers.[8]

For decades, a broad political consensus that included liberal Democrats and conservative Republicans championed a mercilessly punitive War on Drugs.[9] President Bill Clinton, just like President Ronald Reagan, signed legislation giving law enforcement authorities at all levels of government more resources and more incentives to lock up ever more Americans caught up in the distribution and possession of illegal drugs. The African American congressional representative Charles Rangel, whose district included Harlem, was as fierce an advocate of harsh treatment of drug offenders as any of his conservative white fellow members of Congress. For nearly half a century, tens of millions of Americans across social, economic, and political divides agreed that the War on Drugs was one of the US's "good" wars.

Of course, this conventional wisdom functioned in the breach. Americans continued to use illegal drugs, and to raise their voices against repression. In the mid-1970s, in the shadow of President Nixon's declaration of an "all-out offensive" against drugs, a pro-cannabis coalition of mostly white, middle-class users, supported by makers of drug paraphernalia and not a few cannabis dealers, sought to decriminalize the possession of marijuana. They had some success in a few states and locales—before a swelling wave of fearful parents, supported by a range of public health experts, turned the tide against them during the Reagan years. The federal effort to decriminalize cannabis was stopped in its tracks. Similarly, in the late 1970s, as cocaine use soared among a segment of the professional-managerial class—"yuppies"—some politicians began to rethink the logic of the absolute criminal prohibition of that drug. The rise of crack cocaine in the mid-1980s, often distributed by so-called inner-city crews, put a stop to that reformist campaign.

More recently, cannabis reformers have successfully pushed for legalization. Following a flurry of seventeen successful state medical marijuana legalization campaigns between 1996 and 2011, Colorado and Washington made cannabis legal for recreational users in 2012. Now, many other states have followed—though many of them still only allow for "medical" use. Even so, the federal government has refused to budge on its absolute statutory prohibition, creating a legal conundrum that has yet to be resolved.

Similarly, for the past twenty years or so, the opioid epidemic has pushed politicians, medical professionals, and myriad citizens' groups to rethink how drug addicts should be treated. That so many people who became addicted to opioids received their first doses not from back-alley dealers but at their local Walgreens or CVS pharmacies after their physicians prescribed them legal, Big-Pharma, "white market," brand-name products, explains part of Americans' more sympathetic approach to these addicts' travails. That so many of the addicts were (especially in the epidemic's early days) white rural or small-town folks, perceived by many as "respectable" members of their communities, also shaped this particular re-thinking of how drug abusers should be judged.

The War on Drugs has never been static. Reformers and enforcers have fought pitched battles over drug policy throughout its history, with multiple inflection points. And like so many aspects of American life, the War on Drugs has been shaped by issues of racial politics, as well as by fundamental questions about how Americans legally determine their consumer choices in the face of myriad contested cultural beliefs and unequal access to political and economic power.

Obviously, over the past half-century, millions of Americans have refused to abide by the logic of the War on Drugs. In recent years, nearly a million Americans, according to the National Institute on Drug Abuse, have been dependent on or have abused cocaine.[10] Almost 50 percent of twelfth graders in 2018 told pollsters that they had already used one or more illicit drugs at least once in their lives.[11] At the end of the 1970s— peak years for illegal marijuana use in the US—almost 40 percent of high school seniors reported that they had smoked marijuana at least once in the prior month and nearly 12 percent of all Americans over the age of twelve reported that they had done likewise.[12] Illegal drugs have been nearly ubiquitous in modern America, despite the War on Drugs and the opprobrium a range of authorities have rained down on drug users. As this collection demonstrates, America's state-sponsored drug warriors have always battled a guerrilla army of insurgent users, dealers, and traffickers. Anti-drug forces have won many battles in this war, but they have yet to defeat their targeted enemy—which includes tens of millions of Americans.

Despite the many risks associated with obtaining and using illegal intoxicants, throughout the War on Drugs Americans forged a mass market that rivaled almost any other consumer sector of the American economy. Whether they were "yuppie" coke heads or poor heroin addicts, prescription pill–abusing teenagers or the millions upon millions of people from all walks of life who enjoyed getting high on whatever illegal substance was on offer among their set—Thai stick, ecstasy, crank, lean, oxy . . . the list is long—drug buyers have been everywhere.

Illegal drug users in the US created a massive consumer demand that drug traffickers and their retail distributors have been more than pleased to service. The War on Drugs made supplying that demand dangerous in multiple ways, but it also made it extremely lucrative. It created an underground economy with its own global supply chain. As this collection explains, the drug war has created business opportunities in some of the world's most economically challenged nations and has provided employment and entrepreneurial enterprises in poverty-stricken neighborhoods and communities throughout the US.

Overall, in this analysis of the so-called War on Drugs, some of America's leading drug-war scholars examine the hows and whys of America's long and devasting campaign to punish people who want to get high and those who attend to that market demand. As a group, we seek to explain why the War on Drugs received so much broad public support for so long. What, we ask, was its political utility? As we examine how the war was fought both domestically and internationally, we also ask: who benefited from it? We analyze, as well, how forces have aligned to permit some drugs to be legally enmeshed in a willfully impotent regulatory regime—OxyContin, for example—while other drugs, even when championed by a range of credentialled experts, are ruled too dangerous to be legal in any circumstance—LSD, for example. Finally, we consider why so many people were so willing to battle the mighty and punishing force of the War on Drugs, maintaining despite its force a vibrant, dynamic, and expansive market for the illegal substances Americans desired.

Aimed at fellow drug war scholars, university students, and anyone who wishes to better understand the role the fifty-year-long War on Drugs has played in national and international affairs, this collection serves several purposes. Fundamentally, we want readers to understand how profoundly the War on Drugs has figured the history of the United States.

We argue that the War on Drugs, while generally seen by Americans as an internal affair, has also played a fundamental role in shaping US international relations. The US government's attempts to expand its War on Drugs to other nations has been, not surprisingly—and in keeping with other aspects of America's role in the world—an exercise in hegemonic power. But America's international drug-war efforts has also provided governments in targeted countries with opportunities to use American resources to fulfill their own political projects. Thus, the War on Drugs is not and never has been just an American story.[13] As with other economic development and security aid programs, governments across the world have used drug-war policies and programs in their struggles over questions of political legitimacy, the role of state power, and the freedoms to which their citizens are entitled.

Within the US, as well, Americans have seen the War on Drugs as a political weapon, one that has been used both to enforce and to challenge America's social order. Since the Nixon era, politicians have generally used drug war rhetoric to demonstrate their willingness to get tough on people they deem to be marginal and, thus, expendable, and have been willing to turn that rhetoric into policy. As a result, the War on Drugs has had a particularly devastating impact on poor communities. Economically disadvantaged African Americans—doubly marginalized by their race and class—have taken the brunt of that attack. Racial injustice and impoverishment have many causes in the US. As this collection demonstrates, the War on Drugs has produced one of the most devastating columns in that hard accounting.

At the same time, we aim to make clear that the War on Drugs is not just a story of repression and suppression. Illegal drug users and suppliers have helped to forge an enduring alternative culture and economy in the US and, indeed, around the world. Inside the US, Americans have used the illegal drug underground to accumulate capital, often providing opportunities where few others exist. That illegal underground also has fostered some of the nation's most compelling cultural forms, from acid rock to hip hop. Drug advocates insist that getting high is, for the great majority of users, not a pathology but a purposeful pursuit of an alternative, generative state of mind and body. While drug addiction and abuse have been catastrophic for many, drug users and their suppliers have built their own social and cultural landscape. This illegal drug infrastructure is an open secret, an interconnected aspect of everyday life in the US, even as it is officially attacked. Despite the War on Drugs, the illegal drug underground and the above-board legal economy and socially sanctioned culture have, we contend, long been intertwined.

Finally, we argue further that the War on Drugs demonstrates how issues of public health, equitable distribution of medical care, and science-based regulation of drugs are shaped by ideological disputes, interest group politics, and politically and economically motivated moral panics. More broadly, the War on Drugs, as presented in this collection, is a window into some of the most enduring historical challenges Americans face, including racial inequality, economic inequities, and political demagoguery.

The essays that make up this volume tackle a range of aspects of the War on Drugs. While this is by no means a comprehensive survey of the modern War on Drugs, we do attempt to examine some of the most enduring, complicated, and noteworthy pieces of the drug war puzzle. Each essay is intended to work as a stand-alone piece, but the essays are also in conversation with one another as they speak to the collection's common themes.

Collectively, these essays analyze how the War on Drugs has served powerful economic and political interests both inside and outside the US. At the same time, the collection explores how the War on Drugs produced a "deviant" form of globalization that offered economically marginalized people an economic lifeline as players in a remunerative, transnational supply and distribution network. In a related vein, a number of the essays demonstrate how government enforcement of the War on Drugs has disproportionately punished these same marginalized suppliers, as well as their disadvantaged customers. And in a different vein, some of the essays also assess how drug warriors traduced science and medical expertise by encouraging moral panics that contributed to the blanket criminalization of certain drugs, including cannabis and LSD. Finally, the concluding essays speak directly to alternatives to the War on Drugs, even as they also remind us of the powerful, sometimes predatory interests that seek to profit off of the common human desire to get high.

While not every essay takes on all of these issues and themes, as a group, they deliver a shared indictment of the War on Drugs and a common hope that the ongoing search for a more humane and realistic approach to Americans' massive illicit drug marketplace can be achieved.

* * *

The first essay in this collection, "The Advent of the War on Drugs," provides historical background for the essays that follow. It reminds readers that the War on Drugs has its roots in the prohibitionist impulses of the nineteenth century and that Americans have long held an ambivalent attitude toward the perils and pleasures of intoxication. This ambivalence has resulted in episodic campaigns to shut down or at least constrain the market for targeted intoxicants, most commonly in the early twentieth century through regulation, then increasingly through selective enforcement against users and suppliers, and most recently through draconian punishments for local dealers and large-scale traffickers. The essay also foregrounds the racial and ethnic prejudices that contributed to the first legal campaigns against opiates, cocaine, and cannabis at the cusp of the nineteenth and twentieth centuries, a trope that never disappears from the War on Drugs.

The second essay, "Drug Dealers," foregrounds the primary target of the domestic War on Drugs. In this essay, I explore why large majorities of Americans during the height of the War on Drugs in the 1980s and 1990s supported harsh punishment for convicted drug dealers, even including the death penalty. I also argue that historically, within the communities in which dealers worked, a surprising number of people—and not just customers—supported their local drug pushers and distributors, seeing them as "Robin Hoods" or, in historian Eric Hobsbawm's phrase, social bandits. Even at the height of the War on Drugs, a sizeable, if shifting, number of Americans never bought into the demonization of drug "pushers," complicating drug warriors' attempts at eradication. The War on Drugs has always also been a civil war.

The next essay, "The Mexico–Chicago Heroin Connection," is by Elaine Carey. It stems from her prodigious research on transnational, Mexican-originating drug trafficking organizations (DTOs). Her work explains how and why DTOs have often won key battles in the War on Drugs—or at least fought them to a stalemate. Carey counters popular culture stereotypes of "Mexican cartels" with a revealing look at the corporate-like, flexible, and sophisticated management skills of the Herrera DTO, which successfully evaded law enforcement efforts for decades on both sides of the border. Carey argues, too, that US efforts to stop the Herrera DTO and similar operations were hindered by racist and culturally ignorant assumptions about Mexican drug traffickers.

Michael Polson, in "Cultivating Cannabis, Excepting Cannabis," situates the domestic cultivation of illegal cannabis in the US-led global War on Drugs. He argues that in the midst of the movement to legalize cannabis state by state in the US, we would do well to understand how US-led efforts to destroy non-US cannabis cultivation and export from the Global South figured in the rise of domestic growers. These domestic growers, operating in an illegal but often locally accepting environment, transformed the US marijuana market and played a vital role in "excepting" cannabis from the War on Drugs in the twenty-first century. Even as the War on Drugs criminalized tens of millions of cannabis users, growers, and sellers, cannabis cultivation became an economic lifeline for marginalized, often rural populations in the US.

Peter Pihos, in "The Local War on Drugs," recasts the familiar accounting of the War on Drugs. Instead of narrating the drug polices of the federal government, he zooms in on local drug enforcement—the site of the overwhelming number of arrests and subsequent incarcerations. Using Chicago as a case study, he argues that city officials used different drug enforcement regimes, over time, to police Black residents, especially those concentrated in poor, segregated neighborhoods. Chicago's political leaders, he argues, used drug enforcement not simply as a tool to fight "vice," but as a more general mode of governing the economically segmented, racialized city. His case study, in relation to other essays in this collection, speaks to the class-based and race-based nature of the War on Drugs.

Emily Dufton, in "Cannabis Culture Wars," also analyzes the class and race aspects of the War on Drugs—but from a very different angle. She explains how white, middle-class activist parent-citizens groups fought against cannabis legalization or de-criminalization in the first twenty years after President Nixon declared his War on Drugs. The anti-marijuana activists she has researched were less interested in locking up young users—or even their suppliers—than they were in protecting their children from what they perceived to be a dangerous "pro-marijuana culture." Ignoring expert-based evidence on the relatively low risks of cannabis use in comparison with the use of alcohol or tobacco, their efforts, she concludes, set back the cannabis legalization or decriminalization movement by decades and, inadvertently, opened the door to the arrest of millions of cannabis users, who were disproportionately non-white and non–middle class. Her essay aligns with others in the collection that highlight how drug war enforcement has consistently impacted poor people of color, despite the widespread use of illegal drugs across broad swathes of the American people.

Erika Dyck, Lucas Richert, and Alexis Turner, in "Psychedelic Wars," turn to another critical issue in the War on Drugs: who decides the legal status of drugs and on what basis are those decisions made? Focusing primarily on LSD, they analyze the debate within the medico-scientific community over the suitability of the use of psychedelics in diverse settings, including both the therapeutic and the recreational. Pro-psychedelic "experts" were quickly put on the defensive by scientists who doubted the legitimacy of the advocates' more wholistic, spiritual, and non-commercial claims about the utility of psychedelic research and use. Hallucinogenics, the authors argue, did not fit into the market-based parameters of the pharmaceutical marketplace. A range of authorities, inside and outside the scientific community, deemed them irredeemable, dangerous drugs. The War on Drugs had another criminalized target.

The two essays on international anti-drug campaigns—Aileen Teague's "The War on Drugs in Mexico" and James Bradford's "The War on Drugs in Afghanistan"—share a common feature. Teague and Bradford both argue that the US-led War on Drugs never successfully achieved its goals of supply-side eradication because US policy makers failed to understand how foreign governments used the War on Drugs to their own ends. In addition, non-US governments' eradication efforts were constrained by those governments' need to maintain domestic legitimacy and to refrain from undertaking anti-drug activities that threatened their political—and economic—interests. Teague's deeply researched case study of Mexico's role in the War on Drugs documents how American drug war funds in the early years of the campaign often supported the Mexican government's effort to quash internal political enemies. Bradford, in his eye-opening history of US-led efforts to crush Afghanistan's opium production, also stresses how useful US-funded drug eradication efforts were to the expansion of central state power in Afghanistan. He reveals how American aid funds, more generally, have served to increase the productivity and expertise of Afghan opium producers, especially as US drug interdiction efforts progressed in other opium-producing nations. Both essays reveal how difficult it is for American drug agents to destroy international supply given the enormous economic incentives produced by the massive "black market" demand for illegal drugs that exists in the US, as well as in other wealthy nations.

The final two essays in the collection examine the politically and economically fraught relationship between legal "white" market drugs and illegal "black" market drugs. David Herzberg, in "Between the Free Market and the Drug War," draws on his pathbreaking scholarship on prescription drug addiction and pharmaceutical regulatory regimes to offer an alternative history of the War on Drugs. He argues that drug reformers' efforts to rein in prescription drug abuse, while flawed, provide an "example of a path not taken" in overseeing the abuse of such drugs as cocaine and heroin. Herzberg reveals that the punitive, prohibitionist, criminalization approach to the war in drugs was—and is—not the only way to protect consumers from harmful drug abuse and addiction.

Kathleen Frydl, a leading historian of the American state, makes a similar, if less sanguine argument about government oversight of prescription drugs in the collection's final essay. In "The Pharma Cartel," she argues that in recent decades, government officials and politicians have allowed a "neoliberal"—market-first, profits-before-people—approach to drug regulation to unleash the worst addiction crisis in modern American history. Zeroing in on the extraordinarily loose government regulation and oversight of OxyContin, she explains how and why millions of Americans could be preyed on by major pharmaceutical companies. Rather than simply blame Big Pharma for the opioid crisis, she provides a nuts-and-bolts accounting of government complicity in the failure to keep Americans safe in the name of free-market supremacy. While the federal, government-led War on Drugs targeted the poor and the marginal, politicians and government regulators deliberately supported the efforts of Big Pharma to unleash highly addictive prescription opioids on other Americans, whose communities were unraveling economically. Frydl warns that drug reformers need take great care not to unleash a new profit-driven drug crisis, powered by a neoliberal alliance of politicians and corporate executives, even as they battle the inequities and cruelties of the punitive War on Drugs.

This collection's overarching goal is to provide a historical framework for the War on Drugs. By analyzing that war's key issues, debates, events, and actors, we hope to help our readers ask their own questions, based on the resulting deeper understandings of the role the War on Drugs has played in the making of our current political predicament.

NOTES

1 Betsy Perl, "Ending the War on Drugs: By the Numbers," The Center for American Progress, June 27, 2018, www.americanprogress.org.

2 "The Biden Plan for Strengthening America's Commitment to Justice," Biden/Harris website, accessed March 18, 2021, https://joebiden.com.

3 Emily Ekins, "Poll: 55% of Americans Favor Decriminalizing Drugs," Cato Institute, October 2, 2019, www.cato.org. This poll was commissioned by the libertarian Cato Institute, which has long opposed the War on Drugs, so it should be taken with at least a small grain of salt.

4 For an example of this drug law–enforcement institution-building, see the High Intensity Drug Trafficking Areas (HIDTA) program, which was first created in the Anti-Drug Abuse Act of 1988 and which still has an annual budget of around $250 million. This budget is distributed to local, state, and federal agencies in forty-nine states, Puerto Rico, and other US governmental entities. See "High Intensity Drug Trafficking Areas (HIDTAs)," DEA, accessed March 18, 2021, www.dea.gov.

5 It should be noted that the pharmaceutical industry took shape long before any War on Drugs and is highly structured by the federal regulatory regime that began in the US during the Progressive Era. See David Herzberg's chapter in this collection for a nuanced perspective on these issues.

6 David Herzberg explains how Big Pharma addictive drugs, including barbiturates, amphetamines, and OxyContin, have long been legally marketed and sold through an often-abused, profit-based regulatory system as "medicine" to

a primarily white consumer base. Herzberg aptly calls this regulatory-based approach to addictive drug sales the "white market" in opposition to the illegal or "black" marketplace for drugs such as heroin and cocaine. See David Herzberg, *White Market Drugs: Big Pharma and the Hidden History of Addiction in America* (Chicago: University of Chicago Press, 2020).

7 Andrew Daniller, "Two-Thirds of Americans Support Marijuana Legalization," Pew Research Center, November 14, 2019, www.pewresearch.org.

8 For Senator Biden as drug war hawk: David Farber, *Crack: Rock Cocaine, Street Capitalism, and the Decade of Greed* (New York: Cambridge University Press, 2019), 146.

9 Exceptions certainly exist. Libertarian conservatives, including Milton Friedman and William Buckley, never supported a draconian War on Drugs, and a host of liberals, often at the local level, such as Baltimore Mayor Kurt Schmoke, were outspoken opponents, as well.

10 "What Is the Scope of Cocaine Use in the United States?" National Institute on Drug Abuse, May 2016, www.drugabuse.gov.

11 "Monitoring the Future Study: Trends in Prevalence of Various Drugs," National Institute on Drug Abuse, December 17, 2020, www.drugabuse.gov.

12 Andrew Golub and Bruce D. Johnson, "The Rise of Marijuana as the Drug of Choice among Youthful Adult Arrestees," *National Institute of Justice: Research in Brief*, June 2001, 6, www.ojp.gov.

13 Isaac Campos, in *Home Grown: Marijuana and the Origins of Mexico's War on Drugs* (Chapel Hill: University of North Carolina Press, 2012), cogently revises conventional historical accounts to explore how the Mexican government, beginning in the late nineteenth century, well before the US federal effort, condemned marijuana as a dangerous substance and banned the drug in 1920. While the US government took the lead internationally throughout much of the twentieth century in enforcing a War on Drugs, other nations have long played a complicated role in the campaign.

PART I

Background

1

The Advent of the War on Drugs

DAVID FARBER

This brief history of drug policy in the United States lays the groundwork for understanding President Richard Nixon's 1971 declaration of a War on Drugs. It reveals Americans' centuries-long love-hate relationship with intoxicants. From that conflicted relationship emerged abolitionist movements that led to the Eighteenth Amendment to the Constitution, which generally prohibited the sale of alcoholic beverages from 1920 to 1933, as well as a series of local, state, and national laws that first regulated and then punished both the sellers and the consumers of a variety of substances, including opium, cocaine, heroin, and cannabis.

1

As declarations of war go, it was pretty low-key. On June 17, 1971, President Richard Nixon held a press briefing in the West Wing of the White House. In his usual dark suit and striped tie, speaking comfortably from notes, the president branded Americans' rising tide of drug abuse "public enemy number one." He continued: "In order to fight and defeat this enemy, it is necessary to wage a new, all-out offensive . . . This will be a world-wide offensive . . . It will be government-wide . . . and it will be nation-wide."[1] To fund this war, Nixon declared that he would ask Congress to appropriate a minimum of $350 million. In 1969, when Richard Nixon became president, the entire federal drug budget had totaled just $81 million.[2] Today, some fifty years later, the United States has expended approximately one trillion dollars waging war on illegal drugs.[3]

President Nixon was not the first American political leader to mount a campaign against drugs, or against intoxicants more generally; nor was his call to arms politically partisan. In 1966, with New York City reeling from a tidal wave of heroin addiction, the moderate Republican governor of New York, Nelson Rockefeller had called for a "war on narcotics," and asked the state legislature to appropriate $81 million to wage it.[4] Even earlier, in 1962, the liberal Democratic governor of California, Pat Brown, had responded to middle-class, white parents' fears that "Mexican" drug pushers were luring their children into depravity by declaring that he would end the scourge of narcotics trafficking: "in this war we can never declare a truce."[5] And earlier still, in 1954, Presidents Eisenhower's attorney general, Herbert Brownell Jr., spoke to voters' concerns over the concurrent rise of juvenile delinquency and an uptick in heroin and marijuana use by calling for a massive increase in prison time for drug pushers in what he, too, dubbed a "war on narcotics."[6]

President Nixon's rhetoric was, even then, nothing new. Neither were Americans' politically fraught and febrile fascinations with all manner of intoxicants. Still, at the cusp of the 1960s and 1970s, President Nixon was responding directly to the political and social exigencies of his time. By 1971, the American public—the electorate—was being torn apart by a polarizing debate about the reach and meaning of a seemingly ever more permissive youth culture. Countercultural young people's embrace of illegal drug use was at the heart of that raging debate.

Most immediately, Nixon was responding not to young people's use of drugs, in general, but to a very specific scourge: a two-front heroin "epidemic." One front was America's inner cities. In New York, Detroit, Washington, DC and other major American cities, record numbers of heroin addicts were stealing, robbing, and mugging in their desperate search for the money they needed to fuel their drug purchases, contributing to a surging wave of criminality. While these addicts were overwhelmingly drawn from poor Black and Puerto Rican communities, white Americans feared not only the breakdown in "law and order" but also that the epidemic would spread to their communities. The cover of *Time* magazine from March 16, 1970 played to those fears; it featured a middle-class–looking, white teenager and the ominous warning: "Heroin Hits the Young."[7] At the same time, thousands of miles away, young American soldiers in Vietnam were getting high on almost pure "China White" heroin that cost just a dollar a vial. In spring 1971, the Nixon White House heard a report from a Republican congressman just back from Vietnam that as many as 15 percent of servicemen had become addicted; these men, obviously, would be coming home to the US. The

New York Times and other mass media outlets amplified the story: "GI Heroin Addiction Epidemic in Vietnam."[8] Something, President Nixon believed, had to be done to curtail the scourge.

Heroin addiction, both at home and in Vietnam, most directly fueled Nixon's decision to launch his administration's drug offensive. But it was not the only cause. Nixon, like a great many of his "silent majority" supporters, detested and feared the rapid rise of casual drug use among "Sixties Generation," middle-class white youths. Those feelings were put on somewhat bizarre display during an extraordinary Oval Office meeting between Nixon and the legendary Elvis Presley.

Elvis showed up, without an appointment, at the White House in December 1970. He was there, he said, to volunteer his services as a federal agent in the fight against the rising tide of illegal drug use. A bemused President Nixon took the meeting. Wearing purple velvet pants and a matching cape, a largely unbuttoned white shirt, as well as oversized amber sunglasses (Elvis, not Nixon), Presley explained to the president that the Beatles were a major factor in young people's "anti-American spirit." Nixon, proudly "square," replied: "Those who use drugs are also those in the vanguard of anti-American protest." "I'm on your side," Elvis then said. He explained to the president that he had been studying drug culture and communist brainwashing, which appeared to be linked in his mind. President Nixon made sure that Elvis received an official badge from the Bureau of Narcotics and Dangerous Drugs.[9]

Probably for the best, Elvis never deployed his badge in service to the War on Drugs; he died of a heart attack in 1977 after years of abusing massive doses of doctor-prescribed sedatives and amphetamines. Nixon, like a great many Americans, including Elvis, was not interested in targeting people abusing prescription drugs. He was repulsed by young people's embrace of marijuana, LSD, and other mind-altering recreational substances. And while his 1971 "all-out offensive" was not specifically aimed at such drugs and such users, America's "War on Drugs" would, soon enough, expand to include them.

Richard Nixon did not, it's only fair to state, envision the massively punitive War on Drugs that was to come at the hands of the elected officials that followed him. As drug historian Emily Dufton has pointed out, "Nixon's was one of the last administrations to spend more on prevention and treatment than law enforcement."[10] Still, by 1974, the soon-to-resign Nixon had begun to shift the balance of his drug war policies, drastically cutting the federal drug treatment budget while escalating enforcement efforts. The die had been largely cast and, beginning in the mid-1970s and lasting until the early twenty-first century, with only a few critical interruptions at the federal and local levels, the War on Drugs would become ever more gargantuan and fiercely punitive.

Even as a majority of Americans sought the comfort, relief, and pleasures of an array of intoxicants, legal and illegal, a broad anti-drug coalition chose to "let slip the dogs of war." The drug warriors waged an unprecedented campaign to crush drug traffickers, imprison neighborhood drug dealers, and punish drug users. Well, at least *some* drug traffickers, and *some* drug dealers, and *some* drug users—over time, exactly who would pay the price and bear the burdens of America's War on Drugs depended on shifting political pressure and changing economic forces.

Over the past half-century, America's drug warriors supposedly targeted anyone involved with illegal drugs. In practice, on the domestic front, drug warriors mostly targeted overlapping groups of people they perceived to be on society's margins—poor addicts, people of color, and others outside the cultural mainstream. Especially in the 1980s and thereafter, those illegal drug users—and a good many drug dealers—who were *not* on the perceived margins faced a different kind of drug war. The historian Matthew Lassiter has called mainstream, primarily young, white middle-class Americans who were swept up in the War on Drugs "impossible criminals."[11] Despite their large numbers, they would not be the war's primary target and, indeed, influential reformers would begin in the 1970s to protect such drug users—most of whom indulged in cannabis—and even their neighborhood dealers, by providing a separate and often much more discretionary set of punishments for those caught with relatively small amounts of marijuana.

The War on Drugs was never an all-out war. Some protested such limits. The most zealous drug warriors often demanded a far broader and fiercer offensive on an ever larger number of targets: "We need another D-Day. Instead you're giving us another Vietnam: a limited war, fought on the cheap, financed on the sly, with no clear objectives, and ultimately destined for stalemate and human tragedy."[12] That was Joe Biden in 1989, when he was still a senator, complaining about the Bush administration's policy. Biden, in a perverse way, was right: a great majority of those who used and even sold illegal drugs never faced the War on Drugs' punishing power. Others, however, did feel its wrath. Those targeted domestically by drug warriors, at all levels of government, were, especially in the post-1970s period, disproportionately African American and Hispanic.

The modern War on Drugs, first declared at the national level by President Nixon, quickly became a juggernaut, outpacing anything that had preceded it. Even as Americans by the tens of millions created the largest illegal drug market in the world, government authorities, supported by a majority of American voters, began to prosecute and imprison an ever-increasing number of drug users and drug sellers. Within the US, the War on Drugs, certainly by the 1980s, had become a second American civil war. Illegal drug users—tens of millions strong—and their many suppliers, both domestic and international, fought a guerrilla insurgency against the armed and extraordinarily well-funded might of the state. It has been a war as destructive as any Americans have fought.

2

Americans have always had a love-hate relationship with intoxicants. The historian William Rorabaugh concluded that early America was essentially an "Alcoholic Republic," or in the words of contemporary critics, "a nation of drunkards."[13] The numbers bear witness: by 1830, the per capita intake of absolute alcohol in the US reached 7.1 gallons (today it is around 2.3 gallons).[14] George Washington, who had his own whiskey still at Mount Vernon, feared that hard drinking would lead to "the ruin of half the workingmen in this Country."[15]

The first war on intoxicants arose in response to such intemperate drinking. It was led by pietistic Christians, who decried the moral laxity and general immoderate behavior produced, they believed, by excessive drinking. They were joined by nascent medical authorities, who observed the deleterious effects of alcoholism; employers, who understood that drunks tended to be unproductive workers; and moral stewards of various stripes, who feared that widespread alcohol abuse endangered the American ideal of rational self-determination. Then, too, and well before they could vote, women, notably the notorious Carrie Nation, who used a sturdy hatchet to bust up saloons, played a major role in the fight against alcohol. Women saw firsthand the physical abuse and economic havoc drunken men too often inflicted on their families.[16] The first temperance society formed in New York in 1808. By the 1830s, temperance advocates had forged a national movement.

By January 1919, forty-six of the nation's forty-eight state legislatures had endorsed the cause of prohibition. Joined by Congress, these states successfully voted to pass the Eighteenth Amendment, which banned "the manufacture, sale, or transportation of intoxicating liquors" within the US. Prohibition was in some ways a success. It considerably lowered alcohol consumption in the US, demonstrating the ability of the federal government to create sufficient law enforcement authority to reduce supply and drive down demand.

Alas, Prohibition also stimulated the rise of organized crime, fueled by bootlegging. Like later generations of cannabis users, tens of millions of Americans became scofflaws. They turned to criminals to supply them with the liquor they continued to desire.

This particular war on intoxication lasted for just fourteen years. It ended when the legions of pro-alcohol Americans—"wets"—convinced enough Americans that prohibiting alcoholic beverages had created more problems than it had solved. They pressured their political representatives to overturn the ban with the Twenty-First Amendment (1933), which repealed the Eighteenth. While some states and many counties choose to remain "dry" for decades (Kansas completely banned public bars until 1987 and hundreds of localities remain "dry" to this day), no serious effort to ban alcoholic consumption at the national level has risen since.[17]

Alcohol was by no means the only intoxicating substance Americans chose to use with abandon and then, in great numbers, turn against—at least for a while. Opioids are another. Americans have used opioids for as long as the US has existed. By the late nineteenth century, almost one in every two hundred Americans was addicted to opium or morphine. Most addicts, then, were white women from the middle and upper classes, often suffering, in the contemporary parlance, from "uterine and ovarian complications." Their "pusher" tended to be their family doctor.[18]

Americans, at first, turned against opium only selectively. Rather than direct their attention to physician-supplied white women addicts, authorities at the local and then state levels first began to regulate and punish recreational opium smokers. In large part, authorities turned against opium smoking when young white men and women began to frequent commercial "opium dens," often run by Chinese immigrants. These immigrants had brought the practice of recreational opium smoking with them from China. The San Francisco city government was the first to outlaw opium smoking in 1875. By 1915, twenty-seven states had banned opium dens. Enforcement, however, remained sporadic.[19] Goaded by such local regulatory and punitive efforts, but even more by the American government's increasing interest in influencing events in East Asia— where opium trafficking by imperial powers was long a resonant issue (notably in the Opium Wars)—Congress passed a law in 1909 banning "the importation and use of opium for other than medicinal purposes."[20] Here was the first supply-side attack on narcotics. Americans' cross-racial recreational use of opium, greatly intensified by the American government's increasing global interests, had produced national anti-drug legislation. This pattern would be repeated.

Opioid use, however, began to attract a broader set of critics. According to distinguished drug historian David Courtwright, as increasing numbers of better-trained doctors and other health professionals recognized the dangers and disadvantages of opioids—especially their addictive properties—they began to prescribe them with far greater care. As a result, "respectable" opioid users began to decline in number. In Courtwright's words, addicts were increasingly "lower-class urban males, often neophyte members of the underworld."[21] *These* sorts of addicts—unlike "grandma"—were widely pilloried by common citizens as the dregs of society.

These reprobate addicts, in the eyes of many, deserved not sympathy or medical support but, instead, punishment. Courtwright, with appropriate caveats about the need to admit a range of other factors in explaining this punitive turn, argues: "What we think about addiction very much depends on who is addicted."[22] This argument can be neatly extended to the broader subject of drug abuse, in general. Who is using which drugs for what purposes under whose authority often explains a great deal about how government officials, endorsed by great swathes of the citizenry, identify and define illegitimate drug use and the sorts of penalties applied to those who use such socially defined illicit substances. Here, too, is a pattern that will be repeated.

Still, at the turn of the nineteenth century, Americans did not intend to wage any kind of general war on drugs. Drug reformers in the Progressive Era were much more focused on drug regulation than on punishing and incarcerating drug abusers and drug sellers. In response to reformers' demand for greater regulation of drugs and other consumer products, Congress passed the 1906 Food and Drug Act. This act, as implemented within the federal bureaucracy, primarily focused on keeping spoiled and disgusting food products out of the consumer marketplace (motivated, in part, by *The Jungle*, Upton Sinclair's widely popular, muckraking account of the meatpacking industry). Still, the Act did, for the first time, force drug and food producers to list on their products' labels the presence of eleven ingredients considered by reformers to be dangerous, including alcohol, heroin, morphine, opium, cannabis, and cocaine. The need for such labeling was clear to reformers—at the time, many products, including many marketed to children, contained such substances. For example, dozens of peppy "soft drinks"—not just Coca-Cola—packed a dash or more of cocaine.[23] "Cures" for teething infants and colicky babies commonly contained morphine—resulting in a rash of overdose deaths.

Progressive Era reformers did not demand greater drug regulation just to protect children or other vulnerable consumers of soft drinks and commonly sold health remedies—which included the all-purpose pain reliever Bayer Heroin (Bayer Aspirin came just a bit later). The anti-drug coalition was an unlikely-appearing alliance of concerned medical and health professionals, white supremacists, and religious and secular prohibitionists. While most scholars focus on how these various Progressive Era reformers lobbied for greater federal involvement in the drug trade, they were more effective at the state and local levels. State legislatures all over the US passed laws regulating the distribution of cocaine, alcohol, cannabis, opium, and heroin.

How and why those reformers targeted cocaine is instructive. Unlike opium, cocaine was a relative newcomer to the American consumer. Only in 1860 did German chemists isolate the alkaloid that gave coca leaves, long used as a simulant by people in the South American Andes, their potency. Commercial interests quickly thereafter monetized the processed coca leaves—cocaine—by incorporating them into a variety of elixirs and tonics, all of which were readily purchased by any consumer at a multitude of retail establishments. The US, by the late nineteenth century the world's most prosperous nation, dominated the retail cocaine trade. Here, too, is another pattern that will be repeated over the following decades.

Avid cocaine users drew the attention of doctors and other health professionals. They warned that some users were becoming addicted to the substance. Driven by such public health concerns, as well as the desire to sell papers, Progressive Era "muckraking" newspapers headlined stories about dissolute "cocaine fiends" running amuck.

Such anti-cocaine warnings were strengthened by a campaign by white supremacists against Black cocaine users. In the burgeoning era of Jim Crow, white upholders of America's strict racial hierarchy indignantly reported that cocaine use prompted African Americans to act "uppity" and refuse to accept their purported social inferiority. Cocaine, they also asserted, increased Blacks' criminal propensities. In a similar vein, police and other law enforcement authorities noted that denizens of the demimonde, including prostitutes and gamblers, had embraced the cocaine kick. Reformers of many stripes, across the political spectrum and for different reasons, had come to see cocaine use as dangerous and cocaine users as the kind of people in need of policing.

Following the lead of state and local authorities, the federal government began outlawing a range of narcotics. Congress passed the Harrison Narcotics Tax Act in 1914. This act, on its face, simply charged the Treasury Department with registering and imposing a tax on all people involved in the production and sale of opiates and cocaine. In practice, Treasury Department agents, working with local police and supported by the courts, began to prosecute doctors who prescribed narcotics and pharmacists who sold the drugs in order to restrict legal access to opiates and cocaine. In 1922, Congress passed the Narcotic Drugs Import and Export Act, which banned in almost every instance the legal supply of these drugs (though, critically, excepting opium intended for carefully prescribed medical purposes).

The result of these federal acts, as well as a multitude of state and local drug laws, was the rise of underground, criminal trafficking organizations. While authorities' efforts to suppress the supply of opiates and cocaine did diminish the number of users, it by no means stopped demand altogether. Organized criminal networks arose to meet that demand. Notorious gangsters quickly took up the challenge of supplying addicts, as well as recreational users.

These gangsters, in the 1920s and early 1930s, often ran drug distribution operations alongside their more profitable bootlegging operations. New Yorker Arnold Rothstein, best known for his involvement in fixing the 1919 World Series, had his hand in most every illegal enterprise. He ran a well-organized drug smuggling business, bringing in heroin, morphine, and cocaine from European suppliers on cargo ships. He eventually allied with "Lucky" Luciano and soon the Mafia, working with international producers, became a mainstay of the illegal drug business in the US, specializing in the importation and distribution of heroin. The end of Prohibition in 1933 meant that gangsters who had made millions bootlegging alcoholic beverages focused their talents on the illegal drug trade. Generations of oft-times warring organized criminal enterprises maintained and developed the illegal drug business.[24]

The federal government, in partial response to these international trafficking operations, began laying the foundations for the modern punitive War on Drugs in 1930. That year the Federal Bureau of Narcotics (FBN) was born as a spin-off enterprise from the soon-to-be obsolete Bureau of Prohibition. The FBN was charged by Congress with stamping out drug trafficking, which the bureau's champion, Pennsylvania Representative Stephen G. Porter, called "a greater evil than human slavery."[25]

Led for the next thirty-two years by the politically savvy Harry J. Anslinger, the FBN pursued two major missions. First of all, it targeted international drug traffickers. Cutting supply, Anslinger believed, was the best means for ending drug abuse in the US. Working with nations around the world and bolstered by a series of international antinarcotics agreements, the FBN targeted foreign suppliers—albeit with limited success.[26] International interdiction, then and thereafter, became the centerpiece of federal drug enforcement efforts. Secondly, Anslinger personally and with great energy led a massive public relations campaign to demonize illegal drug use in the US in order to suppress demand.

The FBN continued to focus, in particular, on the perils of heroin, but in the 1930s Anslinger expanded the federal anti-drug campaign to include marijuana. Up until that time, cannabis had been largely ignored at the national level and only half of all states had laws prohibiting or controlling its sale. Marijuana users in the US were few and far between.

Anti-cannabis legislation took off first in California as a progressive-era reform and spread somewhat haphazardly around the country. While popular accounts of cannabis criminalization have long insisted that racist state legislators passed such laws to punish Mexican Americans and Mexican sojourners, the historical record suggests a more complicated story. While newspaper stories in the early twentieth century do report the involvement of people with Mexican surnames in the marijuana trade, they also reveal that a diverse, if relatively small number of other people distributed and consumed cannabis. At the turn of the century, for example, African American jazz musicians in New Orleans enthusiastically smoked marijuana and helped popularize marijuana throughout the nation in youthful, cross-racial bohemian circles.[27] By the early 1930s, FBN chief Anslinger observed the growing concern over marijuana's spread and deployed long-standing anti-cannabis rhetoric, which had first been used widely in Mexico, to rally Americans against its use. He described marijuana as the "assassin of youth."[28] In 1937, he wrote a widely distributed article that detailed the deadly perils of marijuana use: "With an ax he had killed his father, mother, two brothers, and a sister . . . Ordinarily a sane, rather quiet young man, he had become crazed from smoking marijuana."[29] Anslinger was a master inciter of anti-drug moral panics. By the end of 1937, the same year the federal government passed the Marihuana Tax Act (as it was often spelled), all states had made marijuana illegal and thirty-five states had signed on to the Uniform Narcotic Drug Act, which criminalized the sale and use of cannabis, as well as opioids and cocaine. The War on Drugs, while poorly funded at the national level and still far from a priority at the state or local enforcement level, was taking form at the threshold of the Second World War.

By 1940, the US had embraced a federal government-sponsored effort to suppress and criminalize the distribution of certain narcotics, most specifically opiates, cocaine, and, as of 1937, cannabis. This effort marked a complete reversal of the nineteenth-century market-based approach to managing drug demand and supply. Until the late nineteenth century, generally speaking, consumers, not government regulators or law enforcement officials, decided what drugs they wanted to purchase from an array of suppliers, who included doctors, pharmacists, local merchants, and major corporations. No "black" market existed, only an unregulated—and sometimes quite dangerous—"white" market. By the mid-1920s, government authorities had begun to craft a strict anti-narcotics regime. Federal policy makers, along with a great many state and local officials, had decided that the narcotics trade was a dangerous business, generally harmful to the public. It needed to be strictly regulated and, in most instances, banned.

This effort, even at the time of the Second World War, was far from what President Nixon would call "an all-out offensive." Enforcement budgets were scant and few law enforcement personnel at any level of government were dedicated to stamping out the drug trade. The Federal Bureau of Narcotics remained a relatively small operation and even Anslinger recognized that the American people were not ready for a major, intrusive national policing of drugs: "Our staff in order to avoid accusations of being like the Gestapo, has remained the same size as it was when the Bureau was established."[30] While state and local officials did arrest and imprison narcotics traffickers, "street" dealers, and users, the number of imprisoned drug criminals was miniscule compared to what came later.

3

Between the mid-1940s and President Nixon's 1971 declaration, the federal government, joined by state and local officials, began to craft a more punitive approach to the illegal drug trade. Historian Kathleen Frydl argues that it was during these years that the modern, state-sponsored War on Drugs came into being, even if it was still relatively under-resourced and laxly enforced. A coterie of historians, including Frydl, point to a number of overlapping causes for Americans' increasingly punitive turn. Frydl, and Peter Pihos in this collection, argue that militant counter-narcotics policy proved increasingly useful in temporarily resolving other dilemmas of governance—like how to police African

American inner-city neighborhoods.[31] Then, too, another major reason was the increasing availability and use of illegal drugs.

At the broadest level, Americans in the post–Second World War era took to illegal drugs for reasons of both supply and demand. The supply side was stimulated by the overall booming American economy. American international tourism and, more importantly, international trade exploded in the 1950s and 1960s, giving enormous opportunities to drug traffickers both large and small to smuggle product into the US.

Young Americans discovered how easy it was to drive into Mexico, play the part of tourists, find a connection, load the side panels of their cars with cheap "mota"—$15 a brick—drive back across the busy border into the US and sell the weed for more than ten times what they had paid for it.[32] By the mid-1960s, young countercultural enthusiasts, taking advantage of inexpensive international flights and the high value of the American dollar, discovered the drug-producing regions of the "hippie trail," and soon Afghan hash and Thai stick were on the menu. At the heavy end of the smuggling business—the "French Connection"—the Mafia worked with Sicilian and Corsican gangsters to smuggle tons of heroin annually into New York City's bustling ports. The "Golden Triangle" in Southeast Asia became a ready source for heroin, especially for American soldiers stationed in Vietnam, some of whom figured out how to get it into the US.[33]

The demand side, too, was figured by America's burgeoning post–Second World War consumer cornucopia. Legally prescribed Big Pharma drugs, such as amphetamines and barbiturates, were heavily marketed. Housewives, truck drivers, salesmen, and most anyone else in need of either a pick-me-up or a good calming down flocked to these easily available prescription "medicines." Valium, the most popular of these brand-name legal drugs, was introduced in 1963. In 1966, the Rolling Stones, unamused by the seemingly arbitrary line dividing legal and illegal drugs, mocked the "yellow pill" in their hit song, "Mother's Little Helper." In 1978 alone, even after some regulatory reform, some 2.3 billion Valium pills were legally sold in the US.[34] Drugs were everywhere in post–Second World War America. The question was: what made some legal and others illegal?

In the "Sixties" era, as the Rolling Stones' song suggests, a number of young people were in open rebellion against the cultural conventions, social authority, and hypocritical behavior of their elders. The social change movements of the era fueled those young people's disdain for the racist and sexist status quo. The increasingly unpopular and stalemated Vietnam War intensified young Americans' disregard for the moral claims and conventional proprieties of their elite elders. In response to these massive social and political pressures, a countercultural lifestyle flowered.

As youth rebellion spread, so did many young people's rejection of the line between legal intoxicants such as alcoholic beverages, legally prescribed "medicines," such as Valium, and underground, illegal highs, such as marijuana and LSD. By 1970, cannabis use was endemic on college campuses and was fast spreading to the nation's high schools. One of the nation's most popular films, *Easy Rider*, featured two dope-dealing protagonists and scenes of beatific stoned "hippies." Illegal drugs, at least in the eyes of many parents, were suddenly everywhere.

Authorities at the state level began to respond. California, at the epicenter of the youth counterculture, helped lead the way. Between 1962 and 1972, law enforcement personnel around the state increased marijuana arrests some twentyfold, with most of those arrested charged with felony possession. Governor Ronald Reagan warned of the "increasing problem of drug abuse" in his January 6, 1970 "State of the State" address. "The physical and mental destruction of youth is far greater than the public is led to believe," he explained. "Just as alarming is the growth of the 'drug culture' which is tolerated—even touted—by many who influence our youth." He then proclaimed that he would take "legislative and administrative steps to wage a war against the peddler and the pusher."[35] Other state governors followed, with New York's Nelson Rockefeller moving the most aggressively.

The US Congress, too, was jumping on the punitive anti-drug bandwagon, though not yet with its full weight. A few months before President Nixon's public declaration of an "all-out offensive" against illegal drugs, Congress passed the Federal Comprehensive Drug Abuse Prevention and Control Act of 1970, commonly known as the Controlled Substances Act (CSA).[36] This sixty-page bill consolidated US federal drug policy and demonstrated American commitment to a US-led 1961

United Nations' Single Convention on Narcotic Drugs, which committed member nations to a coordinated attack on international drug trafficking. The CSA was, significantly, more than just a "law and order" measure. The entire first section of the law spelled out a rehabilitation regime aimed at helping drug addicts, particularly those dependent on heroin. The new law also spelled out a series of measures that better regulated "white market," but often abused, prescription drugs, such as Valium. But much of the rest of the bill set the stage for a harsh War on Drugs.

In particular, the CSA set up a series of "schedules" that determined the medical utility and thus legal status of drugs. Heroin was determined to have no acceptable medical use and was thus completely banned as a Schedule I drug, the highest level of prohibition. Its sale and use, in all regards, was criminal and punishable by imprisonment. So, too, did Congress declare that LSD and marijuana were Schedule I drugs without any medical use and were, therefore, also criminalized in every regard. Cocaine, opium, methamphetamine, pentobarbital were all deemed to have some medical uses and, thus, when properly prescribed, were still legal—though not when they were sold on the "black market." A whole series of other prescriptible drugs were sorted into three additional, relatively low-risk categories. These drug "schedules" became the basis for much of the criminalization of drug use that followed over the next several decades.

Frydl explains: "While lawmakers viewed their labors as an effort to impose logic and coherence upon the sprawling and inconsistent world of drug laws . . . in [completely] severing drug regulation from taxes and the world of trade, they put forward crime, and rejected trade, as the appropriate framework within which to consider and regulate illicit drugs."[37] This process had been developing incrementally since the early twentieth century. By the end of 1970, the federal government had comprehensively overturned its earlier, regulatory approach to all drugs and created instead an often blurry, even arbitrary line between how government authorities would approach "white market" drugs—as medicines to be prescribed and regulated—and "black market" drugs—as dangerous substances to be banned and criminalized. Richard Nixon's June 17, 1971 declaration of a War on Drugs was the last step in this long and not always linear process in which users and sellers of "hard drugs" would come to be treated as dangerous criminals deserving of punishment.

Between 1971 and the present, the War on Drugs would be waged with varying degrees of intensity, always inequitably, often ineptly, on a range of battlefields. The chapters that follow explore some of the most treacherous and telling encounters on that deadly and dangerous terrain.

NOTES

1   A video clip of the press conference can be seen at Chris Barber, "Public Enemy Number One," Nixon Foundation, June 29, 2016, www.nixonfoundation.org.

2   Michael Massing, *The Fix* (New York: Simon and Schuster, 1998), 98.

3   The total government expenditure on the War on Drugs is open to debate. The nicely round one-trillion-dollar amount, circa 2018, comes from a liberal think tank: Betsy Pearl, "Ending the War on Drugs: By the Numbers," Center for American Progress, June 27, 2018, www.americanprogress.org.

4   "Slow War on Narcotics," *New York Times*, March 30, 1966, https://timesmachine .nytimes.com.

5   Matthew D. Lassiter, "Impossible Criminals: The Suburban Imperatives of America's War on Drugs," *Journal of American History* 102, no. 1 (June 2005): 130.

6   Quoted in an astute Yale senior essay by Will Horvath, "The 'War on Narcotics; Harry Anslinger, The Federal Bureau of Narcotics, and Senator Price Daniel's Probe," April 13, 2020, 7.

7   "Heroin Hits the Young," *Time*, March 16, 1970, 11–15.

8   The headline is from a May 16, 1971, *New York Times* story, as recounted in Massing, *The Fix*, 108. I draw on chapter 8 of *The Fix*, for the Vietnam story, more generally.

9   For a charming overview by the man who managed the meeting, see Dwight Chapin, "I'm the Reason Elvis Met Nixon," *Politico*, December 25, 2020, www .politico.com. See also "Bud Krogh Talks 'The Day Elvis Met Nixon' at the Nixon Library," uploaded by Richard Nixon Foundation, November 5, 2013, YouTube video, 41:04, https://youtu.be/jho-XT5YLdY.

10   Emily Dufton, "The War on Drugs: How President Nixon Tied Addiction to Crime," *Atlantic*, March 26, 2012, www.theatlantic.com.

11   Lassiter, "Impossible Criminals," 126–40.

12   Joe Biden, Speech at National Press Club, Washington, DC, July 31, 1989, 04148-022, Stephanie Dance Collection, George H. W. Bush Presidential Library, College Station, TX.

13   W. J. Rorabaugh, *The Alcoholic Republic: An American Tradition* (New York: Oxford University Press, 1981), 5.

14   Bruce Bustard, "Spirited Republic," *Prologue*, Winter 2014, 15.

15   Rorabaugh, *The Alcoholic Republic*, 6.

16   See Mark Edward Lender and James Kirby Martin, *Drinking in America: A History* (New York: Free Press, 1987), chap. 2.

17 For a recent overview of Prohibition, see Lisa McGirr, *The War on Alcohol: Prohibition and the Rise of the American State* (New York: Norton, 2015).

18 An early addiction specialist made this claim: Frederick Herman Hubbard, *The Opium Habit and Alcoholism* (New York: Barnes, 1881), 17. For the number of opium addicts and their gender, see David Courtwright, *Dark Paradise: A History of Opiate Addiction in America* (Cambridge: Harvard University Press, 2001), chap. 1. For a handy article that draws on Courtwright's expertise and my original source for the Hubbard quote, see Erick Trickey, "Inside the Story of America's 19th-Century Opiate Addiction," *Smithsonian Magazine*, January 4, 2018, www.smithsonianmag.com.

19 Courtwright, *Dark Paradise*, 77–82.

20 "An Act To prohibit the importation and use of opium for other than medical purposes," H. R. 27427, Sixtieth Congress, second session, February 9, 1909, chapter 100, https://www.loc.gov/law/help/statutes-at-large/60th-congress/session-2/c60s2ch100.pdf.

21 Courtwright, *Dark Paradise*, 3.

22 Courtwright, *Dark Paradise*, 4.

23 For a roundup of the prevalence of cocaine products at the time, see David Farber, *Crack: Street Capitalism, and the Decade of Greed* (New York: Cambridge University Press, 2019), chap. 1.

24 David Pietrusza, *Rothstein: The Life, Times, and Murder of the Criminal Genius Who Fixed the 1919 World Series* (New York: Carroll and Graf, 2003).

25 Quoted in Matthew R. Pembleton, *Containing Addiction: The Federal Bureau of Narcotics and the Origins of America's Global Drug War* (Amherst: University of Massachusetts Press, 2017), 28. A vitally important work on the pre-1971 federal anti-drug effort. See also Kathleen Frydl, *The Drug Wars in America, 1940–1973* (New York: Cambridge University Press, 2013).

26 In her foundational work, *The Drug Wars in America*, Frydl argues that Anslinger was driven by much more than a desire to end domestic drug abuse. He believed, more ambitiously, that international drug interdiction cooperation would lead to a moralistic framework of international relations in which he would play a vital role.

27 Isaac Campos has taken on what he calls the "Mexican hypothesis," regarding cannabis criminalization, and has compellingly complicated the historical record. See Isaac Campos, "Mexicans and the Origins of Marijuana Prohibition in the United States: A Reassessment," *Social History of Alcohol and Drugs* 32, no. 1 (2018): 6–37.

28 That Mexican, and not US, political and public-health elites first developed fierce anti-cannabis rhetoric is a major theme in Isaac Campos, *Home Grown: Marijuana and the Origins of Mexico's War on Drugs* (Chapel Hill: University of North Carolina Press, 2012), esp. chap. 9.

29 Harry Anslinger, "Marijuana: Assassin of Youth," *Reader's Digest*, February 1938 (a condensed version of the original article published in 1937 in *The American*), www.druglibrary.org.

30 Pembleton, *Containing Addiction*, 71. For a detailed analysis of how Anslinger's bureaucratic work figured in the development of state power and federal administrative reach, see Frydl, *The Drug Wars in America*. The relationship between the FBN and prior federal Prohibition efforts is complicated. Lisa McGirr, in *The War on Alcohol*, notes how federal anti-alcohol enforcement increased state law enforcement capacity and the legitimation of a conservative state-building project, more generally. But the FBN did not simply take over that capacity and Anslinger, at least, believed he faced a backlash against perceived state overreach. Still, this question of federal law enforcement capacity and state-building in the War on Drugs is a knotty one and Frydl is the first scholar who has sought to unravel it, focusing on the pre-1971 era.

31 See, in this volume, Peter Pihos, "The Local War on Drugs."

32 For the classic account of early-1960s smuggling, Jerry Kamstra, *Weed: Adventures of a Dope Smuggler* (Santa Barbara: Ross-Erikson, 1974).

33 For a readable account, see Jill Jonnes, *Hep-Cats, Narcs, and Pipe Dreams: A History of America's Romance with Illegal Drugs* (Baltimore: Johns Hopkins, 1999), chap. 9. Jonnes recounts the role of the CIA in the heroin pipeline. For more, see Alfred McCoy, *The Politics of Heroin: CIA Complicity in the Global Drug Trade* (New York: Lawrence Hill, 1991).

34 Erik MacLaren, "Valium History and Statistics," American Addiction Centers, updated February 19, 2021, www.drugabuse.com. For more on Valium and the "white" market, see David Herzberg's chapter in this volume.

35 Ronald Reagan, "Governor Ronald Reagan State of the State Message to the California Legislature in Sacramento, California," January 6, 1970, www.reagan library.gov.

36 For the official public law, see https://www.govinfo.gov/content/pkg/STATUTE-84/pdf/STATUTE-84-Pg1236.pdf.

37 Frydl, *The Drug Wars in America*, 345.

PART II

Supply and Demand

2

Drug Dealers

DAVID FARBER

The War on Drugs has above all targeted drug traffickers. For decades, drug dealers have been vilified, arrested, and imprisoned. Yet their numbers remain relatively stable. While authorities wage their wars on crack cocaine, heroin, and marijuana, at least some people, and not just drug users, support their neighborhood dealers. The drug dealer is a complicated figure in American society, envisioned through the prism of race, class, and conflicting cultural beliefs.

1

For decades, drug dealers have been part of the American social fabric. For many, they are not shadowy, anonymous figures. People know drug dealers, have neighbors who are drug dealers, have friends who are drug dealers, have done deals with drug dealers.

Nobody has hard-nosed figures on how many people, full time, part-time, or once in a great while, have sold illegal drugs over the past half-century or so. A wily writer at the popular political number-crunching site FiveThirtyEight used a Fermi estimation (don't ask) to deduce that in 2011, at a minimum, 121,600 people dealt illegal cannabis full-time at the retail level in the United States.[1] That number did not include growers, smugglers, distributors, wholesalers, or the elderly couple that grew a few pot plants for home consumption but sold the occasional bud on the side. In the late 1980s, about 35 percent of adult Americans surveyed said that drug dealing was "widespread" or "somewhat widespread" in their neighborhoods.[2] That survey included people who lived in big cities, suburbs, and rural areas. In 1975, the survey data used by the federal government stated that 87.8 percent of twelfth graders claimed that it would be "fairly easy" or "very easy" to get marijuana; that percentage stayed almost unchanged over the next several decades. In the 1970s and, indeed, thereafter, marijuana dealers predominated in the illegal drug-dealing business. Certainly, in the 1970s, other illegal drugs were harder to find for the average seventeen- or eighteen-year-old but a significant number of older high school students then and later, no matter what the substance, reported that an illegal purveyor could be readily found if the need arose.[3] Personally, between 1971, when President Nixon announced the War on Drugs, and now, I have lived all over the US, from the North Side of Chicago to the North Shore of Oahu, from the Upper West Side of Manhattan to rural Kansas. In all that time, I've never resided more than a few hundred yards from someone I know who is in the illegal drug business.[4]

Drug dealers have been and are everywhere in the US, even as America's drug warriors, backed by a majority of the citizenry, have tried to eradicate them. In keeping with the "War on Drugs" metaphor, at least some leaders of the anti-drug movement, during the fiercest decades of the war, have insisted that dealers are not simply neighbors who have crossed into criminality but are murderous combatants of the worst kind, deserving of no mercy. President George H. W. Bush, in a campaign speech in 1988, declared: "Drug dealers are domestic terrorists, killing kids and cops, and they should be treated as such. I won't bargain with terrorists, and I won't bargain with drug dealers either."[5] In 1987, at the height of the crack cocaine crisis, some 38 percent of Americans surveyed told pollsters that convicted "drug dealers," guilty of no other crime and with the quantity and kind of drug being dealt unspecified, should be executed.[6]

Over the past fifty years, Americans accused of drug dealing have been arrested millions of times. Those arrests have led to mass imprisonment at the state and local levels. Between 1980 and 2000, in New York, over 125,000 people went to state prison for drug trafficking, most of them low-level dealers.[7] In many jurisdictions, imprisonment on drug felony charges only increased in the first decade of the twenty-first century. In the Chicago area, between 2000 and 2011, nearly one hundred thousand people—88 percent of them African American—were jailed or imprisoned for drug dealing or possession with intent to distribute.[8] Nationally, during the second decade of the twenty-first century, roughly a quarter of a million people every year have been arrested for distributing or manufacturing illegal drugs.[9] At least until very recently, American politicians could almost always successfully court voters by demanding ever-tougher punishments for drug dealers. And yet, despite the opprobrium and risk of arrest and imprisonment, the dealers just keep on keeping on, supplying a massive demand.

Most dealers ply their trade to make money. Some are in the business to feed their own habits. A few are in it for the thrills, and some—think LSD, peyote, mescaline, DMT, and related entheogens—are missionaries for an alternative consciousness. All dealers in illegal drugs are by definition criminals, operating in a lawless realm in which rip-offs, extortion, and violence are commonplace. During the long decades of the drug war, dealers have fed Americans' demands for the illegal substances that have kept tens of millions of people high. For their sins, venal and mortal, they have been damned by most, celebrated by some, protected by others, and left always to wonder if the business they chose was worth the risks they had taken and the lives they had changed, often for the worse.

Drug dealers do have their supporters—obviously. In a variety of subcultures and countercultures, as well as in suburban basements, outside convenience stores, and on inner-city street corners, at least some drug users have perceived drug dealers as a necessary and even, in some special cases, heroic presence in their communities. They have been, in certain instances and circumstances, accorded a kind of respect. The historian E. J. Hobsbawm has called such criminals "social bandits."[10] While the authorities persecuted such men, people in a host of diverse marginal communities—though by no means everyone in those communities—saw dealers as figures of resistance in a corrupt society, suppliers of commonly used and prized commodities, and, in some cases, tricksters who had figured out how to put one over on the hypocritical society that treated them with disdain and attempted to keep them poor and powerless. For at least some citizens of the Intoxicated State, in which getting high has been both common and illegal, drug dealers have been the Resistance, guerilla fighters waging an asymmetric battle against America's heavily armed, merciless drug warriors.

2

In 1971, the year President Nixon declared his War on Drugs, as the US was wracked with anger and discontent, the singer-songwriter Kris

Kristofferson laid down an elegy, "The Pilgrim, Chapter 33." "See him wasted on the sidewalk in his jacket and his jeans," Kristofferson sang, "Wearin' yesterday's misfortunes like a smile."[11] It's a song about artistry, outlaw life, sorry times, and illegal drugs.

A year later, Kristofferson starred in a small Hollywood film, *Cisco Pike*.[12] Kristofferson plays a just-out-of-prison guitar-playing drug dealer who's forced by a crooked cop (the irrepressible Gene Hackman, whose much bigger drug movie, *The French Connection*, came out the year before) to distribute one more load of weed or go to prison for the rest of his life. In the film, "The Pilgrim" plays as Cisco lays off a pound here and a brick there to a Hollywood director, a bell-bottomed boat builder, a pimp, and a variety of right-on long hairs. While Pike wanders the mean streets, dealing his dope, Kristofferson, in a voice over, sings: "He's a poet, he's a picker. He's a prophet, he's a pusher . . . He's a walkin' contradiction." The drug dealer in this movie and in this song, in 1972, is a tragic hero, forced to break the law by a corrupt society. The cannabis he sells hurts no one; the only one at risk is the dealer.

Dope-dealing heroes, tragic or otherwise, were not just a Hollywood conceit, especially in the late 1960s and early 1970s. In 1968, acid luminary Timothy Leary paid homage to America's countercultural dope dealers. Dealing drugs, he said, is "an ancient and honorable profession." The New York City underground newspaper, the *East Village Other*, publisher of the story in which Leary praised drug dealers, titled the article: "Deal for Real: The Dealer as Robin Hood."[13] Leary, though a self-interested party, was not alone in seeing weed dealers and psychedelic distributors in the 1960s and 1970s as paladins of the ascending counterculture.

In white America's "long 1960s," drug dealers were essential contributors to the countercultural scene. Some became celebrities in their own right, at least among the cognoscenti. Acid dealers, in particular, became living legends.

Augustus Owsley Stanley III, nicknamed Bear, was the first and foremost of the acid dealer visionaries. He, an autodidact of uncanny abilities, along with the academically trained chemist Melissa Cargill, became the first large-scale producers of LSD in the United States. Owsley was not in it for the money. He believed in the spiritual, life-altering power of LSD. He gave away at least half of the acid he made. "None of

the money that came from acid I felt was my money. I was like the custo-
dian of it . . . What I was doing was something for the community," he
told a *High Times* journalist.[14] Stanley used his acid money to subsidize
the early Grateful Dead and to help fund San Francisco's psychedelic
paper of record, the *Oracle*. At the 1967 Human Be-In at San Francisco's
Golden Gate Park, Owsley gave away thousands of hits of "White Lightning." Rock Scully, the manager of the Grateful Dead, looking back some
forty years, described Owsley as "revered because he was a bit of a guru
and an alchemist. He was our good wizard, an extreme Robin Hood-like
outlaw wizard."[15] His acid was everywhere in those early years. Other
chemists of like mind joined in. An acid distribution network, led by
Owsley, took form. Dealers, Owsley instructs, can sell a dose for no
more than $2. "Putting it out through a sales trip," he believed, "allowed
a wide distribution that wouldn't have happened if there had been no
money in it."[16]

Among those who first moved Owsley's acid, and then the acid
produced by like-minded acolytes, was the Brotherhood of Eternal
Love (BEL).[17] The Brotherhood grew out of a hard-knuckled crew
of working-class surfer dudes and petty criminals who first operated
in Southern California. Their leader, John Griggs, had stolen his first
doses of LSD from a Hollywood producer at gunpoint. The acid, as
the saying went, put him through some changes and he decided to
use his outlaw talents to bring acid—and hashish and high-quality
cannabis—to the masses. Surfer legend Mike Hynson describes his
friend: "Griggs had gold flashing out of his eyes and tongue, and those
words; he was just a magical guy."[18] Under Griggs' loose leadership, the
BEL connected with countercultural acid makers. Quickly, and for the
next several years, they distributed massive quantities of LSD—tens
of millions of doses—throughout Southern California, the Bay Area,
and then nationally. They also gave away hundreds of thousands of
doses at be-ins, music festivals, and everywhere the burgeoning counterculture gathered. The BEL set up an above-board headquarters in
Laguna Beach; the Mystic Arts World was a combination head shop,
art gallery, health food store, and community hangout. For all to see, it
represented and disseminated the psychedelic culture the BEL aimed
to foster through the emergent acid consciousness they helped make
possible by dealing drugs.

John Griggs died from a massive overdose of psilocybin in 1969. Timothy Leary, who had spent time with Griggs and the Brotherhood, was
devastated: "He was the holiest man ever to live in this country."[19] The
BEL pushed onward, though some say that, without Griggs, the scene
changed. For some of the dealers, the lure of big money became ever-
more paramount. In the late 1960s and the early 1970s, the BEL, a loosely
coordinated crew that included as many as a couple of hundred people,
distributed millions of hits of Orange Sunshine LSD and tons of hash
and cannabis.

The BEL, at least in its drug dealers-as-countercultural-spiritual-
apostles iteration, took a massive blow in 1972, when a task force comprised of twenty-one law enforcement agencies from up and down the
West Coast targeted the Brotherhood's vast drug distribution network.
On August 5, 1972, a little more than a year into the Nixon Administration's War on Drugs, the task force simultaneously raided some two
dozen BEL houses in Hawaii, California, and Oregon. Fifty-three members were arrested and massive quantities of illegal drugs were seized,
including two and half tons of hashish and 1.5 million doses of Orange
Sunshine.

In the aftermath of the bust, *Rolling Stone* magazine mourned the
takedown of "the hippie mafia."[20] Joe Eszterhas, the twenty-seven-year-
old, sympathetic author of the magazine's lengthy two-part series on
the BEL, mocked how legal authorities portrayed the crew: "They are
all members of an underground counterculture syndicate, the Brotherhood of Eternal Love, corrupted flower children who once preached the
teachings of Jesus Christ, now a cold-blooded family of criminal materialists, a denim Cosa Nostra. Jimi Hendrix was one of their soldiers.
Timothy Leary is their Godfather."[21] In counterpoint, Eszterhas quoted
a BEL sympathizer: "There was no real organization. The Brotherhood
was more a vibe than a group. It symbolized love, understanding, and
dope, and it symbolized freak power in Laguna Beach."[22] Decades later,
Eszterhas, who had become a successful screenwriter, succinctly summarized how divided Americans were over the sale and use of cannabis
and hallucinogenics in the early 1970s: "The country was completely po-
larized, and the Brotherhood became an example of that polarization in
front-line terms . . . In those years in Laguna Beach, there was a kind of

war between the straight residents and the people with long hair—and it was deadly, and occasionally lethally, serious."[23]

The BEL was never just a bunch of peaceful drug-dealing hippies with spiritual inclinations, just as it was never—quite—"a cold-blooded family of criminal materialists." Some of the BEL crew, most infamously Johnny Gale, did follow the money and became stupendously wealthy coke dealers, reveling in "life in the fast lane," to quote the great cocaine-fueled band of the 1970s, the Eagles. Others never gave up on their countercultural virtues. They stayed connected to the less mercenary, more spiritual side of the dope scene, even as they kept running their drug "scams." "We weren't gangsters," insists one of the BEL originals, Michael Randall. "We didn't carry guns, rob banks or hurt people. We were doing this for all the right reasons and we truly didn't benefit economically. We were living in teepees and driving old pickup trucks."[24] When Randall was finally tracked down in the early 1980s, charged, and found guilty of breaking numerous drug laws, the sentencing judge commended the drug dealer for staying true to his beliefs: "I admire that. And by the way, I was at your store [Mystic Arts] in Laguna Beach when I was a law student and I thought it was beautiful. I hate to sentence you to prison right now."[25] Nonetheless, he did.

The Brotherhood of Eternal Love was notorious and, at least in some regards, unique. No other dope crew could claim acid avatar Timothy Leary as its patron saint; no other would be eulogized in *Rolling Stone* magazine. Still, BEL associates were far from the only semi-organized, semi-public countercultural dealers of cannabis and psychedelics, especially in the 1970s. Countercultural dope scammers—smugglers, off-loaders, distributors, and major dealers—often specializing in exotic and high-quality cannabis—proliferated in the 1970s. Many tried to stick to a code of behavior, eschewing the brutality and cutthroat behavior they associated with the heroin trade and other "heavy" drugs. They were self-styled "hippie outlaws."

There was the Coronado Company, another ragged group of Southern California surfers and watermen, who helped introduce Americans to Thai stick, arguably the most potent cannabis available in the US the early 1970s. They dealt in multi-ton loads. On the beaches around San Diego they operated a DUKW, a Second World War–era vintage amphibious landing craft they used to bring in loads from offshore boats. Their derring-do was less than covert. Everyone around their base of operation in Coronado knew who they were and what they did. But, at least for a while, that visibility opened them up to only limited risk. Not only were they a part of the community of surfers and countercultural stoners; they were also major benefactors of it. To get their loads off the beaches and on their way to the marketplace, they paid friends and acquaintances a week's worth of wages and more for a few hours of intense work. "If we take care of them," one of the core crewmembers insisted, "they'll take care of us." As the writer Joshua Bearman observes, "The partners could afford to be generous. Still in their twenties, they were walking around with $50,000 in their pockets, then $100,000, then a quarter of a million dollars."[26] The Coronado Company drug dealers were, in their countercultural community, figures of renown.

Most countercultural dope operations were far more low-key and less remunerative, yet they too, had their circle of admirers. Most every college town had its own crews, whose illegal activities were often an open secret.

In Lawrence, Kansas, home of the University of Kansas, the "Kaw Valley Hemp Pickers" mixed local "ditchweed" with high quality Mexican cannabis and sent loads east and west on Interstate 70 and up and down the heartland on a ribbon of state highways. Like the BEL, the main figures in the loosely confederated drug operation tended to be working-class men with the skills and emotional register to carry off a dangerous and criminal business. But they reveled, too, in the antiauthoritarian, hippie ethos of the times. The broader countercultural community, which both relished the profligate quantities of low-cost weed they supplied and appreciated the money they pumped into local hip and artisanal enterprises, embraced them.[27]

Some of these community-supported and community-supporting countercultural illegal drug operations continued on for years. In places like northern New Mexico, Humboldt County, and up-country Maui, where countercultural communities took deep roots, some cannabis businesses, which were built on broad networks of retail and wholesale customers, were handed off from one generation to the next. The domestic artisanal weed business, at least in some, often secluded parts of the US, maintained its countercultural ethos right up to contemporary times. Local mores and social solidarity kept the illegal operations viable and protected . . . at least until outside authorities stepped in.[28]

More often, however, countercultural drug operations evolved into more mercenary businesses. Sometimes, as was the case with some of the BEL members who evaded the early 1970s busts, more profitable cocaine dealing replaced cannabis and hallucinogenics. And no one could make a compelling case that running cocaine was some kind of spiritual endeavor. Robert "Stubby" Tierney, one of BEL's honchos, insists, "Cocaine destroyed our scene . . . Brothers started taking opium and doing cocaine and amphetamines. That took all the spirituality out and made people selfish . . . the coke would make everyone paranoid . . . When I started really dealing cocaine . . . it made my life miserable."[29]

Whether it was the coke, changing times, or both, the countercultural ethos with its spiritual trappings and communitarian dreams had lost its allure for most by the late 1970s. Some "hippie" dealers, including a few who had run LSD at the highest levels, chose to become deviant "yuppie" millionaires. Seemingly without remorse or any sense of cultural betrayal, they became gold chain–wearing, champagne-drinking, materialist obsessives . . . with a propensity for violence. A young associate of the BEL's Johnny Gale, who had become one of California's biggest coke dealers by the late 1970s, got arrested in Orange County. He was offered a deal to inform on Gale but he refused: "He would have killed me. He had bodyguards and Ferraris and all this crazy shit—a brand-new Mercedes—and you know what? The weird thing was that he was not a nice guy anymore."[30] Customers noticed the difference. Peter Maguire, co-author of the definitive book on the dope smugglers and distributors who created the Thai-stick market in the US, sums it up: "To us pot-smoking teenagers, scammers were heroic Robin Hood characters . . . but by the 1990s those days were over."[31]

The "Robin Hood" era of dope dealing, in which customers and suppliers had understood themselves to be invested in more than just a financial transaction, ended not just as a result of cocaine greed and "yuppie" disillusionment. Throughout the 1970s and especially into the 1980s, as illegal drug markets became ever more lucrative in the US, even the weed and LSD trade become a much harder, more violent business.

Men who had no concerns about using extreme violence to control lucrative, illegal businesses were taking over. While dedicated followers of the Grateful Dead and related countercultural associates continued to play a significant role in retailing LSD, increasingly, heavy underworld gangsters and international criminals become invested in the business, too. In 1978, Frank Ragusa, a major LSD dealer with shady European connections, was murdered in his ritzy Oakland Hills home. He had been stabbed twenty-nine times; his wife and sister were killed, as well. More than a million dollars' worth of ergotamine tartrate (ET), the key ingredient in the making of LSD, was found in his residence. Ragusa was no hippie. As LSD historian Jesse Jarnow notes, "Ragusa flies first class and shaves with a $500 gold-rimmed razor."[32] The Oakland detectives investigating the murder filled in some of the blanks. Ragusa, they told reporters, had bought his ET from a recently busted European criminal network known as the "Judo Gang" (martial arts enthusiasts, they smuggled drugs around the world in Judo mats). Ragusa, the police continued, worked closely, as well, with the Mafia on the East Coast.[33] Maybe the recent bust and the Mafia connections explained his murder—but, they admitted, maybe it did not. Ragusa, just thirty when he was killed, was no stranger to the California youth scene, he had gone to the University of California, Berkeley, but he came from a long line of hard men. Both his father and grandfather had been violently murdered.[34] The "hippie mafia" had been replaced, at least in this case, by the real thing. Countercultural "Robin Hoods" were no match for the Mafia, biker gangs, Mexican cartels, Colombian drug lords, Hawaiian gangsters, and myriad other brutal men.

3

In recent decades, the drug dealer's mercurial, contested status as criminal/social bandit—Kris Kristofferson's "walking contradiction"—has been perhaps most apparent in poor inner-city communities, where underground economies have long been a way of life.[35] In such places, in which the means for achieving social status and economic self-determination are too often in short supply, the successful drug dealer can be both an exemplar and a warning, a sign of desperation and a signal of accomplishment.

In Oakland, California, in 1986, those cultural contradictions surrounding the status and meaning of drug dealing were put on public display when thousands of people gathered to send off one of the city's biggest heroin distributors: Felix "The Cat" Mitchell. Mourners filled the sidewalks and streets outside his East Oakland home. They watched, in silence, as a group of solemn men in black tuxedos carried his bronze casket out of the house to a horse-drawn carriage. Four Rolls Royces, ten white limousines, and a long procession of Cadillacs and Lincolns lined up behind the carriage and rolled slowly from East Oakland, through the downtown area, and then alongside Lake Merritt, snarling traffic for hours as they made their way to the burial site. At the funeral service at Star Bethel Baptist Church, some 1,500 people squeezed inside. Another thousand stood outside. Reverend Ivory Redeaux, at the pulpit alongside a massive floral arrangement in the shape of a dollar sign, preached the gospel: "God is merciful."[36]

Mitchell, age 32, had been murdered August 21, 1986, at Leavenworth Federal Penitentiary, some 1,700 miles from Oakland. An inmate had stabbed Mitchell ten times over a petty drug debt. Mitchell had been in prison for just over a year. For nearly a decade, before he was incarcerated, Mitchell, the undisputed leader of the "69 Mob," had been Oakland's heroin kingpin. His crew had been bringing in some $5 million a year before he was taken out.[37]

Oakland police officers watched Mitchell's funeral procession with disgust. Two of them, plain as day, sat in a bright red Ferrari convertible with the top down, taking photographs of known associates of Mitchell as they drove by. The car had been Mitchell's, seized after his arrest. One of the detectives told a reporter: "They're trying to martyr him, this scumbag, this murderer, this convicted heroin dealer. As far as I'm concerned, justice was served."

Oakland City Councilman Leo Brazille, standing outside Mitchell's house, worried that the lavish spectacle sent exactly the wrong message to the city's young people, calling it "hero worship of a murdering thug." Another councilman, Carter Gilmore, also in attendance, speaking to the throng of reporters, echoed this concern: "I'm very upset by this . . . He used young kids to deal with drugs. I don't think any of us here want our kids to be brought up this way. And I think this is a good example of what happens when you're brought up with drugs."

Several people in the crowd, gathered in a scrum around the television cameras and reporters, took offense at Gilmore's comments.

A young man shouted, "You put some jobs here maybe we won't have this on the streets of Oakland." A young woman agreed: "I know what he done. He was a good man. And we need to tell the city officials that if they get the jobs out here, maybe it wouldn't be so many drugs in Oakland." An eleven-year-old boy, sporting a Yankees cap, was asked what he thought: "It's great. The whole thing is great . . . He was kinda cool. He wore cool clothes. He would give my mother money sometimes. I feel sorry for him, that he was stabbed like that." Another boy, feeling no need to explain, compared Mitchell to Martin Luther King Jr. A middle-aged woman, listening in, added: "You know, he taught the young kids that you don't have to live poor, and you don't have to die poor." A thirty-one-year-old man concurred: "He made this out of nothing. He just made it happen . . . The man was a realist. He worked with what he had. Being a black man in this world, nothing comes easy. He did what he had to do."[38]

Felix Mitchell, in life, had been a tall, slim, charismatic man. He never made it out of high school but, among other signs of his stupendous success, he had sported a necklace with a small hourglass filled with dozens of shiny diamonds. Darryl "Lil D" Reed, a teenage Mitchell protégé who would, in turn, become an Oakland drug kingpin before he turned 21—running crack, not heroin—worshipped the man: "The way he dressed up, I never seen anybody so fly . . . You caught up in the visual."[39]

As Reed knew, Mitchell was far more than a charismatic bon vivant, sporting the latest fashions and high-end jewelry. Because Mitchell's business was illegal and immensely profitable, he also had to be a hard man. As Mitchell's teenage protégé, Reed had watched and learned how the Mob 69 crew operated on Oakland's streets: "They jumped out of their cars with machine guns . . . You couldn't be soft around these guys because these were what you called real gangsters in the streets . . . Them explaining to me what the rules were in the streets, I knew what the consequences were . . . If you jumped in the streets, you had to be prepared for some of the violence what came from the streets."[40] Killing and terrorizing rivals was a necessary aspect of the work. In August 1980, Mitchell's people went to war with a rival crew, the Family, over drug-selling territory. In just three days, six people were shot dead. Such murderous internecine struggles were a part of the price of doing business.[41] As Martin "Chango" Mejias, the leader of the Yellow

Top crack crew on New York City's Upper West Side in the late 1980s, put it: "We did what we had to do . . . to survive . . . In our case, it took killing to survive."[42]

Killing and deploying violence was far from the whole story for any large-scale drug crew. Felix Mitchell brought much more to the game. To run his sprawling business, he developed extraordinary organizational skills. Some of what he needed to know he learned from drug-dealing legend Thomas C. "Tootie" Reese, who began his operation in South Central Los Angeles in 1965. Reese informally mentored Mitchell, teaching him how to manage relationships with his suppliers and his distributors without the benefit of contracts or legal protection of any kind.[43] Mostly, though, Mitchell learned on the job.

Mitchell was inventive. To keep his unschooled and often dangerous associates in line and productive, he regularly gathered his lieutenants together to watch *The Godfather*, using the movie to provide his men with lessons about the benefits of loyalty and discipline. Mitchell was also an inveterate fan of TV crime shows, especially *The Untouchables*. He was much taken by *The Untouchables'* portrait of Prohibition-era gangster Al Capone and, at least according to his protégé "Lil D," he modeled himself after the infamous "Public Enemy No. 1."[44]

Then, too, to minimize deleterious scrutiny of his affairs, he worked hard to maintain beneficial community relations. He developed a relationship with Huey Newton, the leader of the Oakland-headquartered Black Panther Party. Though the Panthers were by the late 1970s no longer a national organization, their power rapidly fading even in Oakland, Mitchell recognized that Newton and the few remaining Panthers remained a force to be reckoned with. Mitchell treated Newton, by this time a prodigious user of cocaine, with respect—though he did refuse Newton's extortionate demands that Mob 69 provide him with "donations." Though Mitchell refused to pay off the Panthers, he was by all accounts a generous local benefactor. He spread around cash, slipping boys money for new sneakers and Fila sportswear; he put on lavish parties that supported the local community.[45]

More practically, to make sure that his business's many revenue streams were accounted for and distributed wisely, Mitchell worked hard to develop the kind of financial acumen for which he had no formal training. Mitchell, somehow, succeeded. Even his law enforcement enemies were impressed by Mitchell's ability to run his massive enterprise: "Felix could have been a CEO," Oakland FBI agent Steiner told a journalist. "He had a knack for business. Unfortunately, that business was heroin."[46]

Taking a page unwittingly from Hobsbawm, "Lil D" Reed emotionally recalled that Felix "The Cat" Mitchell "was like Robin Hood to us." Looking back both at his own years as a drug dealer and at the glory years of his mentor, Reed spoke for many of that era's Oakland street corner boys: "I know that Felix did what he did but at the end of the day I got love for Felix."[47]

Reed understood first-hand, as well, the "love" and renown an inner-city drug kingpin could earn in his community. Before Reed was 18, having learned at the feet of the master, he was making more than $15,000 daily selling crack cocaine in his Oakland neighborhood. Before he was 20, his massive crack ring was grossing millions a year.[48] The big money, he knew, bought him respect, at least among his drug-dealing peers, and admiration, at least from those in his community who benefitted from his willingness to spread the wealth. Reed's operation, which employed dozens of corner sellers, stash-house attendants, cooks, "soldiers," runners, and various part-timers, put good money into people's formerly empty pockets. Such money, Lil D's friend, Stanley Kirk Burrell (better known as rapper/dancer MC Hammer) wrote, was not easily attained in Oakland's ghetto in any other way: "Young men choose the 'game' because they see no hope of the American dream being lived around them without the hustle and grind of the streets."[49]

Reed, self-consciously, worked to foster his image as a "good" drug dealer. Not unlike the countercultural drug dealers who preceded him, he saw himself as part of the community in which he operated. He wanted his dealers to understand that they needed to be decent to their customers, who were often their neighbors. "I stressed to the guys that worked for me, that was hustling in the streets," he explained to an interviewer, "to not be mistreating the people who come and buy drugs. I stressed to the guys that I was dealing with, don't mistreat people, they could be your auntie or your uncle . . . I demanded to the guys that was dealing with them, don't take advantage of them in the situation."[50] Reed, at least at the time, believed that he did his best to supply his community with a highly desired product at a fair price under favorable conditions.

In retrospect, Reed insists, he just wasn't aware that selling crack to desperate neighbors could and should be construed as less than meritorious service. As he saw it, "I just thought I was doing what everybody else was doing trying to find a better way to change my life and change my family life. And I didn't realize I was doing more harm to my community. A lot of young guys at the time they wasn't thinking about that man, we were just trying to get some money."[51] And Reed definitely was getting money.

That money, as was made plain by those who mourned the loss of Felix Mitchell, was at the core of what earned Reed his peers' respect and admiration. That and the fact, too, that he was neither arrogant about his achievements nor selfish with his wealth. Indeed, Reed's public largesse led directly to his downfall.

In 1988, Reed threw himself a spectacular twentieth birthday party. He wanted to show off, for sure. But he also wanted to give his community a night no one would ever forget. It was a black tie-only event. More than three thousand young Black men and women celebrated Reed's big day at the Golden Gate Fields Turf Club, across the Bay from Oakland. There was champagne on ice for everyone. Reed, leaving his teenage years behind, was dressed in an oversized white tuxedo with a jet-black button-down shirt. He flashed a massive gold and diamond medallion. MC Hammer and Too Short ("Too $hort"), the biggest rappers to have come out of Oakland, performed. Too Short brought down the house: "Everybody's got that same old dream / To have big money and fancy things."[52] In the words of Hammer: "It was legendary . . . Cats from all over Northern California came to the party and everybody was dressed to the nines . . . you had cats that came in with all white tuxes, you had cats who came in black and white, you had cats in turquoise tuxes . . . It was a celebration of our little potna . . . Everybody had a ball!"[53] Darryl Reed, the biggest crack dealer in Oakland, was the man for all to see.

The event did not go unnoticed by law enforcement. They already had their eyes—and ears—on Reed. The brazen party was too much. Just days after Darryl Reed's extravaganza, Oakland narcotics officers raided his Adams Point apartment in Oakland. They caught him in the act of cooking some thirty pounds of powder cocaine into crack in a massive soup pot on his stovetop. His hands were covered in cocaine. Another sixteen or so kilos were lined up, readied for the next batch. Reed had always been meticulous in taking personal care of his product, and that commitment led to his downfall.[54] Darryl Reed was charged federally under the Anti-Drug Abuse Act of 1986. This is the notorious law that mandated that crack-cocaine dealers (who were overwhelmingly African American) caught with just 1 percent as much weight as powder cocaine dealers (who overwhelmingly were not African American) received the same lengthy prison sentences. Reed, by both measures, met that standard. Just twenty years old, he received a federal sentence of thirty-five years, even though he had committed no violent crimes. (President Barack Obama commuted Reed's sentence in 2016, after he had served twenty-six years in prison.)

Reed's story is far from unique. In the 1980s and 1990s, crack crews, overwhelmingly dominated by young Black men willing to deploy whatever means were necessary to control drug-selling territories, sprang up all over the US, taking advantage of hard times in inner-city communities to supply a cheap, potent high that had customers lined up nearly 24/7. In New York City, the Supreme Team, the Yellow Top Crew, Sex Money Murder, the Gulleymen, and others got rich fast before being taken down by law enforcement. The same held true in Chicago, Detroit, Los Angeles, Washington, DC and every other big city, as well as many a smaller community that had the necessary consumer base. Crack rings all over the US made millions of dollars. And that crazy money, made by unschooled young Black men operating in their own poor neighborhoods, raised a heated conversation within the African American community.

For some, the drug money—and the power and respect that drug money earned—was all that needed to be understood. A whole hip-hop genre, gangsta rap, emerged to lavish praise on the Gucci-wearing, gold chained, luxury-automobile-owning, murderous crack entrepreneurs who were reinventing the Horatio Alger self-made-man myth for young inner-city men on the make. NWA, a group of artists who came "Straight Outta Compton," explained the lure of the trade: "Young brother getting over by slanging cane / Gold around his neck 14 k he has it / Bitches on his dick 24–7."[55] Scarface, a Houston rapper who hustled drugs before making it as an artist, insisted that dealing crack wasn't much different from what some of American's better known wealthy men did to make their pile: "Nigga rollin' hard stackin' paper like Trump."[56] Nas, a rap lyricist with few peers, who gave up on school after the eighth grade, linked together what he saw as the only two ways a young Black man could get ahead: "Ayo the rap game reminds me of the crack game."[57] The crack hustler, whether the street corner boy with a "Tec" and his Air Jordans or the kingpin rolling down the street in a mint white Cadillac, was a hood celebrity.

Strangest of all, perhaps, was that the gangsta rapper, who often emulated the ostentatious "flossing" and menacing attitude of their gangster peers, became style icons for a not-insubstantial segment of white, middle-class youths. Hip-hop verses celebrating the slinging of crack and the gunning down of rival drug crews became locker room chants and drunken frat boy choruses. A *Washington Post* article in 1992 was one of many that had a journalist reporting back from a fancy suburban high school about the phenomenon: "Asian American boys grab their crotches rap-style . . . and white boys splutter, 'Yo, whassup man? . . . [F]or others—whose contact with blacks is limited to the two dimensions of an MTV video—hip hop's allure runs as shallow as the gangster swagger, the exotic otherness, the aggressive, strong simple beats."[58] The crack dealer, channeled through the gangsta rapper, became a suburban icon.

Some of the fiercest and most successful hip-hop artists did push back against the vainglorious portraits of the gun-toting, "ho"-bashing, money-stacking crack dealer. Tupac Shakur yo-yoed back and forth between celebrating—and living the life—of the drug slinging gangster—and recognizing the "walking contradictions" of the neighborhood-destroying crack dealer. In a track that perhaps only he could have pulled off, titled "Dear Mama," he began, "You are appreciated." And then, loving son to worried mother, he explained: "I ain't guilty 'cause even though I sell rocks / It feels good puttin' money in your mailbox."[59] Todd Anthony Shaw, better known as Too Short, who gave that boffo performance at Oakland crack kingpin Darryl Reed's birthday party, was one of several rappers who knew better. A year after Reed got sent away on a thirty-five-year bid, Too Short released his song "The Ghetto": "Sitting in the jailhouse running your mouth / While me and my peoples try to get out."[60] Dealing crack, even sympathetic hip-hop artists knew, was at best a devil's bargain.

Within poor communities, most people did not countenance crack and heroin dealers. They despised them, even as they often feared them. In the 1960s and 1970s, Black residents of Harlem watched heroin rip through their neighborhood. Dealers sold out in the open. A high school addict told a reporter: "I could walk down 122d Street, between Seventh and Eighth Avenues, and pick up anything I wanted, any time— like a bazaar or something."[61] Junkies robbed and stole and mugged. "Some sections of the so-called Harlem business section after nightfall [look] like a ghost town," the *Amsterdam News* reported to its African American readership. "People continue to be afraid to walk the streets at night."[62] Harlem Congressman Charles Rangel was furious with the dealers, but equally with the police who allowed drug dealers to operate in his district with near impunity: "Drugs affected every part of every life in my town. Senior citizens were assaulted by addicts, while addicts were fighting and killing one another and had taken over whole streets and neighborhoods."[63] Congressman Rangel, alongside a great many other Black elected officials and community leaders, vowed to bring the dealers down. For the next twenty-five years, Rangel would be one of the fiercest of America's drug warriors.[64]

African Americans, especially in poor neighborhoods, were even more torn apart by the scourge of crack cocaine in the 1980s and 1990s. After the young basketball star Len Bias died of a cocaine overdose in 1986 (though many believed he died from crack, he had actually been snorting powder cocaine), the Reverend Jesse Jackson, then America's best-known civil rights leader, launched a searing jeremiad at the people who supplied young Black men and women with drugs. Speaking to a large crowd of mourners at the University of Maryland's Memorial Chapel, Jackson was deadly serious: "Ropes never killed as many of our young people as the pushers of drugs . . . Lenny was vulnerable, but all of us are . . . We must make his death the turning point."[65] Soon after Bias's overdose death, Congressman Charles Rangel, a liberal, worked closely with the conservative Reagan administration to pass the Anti-Drug Abuse Act of 1986, the single most punitive law ever passed during the War on Drugs. At the federal level, it massively increased prison sentences for drug dealers, targeting, above all, the young Black men who sold crack cocaine. It also began a massive increase in the amount of money and resources the federal government would expend on arresting, convicting, and imprisoning drug dealers.

In general, people cheered this more aggressive, more merciless War on Drugs. A June 1989 Gallup poll revealed that, by a 3 to 1 ratio, Americans believed that drugs were Americans' number-one problem. President George H. W. Bush's political advisors told the newly elected president that, in the minds of most voters, no measure could go too far in punishing drug dealers. In response, the Bush administration floated the idea of making certain kinds of drug-dealing offenses capital crimes, something Bush had first raised on the campaign trail.[66]

Letters of support flooded into the White House: "The penalty should be death!" "Put the automatic death penalty to the vote of the people of the USA." "I believe that capital punishment is a better solution rather than spending millions of dollars to build more jails and overcrowd them again." Many, in hopes of bringing the war to a successful conclusion, wanted the military to join the fray: "Why are our armed forces on the ready to serve in a foreign country while our home front is ignored? JUST ASKING," and "Let's make a war of it! Use our entire armed forces as a big war game exercise, crank up the propaganda machine to offset the screams of inhuman treatment that are sure to follow," and "I would very much appreciate an answer telling me why the military cannot eradicate these armed [marijuana] growers." Others insisted that if the US was going to wage a "war" on drugs then it should pull out all stops: "When drug pushers are caught, send them to the POW camp. Don't tie up the courts with these people. We didn't in World War I or II. Let's win the war first and worry about civil rights after the war is over." The Bush White House received thousands of letters demanding an escalation of the drug war.[67] The administration backed off on the death penalty talk—in part, because the Democratic majority in the Senate, led by Joe Biden on this issue, wasn't having it— but it did dramatically increase the federal prosecution of drug dealers and the financial support the federal government provided states and localities in locking them up.[68]

4

Given the strength of popular support for the War on Drugs, at least until recently, it is remarkable how hard it has been to put a stop to drug dealing. Part of the answer, of course, is built into the business equation. Government authorities, for a very long time, have made a number of extremely in-demand drugs illegal and have attached very high risks—basically, imprisonment—to selling those drugs. As a result, to accommodate those sales risks in accord with the hungry demand, profit margins are quite good, even extraordinary. Such profit margins, risks be damned, incentivize the supply chain, from kingpin to street-corner dealer.

In addition, as the tales I have recounted above should make abundantly clear, drug dealers are often enough dangerous people. So even if neighbors, parents, teachers, and ministers want drug dealers to stop peddling in their communities, making them stop is often far from easy. When I was interviewing knowledgeable insiders about the history of the crack cocaine industry in the 1980s and 1990s, admittedly among the most murderous of drug businesses, I was repeatedly told—twenty and more years after the fact—that talking with me about specific dealers and their networks was not a smart play. One man, who shall remain anonymous, explained the situation to me as simply as he could: "I do know that one thing is for certain with the XXXXXX organization; you can be 100 percent for certain that if I get caught telling, that is the end of it."[69]

Community leaders and neighbors sometimes did take on the dealers. In some places, in some cases, those campaigns worked. In the Mantua neighborhood of West Philadelphia, Herman Wrice became a local hero in the 1980s and 1990s by standing up to the crack dealers that operated openly in his community. He and a stalwart group of his neighbors boarded up abandoned "crack houses," posted flyers showcasing "the dealer of the week," and directly confronted street corner sellers. "Stand up to them and they'll leave," Wrice told his neighbors. Though the dealers threatened Wrice's life, at least some of them eschewed the public shaming and did leave, though many simply opened up shop elsewhere.[70]

Sometimes, horrifically, such community efforts did not work. In East Baltimore in 2002, Angela Dawson, her husband, and their five children were burned to death by their drug-dealing neighbor after she contacted the police about his business. In part, Ms. Dawson had acted in response to Baltimore Mayor Martin O'Malley's "Believe" campaign, which had urged the city's residents to take their city back from the murderous drug crews that ran the streets.[71] In 2000, in the Venice neighborhood of Los Angeles, the community's most vocal anti–drug dealer activist, James Richards, was gunned down right outside his modest home. "They took his life to show that they are the winner," his domestic partner told reporters. Even as Mr. Richard's body still lay on the ground, an onlooker sneered, "I'm glad he's dead." Others agreed, condemning the 55-year-old man as a "snitch" who had gotten what he deserved.[72] Such tragic stories can be multiplied.

Within the hip-hop community, there is an entire genre of anti-snitching rap songs. Some of the most celebrated artists, including Snoop Dogg, Lil Wayne, Scarface, Mobb Deep, Pusha T, and many more, have spit out verses condemning any and all who would cooperate with the police against neighborhood drug dealers. Few of these rappers openly encourage the murder of local people who speak out against drug dealing in their neighborhoods, saving most of their bile for arrested dealers who roll over on their own networks. Still, they make the case repeatedly in their verses that cooperating with the police, whom they condemn as a racist occupying force in inner-city neighborhoods, is a greater offense than selling drugs in the street. So, while the fear of physical—even murderous—retaliation is very real for those who would stand up to drug dealers in poor communities, so, too, is homegrown cultural opprobrium. In 2018, Philadelphia's African American newspaper headlined a story "'No Snitching' Culture Cripples Community," recounting numerous unsolved crimes by drug crews.[73] Drug dealers, for some, are less "domestic terrorists" than local people caught up in a tough business doing their best to survive and even prosper in a society that has given them too few ways to craft an upright life of dignity.

The inner-city drug dealers who figured so prominently in the crack-cocaine business of the 1980s and 1990s seemingly had little in common with the hippie weed and acid dealers of the early 1970s—except for the social reality that all were criminals by law. And except for the shared cultural perception—among at least some of their peers and compatriots—that such outlawry was not without cause and reasonable intention. "Robin Hoods," said Darryl "Lil D" Reed. "Robin Hoods," Timothy Leary agreed.

A majority of Americans, then and now, would have none of it. Then, too, once past the overly capacious label—drug dealer—people have perceived purveyors of illegal substances through a prism of all the usual social categories: race, class, ethnicity, age. Even in the fiercest days of the War on Drugs, few white Americans wanted to see white teenage neighborhood weed dealers spend decades in prison. Many had fewer qualms about destroying the lives of inner-city, Black crack dealers.[74] In the abstract, large majorities of Americans have directed an extraordinary animus toward drug dealers. In practice, unsurprisingly, that rage has largely targeted poor, Black dealers who have filled our prisons for decades. Darryl Reed asks why he got thirty-five years and the Big Pharma executives and investors who deluged America with opioids got nothing but rich: "They ruining more people's lives than cocaine or heroin. Those pharmaceutical companies they drug dealers . . . So let us question what their drugs are doing to society, too!"[75] Sure, it's a self-serving observation and yet . . .

Kris Kristofferson, back in 1971, sang about the drug dealer as a "walkin' contradiction." That contradiction—a man needed, even respected, but often reviled, a man who without judgment simply sells what people seek—is at the heart of American society's conflicted and confounding War on Drugs. The American people, with their unparalleled hunger for intoxicating substances—a demand that extends across the social map—created a criminal class to feed that need and then declared war on it. That battle spread internecine violence throughout the land. Millions, cumulatively, become prisoners of that war. And still the dealers keep on keeping on, in a war without end.

NOTES

1 Walt Hickey, "The Number of Marijuana Dealers in the United States," July 16, 2014, FiveThirtyEight, www.fivethirtyeight.com.

2 The George H. Gallup International Foundation, "Surveys on the Drug Crisis, August 4, 1989—briefing provided to ONDCP," OsNDCP Strategy ll—[4] 02301-009, George H. W. Bush Presidential Library.

3 *Monitoring the Future: National Survey Results on Drug Use, 1975–2019* (Institute for Social Research, University of Michigan: 2020). A summary of the data on

marijuana and twelfth-graders appears on page 11, with critical data appearing throughout this incredibly valuable 131-page source.

4 Well, in Kansas it might be a bit farther, but not much.

5 George H. W. Bush, campaign speech, Los Angeles Police Academy, May 18, 1988, Michael P. Jackson Files, 02301–010, George H. W. Bush Presidential Library.

6 Aaron Dugan, "Gallup Vault: Executing Drug-Users Unpopular in 1987 Poll," Gallup, March 21, 2018, https://news.gallup.com. The title strikes me, at least, as somewhat ironic given that only 55 percent of people thought the death penalty was a tad too punitive. It is worth noting that the crack crisis was in full force in 1987 when the poll was taken.

7 "Who Goes to Prison for Drug Offenses? A Rebuttal to the New York State District Attorneys Association," Human Rights Watch, 1999, www.hrw.org. It is really hard to find accurate historical and cumulative numbers on state and local drug trafficking imprisonments. Federal prison numbers are available, but they account for less than 10 percent of people imprisoned on drug charges.

8 Angela Caputo, "Road to Ruin," *Chicago Reporter*, March/April 2013, 10.

9 "Drug War Facts," accessed March 9, 2021, www.drugwarfacts.org.

10 E. J. Hobsbawm, *Primitive Rebels* (Manchester, UK: University of Manchester Press, 1959), 13–29.

11 Kris Kristofferson, "The Pilgrim, Chapter 33," *The Silver Tongued Devil and I*, Monument Records, 1971.

12 *Cisco Pike*, directed by Bill L. Norton (Columbia Pictures, 1972).

13 Timothy Leary, "Deal for Real," in *Underground Press Anthology*, ed. Thomas King Forçade (New York: Ace Books, 1968), 13. As noted in the text, the article was originally published in the *East Village Other* under the title, "Deal for Real: The Dealer as Robin Hood."

14 Quoted in Jesse Jarnow, *Heads: A Biography of Psychedelic America* (Boston: Da Capo, 2016), 17. Bear figures in many of the key works by and about the early counterculture. I am mostly following the account given by Jarnow in his superb history of LSD in the United States.

15 Quoted in Robert Greenfield, *Bear: The Life and Times of Augustus Owsley Stanley III* (New York: St. Martins, 2016), 85. Greenfield has written many of the best biographies of key Sixties-era counterculture icons and the interviews he has done for his books are, for the era, unrivaled.

16 Jarnow, *Heads*, 23.

17 Some veterans of the Brotherhood of Eternal Love maintain an extraordinary, anarchic website, accessed March 19, 2021, https://belhistory.weebly.com.

18 Quoted in the definitive work on the Brotherhood: Nicholas Schou, *Orange Sunshine: The Brotherhood of Eternal Love and Its Quest to Spread Peace, Love, and Acid to the World* (New York: St. Martin's Press, 2010), 48.

19 Schou, *Orange Sunshine*, 192.

20 Joe Eszterhas, "The Strange Case of the Hippie Mafia, Part 1" *Rolling Stone*, December 7, 1972, 28–34, and Joe Eszterhas, "The Strange Case of the Hippie Mafia, Part 2," *Rolling Stone*, December 21, 1972, 48–56.

21 Eszterhas, "Part 1," 28.

22 Eszterhas, "Part 1," 32.

23 David Browne, "50th Anniversary Flashback: The Drug Chronicles," *Rolling Stone*, August 17, 2017, www.rollingstone.com.

24 Quoted in a glowing piece in *People* magazine celebrating the 2017 release of the documentary film, *Orange Sunshine: The True Story of Friends, Family and One Hundred Million Hits of Acid*: Johnny Dodd, "Memories from the Summer of Love," *People*, September 4, 2017, www.people.com.

25 J. Macon King, "Interview with Michael Randall of the Brotherhood of Eternal Love," *Mill Valley Literary Review*, 2019, accessed June 1, 2020, www.millvalleylit.com.

26 The best overview of the Coronado Company is by Joshuah Bearman, "Coronado High," *The Atavist*, no. 27, July 2013, https://magazine.atavist.com.

27 For the dope scene in Lawrence, see *Cows Are Freaky When They Look at You*, comp. and ed. David Ohle, Roger Martin, and Susan Brosseau (Wichita: Watermark Press, 1991).

28 For more, see Michael Polson's chapter in this volume.

29 Nick Schou, "Lords of Acid," *OC Weekly*, July 7, 2005, www.ocweekly.com.

30 Schou, "Lords of Acid."

31 Peter Maguire and Mike Ritter, *Thai Stick: Surfers, Scammers, and the Untold Story of the Marijuana Trade* (New York: Columbia University Press, 2014), xxi-xxii, xxx.

32 Jarnow, *Heads*, 113.

33 "Inquiry into Killings Discloses Drug Link," *New York Times*, March 28, 1978, www.nytimes.com.

34 "Mafia Ties? Suspect Held in Murders, Dope Racket," *Desert Sun*, March 22, 1978, https://cdnc.ucr.edu.

35 For an acclaimed book on the subject: Sudhir Venkatesh, *Off the Books: The Underground Economy of the Urban Poor* (Cambridge: Harvard University Press, 2009).

36 The quotes and description that follow are drawn from two key sources: Channel 7 News (Oakland, California), "Drug Lord Felix Mitchell funeral ('The 69 MOB'☆1986)," uploaded by Vinmoonsu, March 16, 2019, YouTube video, 2:46, https://www.youtube.com/watch?v=qnVtwzaw6lM; Dan Morain, "Garish Oakland Funeral," *Los Angeles Times*, August 30, 1986: 1, 30.

37 The group took its name from Oakland's 69th Avenue San Antonio Village Housing Projects. For Mitchell's heroin sales figures, see "Garish Oakland Funeral."

38 "Felix's Funeral" and Morain, "Garish Oakland Funeral," 1, 30.

39 "Lil D on Becoming Crack King, Getting 35 Years, Obama Clemency (Full Interview)," uploaded by djvlad, January 23, 2019, YouTube video, 2:18:59, https://www.youtube.com/watch?v=Hc9kOILif54.

40 "Lil D on Becoming Crack King."

41 Walker, "Drug Kingpin's Sentencing Ends Bloody Era in Oakland."

42 "The YTC Story - Director's Cut (Plus Narrated Version)," uploaded by Infominds, January 8, 2018, YouTube video, 42:00, https://youtu.be/3PGoSsbHKHs. The quote is from YTC co-leader Chango.

43 Tootie Reese was convicted in 1984 of cocaine trafficking. For a portrait or Reese, see Seth Ferranti, "LA's Original Gangster—Tootie Reese," Gorilla Convict, April 22, 2015, www.gorillaconvict.com.

44 "Lil D on Becoming Crack King." For a guide to Chicago drug crews' corporate culture in the same era, see Andrew Martin, "Instructions Required for Gang Membership," *Chicago Tribune*, May 13, 1995, www.chicagotribune.com.

45 "Lil D on Becoming Crack King" and Thaai Walker, "Drug Kingpin's Sentencing Ends Bloody Era in Oakland," February 16, 1999, SFGATE, www.sfgate.com.

46 Walker, "Drug Kingpin's Sentencing Ends Bloody Era in Oakland."

47 "Lil D on Becoming Crack King."

48 Daryl "Lil D" Reed published a 154-page memoir, *Weight* (Pasadena: Concrete Jungle Publishing, 2010). He was pardoned from a 35-year prison sentence by President Obama in 2016 and subsequently did many interviews, which are available on YouTube.

49 Hammer grew up in public housing in East Oakland and wrote the brief introduction to *Weight*. Hammer actually stayed on the straight and narrow throughout his youth, displaying his abundant talents in multiple legit ways before joining the Navy and then, after an honorable discharge, becoming a successful performer. Still, he understood.

50 "Lil D on Becoming a Crack King."

51 "Lil D on Becoming a Crack King."

52 Too Short, "Life is . . . Too Short," track 1 on *Life is . . . Too Short* (Jive Records and RCA Records, 1988). This was Too Short's breakout track on the breakout album of the same name.

53 "Mc Hammer Reflects Back on Lil Potna's 1st Black Tie Party 28 Years Ago," uploaded by Fulani Muhammad, March 13, 2017, YouTube video, 2:36, https://www.youtube.com/watch?v=OxknomXyLrE.

54 Pamela A. MacLean, "Millionaire Street 'Crack' Dealer Charged," UPI, December 9, 1988, www.upi.com; David Debolt, "Oakland Crack King, Darryl Reed Gets Clemency from Obama," *Mercury News*, September 5, 2016, www.mercurynews.com.

55 NWA, "Dope Man" [1988], track 3 on *The Best of NWA, "The Strength of Street Knowledge"* (Priority Records, Ruthless Records, 2006).

56 Scarface, "Money and the Power," track A1 on *Money and the Power* (Rap-a-Lot Records, Priority Records, 1992).

57 Nas, "Represent," track 1-9 on *Illmatic XX* (Columbia Records, Legacy Records, Sony Records, 1992).

58 Laura Blumenfeld, "Black Like Who? Why White Teens Find Hip-Hop Cool," *Washington Post*, July 20, 1992, www.washingtonpost.com.

59 Tupac Shakur, "Dear Mama" [1995], track C1 on *2Pac: Me against the World* (Interscope Records, Ume Records, Amaru Entertainment, 2020).

60 Too Short, "The Ghetto," track 3 on *$hort Dog's in the House* (Jive Records, 1990).

61 Thomas A. Johnson, "Heroin 'Epidemic' Hits Schools," *New York Times*, February 16, 1970, www.nytimes.com.

62 Michael Javin Fortner, *Black Silent Majority* (Cambridge: Harvard University Press, 2015), 141.

63 Charles Rangel and Leon Wynter, *And I Haven't Had a Bad Day Since* (New York: Thomas Dunne Books, 2007), 189.

64 For more see Fortner, *Black Silent Majority*, and David Farber, *Crack: Street Capitalism, and the Decade of Greed* (New York: Cambridge University Press, 2019), chap. 5.

65 Roy S. Johnson, "At Services for Bias, Tributes and Warnings Offered," *New York Times*, June 24, 1986, 5.

66 Bush's first drug czar, William Bennett, led the charge: "Two words sum up my approach: consequences and confrontation. Those who use, sell, and traffic in drugs must be confronted and they must suffer the consequences . . . in law enforcement, they include policies such as . . . the death penalty for drug kingpins." This example is from William Bennett, "Drug: Consequences and Confrontations," Washington Hebrew Congregation, May 3, 1989, Steve Danzansky Files, 02183–001, George H. W. Bush Presidential Library. Bush called for the death penalty for drug traffickers at a speech he gave at the Los Angeles Police Academy, May 18, 1998, Michael P. Jackson Files, 02301–010, George H. W. Bush Presidential Library.

67 Office of Correspondence, Public Mail Files: DRUG WAR, 2018–0038-F, George H. W. Bush Presidential Library. At the Bush Library, I used a FOIA request to have a sample of the White House mail, catalogued under "DRUG WAR," opened up for my perusal. There were so many tens of thousands of letters that the archivists and I worked out an arrangement to have a sample of just some of the boxes prepared. I read around a thousand, most of which were sent soon after President Bush's Oval Office speech in which he waved around a big bag of crack cocaine. Many people simply expressed support for Bush's speech and the War on Drugs, in general. A lot of people offered to pray for the president. But a sizeable number do reflect the comments I have used here and very few offered any opposition to a punishing War on Drugs. I did not read a single letter that expressed any sort of racism or racializing of the War on Drugs, which surprised me given the public focus at that time on African American crack dealers.

68 Biden was no "dove" in the War on Drugs, but he did oppose the death penalty. His 236-page plan released in January 1990 was otherwise very similar to that of the Bush administration, as was approvingly pointed out in a *New York Times* editorial, "First Victory in the Drug War," *New York Times*, January 26, 1990, clipping, 02301–006, Michael P. Jackson Files, George H. W. Bush Presidential Library.

69 Anonymous, interview with author, May 2018.

70 Wrice became nationally known for his efforts. He embraced the most punitive aspects of the War on Drugs. For a good overview see John L. Puckett, "Mantua

against Drugs," West Philadelphia Collaborative History, accessed March 9, 2021, https://collaborativehistory.gse.upenn.edu.

71 Jeffrey Gettleman, "In Baltimore, Slogan Collides with Reality," *New York Times*, September 2, 2003, www.nytimes.com.

72 Gina Piccalo and Kurt Streeter, "Venice Anti-Gang Activist Killed in His Driveway," *Los Angeles Times*, October 19, 2000, www.latimes.com.

73 Ashley Caldwell, "'No Snitching' Culture Cripples Community," *Philadelphia Tribune*, October 1, 2018, www.phillytrib.com.

74 I discuss this problem in *Crack*, chap. 6.

75 "Lil D on Becoming a Crack King."

3

The Mexico–Chicago Heroin Connection

ELAINE CAREY

With the heightened War on Drugs beginning in the 1970s, drug trafficking organizations embraced new technologies and transportation modalities while constructing cross-class and cross-ethnic alliances that reflected shifting power dynamics. The Herrera family organization was a nexus between old and new United States–Mexico organizations. Operating from Mexico's Golden Triangle and Chicago, it evaded the attention of law enforcement due to its complex structures and flexible business practices. Even when enforcement agencies focused on taking down the Herreras, the family remained one step ahead by adapting certain practices, diversifying markets, shifting locations, expanding territories, and modernizing money laundering. The policing of the Herreras had a significant impact on the 1984 Comprehensive Criminal Control Act.

1

During the 1970s, the downsizing, closure, or relocation of local steel and heavy industries economically shattered the old industrial communities of Roseland and Pullman, on the far South Side of Chicago. These once vibrant working-class neighborhoods, whose residents had worked for generations in well-paid union jobs, saw their employment disappear, housing prices plummet, and commercial establishments close their doors. In the midst of the economic downturn, one major business did thrive in Roseland and Pullman, belying the many shuttered stores and factories. In the mid-1970s, these two economically depressed Chicago neighborhoods had become major distribution stations in the United States–Mexican transnational drug trade.

Some of the highest-ranking members of the Herrera drug trafficking organization (DTO), one of the most lucrative illegal drug operations originating in Mexico, made their home in the down-on-its luck, working-class communities of Roseland and Pullman. While the Herrera organization was based in Durango, Mexico, its US-based distribution ring operated commercially out of Roseland, Pullman, and other scattered neighborhoods in southwest Chicago. They also set up shop in the far west Chicago suburb of Aurora, farther north in Milwaukee, and east in economically depressed communities in neighboring northwest Indiana. From the 1950s onward, the organization smuggled, distributed, and wholesaled thousands of kilos of heroin that originated in Durango and other parts of Mexico and that flowed to the Chicago area through US–Mexican border towns such as El Paso–Ciudad Juárez.

The Herreras had begun to use Chicago as their primary US distribution base for heroin in the late 1950s. The city had drawn Herrera family members because they recognized the utility of Chicago, nationally known then as "the city that works," as a well-developed transportation and distribution hub. They took the heroin that arrived in Chicago, cut it, and, after reserving a large amount for the local market, distributed it to other major Midwestern cities, such as St. Louis, Milwaukee, Gary, and Detroit, as well as into numerous towns and cities throughout the Northeast.[1]

While the Herrera DTO's origins were Mexican, its workforce resembled that of a modern transnational corporation, comprising Mexican Americans, Puerto Ricans, African Americans, and European Americans, men and women alike, all of whom became trusted members of the organization. The organization readily diversified its offerings when demand shifted, and it strategically expanded its market share over years. The Herrera DTO ran for decades like a well-oiled money-making machine.

Journalists have often glorified and celebrated the spectacular rise and fall of notorious Mexican cartels, regaling readers with tales of violence, gun battles, wild parties, and, finally, the gaudy, lavish narco-mausoleums that hold the remains of murdered drug lords—common sites across Mexico nowadays.[2] Such accounts are not inaccurate, but they hide another aspect of the drug trade: some of the more enduring DTOs are sophisticated operations that shun public notoriety. The Herrera DTO operated for decades while avoiding the limelight and insisting that its members keep a low profile. The Herrera organization was always innovating to stay one step ahead of law enforcement; it

embraced new technologies and transportation modalities. They constructed cross-class and cross-ethnic alliances that reflected shifting
power dynamics in the global drug trade. Like many other major corporations, the Herrera DTO used complex management structures to
run its business. To evade unwanted attention, its leaders insisted that
its members maintain modest lifestyles. The Herrera DTO looked and
acted little like the glorified narco-dramas that circulate in telenovelas,
films, and other forms of popular culture.

The Chicago Police Department (CPD) and, later, the Drug Enforcement Administration (DEA) for decades failed to recognize that the Herrera DTO was the model many future drug traffickers in the US would
embrace. This family-based organization was a narco-pioneer. The Herrera family successfully created a DTO that was transnational, bilingual,
bicultural, and immensely profitable. While they remained rooted in a
working-class, Mexican-American environment in the US, the Herreras
readily adapted to transnational business opportunities and law enforcement threats. They constantly diversified their markets and productions.
They steadily forged new alliances. And they relocated to new locations
when threats or opportunities arose. All the while, they maintained a
free-flowing heroin pipeline that fed the massive demand of their US
consumers, who rejected the strict drug prohibition and fierce punishment strategies their elected representatives sought to enforce.

2

The Herrera DTO in the 1970s and America's War on Drugs

After his inauguration in 1969, President Richard Nixon sought to
fulfill his campaign promise to undermine illegal drug use and crush
the criminal drug trade. That promise led the federal government to
expand and reorganize the Bureau of Narcotics and Dangerous Drugs;
its much beefed-up successor organization, the DEA, was formed in
1973.[3] It understood that one of its primary responsibilities in waging a war against drugs was to take on the massive flow of contraband
that was being brought into the US by Mexican drug traffickers. As a
result, by 1974, the DEA had six offices in Mexico, and 157 agents on
the US–Mexico border.[4] Based in Mexico, fifty-four agents worked with
Mexican authorities and trained 250 of the 350 members of the Mexican

Federal Judicial Police (*Policía Judicial Federal*, PJF, colloquially known as the *federales*) in drug enforcement procedures. The PJF disbanded in 2002 after its agents' ties to DTOs became impossible to ignore.[5]

Abraham L. Azzam, the deputy regional director of the DEA for the Chicago area testified in 1977 that the DEA had a strong working relationship with the PJF in Mexico.[6] Azzam seemed not to know, or perhaps didn't care, that the *federales* had long been despised by many Mexicans for their history of corrupt and violent practices. It is clear that the DEA worked with PJF officers on drug interdiction and policing without regard for or understanding of how Mexicans viewed the PJF.[7]

In the early 1970s, the DEA rediscovered an open secret that had been common knowledge among US drug agents in the 1950s: that a large percentage of all heroin in the US came from or through Mexico and virtually all marijuana seized in the US came from Mexico and Central America. In 1974, the DEA concluded that cocaine was also being moved through Mexico into the US.[8] While the Colombian Medellín DTO based its US operations initially in the borough of Queens in New York City, where its members received shipments of cocaine by sea and by air from multiple, non-Mexican smugglers, the Medellín DTO also supplied the US cocaine market with product smuggled across the US–Mexico border crossings.[9] By the mid-1970s, the Medellín organization moved its US operations from New York to Miami, Florida, and worked even more closely with several cocaine smuggling Mexican DTOs, including the Herreras.[10]

By 1974, the DEA knew that its earlier reports had underestimated the amount of heroin being supplied by Mexican traffickers. In 1971, the DEA had claimed that only 2 percent of the heroin consumed in the US came from Mexico; but by 1974 they estimated that 50 to 70 percent of all heroin consumed in the US came from Mexico. Any capitalist titan would be envious of such market growth. The DEA actually took credit for the tremendous success of Mexican DTOs, arguing that the increase was due to "successful action against heroin entering the US from Turkey and Western Europe." In 1974, a DEA report argued that Mexican chemists "follow a less sophisticated opium process formula than the European chemists, which gives their heroin a brown color as opposed to a white color."[11] Allegedly, Mexican chemists processed 70 percent of the heroin consumed the US in *cocinas* or "kitchens." The DEA's erroneous—and racist—assumption about the primitive nature of Mexican heroin production, ignored Mexico's robust pharmaceutical industry and vibrant and sophisticated university programs in chemistry.[12] The DEA based its assumptions on a growing body of evidence that repeated the stereotype of the "primitive" nature of the Mexican drug trade. In 1975, the Illinois General Assembly's report on Mexican heroin, commonly referred to as "The Heroin Highway," crowed about the perfectionism of French chemists in processing heroin compared to Mexican "cooks."[13] The report juxtaposed descriptions of French and Mexican labs:

> The French chemists, perfectionists, proud of their work would set up in an empty farmhouse, take several suitcases full of raw materials with them, tape the windows shut, don surgical masks so as not to inhale fumes (which in itself can create addiction), and then stay with the process for as many days as it took to produce 100 percent pure heroin. Then they would untape the windows, clean everything up, and not return for several weeks or months.
>
> The Mexicans, with good reasons, are satisfied with something less than perfection. Their heroin is brown rather than white, and is only 60–90 percent pure rather than 100 percent. On the other hand, their simplified refining procedures take much less time and can be done by people other than professional chemists. The impurity prevents too many middlemen from cutting the product further. And most important, the product sells: there is simply no need to market a pure heroin.[14]

The report referred to Mexican drug processing taking place in "kitchen labs" in houses, cellars, and barns, not dramatically different from a French farmhouse. The report reflects Illinois policy makers' inability to recognize that Mexican drug traffickers operated the same way as their European counterparts. Moreover, French and Corsican crime organizations had operated in Mexico and had partnered with Mexican DTOs since the 1920s.[15] Lastly, the report ignores that much of the pharmaceutical industry in Mexico had ties to European and American methods and training. Since the 1950s, policing agents on the US–Mexico border had argued that the purity of brown Mexican heroin surpassed that of European heroin.[16] Yet concepts of whiteness and purity in the racialized US imagination became a basis for chemical analysis: brown heroin equaled impurity and hence a lower-quality product than European-produced "white" heroin.[17]

In its official reports to Congress in the mid-1970s, the DEA seemed to have ignored decades of work and research on Mexican drug traffickers conducted by its predecessors, as well as by the US State Department and the Mexican government.[18] All of these entities had long documented illegal drugs flowing out of Mexico and into the US, whether Mexican-grown poppy and processed heroin or non-Mexican-originated drugs that were transshipped through Mexico by a broad array of international DTOs. Regardless of this institutional failure to build on other efforts to understand the role of Mexican traffickers, by the mid-1970s, the DEA was building on investigations conducted by the CPD, and knew that it had to do more to stop the Mexican drug-supply pipeline. The Herrera family, they quickly came to understand, had to be one of their major targets. Understanding the organization took years of investigative work.

In the late 1950s, the Herrera organization had begun trafficking to Chicago and Los Angeles through the land ports of El Paso–Ciudad Juárez, Mexico; Del Rio, Texas–Ciudad Acuña, Mexico; Eagle Pass, Texas–Piedra Negras, Mexico; and Laredo, Texas–Nuevo Laredo, Mexico. Mexican bootleggers and smugglers had pioneered the use of these ports during Prohibition.[19] These border towns had also long hosted Americans in search of fun—whether alcohol, drugs, or sex—and thus had vibrant "black" and "gray" marketplaces. Law enforcement in these towns, on both sides of the border, tended to be lax and/or corrupt. When Prohibition ended in 1933, Mexican smugglers, in search of new customers, refocused their efforts on bringing marijuana and heroin to the lucrative American market. The Herrera family returned to those old and established smuggling ports of entry when they began their operations. They also relied on the other technological and economic changes, especially American and Mexican emerging interstate and highway systems, which allowed the Herrera DTO to efficiently move their commodities north to major US cities.

In Mexico, the Herrera family extended from cities and towns across Mexico's own Golden Triangle: the northwestern states of Sinaloa, Durango, and Chihuahua.[20] While the Herrera family has been identified by journalists with the small Mexican town of Los Herrera in Durango, the family was not bound to a single small town.[21] It was a large, extended family that spread across Mexican states that facilitated drug production, distribution, and transborder trafficking. In the US, the organization spread from California to Texas to Chicago and, later, further east. By the late 1970s, the DEA had hired a few bilingual researchers who were able to better understand the complexity and sophistication of the Herrera DTO despite the savvy operators' cover as modest immigrants living in working-class towns and communities in and around Chicago. By the time the DEA began focusing on the Herrera heroin operation, the family had been in the drug business for over twenty years.

In 1973, twenty-five members of the Herrera family were arrested by the Chicago Police Department's gang unit after a two-month undercover investigation. In a *Chicago Tribune* article that year, journalist Bob Wiedrich argued that high-grade brown heroin had started to appear on the streets a year prior to the raid. In an interview with Wiedrich, CPD Captain Vrdolyak argued that the ring, based in Roseland and Pullman, had started on a small scale four to five years earlier and was led by fifty-nine-year-old Reyes Herrera. The police raided Herrera's home and his tavern, arresting family members and associates. At the tavern, the police discovered cars that had recently arrived from Mexico with heroin. They also uncovered bank books indicating large deposits that were out of scale for a small neighborhood tavern. Vrdolyak told reporters that drug mules were paid $4,000 dollars (worth $23,000 in 2020) to drive drug-laden vehicles to Chicago.[22] Overall, the police raid yielded a million dollars in drugs, $10,000 in cash (worth $57,700 in 2020), six .38-caliber handguns, and a rifle. More significantly, that investigation and the raid ensured the Herreras were no longer anonymous and that their businesses, both licit and illicit, were being monitored by law enforcement.

In attempting to understand the structure of this drug enterprise, the CPD reported that Reyes Herrera headed the organization with his sons, who in turn coordinated with four "lieutenants," which the report referred to as "coyotes."[23] The CPD had misunderstood the word. A *coyote* is not a lieutenant, but rather a person who coordinates the movement of drugs or people. The CPD and other law enforcement agencies had a lot more to learn about the Herreras' operations.

The arrest of Reyes, his wife Maria, their children, and their coyotes and mules was a blow to the organization. And the raid would trigger more research by the Chicago police into the DTO and its members. At the time, however, the Chicago police were operating under a veil of ignorance. The CPD believed that the Herrera DTO was a small-time gang, with only a few years in the drug business. Reyes and Maria Herrera took advantage of such ignorance. Bail was set at a relatively modest sum and the couple immediately posted it and fled to Mexico. Their sons got off with a relative slap on the wrist. By 1977, Reyes and Maria were rumored to be working in Guadalajara Mexico, the growing hub of the Mexican drug trade in the 1970s, while their sons were still living and working in Chicago where they owned a growing array of businesses in working-class neighborhoods, even as they continued their drug operations.[24]

Nonetheless, the Herreras' exposure in Chicago led to growing surveillance and analysis of the organization and its operations. It also drew the attention of policy makers in Washington, DC and Chicago. Representative Cardiss Collins, a vital and vibrant presence in Chicago, was serving on the US House of Representatives Select Committee on Narcotics Abuse and Control.[25] In her twenty-four-year career in the US House, Collins was recognized for her advocacy for African Americans, people of color, and women.[26] The growth of heroin in Chicago became an ongoing focus of her work on the committee. She focused committee hearings in 1977 on the Herreras' operations and in 1985, she invited the select committee to return to Chicago for further hearings on the Herrera DTO. Cardiss played a key role in the hearings that brought greater attention to the crime organization, and ultimately led to further investigations by showcasing the DTO's control over the Midwest. Journalists reported on the hearings, and police departments across the Midwest learned about how Chicago was the base for Midwest heroin distribution. The politicians came to realize, moreover, that the Herreras were not a mere gang, but a vast operation with thousands of employees.

In the mid-1970s, building on information obtained in the 1973 raid, the DEA and CPD began researching the Herreras in earnest. In 1977, DEA analyst Mary Hohler informed the House Select Committee on Narcotics Abuse and Control that the Herrera DTO had over a thousand members. She compared it to General Motors. The Herreras, she made clear, were far more than a neophyte gang. To demonstrate their organization's complexity, she included a copy of *Forbes* magazine's list of the "Fifty Largest Retailing Companies," and placed the Herrera DTO's wealth between Safeway Stores and May Department Stores, estimating that the DTO yielded an annual profit of approximately $100 million.[27] In 1977, the DEA, Customs, and the IRS agents who also testified before the committee noted that over the prior twenty years, the Herrera DTO had made billions of dollars selling heroin in Chicago and around the Midwest.

3

The Herreras' wealth and the sophistication of their business model ensured their success for many years. Leading family members strategically occupied the upper echelons of the drug business and were far removed from direct interaction with the organization's illegal product, keeping them well insulated from arrest and prosecution. In their role-proliferation analysis of New York City crack dealers in the 1990s, Bruce Johnson, Eloise Dunlap, and Sylvia Tourinay documented this pattern.[28] They noted that those on the lower levels of the drug business endured the highest risks for arrests (except for those who served in positions such as "lookouts" or "counters"). Because street vendors worked at the most visible point of the drug supply line, they were far more likely to be arrested than high-ranking members of the organizations, who avoided direct and especially public involvement with illegal drugs. The Herreras' leaders understood this dynamic and avoided direct involvement with the selling of their wares. They went even further in their efforts to evade law enforcement attention by avoiding the public spotlight.

In addition, the Herrera DTO leadership skillfully crafted and manipulated a series of advantages that supported the longevity of their business. For example, the DTO employed certain Mexican cultural practices to their advantage. The DEA, its organizational predecessors, and other US-based policing agencies had a limited number of Spanish-speaking employees and even fewer experts on Mexico. Like other organized crime figures, the Herrera family routinely used nicknames as first names. For example, the notorious Joaquín Archivaldo

Guzmán Loera, known as "El Chapo," was not the first Chapo that DEA agents tracked. Moreover, policing and government agents had long embraced stereotypical and racist tropes regarding Mexican and Mexican Americans. These prejudices clouded their ability to recognize that the Herrera DTO was a sophisticated transnational criminal organization that rivaled the Italian mafia or Jewish organized crime. In this case, American officials' racism resulted not in more arrests of people of color but rather in helping the Herrera DTO to operate for years free from serious surveillance or intervention.

Even their very name, Herrera, served the organization because it confused Anglo law enforcement agents and allowed the family to hide in plain sight among other Mexicans and Mexican Americans living in the Midwest. Herrera is a common family name in Mexico. Mexicans use their paternal and maternal surnames, but in the US members of the family commonly just used Herrera. In Chicago alone, in 1974, some 659 legal residents—and an unknown number of undocumented residents— shared the Herrera surname. By the mid-1970s, the DEA struggled to track the Herrera DTO by tracing the full names of suspected members in order to create US-based family trees.[29] In Chicago, in fact, the DTO included six extended families: Herrera-Diaz, Herrera-Herrera, Herrera-Medina, Herrera-Nevarez, and Herrera-Venegas. These six families included siblings, cousins, and their children, and were also all extended to include twenty-six different family-run operations in different sections of Chicago with different configurations of families and surnames. Members of the Herrera-Venegas family lived and operated in Aurora while members of the Herrera-Nevarez family lived in Roseland.[30] Another Herrera-affiliated family, which did not share the paternal or maternal surname Herrera, controlled the trade in Milwaukee. The Chicago police, as well as the DEA, with little knowledge of Spanish or Mexican culture, had an extremely difficult time just figuring out who was who in the DTO and which Herreras they needed to surveil and investigate.

By 1975, the Illinois legislative investigating committee understood that the inability to understand nomenclature within the network of Herrera families was hindering the investigation. Misreporting names or using nicknames provided by someone in custody also hindered the ability of investigators to understand the family network.[31] For example,

Nevarez, the family maternal name, was frequently written with a "z" in the US. In Mexico, the family name ended with an "s" rather than a "z." These slight differences made careful recordkeeping—and thus investigations and prosecutions—difficult because both spellings exist in Mexico and the US.

The family's origin and well-established place in the state of Durango also helped the Herrera DTO to thrive and succeed. Poppy was introduced to the state in the 1800s and it flourished due to the climate. Despite attempts at eradication by the Mexican government that began in the 1920s, the ruggedness of the landscape in the Sierra Madres, the climate, and the favorable support from local politicians allowed *gomeros* (poppy growers) to flourish. Most senior Herrera family members lived in Durango, while their children lived in the US or split their time in between the two countries. Jaime Herrera-Nevares, the patriarch of the family, was a well-respected former police officer who had also served as a mayor of the small town of Los Herrera.[32] Born in 1927 to a farming family, he and his seven siblings grew corn, beans, and other products. Like many *gomeros*, the family first grew marijuana and then diversified to the more lucrative poppy. They thus climbed the narco-hierarchy through a strategic decision to shift to poppy, which was far more profitable than marijuana.[33]

Don Jaime, as he was known, collaborated with his brothers Elias and Manuel; his cousins also entered the business. His brother Reyes had set off to Chicago years before and started the Chicago-based operations for the family with various other cousins.[34] Reyes was the one who was arrested in 1973. Other family members served in state and local government positions, such as mayors or police chiefs of cities and towns in Durango.[35] The growing family expanded their ranchos and businesses into other cities: Culiacán, Sinaloa; Victoria de Durango, Durango; Ciudad Obregón, Sonora; Ciudad Juárez, Chihuahua, and El Paso, Texas. Thus, the well-entrenched extended family lived and worked in the richest poppy-producing Mexican states, while the family was also located on the US–Mexico border at one of the largest land ports and members lived in a key distribution city in the US.

The Herrera family quickly became one of the modern pioneers and innovators of the modern US–Mexico drug trade. Of course, it did not work in isolation. Herrera-Nevares closely coordinated his family's DTO with Pedro Avilés Pérez. Known as *el León de la Sierra* (Mountain Lion) in the narcocorridos, Avilés is, arguably, the most important architect of the modern drug trade because he, like Herrera-Nevares, controlled the trade from production to distribution. Avilés has returned to the popular imagination through Netflix's *Narcos: Mexico* and the growing number of accounts of his career by Mexican journalists.[36] Avilés coordinated the Mexican drug trade through the 1960s with his *clicas* (cliques) comprised of Ernesto Fonseca Carrillo in Sinaloa, Miguel Urías Uriarte in Sonora, and Herrera-Nevares in Durango. Avilés grew and trafficked marijuana and heroin, and he is recognized by Mexican journalists as the first Mexican trafficker to work with the Colombians to move cocaine through Mexico. Urías Uriarte was a nexus between ex-Mexican revolutionary generals involved in the drug trade and the modern drug trade in Sonora.[37] Fonseca Carrillo founded and led the Guadalajara DTO with Miguel Ángel Félix Gallardo and Rafael Caro Quintero, who were tied to the murder of DEA agent Enrique Camarena.[38] Herrera-Nevares was thus working closely with many of the most significant Mexican drug barons. These connections and cooperative structures contributed significantly to the Herreras' success and their ability to build their organization in Chicago. They made Chicago one of the most powerful bases of the contemporary Mexican drug trade—a major heroin distribution hub for much of the US.

A final factor in the longevity of the Herrera family: in Mexico, as in Chicago, the Herrera family held a multitude of legitimate businesses. The family owned ranches, where they raised cattle. They farmed extensively and sold a wide range of agricultural products. They also owned and leased land and owned properties, including a great many apartment buildings. Moreover, members worked in politics, policing, and other official and legitimate enterprises. All of these above-board activities whitewashed the family name and integrated their affairs into the economy and government of the states in which they operated, as well as in Mexican society, more generally.

While successful, their legitimate businesses were not nearly as lucrative as the heroin industry. Their drug operations always came first. On their farms and ranches in Durango, Sinaloa, and Chihuahua the family not only raised cattle and harvested corn; they grew poppy. On the land and properties they controlled, they built an industrial narco-enterprise.

Their paid workers harvested and extracted the poppy gum, and their chemists processed the heroin in their modern laboratories. Herrera family members owned laboratories in different cities in the Mexican Golden Triangle and brought chemists from major cities to their labs for weeks at a time to process heroin.[39] Mixing their legitimate and illicit businesses in a synergistic fashion, the Herrera DTO built a highly lucrative, multifaceted, vertically and horizontally integrated business.

4

By the 1970s, major Mexican DTOs used a shifting array of boats, airplanes, cars, and all methods of transportation in their trafficking operations, making it difficult for law enforcement agencies to shut them down. The Mexican government reported that from February 1973 to February 1974 it had arrested 467 farmers for growing poppy and marijuana. In the same period, however, the government confiscated two launches, forty-one airplanes, and 735 cars.[40] The confiscation, especially of airplanes, caused major concern in the US because the number of private airplanes that traveled across the US–Mexico border exceeded five hundred a month. This air-based smuggling between the US and Mexico led the DEA to create a dedicated Air Intelligence Program and the El Paso Intelligence Center.

Herrera-Nevares and his colleagues, beginning with Avilés Pérez and Fonseca Carrillo of Sinaloa, had pioneered the use of airplanes to smuggle large amounts of drugs. Later, the Ciudad Juárez DTO became known for the use of planes to smuggle heroin, marijuana, and cocaine. It was led by Amado Carrillo Fuentes, the "Lord of the Skies," who was the nephew and protégé of Fonseca Carrillo. Carrillo Fuentes became more recognized for his use of planes after Avilés Pérez was killed during Operation Condor in Mexico in 1978.[41]

While planes had longed been used by traffickers, including during the Prohibition era, the Herrera family mostly relied on cars and trucks to get their drugs into the US market. They hired drivers or "mules" who transported the heroin from Durango on direct, forty-nine-hour car trips to Chicago. According to DEA analyst Hohler, the Herrera DTO compensated their mules well. She reported that in 1977, mules received $800 to $1,000 (2020: $4,611) per kilo that they moved from Mexico to

Chicago. They drove large American cars and trucks to Chicago. The heroin packages were hidden in gas tanks, drive shafts, seats, and side panels. Illinois enforcement agents joked about the heroin-concealing "Durango Driveshaft."[42] Mules often returned to Mexico with large amounts of American dollars concealed in their car's hiding places. Because the car, with its relatively small load capacity, was the Herreras' preferred mode of transportation, the DTO had to use many mules. These mules regularly drove across major border crossings in Texas and on to distribution points in the Midwest, Northeast, California, and Arizona. Once in Chicago, Los Angeles, or elsewhere, the heroin was distributed to different family-run safe houses to be cut, repackaged, and sold wholesale to other organizations.

The Herrera organization resembled other modern companies. It readily expanded, when necessary, to include highly skilled workers, regardless of race, gender, or national origin. The DTO employed both male and female members of the Herrera family. It also recruited and worked with trusted non-Mexican lieutenants.

By the late 1960s, the Herreras were working closely with Puerto Rican organized crime in Chicago and in the Northeast. In Indiana, they collaborated with both African American and white gangs. They sold directly to heroin dealers of all races and ethnicities. In Chicago, the Herrera-connected Puerto Rican gang, the Latin Kings, followed the Herrera model and soon recruited Mexican street gangs to help manage their territorial expansion.[43]

Women in the Herrera DTO usually had higher levels of education than the men in the organization and tended to do money laundering and accounting work. This gender inclusivity, too, became a regular feature of the organizations that sprang from the clicas and the Guadalajara cartel. One of these offspring, the Arellano Félix DTO, developed equal partnerships among the siblings, including Enendina Arellano-Félix, an accountant who became essential to the DTO and ultimately led it.[44]

Despite the immense profitability of the Herrera DTO, the men and women in the organization appeared to outside observers to be modest, working-class people. They lived in bungalows or clapboard houses in working-class neighborhoods in the Chicagoland area. They drove older-model American cars and dressed modestly. Journalist John

O'Brien, using a racially charged analysis, described the Herreras as follows: "While some Chicago dope dealers flaunt their immense wealth
with luxury cars, diamonds, and flashy gals in ankle-length furs, the
Mexicans who actually control the heroin traffic here are as inconspicu-
ous as peons."[45] Quite deliberately, the Herrera family's modest lives
served as a cover for their organization.

Like in Mexico, the US-based family had an executive board that
represented the different distribution hubs: Boston, MA; Los Angeles,
CA New York, NY; Springfield, MA; San Juan, Puerto Rico, and Washington, DC. This board was charged with responding to changing opportunities, as well as to threats. The Herreras were good at what they
did and their ability to respond quickly to their business environment
percolated down the organizational chart. The DTO member-cells' abilities to respond rapidly to law enforcement threats by moving safe houses
and distribution sites helped ensure their continued success. After the
arrests of Reyes, his wife, and family members, for example, the DTO
moved parts of its operations into quiet, respectable-appearing suburbs
and to nearby states where law enforcement officials had no idea who
they were.[46] The members communicated using coded language via telephone. This tactic complicated police surveillance because speakers of
Mexican Spanish can often use indigenous words that are not commonly
understood, even by other Spanish speakers. Such indigenous-derived
words and phrases, combined with their use of northern Mexican collo-
quialisms that are not taught in Spanish classes or used in Castilian and
Caribbean Spanish, also helped the DTO to evade surveillance.

The Herrera family successfully deployed a great many tactics in their
battle against US law enforcement agencies. As a result of their ability
to evade prosecution, they made a lot of money for a long period of
time. In 1977, hearings held by the House Select Committee on Narcotics
Abuse and Control focused on the ability of the Herrera DTO to bring
that massive amount of money back to Mexico and to "launder" it. Here,
too, the Herrera family had long outwitted law enforcement.

The Herrera DTO in Chicago, like the Medellín DTO in New York
City, primarily used currency exchanges to send their money back
to their native country.[47] Currency exchanges were common in US
working-class immigrant neighborhoods, where few banks existed,
and these continue to be commonly used in in Mexico and Colombia.

Working-class people use them to pay their utility bills and cash checks. In the US, they also receive food stamps there, and in Mexico and Colombia currency exchanges are used to convert dollars to pesos or pesos to dollars. A money order issued at a local currency exchange moved with no regulatory oversight through banks in Chicago or New York and then arrived safely in Mexican banks.

These exchanges moved money orders circulated through the National Lincoln Bank in Chicago to branches of major Mexican banks such as Banamex (Citibank) and Banco Nacional de Mexico, among others. Hundreds of thousands of dollars moved through these currency exchanges from Mexican immigrants living in the Midwest, who helped their families at home through their monthly remittances. Working people sending small sums comprised the majority of money orders and transfers, which helped to hide the large sums being laundered by the Herreras. In testimony taken in 1977, congressional leaders seemed confused as to why the Herrera DTO used currency-exchange wholesalers. Russ McDougall, a DEA analyst and former IRS special agent, then explained that the Herreras needed to launder anywhere between $300 million to a billion dollars per year back to Mexico.[48] That meant that the DTO also had a great many people on the payroll whose job was simply to purchase a multitude of money orders in an array of amounts that were ultimately deposited in Mexican banks.

5

The Chicago police raid in 1973 and the US congressional hearings in 1977 introduced the Herrera DTO to a growing number of people. The organization lost much of the anonymity that its members had cultivated over the prior twenty years in the heroin business. Over the next two decades, the Herrera DTO became a poster child for drug warriors' efforts to strengthen and expand federal drug laws.

In 1986, the Herrera family again re-emerged as a central focus of the DEA for heroin, marijuana, and cocaine distribution in the Midwest. By the mid-1980s, the DEA had been in existence for more than a decade and had been able to recruit bilingual and bicultural agents who allowed it to develop conspiracy cases against the Herrera operation using the resources of the CPD, the Indiana State Police, and local law enforcement.

Moreover, the DEA found another champion and additional resources following the election of Ronald Regan, who had campaigned on the promise to control the flows of drugs into the US.

Working the Ranch in Gary, IN: The Herrera DTO in the 1980s and 1990s

The 1980s gave birth to a far more aggressive and better resourced War on Drugs. In part, the accelerated drug war was precipitated by the hyper-violent battles over cocaine that were raging in the streets of Miami.[49] While far less violent, the Herrera DTO, too—by then known widely in law enforcement circles as the architects of the "Heroin Highway"—came under greatly increased pressure.[50]

In 1978, the House Select Committee on Narcotics Abuse and Control had published a report detailing just how the Herrera family had made Chicago a national hub for Mexican heroin and marijuana distribution. Investigators systemically ripped away the cloak of anonymity that the Herrera DTO had worn to cover up its American operations. The report stated that the Herrera family "is similar to traditional organized crime families as evidenced by the magnitude and complexity of its criminal activity. It also shares the common trait of having many of its members related by blood and by marriage."[51]

The 1978 report recommended a number of measures that would impact not only the Herrera DTO but also Colombian and other Mexican DTOs. The report recommended that the DEA and the CPD increase their efforts to infiltrate the organization. It also recommended that law enforcement agents and officers strengthen relationships within the Mexican American community in Chicago so as to gain local cooperation. It encouraged the DEA and the State Department to pressure the Mexican government to cooperate more closely with the US and to increase its independent drug-interdiction efforts. The committee also called for stronger banking regulations and laws to hinder drug money–laundering operations, including greater oversight of currency exchange transactions.[52] In addition, the committee proposed that Congress amend the Bail Reform Act to make it easier for judges to deny bail to defendants involved in narcotics—this recommendation was in direct response to the Herrera family's prior abuse of the bond system.[53]

All told, this series of recommendations, many of which emerged from investigations of the Herrera DTO, built the infrastructure for the 1984 Comprehensive Criminal Control Act.

With the election of Reagan and a renewed focus on drug trafficking and the increasing violence associated with the drug trade, the Comprehensive Criminal Control Act created civil and criminal sanctions related to drug trafficking and established determinate sentencing for drug offenses.[54] The 1985 murder of DEA agent Enrique Camarena also led to far greater scrutiny of Mexican traffickers, in general. Moreover, the Mexican drug trade's diversification into the cocaine market further intensified American law-enforcement agencies efforts to crack down on the Mexican DTOs.[55]

This intensified pressure affected the Herreras' operations. Despite the raids and investigations of the 1970s, by the mid-1980s the Herrera DTO had well over three thousand members with fifty different family names.[56] Building on the work of Avilés Pérez, the younger members of the Herrera DTO had successfully expanded into cocaine trafficking. Chicago served as their wholesale hub for cocaine, along with heroin and marijuana.[57]

By this time, Don Jaime's numerous children and those of his brothers and sisters had developed phenomenal wealth. A 1984 expose by journalist Bob Wiedrich revealed that, in Mexico, Don Jaime owned "two hotels, a pharmacy, a truck stop and restaurant, a construction firm, a bowling alley, disco, taco restaurant complex, and several bars, one of which was favored by local police."[58] His article was part of a series that year exposing the Chicago-Mexican heroin connection and trade.

The Chicago police were well aware of the heroin problem and the overwhelmingly dominant role the Herrera family played in fostering it. They were not pleased by the newspaper exposé, as they were hard at work building a case against the Herreras. Through the 1980s, the Chicago police department and DEA had gathered evidence about the organization from wiretaps that had been planted in Herrera DTO properties in Gary, Indiana. Those wires included calls between members in Indiana and Illinois and other locations in the US, Puerto Rico, and Mexico.[59] The DEA and the CPD had focused on Jesús Herrera-Diaz, who lived in Calumet City, a working-class, southeast Chicago suburb that borders on the state of Indiana.

The case focused on Herrera-Diaz, but it also extended to couriers, mules, safe-house operators, and dealers. Allegedly, the case was triggered by a disgruntled gambler who lost money at a rigged cockfight in Gary, Indiana at one of two warehouses that the Herrera family used and operated. Indiana state police had raided the locations for illegal gambling. Operated by the Herrera DTO and run by a Puerto Rican member, Jesus Zambrana, the two locations in Gary were referred to as *la finca* and *el rancho* by members of the organization. The sites were (and are) industrialized warehouse areas that are close to Interstate 80/94, the Chicago Skyway, and I-65. Thus, deliveries from Durango directly to *el rancho* and *la finca* could be easily cut, repackaged, and moved north to Chicago and Milwaukee, east to Cleveland and New York City, and south to Indianapolis and Nashville. Two months after the raid, federal and local police raided over forty locations connected to the Herrera DTO, arrested and indicted 132 suspects, and confiscated properties and business in Illinois, Indiana, California, Colorado, Florida, Texas, Mexico, and Puerto Rico.[60]

The two-year investigation, called Operation Durango, brought together the DEA; the FBI; the US Marshals Service; the Bureau of Alcohol, Tobacco, and Firearms; the US Customs, Immigration and Naturalization Service, the CPD, and the Lake County, Indiana Police Department. This collaboration between different enforcement agencies stemmed from recommendations made during the 1977 House Select Committee hearings. The bill that emerged from those hearings, sponsored by the fiercely conservative Senator Strom Thurmond of South Carolina, called for the creation of a National Drug Policy Board to coordinate international and criminal justice issues related to drugs and the drug trade.

Differing from the Herrera DTO arrests in the 1970s, the 1982–84 investigations, raids, and indictments were facilitated by changes in US federal laws, especially the 1984 Comprehensive Criminal Control Act. This act allowed for expansive federal and civil asset forfeiture penalties. These penalties have become a major weapon against DTOs; because a percentage of the confiscated assets go directly to enforcement agencies, thus incentivizing their deployment, they have become a controversial tool in the War on Drugs.[61]

The 1984 Act also toughened up bail procedures for high-level drug traffickers, making it far more difficult for defendants to be released, at any price, before they go to trial.[62] While lawmakers claimed the 1984 Act would target high-level traffickers, in practice it hit lower-level drug dealers the hardest, a majority of whom were African American and Hispanic. Many of the policies enacted in the 1984 Act were made even more punitive in the 1994 Violent Crime Control and Law Enforcement Act, which included the infamous "three strikes" provision imposing mandatory life sentences for repeat drug offenders.[63]

Shortly after the raid on the Herrera organization, Anton Valukas, US Attorney for the Northern District of Illinois, Phillip Fisher, Special Agent-in-Charge of the Chicago Field Office of the DEA, and Edward Hegarty, Special Agent-in-Charge of the Chicago Division of the FBI, announced the indictments of ninety-nine people in Illinois, thirty-three in Gary and Dyer Indiana, and others in California, Mexico, and Puerto Rico. The 132 people arrested comprised six different networks within the Herrera DTO. All of the indictments referenced the use of court-authorized listening devices that had recorded hundreds of telephone conversations related to drug trafficking.[64]

The wiretaps demonstrated that Herrera-Diaz of Calumet City collaborated with his brothers Ruben and Pancito ("Cubby"), along with nephews, sons, wives, and in-laws. All thirty-four were charged with "using the telephone to commit and facilitate the commission of narcotics offenses," particularly with family members in El Paso, Texas. In Chicago, Miguel Medina, another member of the Herrera DTO, the indictment stated, used his multiple businesses to distribute cocaine and heroin in concert with eighteen co-defendants. Luis Armando Villela and eleven co-defendants, the indictment further declared, coordinated with members in El Paso to distribute heroin. Rodolfo Herrera-Medina and thirteen co-defendants were indicted on similar charges. David Ercoli of Dyer, Indiana was also indicted with ten codefendants. Gino Zanin, Peter Soto, and Gilberto Gonzales were all charged, along with all the other codefendants, with "using a telephone to commit and facilitate the commission of a narcotics offense."[65]

The 1984 Comprehensive Criminal Control Act allowed local and federal police to seize forty-seven properties, as well as hundreds of cars. The seized properties included the homes of members of the Herrera DTO and their businesses, including two gas stations, five bars, two restaurants, two jewelry stores, a flower shop, and multiple apartment buildings.[66]

The arrests in Chicago had a domino effect. The evidence they collected allowed the DEA and US law enforcement to place more pressure on Mexican officials to go after the Herrera DTO in their jurisdictions. The pressure worked. In 1987, Don Jaime and his son Jaime Herrera-Herrera were arrested by the commander of the PJF, Guillermo González Calderoni.[67]

The arrest and subsequent prosecutions in Durango, Chicago, and other cities gave the public the sense that the Herrera drug operation, after a thirty-year reign, had been vanquished. It had not been. Law enforcement had arrested just over 130 people associated with the DTO; it had over three thousand members. After the busts, the Herrera DTO, though weakened, continued to distribute heroin and other drugs from the Chicago metropolitan area, Los Angeles, Durango, and towns and cities along the US–Mexico border.[68] By 2001 the DTO has expanded, growing to twelve family cell/networks in Chicago that trafficked marijuana, heroin, cocaine, and methamphetamine.[69]

6

Many of the current Mexican DTOs are branches of the earlier *clicas* that emerged in the 1950s and 1960s. The Herrera DTO's transnational network became the model for many that have followed or continue to work alongside the Herreras, such as the Ciudad Juárez cartel, the Tijuana cartel, and the Sinaloa cartel. Their farm-to-arm business model remains intact but is ever evolving. The DTO was and continues to function as a large-scale distributor with an uncanny ability to work with other organizations while running its own operation.

Don Jaime, his brothers, and their families created much of the business plan for transnational drug trafficking with their Mexico–Chicago connection. Raids, arrests, indictments, hearings, recommendations, and numerous national and state crime acts and legislation, despite a $27.8 billion annual price tag, have done little to disrupt that business model.[70] Given the massive drug demand in the US and the immense profits that are made servicing it, this aspect of the War on Drugs has, at least so far, been doomed to failure. Drug traffickers, such as the Herrera organization, adapt, reorganize, relocate, and respond to whatever law enforcement throws at them. And so far, at least for the past sixty-plus years, even when it has been laid low, it has risen up again to work alongside other DTOs or distribute a new product to meet evolving consumer demand, whether in Mexico or the neighborhoods of Chicago.

NOTES

1   Illinois Legislative Investigating Commission, "Mexican Heroin: A Report to the Illinois General Assembly ['The Heroin Highway']" (Chicago: Authority of the State of Illinois, 1976), www.idaillinois.org.

2   Terrence E. Poppa, *Drug Lord: The Life and Death of a Mexican Kingpin* (New York: Pharos Books, 1990); Don Ford Jr. with Charles Bowden, *Contrabando: Confessions of a Drug-Smuggling Texas Cowboy* (New York: Harper and Row, 2006); Ioan Grillo, *El Narco: The Bloody Rise of Mexican Drug Cartels* (London: Bloomsbury, 2017) and Grillo, *Gangster Warlords: Drug Dollars, Killing Fields and the New Politics of Latin America* (London: Bloomsbury, 2017). See also Natalia Almada, dir., *El velador* (Paris: Les Films d'ici, 2015).

3   "Task Force Report: Narcotics, Marijuana and Dangerous Drugs Special Presidential Task Force," June 6, 1969. National Archives, Nixon Presidential Materials, White House Special Files: Staff Members and Office Files Egil Krogh, Box 30, "Operation Intercept," National Security Archive, accessed March 20, 2021, https://nsarchive.gwu.edu. For policies that impacted Mexico during the Nixon years, see Lawrence A. Gooberman, *Operation Intercept: The Multiple Consequences of Public Policy* (New York: Pergamon Press, 1974) and G. Gordon Liddy, *Will: The Autobiography of G. Gordon Liddy* (New York: St. Martin's Press, 1980). For a history of the DEA, see "DEA History 1970–1975," accessed March 9, 2021, www.justice.gov; US Drug Enforcement Administration, *Drug Enforcement Administration: A Tradition of Excellence, 1973–2008* (Washington, DC: DEA, 2008).

4   US General Accounting Office, "Efforts to Stop Narcotics and Dangerous Drugs Coming from and Through Mexico and Central America," Drug Enforcement Administration, Department of Justice, Department of State: Report to the Congress (Washington: US General Accounting Office, 1974), 2, http://dp.la.

5   Tim Weiner, "Mexico Indicts Former Chief of Secret Police," *New York Times*, March 30, 2003.

6   US Congress, House Select Committee on Narcotics Abuse and Control, "Investigation of Narcotics Trafficking Proceeds, Chicago, Illinois," Hearings Before the Select Committee on Narcotics Abuse and Control, House of Representatives, Ninety-fifth Congress, first session, September 30, 1977 (Washington: US Govt. Print. Office, 1978), http://dp.la.

7 The DEA acknowledged a concern of police involved in the drug trade. US General Accounting Office, *Efforts to Stop Narcotics and Dangerous Drugs*, 20.

8 US General Accounting Office, *Efforts to Stop Narcotics and Dangerous Drugs*, 20.

9 Wiretap transcripts, United States v. Alberto Bravo et. al. United States District Court, Southern District, S75 CR-429, in possession of author. For a discussion, see Elaine Carey, *Women Drug Traffickers: Mules, Bosses, and Organized Crime* (Albuquerque: University of New Mexico Press, 2014), 187.

10 Max Mermelstein, with Robin Moore and Richard Smitten, *The Man Who Made it Snow: By the American Mastermind inside the Colombia Cartel* (New York: Simon & Schuster, 1990) and Carey, *Women Drug Traffickers*, 177–93.

11 US General Accounting Office, "Efforts to Stop Narcotics and Dangerous Drugs," 22.

12 The DEA's misunderstanding of Mexican heroin is a historical continuity. For decades, police agents in Texas and California had tried to disrupt the narratives of the supposed lack of purity of Mexican heroin or that Mexican chemists only produced brown heroin. For example, in 1955, W. E. Naylor, Chief of Narcotics Division of Public Safety for the state of Texas, testified that white Mexican heroin was actually available in Houston or anywhere else in Texas, and he argued that Mexican heroin was far purer than Asian. Mexican heroin, he testified, was less likely to be cut, so it was far more concentrated for its price. Mexican brown heroin was not less potent; it was simply not as highly refined. Testimony of W. E. Naylor, Chief of Narcotics Division of Public Safety, State of Texas, Hearing Before the Subcommittee on Improvements in the Federal Code of the Committee on the Judiciary, US Senate, Eighty-fourth Congress, Illicit Narcotics Traffic (Austin, Dallas, Fort Worth, Houston, and San Antonio, Texas) (Washington, D.C: Government Printing Office, 1956), 2381–85.

13 Illinois Legislative Investigating Commission, "Mexican Heroin," 11.

14 Illinois Legislative Investigating Commission, "Mexican Heroin," 11. Emphasis in original.

15 US Senate, Organized Crime and Illicit Narcotics Traffic, hearings before the Subcommittee on Investigations of the Committee on Government Operations, July 30, 1964, pt. 4 (Washington, DC: Government Printing Office, 1964), 919–20, 989. See also "Cohen Aide Gets 5 Years," *New York Times* (June 16, 1951) and Juan Alberto Cedillo, *La cosa nostra en México, 1938–1950* (México: Grijalbo, 2011). This is a topic of ongoing research by the author.

16 Testimony of W. E. Naylor, 2381–85.

17 Gloria Anzaldúa, *Borderlands/Frontera: The New Mestiza* (San Francisco: Aunt Lute, 2007); Lee Bebout, *Whiteness on the Border: Mapping the US Racial Imagination in Brown and White* (New York: New York University, 2016); and Laura Gómez, *Manifest Destinies: The Making of the Mexican American Race* (New York: New York University, 2007). For a broader discussion on racialized narratives of drugs, see Carey, *Women Drug Traffickers*.

18 Ethan Nadelmann, *Cops across Borders: The Internationalization of US Criminal Law Enforcement* (University Park, PA: Penn State University Press, 1993), 105.

For a discussion of the contemporary exchange of information as well as DEA activities in Mexico, see Maria Celía Toro, "The Internationalization of Police: The DEA in Mexico," *Journal of American History* 86, no. 2 (1999): 623–640. For a discussion of Mexican and US enforcement in the 1920s and 1930s, see William Walker III, "Control Across Border: The United States, Mexico, and Narcotics Policy, 1936–1940," *Pacific Historical Review* 47, no. 1 (1978): 91–106.

19 George Diaz, *Border Contraband: A History of Smuggling across the Rio Grande* (Austin: University of Texas Press, 2015); José M. Almamillo, *Making Lemonade out of Lemons: Mexican American Labor and Leisure in a California Town, 1880–1960* (Urbana: University of Illinois Press, 2006), 57–78. For an account of bootlegging and socioeconomic advancement along the border and in California, see Victor Villaseñor, *The Rain of Gold* (Houston: Arte Publico Press, 1991).

20 Guillermo Valdés Castellanos, *Historia de narcotráfico en México* (Mexico City: Aguilar, 2013), 100.

21 Elaine Shannon, *Desperados: Latin Drug Lords, US Law Men, and the War America Can't Win* (1995; repr., IUniverse, 2015); Charles Bowden, *Down by the River: Drugs, Money, Murder, and Family* (New York: Simon & Schuster, 2002); and Peter A. Lupsha and Kip Schlegal, "The Political Economy of Drug Trafficking: The Herrera Organization," Working Paper 2 (Albuquerque, NM: Latin American Institute, 1980).

22 Bob Wiedrich, "Police Infiltrate Gang, Seize $1 Million in Drugs," *Chicago Tribune* (October 18, 1973).

23 Wiedrich, "Police Infiltrate Gang."

24 Guadalajara has been known as a processing site for narcotics since the 1940s. For example, see Affidavit of H. B. Westover, *United States vs. Ignacia Jasso González et al.*, September 16, 1942, State Department (RG 59) Central Decimal Files, 1940–1944, 212.11, González Ignacia Jasso, Box 105, National Archives II, College Park, Maryland. Ignacia Jasso la viuda de González, a boss in Ciudad Juárez, Chihuahua was associated with Guadalajara for much of her career. Her processing laboratories were in the city. See Carey, *Women Drug Traffickers*, 126–56.

25 US Senate, Committee on the Judiciary, Hearings Before the Subcommittee to Investigate Juvenile Delinquency, "The Mexican Connection: Hearings before the Subcommittee to Investigate Juvenile Delinquency on Untied States Efforts to Halt Heroin Importation: Eradication, and Enforcement in Mexico, Southwest Border Control," Ninety-fifth Congress, second session, February 10 and April 19, 1978, 13, www.hathitrust.org.

26 "Cardiss Collins, 1931–2013," History, Art, and Archives: US House of Representatives, accessed March 20, 2021, https://history.house.gov; Marie Garrett, "Cardiss Collins," in *Notable Black American Women*, ed. Jessie Carney Smith (Detroit, MI: Gale Research, 2003), 204.

27 House Select Committee on Narcotics Abuse and Control, "Investigation of Narcotics Trafficking Proceeds," 267; "50 Largest Retailing Companies," *Forbes*, July 1977, 168–69.

28 Bruce Johnson, Eloise Dunlap, and Sylvia C. Tourigny, "Crack Distribution and Abuse in New York," *Crime Prevention Studies*, 11 (2000), 28–30. For a study of family-based business, see Eloise Dunlap and Bruce D. Johnson, "Family and Human Resources in the Development of a Female Crack Seller: Case Study of a Hidden Population," *Journal of Drug Issues* 26, no. 1 (1996): 175–98.

29 House Select Committee on Narcotics Abuse and Control, "Investigation of Narcotics Trafficking Proceeds," 262, 264, 265, 267, and 269.

30 House Select Committee on Narcotics Abuse and Control, "Investigation of Narcotics Trafficking Proceeds," 275.

31 Illinois Legislative Investigating Commission, "Mexican Heroin." See also Lupsha and Schlaegel, "The Political Economy of Drug Trafficking," 6.

32 Sam Quinones, *Dreamland: The True Tale of America's Opiate Epidemic* (New York: Bloomsbury Publishing, 2015), 58.

33 This has also been noted in the US. See Santiago Ivan Guerra, "From Vaqueros to Mafiosos: A Community History of Drug Trafficking in Rural South Texas" (PhD diss., University of Texas at Austin, 2011).

34 Illinois Legislative Investigating Commission, "Mexican Heroin," 7.

35 House Select Committee on Narcotics Abuse and Control, "Investigation of Narcotics Trafficking Proceeds," 275. See also Bowden, *Down by the River*, 165–72; Lupsha and Schlegel, "The Political Economy of Drug Trafficking," 5–9.

36 See Dave Jubera, "Drug Lord," *Texas Monthly* 15, no. 7 (1987): 100–104, 155–58. For mentions of Avilés, see Diego Enrique Osorno, *El cártel de Sinaloa: Una historia del uso político del narco* (México: Grijalbo, 2009), 127; Anabel Hernández, *Narcoland: The Mexican Drug Lords and Their Godfathers*, trans. Iain Bruce (New York: Verso, 2010), 17.

37 Luis Astorga, *El siglo de drogas: Del Porfiriato al nuevo milenio* (México: Grupo Editorial México, 2016), 97; Luis Astorga, "Organized Crime and the Organization of Crime," in *Organized Crime and Democratic Governability: Mexico and the US Mexican Borderlands*, ed. John Bailey and Roy Godson (Pittsburgh: University of Pittsburgh Press, 1999), 58–82. See also Elaine Carey, "A History of Organized Crime in Mexico," in *Organized Crime Causes and Consequences*, ed. Robert M. Lombardo (Hauppage, NY: Nova Science Publishers, 2019).

38 Francisco Cruz, *El cártel de Juárez* (Mexico City: Planeta, 2008); Diego Enrique Osorno, *El Cártel de Sinaloa: Una historia del uso político del narco* (Mexico City: Grijalbo, 2010); Rafael Rodríguez Castañeda and Luciano Campos Garza. *El México narco* (Mexico City: Planeta, 2010); and Rafael Rodríguez Castañeda, *Los rostros del narco* (Mexico City: Planeta, 2011).

39 House Select Committee on Narcotics Abuse and Control, "Investigation of Narcotics Trafficking Proceeds," 263.

40 US General Accounting Office, "Efforts to Stop Narcotics and Dangerous Drugs," 16.

41 Diego Enrique Osorno, *El cartel de Sinaloa*, 133–34.

42 Illinois Legislative Investigating Commission, "Mexican Heroin," 15.

43 In an interview, Gloria Rosario described how the Latin Kings undermined the Young Lords' social programs in the Lakeview and Wicker Park neighborhoods. "Gloria Rosario video Interview and Biography," March 28, 2012, http://dp.la. For more information on Mexican gangs operating in Chicago, see F. Milton Thrasher, *The Gang: A Study of 1,313 Gangs in Chicago*, ed. J. F. Short (1936; repr., University of Chicago Press, 1963). This book describes Mexican and Puerto Rican gangs as "white."

44 Ioan Grillo, "Meet the First Woman to Lead a Mexican Drugs Cartel," *Time*, July 2015, www.time.com, and Elaine Carey and José Carlos Cisneros Guzmán, "The Daughters of La Nacha: Profiles of Women Traffickers," *NACLA Report on the Americas* 44, no. 3 (May 2011): 23–24.

45 John O'Brien, "Herreras: Family Firm with a Low Profile," *Chicago Tribune*, January 8, 1978, www.chicagotribune.com.

46 Interview with Brian Miller, chief of Hammond Police Department from 2004 to 2014, Hammond, IN, March 2020.

47 House Select Committee on Narcotics Abuse and Control, "Investigation of Narcotics Trafficking Proceeds," 122–29. See also Carey, *Women Drug Traffickers*, 185–89.

48 House Select Committee on Narcotics Abuse and Control, "Investigation of Narcotics Trafficking Proceeds," 67–70.

49 See Carey, *Women Drug Traffickers*, 177–93. The term "cocaine cowboys" was also used by law enforcement. See a statement by Michael Horn, Chief Officer of International Operations, DEA, US Senate Committee on Foreign Relations, Subcommittee on Western Hemisphere, Peace Corps, Narcotics, and Terrorism, "The Drug Cartels and Narco-violence: The Threat to the United States," One Hundred Fifth Congress, first session, July 16, 1997, 41, http://dp.la. The Miami drug wars were essential to the show *Miami Vice*; see also David Cupkin, Alfred Spellman, Billy Corben, and Charles Cosby, *Cocaine Cowboys 2* (Australia: Madman Entertainment, 2009).

50 Illinois Legislative Investigating Commission, "Mexican Heroin," and US Congress House Select Committee on Narcotics Abuse and Control, "1986 Major City Survey on Drug Arrests and Seizures: Report of the Select Committee on Narcotics Abuse and Control," One Hundredth Congress, first session (Washington: US G.P.O., 1987), 17.

51 US Congress House Select Committee on Narcotics Abuse and Control, "Investigation of Narcotics Trafficking and Money Laundering in Chicago: A Report of the Select Committee on Narcotics Abuse and Control," Ninety-fifth Congress, first session (Washington: US Govt. Print. Office, 1978), 24.

52 US Congress House Select Committee on Narcotics Abuse and Control, "Investigation of Narcotics Trafficking and Money Laundering in Chicago," 24–25.

53 US Congress House Select Committee on Narcotics Abuse and Control, "Investigation of Narcotics Trafficking and Money Laundering in Chicago," 32.

54 Kristin M. Finklea, "Organized Crime in the United States: Trends and Issues for Congress," Congressional Research Service, January 27, 2010, 7, https://crsreports .congress.gov.

55 Testimony of Mayor Washington, US Congress House Select Committee on Narcotics Abuse and Control, "Drug Abuse and Drug Trafficking in Chicago," Hearings before the Select Committee on Narcotics Abuse and Control, Ninety-ninth Congress, first session, May 31–June 1, 1985 (Washington: US G.P.O, 1986), 9–10, https://dpa.la.

56 Bob Wiedrich, "Agents Tie Chicago Heroin to Mexican 'Godfather,'" *Chicago Tribune*, April 1, 1984, www.chicagotribune.com.

57 Lynn Emmerman, "1ˢᵗ Family of Dope into Cocaine," *Chicago Tribune*, September 14, 1980, www.chicagotribune.com.

58 Weidrich, "Agents Tie Chicago Heroin to Mexican 'Godfather.'"

59 US Congress House Select Committee on Narcotics Abuse and Control, "Drug Abuse and Drug Trafficking in Chicago," 32–33.

60 E. R. Shipp, "134 Indicted in Nationwide Drug Distribution Case, *New York Times*, July 24, 1985.

61 Police auctions have been practiced throughout the twentieth century. For an example, see the image from the *Detroit News*, "Auctions; Detroit. Police Auction," October 26, 1939, http://dp.la. In more recent decades, drug forfeitures have been a source of revenue for local, state, and national agencies. See "DEA Asset Forfeiture," accessed March 20, 2021, www.dea.gov. For a Chicago example, see Bill Bird, "Cars Seized in Crimes Generate Lucrative Income for Police and Governments," *Chicago Tribune*, July 23, 2016, www.chicagotribune.com.

62 Ronald Ostrow, "1984 Crime Control Act Leads to a 32% Rise in Prisoners," *Los Angeles Times*, January 9, 1986, www.latimes.com.

63 For the impact of both acts, see Todd R. Clear and Natasha Frost, *The Punishment Imperative: The Rise and Failure of Mass Incarceration in America* (New York: New York University Press, 2014); Michelle Alexander, *The New Jim Crow: Mass Incarceration in the Age of Colorblindness* (New York, NY: New Press, 2012).

64 US Department of Justice, US Attorney, Northern District of Illinois, Information Release, in "Drug Abuse and Drug Trafficking in Chicago," 212–16.

65 Indictments published in "Drug Abuse and Drug Trafficking in Chicago," 216–30.

66 List of Properties for Forfeiture, "Drug Abuse and Drug Trafficking in Chicago," 232–33.

67 Calderoni, as he was known, frequently collaborated with the DEA. He was involved in the death of Pablo Acosta in 1987. A controversial figure, he argued that President Carlos Salinas de Gotari and his brother Raúl were involved in the drug trade. Calderoni later retired in McAllen, Texas where he would be killed in 2003. See Poppa, *Drug Lord,* and Christopher Lee, "Former Mexican Police Official Shot to Death in Texas," *Washington Post*, February 6, 2003, www.washingtonpost.com.

68 Miller, interview. US Department of Justice, National Drug Intelligence Center, Illinois Drug Threat Assessment, product no. 2001-S0382IL-001, January 2001, www.justice.gov.

69 NDIC, Illinois Drug Threat Assessment, 10. See also "Mexico Drugs: Cartel 'Meth Boss' Jaime Herrera Arrested," BBC News, February 14, 2012, www.bbcnews.com.

70 See "Federal Drug Control Spending by Functions FY2013 through FY 2018 (Un-Adjusted)," Drug War Facts, accessed March 10, 2021, www.drugwarfacts.org.

4

Cultivating Cannabis, Excepting Cannabis

MICHAEL POLSON

Cannabis is often framed as an exception to the War on Drugs. Legalization would simply remove "soft drugs" from prohibition while leaving the rest of the drug war apparatus in place. This "cannabis exceptionalism," however, elides the centrality of cannabis in the global drug war. This chapter outlines the pivotal role of cannabis in global prohibition and how its supply-side tactics produced a modern, global, and illegalized peasantry. Relying on ethnographic data from California, this chapter illuminates the "exceptional" factors that shaped cultivation in the United States, leading toward the surprising advancement of legalization at the heart of the drug war empire. Despite its benefits, US legalization now marks US cannabis as an exception in a still-global drug war, perpetrated by the US, with consequences for illegalized farmers and market actors worldwide. A holistic perspective on (US) legalization thus requires a "de-prohibition" politics at a scale equal to that of the sweeping, global War on Drugs.

Cannabis Exceptionalism

The global War on Drugs could not exist in its broad scale and granular intensity without cannabis. The 2019 UN *World Drug Report* estimates that 188 million people (3.8 percent of the world's population) used cannabis in the previous year. That's 50 percent more than consume the four other most frequently used drugs combined. Cannabis is the most widely grown illegalized plant, covering 159 countries and 97 percent of the global population (unlike opium, which is grown in fifty countries, and coca, grown in a handful of Latin American countries). Even in 2017, when states and countries around the world were liberalizing cannabis, the plant accounted for approximately 50 percent of seizure cases globally and 60 percent of seized tonnage.[1] That is 60 percent more seized tonnage than 1998. In the United States, where most states have liberalized cannabis, one person is still arrested for cannabis-related charges every forty-eight seconds (92 percent of them for simple possession) as late as 2018.[2] That's more than twice as many arrests as 1991.[3] On the Southwest US border, the amount of cannabis seized is drastically larger than heroin, cocaine, and meth combined and continues to be the most common drug found in border stops.[4] With global cultivation increasing between 2014 and 2017, these trends will likely continue.[5] Cannabis remains the workhorse powering the global War on Drugs.[6]

And yet one would hardly know the power behind this seemingly innocuous, "soft" drug—and for good reason. President Bill Clinton winked, nudged and never inhaled, but cannabis arrests under his presidency more than doubled, partly a product of his epic expansion of policing and mass incarceration in the 1994 Violent Crime Control and Law Enforcement Act (commonly known as the "1994 crime bill"). President George W. Bush admitted he smoked cannabis, even as he vigorously blocked cannabis' medicalization, escalated the militarization of police, and resuscitated anti-drug operations in the Andean region.[7] Meanwhile, President Barack Obama inhaled and promised to not intervene in state cannabis laws, but then federal prosecutors did just that, sending the emerging medical sector into disarray, and prompting Congress to bar the use of federal funds to impede state medical laws in 2014.[8] As an anthropologist doing fieldwork at that time, I narrowly missed a federal raid on Oaksterdam University, an early starter in cannabis education, where I was taking a course, and I watched as California medical dispensaries—particularly those with vocal, activist leaders—were shut down directly or indirectly through threats to landlords, local officials, or operators. Cannabis, it seems, is not a big deal. Until it is.

As the US led the global war on cannabis, and drugs more generally, its residents were taught to make light of cannabis in movies from *Dazed and Confused* and *The Big Lebowski* to *Up in Smoke*, *Friday*, and *Harold and Kumar Go to White Castle*. These cult favorites articulated a kind of subcultural resistance to the insidious pervasiveness of drug war culture, but something shifted in 2005, when Nancy Botwin, the single white mother and sympathetic widow of the award-winning, highly watched TV series *Weeds* (2005–12), accompanied the US through a period of transformation of public opinion, culminating in two legal-weed states. What was so bad about people in the cannabis economy, anyhow, when the legal economy—from Enron and Bear Stearns to Cambridge Analytica and the roster of banks involved in embezzling drug money (e.g., Wachovia, HSBC, US Bank, Wells Fargo)—seemed to be just as criminal?[9]

Our collective fascination with the cannabis outlaw has been reflected back to us in documentaries, news specials, and confessional reality TV. In the circular fashion of the "Synopticon 2.0," where "the many watch the many,"[10] citizens watch criminals and criminals watch back, a viewing practice that peers across legal lines, uniting viewers through a binding neoliberal commonsense of entrepreneurialism and risk. Representation and reality intermingled when my study participants were recruited by reality shows, law enforcement officials became mini-celebrities, and cultivators, caught between fame and enforcement, stopped talking. The fascination with cannabis realms continues in shows like *Murder Mountain*, which reinjected moralizing concerns about criminality and (poor, rural, white) dysfunction in California, right at the moment when cannabis liberalization proffered an opportunity for substantive rural development and de-stigmatization. From crime thriller to quirky comedy, cannabis was there to entertain. Cannabis was the US's open secret, its favorite primetime criminal indulgence.

For academics, those arbiters of the serious, cannabis has merited relatively little attention. In 2001, an anthropological review noted a "surprising" dearth of research on cannabis.[11] In 2019, geographer Pierre-Arnaud Chouvy could still note that opium and coca byproducts receive the lion's share of academic attention. Outside of a significant wave of recent historical and ethnographic accounts (which I explore below), existing studies mostly focus on consumption (often termed, a priori, "abuse"), a priority of the US's National Institute on Drug Abuse, which self-reportedly funds 85 percent of global research on "drugs of abuse." This research explicitly focuses on negative effects, a focus clarified after the institute funded three ethnographic "natural experiments" in the 1970s (in Jamaica, Costa Rica, and Greece) that found cannabis use to be neutral in effect, if not beneficial.[12] Given the relative neglect of cannabis research and the primary focus on abusive consumption within the cannabis research that does exist, it is unsurprising that research on cannabis *production* in recent times is a rare endeavor, especially to the degree it retains an openness to understanding its importance, even benefit, to society.

So, here we have a drug that is either laughed at or left understudied, yet has (tacitly) fueled the devastation of a global War on Drugs for the past fifty years. As cannabis liberalizes, we might think the plant is an exception to, rather than formative of, the War on Drugs. No need to stop that war when we can simply remove cannabis from the battle plans. After all, isn't cannabis the good, soft drug, bringing mirth, relaxation, even elevated consciousness, to its users?[13] This argument is similar to one made in the US in the 1970s: as white youth began using and getting arrested for cannabis use, concerned voices rose to decriminalize the plant—for well-intended user-victims, but not dangerous dealers and producers. Today, wholesome (mostly white) farmers do for legalization, what the white, experimenting teenager did for decriminalization—legitimatize cannabis in opposition to other shadowy entities, like Mexican cartels or Asian or Eastern European "drug trafficking organizations." *Excepting* cannabis from the drug war enables the *accepting* of cannabis as legal.

This chapter unearths the fallacies behind "cannabis exceptionalism." When we focus further up the commodity chain from the blissed-out consumer and further afield from US representations, we find that cannabis has been—and remains—part of a global drug war system. To see the ways cannabis is *un*exceptional, we must look beyond what we think we know of the (soft) drug and its (harmless) users, and instead take account of (to riff off of Timothy Leary) the drug, set, *and* historical-social "setting,"[14] or context, within which that drug exists. This chapter explores the US-led War on Drugs as the setting that instituted common constraints on cannabis globally and then analyzes how the particular setting of cannabis *inside* the US is playing a unique role in undermining supply-side criminalization—at least for US cultivators. By accounting for this setting, the purpose of legalization might be thought of not just as establishing a legal market like any other, but rather as a mechanism to account for and replace a global system that has caused many harms and, as I will explore, supported many people.

Cannabis cultivation looks different in Argentina than in Albania, yet the War on Drugs establishes similar constraints across places, especially since the US, that imperial hegemon, steered the world into harmonizing with its prohibition regime. After tracing how cannabis became a central component of the international drug control system, I will argue that, since the 1970s, the drug war created a common economic architecture for cannabis cultivators worldwide through drug premiums—inflated prices generated by supply-side tactics and the risks they imposed. In doing so, I aim to counter the often exceptionalist, myopic focus in legalization debates on domestic matters by illuminating the latent, criminalized solidarities and common political lots of cultivators across borders. Then, drawing from fieldwork in Northern California, I explore what makes US cannabis cultivators *different* from (even exceptional to) cannabis producers around the world. Supply chain differences, legal citizenship status, and medicalized politics set US cultivators apart, affording them relative privileges as well as particular importance in challenging supply-side tactics and the War on Drugs "at home." This unique position holds transformative political potentials and unfortunate perils, at least in regard to a just transition to legalization. The question then returns: will cannabis simply be excepted from the drug war or can we imagine a different future, one that challenges the extant drug war, addresses the fundamental inequalities it created and managed, and does all this across borders?

Colonialism, Bourgeois Nationalism, and the Rehearsals of US Empire

In a sign of things to come, the US delegation to the 1912 International Opium Convention was among the first to raise the prospect of international cannabis prohibition during negotiations.[15] The convention, called by the US, aimed to address opium and coca products, two addictive drugs that were often allowed, even propagated, by other colonial powers. With neither data nor authorization to discuss, the matter was nonetheless pushed by morally enterprising delegates, who feared pollution of "our whites" and worried that "fiends" would hunt for cannabis once opium and coca were restricted.[16]

It would take another decade for cannabis[17] to be revisited at the 1925 International Opium Convention, where the terms of cannabis debate were set for the next several decades. On one side were traditional colonial powers—Britain, the Netherlands and France, along with India (under British rule), where cannabis use was historically rooted—opposing universal prohibition, arguing it was an unwarranted incursion on internal affairs. Colonial powers already profited from organized sales of opium and coca, fought for the ability to market them freely (as in the Opium Wars between Britain and China), and placated colonized populations by tolerating the plants' use.

Cannabis was no different. In Morocco and Tunisia, France required cannabis products to be sold through a French capitalized company. Spain, concerned with winning over Berber tribes to their Moroccan protectorate (1912–56), allowed cultivation, too. Both colonial powers would later, half-heartedly, attempt to ban cannabis in their colonies, but the *realpolitik* of colonial rule won out. Despite nominal prohibition, Spain and France designated areas of Morocco's Rif for cultivation and France allowed cannabis cultivation to persist in Lebanon's Beqaa Valley, where cannabis rents might subdue politically agitated chieftains.[18]

Colonial tolerance was not universal. While the colonial government of India (like British Guiana and Mauritius) saw cannabis regulation as key to maintaining order, British-colonized Jamaica implemented prohibition in 1913, fearing use among Indian laborers and disruptions to racializing systems of labor control and colonial extraction.[19] Portuguese-occupied Angola implemented the world's first colonial prohibition in 1857, despite Portugal's earlier tolerance of cannabis in Brazil.[20] Angola was followed by other colonized nations like Gabon (France), Mozambique (Portugal), and the French Congo. Colonial prohibitions emerged as moral-civilizational reform projects and a means to increase labor control and productivity.[21] With cannabis prohibited here, tolerated there, cannabis policy became a tool of colonial statecraft in pacifying and controlling populations through *either* tolerance or bans.[22]

If colonial nations dragged their feet, it was emergent bourgeois republics—Egypt, Greece, Turkey, Brazil, the Union of South Africa—that advanced prohibition at the 1925 convention. Whether emerging from colonization (Egypt), wartime conflict and territorial reordering (Greece, Turkey), or into race-based self-rule (Union of South Africa), each nation resonated with the Wilsonian post–First World War spirit of self-determination. Rising national bourgeoisies latched onto cannabis prohibition as a mechanism of modernization, nation-state building, and sociopolitical pacification, particularly of youth, urban workers, peasants, and the racialized poor.[23]

While some theorize that the ensuing history of cannabis prohibition was simply "the international diffusion of a national policy,"[24] this theory elides the interstate competition emerging between European colonial powers and the US over the form of drug control. The US, a latecomer to colonialism, laid the bases of postcolonial but still imperial statecraft in its colonies, especially the Philippines. Via internally administered programs of drug prohibition and policing, the US could operate through and with moralizing national bourgeoisies, not over them, to discipline poorer, ethnic and rebellious populations and establish what Alfred McCoy calls a "nonterritorial American imperium."[25] Its imperial ambitions would be frustrated for some time, however. It walked out of the 1925 and 1936 conventions, galled at not getting its preferred hardline policies and leaving the remaining nations to find compromise.[26] It would take many years, a second world war, and the establishment of a United Nations coordinating body for the US to be in position to transform its imperial stylings into a global system.

Harmonizing Prohibition, Globalizing Cannabis

The US failed in 1936 to institute an international prohibition on cannabis, a move that might have cleared the way for domestic cannabis prohibition.[27] Undeterred, the US delegate and head of the newly formed Federal Bureau of Narcotics (FBN), Harry Anslinger, furthered a racializing campaign against "marihuana" that has become a textbook (if overstated) case in moral entrepreneurialism.[28] The result: the Marihuana Tax Act of 1937, which effectively prohibited cannabis through the levying of nominal taxes,[29] astronomical violation fees, and draconian enforcement.

In the ensuing years, the US launched bilateral efforts to incrementally implement and enforce supply-side drug prohibition, thereby making an end run around colonial powers and compromise treaties. Through moralistic and often extralegal practices, the FBN's efforts presaged the post-Nixon War on Drugs by acting preemptively and blurring lines between military and police, official and covert state action, and foreign and domestic jurisdictional provenance.[30] Anslinger fashioned the FBN as "a cop at the crossroads of the world" and advocated for a new single convention to replace the multiple narcotics treaties signed since 1912. The UN resolved to do this in 1948 and the US flexed its postwar muscles by pushing total cannabis prohibition, discounting its medical and cultural value.[31] The United Nations' 1961 Single Convention on Narcotic Drugs established the world's first coordinated prohibition regime and the first unambiguous international prohibition of cannabis (as opposed to mere trade controls). As a signatory, the US is still obligated to continue its criminalizing prohibitionist approach, which was domestically implemented through the Controlled Substances Act of 1970.

The Single Convention was an achievement in postwar international cooperation. It went beyond previous treaties, which had largely established rules of international trade, and instead implemented a global system of drug control, mandating that signatories—which included 95 percent of all nations by 2018—prohibit listed drugs, with few exceptions. As overseen by the UN, it follows a two-pronged strategy: prohibit and develop alternatives. In its first report, released in 1968, the International Narcotics Control Board (INCB), the treaty's multilateral monitoring body, noted that drug producers depend on crops for their livelihoods and production takes root in "underdeveloped areas not under government control." It called for a "long drawn out campaign" of economic and infrastructural investments (as opposed to a singular focus on punishment), which led to crop-substitution programs, such as the effort to replace cannabis production in Lebanon with sunflowers. By 1977, the INCB declared Lebanon a failed project, the first of many underfunded and ineffective crop substitution programs. Regardless, as late as 2014, the UN's Secretary General was still advocating crop substitution, despite evidence of their inefficacy in altering farmer decision-making and inability to achieve substantive, long-term economic development with ecological safeguards.[32]

In practice, prohibition contradicts the UN's developmentalist vision as well as its ethical mission of protecting sovereignty and promoting security, human rights, and peace.[33] There is also a functional contradiction at work: prohibition generates risk-induced market premiums that make drug production lucrative. Few, if any, substituted crops could outperform "prohibition premiums," but aspirational (and failing) programs transformed the UN into a perpetual development machine, forever striving to develop further and intervene deeper.[34]

For cannabis, the globally harmonized and instituted prohibition premium that emerges out of the Single Convention was transformative. By 1972, the INCB noted that cannabis commerce had jumped to a global scale, beyond its previous intraregional character. Soon, global cannabis seizures hit a historic high: in 1977, seizures from Mexico, Colombia, and the US alone exceeded the total amount that was seized globally in 1976. By 1979, cannabis had become, "quantitatively," the most trafficked drug. Cannabis cultivation exploded not despite prohibition but *alongside* of it and its risk-based incentives to produce.

Expanding global production was also a response to an expanding consumer base. In industrialized nations, the INCB theorized, countercultural youth, in "revolt against the established order of things,"[35] provided just that mass base. The Single Convention originally obliged signatories to criminalize that consumption. For instance, California, which led the push toward draconian punishment for cannabis "pushers" in the 1950s, saw a twentyfold increase in cannabis arrests from 1962 to 1972, of which 95 percent were felony charges, mostly for possession.[36] With such high consumption and criminalization rates, cannabis had the potential to delegitimize drug prohibition broadly in developed nations, leading UN members to pass a 1972 amendment to the Single Convention that achieved two critical reforms. First, it allowed signatories to rehabilitate and treat (rather than incarcerate and punish) drug users—thus, in the US, easing the threat that middle-class, white consumption posed to prohibition. Second, it recommitted nations to punishing suppliers. The INCB called for upstream economic activities (production, trafficking, financing) to be "severely punished" and a "clear distinction" to be drawn between users and supply-side actors.[37]

The US worked within the developmentalist UN process but it also pushed its militaristic, interventionist supply-side strategies through bilateral agreements with nations from Turkey to Burma, Colombia to Thailand to Mexico. The agreements became a critical part of the US foreign assistance apparatus and were codified in 1986 when President Reagan signed an order declaring drug trafficking and production a national security threat and requiring any foreign aid recipient to first be certified as cooperative or uncooperative with US anti-drug policy.[38]

Drug policy harmonization was a requirement for receiving aid, while enforcement of drug policies facilitated the US economic aims of extraction, privatization, and investment,[39] and fiscally fortified and morally legitimated national bourgeoisies as they pursued inequitable market liberalization agendas.

The cannabis trade only expanded, coming to be the quantitative anchor for the ever-expanding global drug war in ways opium and coca never did. While the Single Convention created a unified global prohibition price premium for cannabis, thus inciting expanded production, US-led militarization of the trade heightened consequences, risks, and thus prices for supply chains. This led to two developments. First, the globalized trade in cannabis returned to an expanded, deepened "intra-regional" patterning as traffickers shortened risk-laden supply chains.[40] Long supply chains were not only riskier and more expensive; they were increasingly unnecessary since cannabis could be grown in almost any environment. Second, and correlatively, US militarization instigated a turn toward "import substitution," or the global rise of domestic production, particularly in developed consumer nations.[41]

In short, by the mid-1980s the War on Drugs had fostered a global cannabis cultivation sector—a shadow economy into which developmentalist and militaristic-imperial interventions could be made. Though "hard" drugs (opium, then coca products) were the tip of the drug war spear, justifying its most intensely violent and invasive expressions, cannabis was the drug war's shaft. Its quantitative heft and geographical ubiquity made it a truly global object of state interventions.

US legalization debates often occlude this global setting (and the US's role in creating it): cannabis exceptionalism meets American exceptionalism as cannabis is parochially shorn of its global bearings. Is there a way to speak of what is common to cultivators globally? What, if anything, sets apart US cultivators (and cultivators in higher-income nations) from cultivators elsewhere? In the next two sections, I address these questions in turn. Rather than rely on state-generated statistics and data points, often seen as the only reliable data on illegalized realms, I turn instead to the ethnographic record, where the realities of cannabis cultivation are assembled from everyday lives.[42] By centering lives lived under prohibition, something invaluable appears for the consideration of de-prohibitionist paths: we see not only the harms caused by the drug war but how illegalized peoples forged ways of worth and life in illegalized realms.

Social Architectures, Prohibited Lives, and the Modern Peasantry

The drug war lent a coordinating economic logic to global cannabis cultivation, chiefly through a mechanism I call the *prohibition premium*.[43] Prohibition generates risks for cultivators, and these risks elevate the prices retrieved for product, which in turn draws more people into production. While cultivators may exhibit all kinds of motivations,[44] ranging from poverty to thrill-seeking to political-ethical commitments, all cultivators are placed in a criminalized relationship with the state. Being outside the law, however, does not mean being ungoverned.[45] Rather, as geographer Dominic Corva argues, criminalized realms are able to be governed differently. In terms set by liberal jurisprudence, criminals are regarded as free, choice-making individuals whose actions enable them to be governed illiberally, often through violent state interventions.[46] The drug war projected this illiberal interventionism to the global level, justifying all kinds of interventions into varied places and populations. Yet extralegality also allowed cultivators a certain kind of negative liberty, a freedom *from* liberal society and its norms, to craft other ways of life. Prohibition premiums facilitated and amplified that creative capacity, even if they imported a marketizing logic of supply, demand, and risk around which people were compelled to conceptualize themselves and their worlds. Born of coercion, capitalism, and human creativity, the shadow economies generated by prohibition and its premiums were much more than abstractly criminal or tragically criminalized. They were, instead, lived spaces. If legalization proposes justice for drug war targets, it must account for these spaces. After all, legalization is not just the advent of new legal markets and social realms but the transformation and upheaval of prior ones.

The cannabis market provided livelihoods for cannabis cultivators globally. The prices one could retrieve far exceeded the costs of physical inputs and what one might earn with other crops. Members of the Nasa tribe in Colombia consistently earned more from cannabis than from food and specialty crops, like coffee, as did Mayan farmers in southern

Belize.[47] Residents in Morocco's Rif turned to cannabis when the state took over the forestry industry, seasonal work in Algeria evaporated, and emigration and remittances became the only other viable income option.[48] Declines in extractive industries in Lesotho and rural, mountainous regions of Kentucky and California made cannabis a key livelihood strategy.[49] Among farmers in post-socialist Kyrgyzstan and India's Himachal Pradesh state, cannabis was a way to stabilize an unstable transition to neoliberal capitalism.[50] At times, too great a dependence on cannabis cultivation has led to declines in traditional agricultural practices and food security, but more often cannabis has allowed cultivators to utilize lands otherwise unfit for food cultivation or cash crops, access cash to purchase supplemental food, and even use cannabis itself as currency.[51]

A "weed" after all, cannabis can be grown in many environments and requires relatively little capital to begin. Low barriers to entry enable all kinds of people to participate, from marginalized youth in Papua New Guinea to women seeking alternatives to welfare in California.[52] Though some invest heavily in facilities to shield cannabis from detection, particularly in higher-income consumer nations, growers often avoid fixed capital investments for fear they may be destroyed in unstable environments, or seized and used as evidence in areas of intensive enforcement.[53] Land is a key capital input necessary for cultivation as well as protection, whether through the anonymity of growing on public lands or the seclusion of private property.[54] Knowledge of agronomy and access to land and markets can become axes along which cultivators are stratified, as, for example, in Sierra Leone, where those with land access (as well as knowledge of cultivation techniques) sat atop a system of labor tutelage, market access, and protection from police. Similar dynamics exist in Canada, where contact with mentors was key for advancement, or in the US and South Africa, where indigenous farmers have suffered for lack of market access.[55]

High profits and low investments not only stabilized economic life but scaffolded spaces for new formations of subjectivity, community, and politics. Cultivation could be disruptive, whether of traditional agricultural practices in Nepal, caste orders in the Indian Himalayas, or conservative and racialized notions of agriculture and rurality in the US West.[56] It fostered countercultural notions of ecological consciousness and conceptions of well-being among quasi-legal medical cultivators.[57] Conspicuous consumption, afforded by cannabis, often signaled independence and modernity and enabled status and identity shifts, as in Colombia, where youthful cultivators acquired motorcycles and mobility, or in Kyrgyzstan, where profits brought nicer foods and clothes, or in Northern California, where new trucks indexed success, or in Papua New Guinea, where cannabis growing became a vehicle for young men to insert themselves into the commodity flows promised by unrealized development.[58] Cultivators generated codes of professionalism (Canada), autonomous, safer spaces for cultivation (Spain, Belgium), communal systems of protection (Kentucky), ethical norms (Norway), leisure and passion (Florida), apprenticeship systems (Sierra Leone), and conflict resolution protocols (California), though cultivation scenes could be riddled with sexism, and racial-ethnic markers could pattern who one trusted and how networks formed.[59]

Cannabis often took root amid war, economic transformations and crises, political unrest or other conditions that inhibit the state's politico-territorial control.[60] It figured centrally into radical political organization, whether of Kurdish separatists in Turkey, armed groups in central Africa, Rastafarian resistance to colonial rule in Jamaica, tribal struggles for autonomy from colonial or national governments, and Maoist rebellion.[61] These political assemblages might cultivate cannabis themselves or reap revenue through taxation and protection fees, thus giving them financial bases of operation.[62] People in Lebanon's Beqaa Valley turned to cannabis to compensate for an absence of infrastructural development and as an income strategy during periods of conflict.[63] This was also the case in the Democratic Republic of Congo, Nepal during the Maoist insurgency, and Afghanistan, particularly since the US invasion in 2001,[64] where periodic bouts of violence and political instability necessitated innovative livelihood strategies. In Northeast Brazil, cannabis cultivation grew amid instability caused by market liberalization and commodity price declines.[65] It grew in spaces of failed development, as in Colombia, extractive and agricultural decline in rural regions, and amid the decimation of social welfare systems.[66] For developing nations, it became an "alternative to development,"[67] while in industrialized nations it became a "shadow welfare state" and criminalizing successor to Keynesian policies of managing postindustrial poor and working classes.[68]

Battling cultivators in unstable environments spawned state-formation activities—state-run extortion and protection rackets, institution-building funded by anti-drug foreign aid, federal transfers to local governments, or arrangements to ensure peace between national governments and unincorporated hinterlands.[69] By stabilizing marginal populations and building state capacities, prohibited cultivation produced a kind of "war system" in which cultivators and state actors were invested, often antagonistically, in maintaining the status quo.[70]

In this whirlwind tour, I purposefully scrambled the geography of ethnographic citations with an aim to illuminate the social architecture generated by the drug war worldwide. As its coordinating mechanism, the prohibition premium lured people at the edge of market societies into production, structured semi-autonomous spaces of extralegal life, and justified illiberal interventions that policed those spaces and peoples.[71] Out of the drug war's architecture, a figure emerged in the shadows of market globalization, a ghost of developmentalism, welfarism, and industrialism haunting neoliberal society. This figure was an abject reminder of capitalism's failures and, at times, a symbol of its core values—risk, unregulated markets, and the bending of law for profit. Cannabis cultivators were a distinctively modern global peasantry, produced from, yet marking the frontiers of, late capitalism.

At a moment when legalization is reintegrating this modern peasantry into national (agri)cultural orders, we might remember the common architecture constructed by the drug war—an architecture in which cultivators worldwide have lived, often adversely but always creatively. Legalization is much more than the lifting of prohibitive, punitive practices. It is the transformation of ways of life carved out in prohibition's shadows. Without forethought, legalization may simply take away "economies that were largely imposed on [cultivators] and on which they have now become dependent,"[72] and in doing so, double down on the drug war's negative impacts for cultivating populations.

The Particular Qualities of US Cultivation: Supply Chains, Criminal-Citizens, and Medicalization

Despite the commonalities generated by prohibition globally, the world is not flat. The "globalization of cannabis cultivation" has occurred across uneven geographies, particularly the unevenness between higher- and lower-income nations, or the global North and South, as geographer Chris Duvall has framed it.[73] This matter is particularly important for the US, which has played an outsize role in generating drug war geographies and is now positioned at the helm of a new uneven geography of legalization. What, then, is particular to US cultivation?

When Gerri moved to Northern California's Lost Coast in 1968 with "some hippies" who had turned her on to Bob Dylan, she came with "an idea of self-reliance, self-sufficiency, with no intentions of coming up here to start a marijuana industry." Heeding Leary's call to "tune in, turn on, drop out," Gerri's move was part of an urban-to-rural migration of disaffected youth popularly dubbed the Back-to-the-Land movement, an offshoot of the general countercultural protest against middle-class orthodoxy and part of what the philosopher Herbert Marcuse would call the Great Refusal in industrialized nations. On the Lost Coast, a wind-swept, rugged, remote oceanfront at "the edge of the world," as Gerri, a single African American mother from the Jim Crow South has described it, people "came with cows and chickens and goats. And marijuana was always our little side project, our hidden medicine."

Gerri's medicine was just that for the first few years—a symbolic, consciousness-altering plant around which she and her neighbors communed and relaxed in this retreat from regulated society. Growing her own also meant she could eliminate another expense from her household balance sheet. With the introduction of cannabis seeds (reportedly imported from Afghanistan and suited to the Lost Coast's latitude and environment) and *sinsemilla* growing techniques (i.e., sorting males and females to produce more potent flowers) Gerri and her contemporaries soon realized they had a valuable crop on their hands. The green, freshly cured, seedless buds could not have looked or felt more different than the compressed bricks of Mexican brown weed, often full of seeds and stems, that dominated the US market at the time.

But the market for this crop did not exist. Gerri remembers, "We drove it by the pounds to the city and the cops didn't even know what it was. We had to introduce it to people so they would stop buying Mexican. We actually had to go to San Francisco and show people good herb, and create the need for it. I remember going to a bar and hustling little buds to people, slowly, getting numbers, introduc[ing] it like Campbell's

Soup." While Mexican brown generally moved for a hundred dollars a pound, this new product eventually pulled $1,500 a pound, Gerri remembers.

For Jim, a white marijuana broker from Marin County, north of San Francisco, this domestic product—and the price it retrieved—was transformative. As a kid, he would marvel at his friend's parents as they sorted imported buds at their kitchen table, intrigued by this international market. When he became a cannabis broker as a college student in 1970s Humboldt County, he reveled in the increasingly cosmopolitan trade, the smells and varieties of plants from Colombia, Afghanistan, and Lebanon, the differences among African varietals and strains from Michoacán versus Zacatecas in Mexico, and his colorful suppliers, often Vietnam vets and private sailors who smuggled cannabis by plane and boat from Mexico, Thailand, and Vietnam. He fondly remembers $400 Colombian brown, the splash that Hawaiian and Afghan strains made among connoisseurs. When the price of domestic pounds skyrocketed, his import business supplying students and locals turned to an export business. With packs of Humboldt cannabis streaming across the country, the county's reputation as a weed epicenter grew.

The escalating price of cannabis helped back-to-the-landers achieve their utopic dreams of communal living, dis-alienated labor, and renewed connection to the land. Stevie, a white UC–Berkeley dropout, reminisced about restoring denuded timber lands, building yurts, and living off the grid with gardens for food and cannabis. Stevie came to the Lost Coast with five friends after having been fired from his substitute-teaching job in Colorado for sporting an "Afro" and a beard. Logged into ragged oblivion, his twenty acres of land were monetarily cheap but socially difficult to sustain in a rugged region averse to "newcomers." With cannabis earnings, he and his neighbors built, volunteered for, and fiscally supported schools, fire departments, and community centers. They established watershed restoration programs, a radio station, and a community health center, and contributed funds to maintain roads. They invested in business ventures, like solar panels, mountain bikes, and sustainable agriculture technologies, that may not always have been profitable (cannabis made profitability somewhat incidental) but tended to materialize utopic ideals. To Stevie, this was the "golden era of marijuana," a several-year window of time in which the price of cannabis was increasing, making possible an efflorescence of community institutions and a rich cultural life.

This golden era, however, was short lived. Limited eradication efforts in the late 1970s grew into a full-grown eradication campaign in Northern California in 1983 under the tenure of President Ronald Reagan. As California's governor from 1967 to 1975, Reagan had squared off with the counterculture in struggles over UC–Berkeley funding and leadership, culminating in the notorious battle over People's Park (among other episodes). It seemed to Hannah, a white woman, that cannabis gave President Reagan a justification for pursuing that counterculture into the hills of California. A surfer from Laguna Beach, Hannah's first political awakening occurred with the police raid of the New Age Christmas Happening in 1970 thrown by the Brotherhood of Eternal Love, whose avatar Timothy Leary had successfully challenged the US Marihuana Tax Act the year prior. This raid may have been unsurprising, given that the Happening occurred mere miles from President Nixon's "Western White House," just as his advisor, John Ehrlichman, was postulating cannabis as an efficient means to criminalize anti-war activists.[74] In the early 1980s, Hannah fled Southern California for Humboldt when a Central American solidarity organization she was involved with crumbled under investigations and infiltration by the FBI's Counter Intelligence Program (COINTELPRO), as court documents later revealed. Adept at recognizing the characteristic white Ford driven by "the Narcs" and becoming increasingly paranoid in her Latin American solidarity activism, she packed up her car, "held together by bumper stickers," and headed north. Humboldt, she thought, would be a reprieve and cannabis cultivation a way to "keep off welfare." Nine months after her arrival, however, California, now governed through a bipartisan, anti-drug, tough-on-crime consensus, launched the federally supported Campaign Against Marijuana Planting (CAMP) to hunt and eradicate cannabis. Hannah regards these political pursuits as part of a war-making machine aimed at those who proposed to stop it: "They undermined a whole culture, and when we all ran away they chased us up here and keep trying to swat us down like ants." She maintains that "the War on Drugs is an arm of the War on Culture"—a *counter*culture, to be precise, which, in Humboldt County, had developed robust, if criminalized, networks, institutions, and modes of communication.[75]

Though prohibitionist enforcement drove these off-grid communities deeper underground, they also drove cannabis prices to new heights. If $1,500 had once been an unheard-of amount for a pound of homegrown, soon prices of $5,000 to $6,000 per pound were commonplace. With this shift in prices, domestic cultivators became differentiated from—and gained significant comparative advantages over—international suppliers. Imported brown (or red or gold) bricks were often packaged to ship across borders. They were easier to smuggle than fluffy, smelly bags of bud, but consumer preferences increasingly favored those fragrant buds. Easier to smuggle were cocaine and heroin, which packed more value per unit with less pungency. As international eradication (particularly in Mexico) and interdiction (particularly in the Caribbean) intensified, new routes and substances took the place of cannabis. Meanwhile, US cultivators continued to feed demand, driving that shift toward import substitution.

The most significant comparative advantage held by intensifying domestic supply chains was that they could avoid the costs of international traffic and smuggling—planes, boats, processing, packaging, personnel, bribes, and so on. While US producers paid for transport to market, those costs were significantly lower than for cultivators outside high-income consumer markets. Put differently, US cultivators were able to pocket a larger percentage of their earnings than their foreign cannabis-producing counterparts, who, if they took part in international trade, would generally pass it through the bottleneck of trafficking organizations. These intermediating organizations were necessitated, enriched, and empowered by supply-side interdiction strategies that made international movement especially risky, capital-intensive, and organized. Though foreign cultivators could turn to intraregional or domestic consumer markets in their own locales—after all, cannabis consumption was increasing virtually everywhere—the US and other industrialized nations were the highest-paying consumers. Weirdly, then, global prohibition, as a system that intensively policed international borders, served as a protectionist policy for higher-income countries and their cultivators, while often consigning cultivators elsewhere to subordinated participation in trafficking networks or lower-value intraregional trade.

With the shift to an increasingly valuable domestic supply chain, local cultivation also shifted, widening from a utopic hobby of countercultural migrants to a common rural livelihood practice. Higher risks, bringing higher prices, had a transformative effect on the determination of who cultivated, in what ways, for what reasons. For many, these new conditions were a cue to leave. Stevie, the yurt-building Berkeley dropout, left the area when he began to worry it only offered his children a limited, precarious future. As a teacher, he noted, "a lot of the boys weren't interested in studying because their attitude was, 'Well, I'm going to be a millionaire when I'm twenty anyways.'" Once-rich interactions with his neighbors increasingly focused on growing techniques, gates appeared where none existed before, semi-automatic gunfire echoed in the watersheds, Rottweilers and four-wheelers roamed property perimeters, and Stevie's roving hikes through the countryside became a thing of the past.

Another cultivator who grew up in the life confirmed Stevie's fears, noting that he and his peers had grown up "in rundown houses with unreliable cars. No electricity. Cold water. It made those kids really yearn for the luxuries. For the amenities. You know, flip the switch and a light goes on, hot water. All suburban amenities. That was what people wanted." Soon, another cultivator and environmentalist observed, the social solidarities hewed in the back-to-the-land migration suffered: "Maybe only one person had a chainsaw and it would be loaned around. Two persons would have a working vehicle and they would drive us around. It was far more convenient. First, then, people got a little bit of money and bought a chainsaw. This began the process of closing themselves off. It really wasn't obvious. It was very gradual." The escalating price, for one local dealer, debased the ethics and values that had drawn him into cannabis commerce—the cosmopolitanism, the trust, the low-stakes intrigue. "I knew the value of the experience people were getting from it, and it [was] not worth it," he told me. He left the market behind.

Others, however, found new purpose in the transformed market. Cole, a white trafficker-turned-cultivator and back-to-the-lander from the agricultural Central Valley, stayed, relishing the thrills of international trafficking, even as he watched his compatriots face jail sentences and lose properties to seizure. Vince, another trafficker turned cultivator, came to California via an East Coast crime family, after being sent to juvenile corrections for drug dealing. For him, crime was not thrilling, per se, but was a matter of mundane money making and trust building. While he missed the simpler cosmopolitan commerce of the 1970s, he adjusted to the higher stakes of the new cannabis economy by moving his life from an increasingly violent urban center, Oakland, to rural Humboldt, where he found a new vocation in cultivation.

Gerri, who had been building cannabis markets since 1968, felt she had no place in mainstream US society, a logical conclusion for someone who had directly experienced the terror of state-sanctioned racism and had now witnessed state-sanctioned violence against her neighbors in California and her other home, Jamaica, for growing cannabis. She acknowledged the dangers that the emerging high-stakes cannabis industry held—federal raids, robberies, an occasional murder—but she saw no less danger in living legally. For her, the answer was not to leave but to weave the threads of community tighter, even as she prepared her children to cultivate talents beyond cannabis. "Pot seeds," she observed, "don't grow feed."

While the golden era of back-to-the-land communalism was drastically affected by prohibition, intensified drug warfare was generative of new cultural forms. Karyl, a white woman, had grown up on the Lost Coast. Born between two mid-century floods that devastated local communities and inaugurated the decline of the local timber industry, she regarded local life in seemingly timeless rhythms, where family names were "everything. Your last name—that's who you are. [They] stuck not just in how people perceived you, but [how] you perceived yourself." Regardless of local differences in status, though, one's status as a "local" was "just a shorthand for 'I know all the stuff.'" She explains, "People that weren't here [before the 1970s] don't know what it was like—you have a shorthand way of saying, if you're an old-timer, 'I know what it was like to think about the trees a certain way, going to church, and cussing.'" As the timber industry slowly deflated, this local culture was thrust back into history. The scapegoats for the ensuing ruination were back-to-the-landers, who found themselves as targets of discrimination, arson, vandalism, code enforcement actions, and law enforcement attentions. Karyl remembered how locals "united against the hippies. It was dramatic." Karyl pantomimes her disgusted reactions as she recounts, "The patchouli oil smell at this market, their smells, everything—their smell was foreign! They got in the river nude! The horror! [. . .] It was beyond the pale!" When Karyl's boyfriend in high school first smoked marijuana, she says, "I imagined his life was just destroyed!"

By the early 1980s, however, the timber industry was in freefall, with prices plummeting 48 percent between 1979 and 1982.[76] Amidst mergers, layoffs, and offshoring, cannabis became the shadow core industry of a region that was increasingly known as "the Emerald Triangle" in honor of its new crop. In this new economic realm, hippies, environmentalists, locals, loggers and rednecks began to find common cause. Karyl watched in high school as differences melted away and her "redneck friends" picked up tips from the kids of hippies and became successful pot growers, even if they didn't get into "all that peace and love [stuff]." This all took on an intensely personal hue for Karyl, when she, the daughter of a church-going Republican Mormon family, married the son of former members of Students for a Democratic Society. "You can *see* the divisions," she says, showing me a wedding picture, where she itemizes the stylistic differences between her father, the heavy equipment operator, and her husband's father, the college drop-out. At their wedding, each set of parents poured a cup of water for their children-to-be, from which Karyl and her husband drank, symbolizing not only the coming together of two families but the union of two sides of a county long divided. By 2011, her husband was working highway construction, like Karyl's father, and she tended the marijuana garden, like her husband's parents. In cannabis, the spark of a new local society was born.

"Without marijuana, this community would be dead," says Gerri. As prices spiked, cannabis employment absorbed unemployed timber workers, stabilized ranch incomes, continued supporting countercultural communities, cycled cash through ancillary, community-based businesses, and provided complementary incomes to teenagers, single mothers, welfare recipients, veterans, felons, tribal members and others whose relation to the formal market was already tenuous. Cannabis cultivation gave new, though covert, value to land, which was realized in shadowy transactions among a new array of industry actors into the cannabis industry—real estate professionals, property speculators, latter-day timber operators, and ranchers.

While cannabis premiums insinuated themselves throughout the region's social hierarchies, as any core industry might, its economic presence had political ramifications for the region, where opposition to clear-cutting and logging of ancient redwood had catapulted Humboldt to the forefront of a burgeoning, radical environmentalist movement.

Hannah, the antinuke surfer, argues cannabis prohibition was an attack on that movement: "They'd identified [cannabis] as a source of large financial support for anti–clear cut, responsible harvesting, sustainable forestry movement. Pot was valuable and it was going to fund the environmental movement."

Criminalization had the insidious effect of curtailing the emergent solidarities between (unemployed) loggers and environmentalists, locals and newcomers, rednecks and hippies. This nascent solidarity, built not only around cannabis but care for community and land, was pre-empted in 1990 when the Redwood Summer campaign, a grassroots effort to build unity among the rural white working class and environmentalists, was shattered. Judi Bari, the campaign organizer, was seriously injured by a mysterious car bomb, thus hobbling the campaign, and the US government launched a coincident military campaign, Operation Green Sweep, against the region's cannabis cultivators. Facing criticism from Andean nations over the eagerness of US forces to implement supply-side tactics abroad but not at home, the US deployed the Army's Seventh Infantry to Northern California to eradicate cannabis in the Emerald Triangle. This was a unique moment in drug war history, when US military capabilities abroad were brought to bear on US citizens using authorizations that loosened posse comitatus restrictions for domestic drug enforcement. Though environmentalists and many of the fifteen thousand Reggae on the River festival-goers protested the militaristic operations, Green Sweep had a chilling effect on cultivators. Domestic cultivators were momentarily branded not simply as criminals but as enemy combatants, a framing applied often to cultivators globally. Politically, anti-cannabis enforcement actions pressured cultivators who chose to engage in overt activism, environmental and otherwise, as it might endanger their economic livelihoods. Socially, punitive enforcement encouraged more insularity and the breakdown of networks that structured community life. Environmentally, the breakdown of community networks and norms fostered spaces within which egregious abuse of the land could occur.[77] Meanwhile, the timber industry clear-cut its way through remaining redwood stands, only slowing once the region's forests had been wrung of most of their value.

In the end, however, the overt military enforcement against cannabis cultivation did not stick (even if domestic police forces became more militarized).[78] Lawsuits were levied to contest the abrogation of civil rights, public outcry was vocal, funding for state eradication efforts declined in the ensuing five years, Humboldt County's sheriff pronounced military involvement to be counterproductive and ill-advised, and even military strategists agreed, questioning the wisdom of military operations on domestic soil.[79] US cultivators were criminals but also rights-bearing citizens whose status afforded them different treatment—and a different degree of political voice—than cultivators elsewhere. In addition to their relative power in the supply chain, cannabis cultivators were exceptional to the degree that they could claim US citizenship, albeit a criminalized citizenship, which protected them from some of the most intensive activities of the US-driven global War on Drugs.

It was a third kind of exception, the medicalization of cannabis in the US, that made it possible for cultivators to become legalized and proffer a domestic challenge to supply-side prohibitionism. The 1961 Single Convention left signatory nations some leeway to designate cannabis for medical-scientific research, provision, and use. This led, in the US, to a successful challenge in the late 1970s by a glaucoma patient who claimed cannabis as a "medical necessity." The federal government subsequently cultivated and provided cannabis for this patient and others, but when the program faced being overwhelmed by HIV/AIDS patient-activists who had discovered the treatment potential of cannabis, the federal government closed cannabis access to patients. In San Francisco, patient-activists founded a medical buyers cooperative, won a city-wide ballot approving medical cannabis, and laid the groundwork for a statewide ballot initiative in 1996 making California the first state to adopt cannabis medicalization.[80]

Patient-activists had primarily organized around the right to consume and access medicine, but someone, somewhere had to provision that medicine. Rights to cultivate were slower in the making, however. California legislators were especially nervous about regulating, and thereby legitimating, cannabis cultivation in light of the federal government's saber-rattling and fierce protection of supply-side controls. In 2004, eight years after voter passage of medical cannabis, the California legislature finally passed clarifying legislation allowing people to grow in legally-undefined medical "collectives," though even this was not unequivocally recognized judicially until a 2015 ruling. In the absence of state protection, cultivators acquired medical recommendations for themselves and often gathered recommendations of other patients in order to grow larger gardens. Cultivation, in other words, was medicalized. And it spread, becoming a ubiquitous, if controversial, activity even in the most conservative parts of the state.[81] The medical exception, that Achilles' heel of the Single Convention, was undermining prohibition not just for consumers but producers, those universal targets of supply-side strategies.

By the late 2000s, amid an economic recession, initial signs of liberalization by the Obama administration, and a growing acceptance of cannabis, many new cultivators broke ground, contributing to a downward trend in wholesale prices (and, incidentally, marking a motion toward a new economic logic of supply–demand pricing rather than risk-induced pricing, given that risks and risk perceptions were significantly declining). A 2010 legalization ballot initiative, which would be defeated that year, threw the cultivation sector deeper into disarray. Anticipating legalization, some cultivators went for broke by planting more, flooding the market, and crashing prices. Economic anxiety dovetailed with geopolitical worries when it became clear that the man bankrolling and organizing the ballot was angling to open at least one of four proposed one-hundred-thousand-square-foot indoor cultivation facilities in Oakland. Much closer to consumers and capable of pumping out massive quantities of high-grade cannabis all year, competition of this sort would devastate rural growers. This perception likely led nearly two-thirds of southern Humboldt County, the epicenter of California cannabis growing, to vote against legalization. A much-discussed bumper sticker exhorted voters to "Save Humboldt County—Keep Pot Illegal." Though growing acceptance had decreased risks, criminal-citizens depended on prohibition premiums and the benefits they gave to remote, consumer-distant cultivation locales. One might regard this as privilege and greed, or as the hard-earned caution of a rural population eager to avoid yet another bust in the boom-bust cycles that have defined the California hinterlands.

Though the 2010 legalization ballot initiative failed, many sensed that the "writing [was] on the wall," as one cultivator expressed it. Growers needed to claim a "seat at the table" if they didn't want to wind up "on the menu." If underground growers wanted to survive in a legal market, they needed to position themselves early and well. At a microeconomic level, positioning meant intensifying competition among cultivators. Growers dropped prices to retain business with increasingly choosey brokers, and cut the wages of trimmers or replaced them altogether with trimming machines. They chased the latest strains popular in dispensaries or the pages of *High Times* magazine, hoping they would still be popular at harvest time, implemented new horticultural methods, like light deprivation techniques that sped up outdoor growing cycles, and created derivative markets for otherwise-wasted plant matter, like the plant "trim" that fueled concentrates.

At a broader level, through the anticipatory machinations of cultivators in policy debates throughout the state, the discursive contours of a new, ready-for-legality cultivation sector took shape. Emerald Triangle cultivators, in some of the first efforts by US producers to build overt political organizations since the drug war began, auditioned new ways of conceptualizing cultivation for a legalizing era. One renowned environmentalist urged cultivators to recognize the legacy of pioneering, back-to-the-land cultivators and the ethical values they cherished: care for the land, community participation, and the struggle against Big Business and Big Government. In community meetings, legislative hearings, op-eds, and, increasingly, the speeches of politicians and even the comments of local law enforcement, people valorized "Mom and Pop," "homestead," and "small" farms, imbuing them with a righteousness that demanded protection in the transition out of illegality. These advocates generated a move toward "sun-grown" (rather than indoor) cannabis, an argument for "boutique," appellation-protected cannabis, a demand for "sustainable," "green," "local," and "organic" certifications, and a politics to insulate smaller farmers in California from the increasing pressure to increase farm size (even if people's definition of "big" and "small" farms was contentious). All of these demands have shaped the development of local and statewide political geographies of legalization in enduring, yet still fragile, ways.[82]

Seeking legitimacy and legibility as they were inducted into public and (agri)cultural life, growers went through a cleansing process to shed negative associations, much like white youth and medical consumers were cleansed of criminal intent in decriminalization debates in the 1970s and medicalization in the 2000s, respectively. This cleansing, however, came at a price, namely the generation of new negative stigmas against which respectable cultivators would be defined. Discursive lines were drawn between environmentally sustainable, law-abiding, citizen cultivators and those labeled as polluting, law-flouting criminal cultivators, who were perceived as dealing in harder drugs, acting violently, polluting public parks, and violating community norms. What sutured this new imaginary of criminal cultivators together was their supposed foreignness and potential relation to international organized crime, whether it was Bulgarian human trafficking rings, violent Mexican cartels on public land, or deviant Hmong farmers flouting norms and laws.[83] The reality underlying these accusations of organized crime is debatable, if not dubious, yet one effect is undeniable: legal market involvement entails a moral sorting of domestic from foreign actors. This is yet another iteration of the historic work of the War on Drugs in generating criminalized and stigmatized populations. As some cultivators are granted a conditional exception to the drug war and disciplinarily ushered into legal markets defined by citizenship, legibility, and respectability, legalization politics are evacuated of their radical demand for global justice for all those ensnared by the drug war.

For those opposed to drug wars, US cultivation was importantly positioned to challenge the supply-side logic of the war in the very belly of the beast. The unique position of US cultivators in the supply chain, and in relation to political claims-making capabilities, made that challenge possible.

Exceptionalism, however, hinders the promise of legalization. Cannabis is simply miscategorized, the line goes, and need only be rescheduled and removed from prohibited status. Meanwhile, the apparatus of the drug war continues apace, applied with equal fervor to other substances. Exceptions to the drug war are crafted along national borders, producing an uneven geography of legality and illegality as the otherwise relatively even geography of global prohibition crumbles. Legalization becomes yet another form of US market capture. Political demands for legalization are shorn to a basic demand for integration into legal-domestic markets. This market focus not only sidesteps demands for repairing harms done by a century of prohibition, but also sidesteps the inequities created by markets themselves. Simply removing cannabis from national prohibitions will not alter the structural purpose that prohibition served in managing inequality, and legal markets will not necessarily be more just. In fact, research I recently conducted with others demonstrates that current legalization may not even, as a baseline, consistently help the people who have labored under and been put at risk by prohibition.[84]

Globalizing Legality, Dismantling Prohibition

Whether in Colombia, Africa, Canada, or California, legalization is, despite all of its improvements, eliminating livelihoods from marginalized people who have depended on prohibition premiums.[85] Without countervailing measures, legal profits will accumulate in more predictable ways to more predictable actors—presumably along the lines of larger-scale monocropping agribusiness, with devastating consequences for producers, workers, communities, and the environment.[86] Generating those countervailing measures, however, will require a robust role for the state in mediating markets. Curiously, this is not an impossibility for cannabis, a plant that is no stranger to intensive state intervention. In California currently, stringent, thorough regulations have been explicitly designed for environmental protection. Yet these are having adverse, perhaps unintended consequences for smaller-scale farming and economic development in producer communities.[87] The question in California and elsewhere, then, is, not just whether robust state actions exist, but rather in whose interests and for which public good(s) will cannabis cultivation regulation be designed? And how will multiple interests and goods be balanced?

A core issue requiring attention is how to distribute the common wealth created by criminalized people over the past century. Because it is unprotected by law, the properties—intellectual, social, biological, horticultural, epistemological, cultural—created by cannabis cultivators under the restraints of prohibition are turned by legalization into unclaimed common property waiting to be appropriated by those with the access, capital, and wherewithal. These properties, developed by illegalized cultivators, are bearers of the immense labor invested in cannabis: building networks, creating markets, accumulating knowledge, sharing resources, protecting each other, refining techniques, breeding seeds, forming medical collectives, generating a culture, protesting, building political relationships, challenging laws, debating neighbors, and publicizing the plant's worth, not to mention taking risks, getting arrested, having property seized, and paying enormous fines. It is only through these historic and political labors taken by cannabis growers and activists that the plant, today, is valuable and legal. Without forethought, legalization may just be a legal sleight of hand to expropriate this collective labor.

So, is there a different path out of prohibition, not only in the US but around the world? One that does not merely expropriate but lifts up producers, communities, and the environment? One that does not merely extract cannabis from a broken prohibition system and render it legal without any regard for what is being taken away from already-marginalized peoples who took great risks to cultivate cannabis? Environmental scientists Liliana Dávalos, Karina Sanchez, and Dolors Armenteras have surveyed the destruction left by drug prohibition and resource extraction across Colombia, Peru, and Bolivia. They ask that we recommit society to substantive, thorough, and ecologically oriented development for rural communities. Duvall points to the need to recognize and protect cannabis seeds and genetics in Africa and elsewhere that are being pilfered by multinational corporations. In the US, as legalization progresses, advocates of equity policies, focused on people impacted by the drug war, attempt to ameliorate high costs and barriers to entry.[88] Activists also advocate for protective policies, like appellation designations, that generate market rents for cultivators to protect places, ecologies, styles of growing, cultural heritage, labor practices, and the like.[89] A broader protective policy would facilitate producer cooperatives, which allow cultivators to share material and intellectual resources, quell competition, and enable collective marketing efforts that make cultivation more affordable and economically sustainable.

More systemic policies would rework how cannabis cultivation meets markets. Looking to US tobacco leaf programs that have supported hundreds of thousands of small farmers for decades, policymakers might explore the potential of market-adjustable allotments, minimum prices, product grading, and cultivator-funded auctions to ensure that a maximum number of productive farmers can afford production costs, environmental protections, and fair farmworker wages. These programs are possible specifically because of cannabis' prohibition-elevated prices and they might be coupled with accountable distribution systems, like the not-for-profit collective systems that California had prior to 2019, which can guard against price gouging, ensure access for the indigent and ill, and are guided by public health principles, not commercial ones. These systemic policies go beyond ameliorative and protective programs by recognizing and replacing what was (perversely) beneficial about prohibition, namely, its provision of small farmer livelihoods and economic development. Designed well, they may also assure the health of workers and the environment, as well as indigent and ill consumers.

These proposals, however, operate within domestic borders. No matter how just the proposals may be internally, they would still be haunted by an active global prohibitionism that prevents cultivators worldwide from participating in legal economies and sharing in the fruits of legalization. The result: market capture by the Global North and a new round of dispossession and marginalization of those in the Global South, that historic object of supply-side interventions. Can "we," however constituted, generate a just legalization and collaboratively support it across the globe with the same gusto as the US did in the War on Drugs?

In this essay, I have illuminated the relationship of US cannabis cultivation with the world. Yet cannabis exceptionalism severs the connection of the plant with the drug war and its global provenance, myopically refocusing US Americans on domestic markets. It is here that cannabis exceptionalism lapses into American exceptionalism, tantalizing US Americans with fantasies of market achievements and divorcing them from the debts owed to one another and the world. It may be that cannabis is now allowed in that city upon a hill. Yet, as the War continues, one might be drawn to wonder who lies in the valleys below—and what it is they may be growing next.

NOTES

1 United Nations Office of Drug Control (UNODC), *World Drug Report* (Vienna: United Nations, 2019). In descending order, cannabis seizure cases were recorded in Paraguay, the US, Mexico, Spain, Pakistan, and Morocco. India reported the second highest number of plants eradicated, Guatemala reported the highest numbers of plants seized, and Brazil and Egypt reported high numbers seized.

2 Tom Angell, "Marijuana Arrests Increased Again Last Year despite More States Legalizing, FBI Data Shows," *Forbes*, October 1, 2019, www.forbes.com.

3 Jacob Sullum, "Marijuana Arrests Hit a Two-Decade Low but Are Still an Outrage," *Forbes*, September 29, 2019, www.forbes.com. Arrest numbers are down from 2010, when cannabis arrests accounted for 52 percent of the nation's total, yet cannabis still comprises 40 percent of all arrests.

4 Drug Enforcement Administration (DEA), *National Drug Threat Assessment Summary* (DEA Strategic Intelligence Section, 2016), 120.
5 UNODC, *World Drug Report.*
6 I borrow the term "workhorse" from Kathleen Frydl, personal communication, July 20, 2020.
7 Arthur Rizer and Joseph Hartmann, "How the War on Terror Has Militarized the Police," *Atlantic*, November 7, 2011, www.theatlantic.com; Winifred Tate, "Into the Andean Quagmire," *NACLA*, September 25, 2007, https://nacla.org.
8 Russell Berman, "Why Congress Gave into Medical Marijuana," *Atlantic*, December 17, 2014, www.theatlantic.com.
9 James Carrier, "Economy, Crime and Wrong in a Neoliberal Era," in *Economy, Crime and Wrong in a Neoliberal Era*, ed. James Carrier (New York: Berghahn Books, 2018), 1–39.
10 Nicholas Gane, "The Governmentalities of Neoliberalism: Panopticism, Postpanopticism and Beyond," *Sociological Review* 60, no. 2 (2012): 623.
11 Mac Marshall, Genevieve M. Ames, and Linda A. Bennett, "Anthropological Perspectives on Alcohol and drugs at the Turn of the New Millennium," *Social Science & Medicine* 53, no. 2 (2001): 153–64.
12 Martin A. Lee, *Smoke Signals: A Social History of Marijuana* (New York: Simon and Schuster, 2012). On the National Institute on Drug Abuse and negative hypotheses, see also Donald I. Abrams, "Medical Marijuana: Tribulations and Trials," *Journal of Psychoactive Drugs* 30, no. 2 (1998): 163–69; Clinton Werner, "Medical Marijuana and the AIDS Crisis," *Journal of Cannabis Therapeutics* 1, nos. 3–4 (2001): 31. Recently, the Drug Enforcement Administration has issued rule changes to expand beyond the single authorized cannabis cultivation lab to multiple cultivators. Only one cannabis derivative has been approved for medical use.
13 The answer is "not necessarily," according to drug historian Isaac Campos, who argues that the actual experience of cannabis use is significantly shaped by one's social context. Isaac Campos, *Home Grown: Marijuana and the Origins of Mexico's War on Drugs* (Chapel Hill: University of North Carolina Press, 2012).
14 Norman E. Zinberg, *Drug, Set, and Setting: The Basis for Controlled Intoxicant Use* (New Haven: Yale University Press, 1984).
15 UNODC, "The Cannabis Problem: A Note on the Problem and the History of International Action," *UNODC*, January 1, 1962, www.unodc.org.
16 Dale Gieringer, "The Forgotten Origins of Cannabis Prohibition in California," *Contemporary Drug Problems* 26, no. 2 (1999): 237–88. Italy also raised concerns over cannabis as it sought a tighter grip on its North African colonies after wresting them away from Turkey in 1911. Transnational Institute, *The Rise and Decline of Cannabis Prohibition*, March 7, 2014, www.tni.org.
17 For the purposes of this article, I do not distinguish between hashish, cannabis flower, and other psychotropic cannabis products directly derived from the plant, the definitions of which are repeatedly conflated and confused in drug policy debates. While there are important differences in the history of each product, I am

focused on the political histories that produced "cannabis" as a singular, dangerous, policed plant source.

18 Kenza Afsahi and Salem Darwich, "Hashish in Morocco and Lebanon: A Comparative Study," *International Journal of Drug Policy* 31 (2016): 190–98. On French cannabis policy and colonialism, see David A. Guba, *Taming Cannabis: Drugs and Empire in Nineteenth-century France* (Montreal: McGill-Queen's University Press, 2020).

19 James Mills, *Cannabis Brittanica* (Oxford: Oxford University Press, 2004); Vera Rubin and Lambros Comitas, *Ganja in Jamaica: The Effects of Marijuana Use* (Norwell, MA: Anchor, 1976).

20 Transnational Institute, *Rise and Decline*.

21 Chris Duvall, "A Brief Agricultural History of Cannabis in Africa, from Prehistory to Canna-Colony," *EchoGéo* 48 (2019), https://doi.org/10.4000/echogeo.17599.

22 For instance, Ram Haggai, *Intoxicating Zion: A Social History of Hashish in Mandatory Palestine and Israel* (Stanford: Stanford University Press, 2020).

23 Liat Kozma, "Cannabis Prohibition in Egypt, 1880–1939: From Local Ban to League of Nations Diplomacy," *Middle Eastern Studies* 47, no. 3 (2011): 443–60; C. Stefanis, C. Ballas, and D. Madianou, "Sociocultural and Epidemiological Aspects of Hashish Use in Greece," in *Cannabis and Culture*, ed. Vera Rubin (Mouton Publishers, The Hague, 1975), 303–26; Transnational Institute, *Rise and Decline*; Utathya Chattopadhyaya, "Dagga and Prohibition: Markets, Animals, and the Imperial Contexts of Knowledge, 1893–1925," *South African Historical Journal* 71, no. 4 (2019): 587–613; Campos, *Home Grown*; Maziyar Ghiabi, *Drugs Politics: Managing Disorder in the Islamic Republic of Iran* (Cambridge: Cambridge University Press, 2019). This literature is part of a general historiographic move challenging unilateral notions that the War on Drugs was simply imposed by colonial or imperial forces. I share this assessment, though I am concerned here with outlining how cannabis (in particular) came to be integrated into international prohibition regimes.

24 K. Bruun, L. Pan, and I. Rexed, *The Gentlemen's Club: International Control of Drugs and Alcohol* (Chicago: University of Chicago Press, 1975), www.drugtext.org.

25 Alfred McCoy, *Policing America's Empire: The United States, the Philippines, and the Rise of the Surveillance State* (Madison: University of Wisconsin Press, 2009), 19. On prohibition and morality, see Jessica Kuperavage, "Petitioning against the 'Opium Evil': Economic Policy as Humanitarian Intervention in Early Antidrug Rhetoric," *Southern Communication Journal* 79, no. 5 (2014): 369–86.

26 David Musto, *American Disease: Origins of Narcotics Control*, rev. ed. (1973; repr., New York: Oxford University Press, 1999).

27 Musto, *The American Disease*.

28 Jerome Himmelstein, *The Strange Career of Marijuana* (Westport, CT: Praeger, 1983).

29 This relatively weak power to tax (rather than affirmatively regulate and restrict) undergirded some early prohibitionist efforts (e.g., the 1914 Harrison Narcotics Tax Act). Only later, when the Marihuana Tax Act was struck down in 1969, was prohibition fully organized under the Commerce Clause, which itself had become

more central to national policy since the national economic reforms of the New Deal and Second World War eras. Even after an era of the expansive Commerce Clause utilization (from 1942's *Wickard v Filburn* to 1995's *US v Lopez*), the Commerce Clause is still used to justify federal cannabis prohibition. See David Crowell, "*Gonzalez v. Raich* and the Development of Commerce Clause Jurisprudence," *Rutgers Law Journal* 38 (2006): 251–320.

30 Matthew Pembleton, *Containing Addiction: The Federal Bureau of Narcotics and the Origins of America's Global Drug War* (Amherst: University of Massachusetts Press, 2017).

31 UNODC, "The Cannabis Problem"; Transnational Institute, *Rise and Decline*.

32 T. David Mason and Christopher Campany, "Guerrillas, Drugs and Peasants: The Rational Peasant and the War on Drugs in Peru," *Terrorism and Political Violence* 7, no. 4 (1995): 140–70; Liliana Dávalos, Karina Sanchez, and Dolors Armenteras, "Deforestation and Coca Cultivation Rooted in Twentieth-Century Development Projects," *Bioscience* 66, no. 11 (2016): 974–82.

33 David Bewley-Taylor, "Emerging Policy Contradictions between the United Nations Drug Control System and the Core Values of the United Nations," *International Journal of Drug Policy* 16, no. 6 (2005): 423–31.

34 Teo Ballvé, *The Frontier Effect: State Formation and Violence in Colombia* (Ithaca: Cornell University Press, 2020).

35 International Narcotics Control Board, *First Report of the International Narcotics Control Board* (Geneva: UN, 1968).

36 Matthew Lassiter, "Pushers, Victims, and the Lost Innocence of White Suburbia: California's War on Narcotics during the 1950s," *Journal of Urban History* 41, no. 5 (2015): 787–807; Michael Aldrich and Tod Mikuriya, "Savings in California Marijuana Law Enforcement Costs Attributable to the Moscone Act of 1976: A Summary," *Journal of Psychoactive Drugs* 20, no. 1 (1988): 75–82.

37 International Narcotics Control Board, *Report of the International Narcotics Control* Board (Geneva: UN, 1975), 7; International Narcotics Control Board, *Report of the International Narcotics Control Board* (Geneva: UN, 1977).

38 William Walker III, "The Foreign Narcotics Policy of the United States since 1980: An End to the War on Drugs?" *International Journal* 49, no. 1 (1994): 37–65; Dominic Corva, "Neoliberal Globalization and the War on Drugs: Transnationalizing Illiberal Governance in the Americas," *Political Geography* 27, no. 2 (2008): 176–93.

39 Paul Gootenberg, "Secret Ingredients: The Politics of Coca in US-Peruvian Relations, 1915–65," *Journal of Latin American Studies* 36, no. 2 (2004): 233–65; Julien Mercille, "Violent Narco-cartels or US Hegemony? The Political Economy of the 'War on Drugs' in Mexico," *Third World Quarterly* 32, no. 9 (2011): 1637–53; Nazih Richani, "Multinational Corporations, Rentier Capitalism, and the War System in Colombia," *Latin American Politics and Society* 47, no. 3 (2005): 113–44.

40 UNODC, *World Drug Report*.

41 Tom Decorte and Gary Potter, "The Globalisation of Cannabis Cultivation: A Growing Challenge," *International Journal of Drug Policy* 26, no. 3 (2015): 221–25.

42 Michael Polson, "Marketing Marijuana: Prohibition, Medicalization and the Commodity," in Carrier, *Economy, Crime and Wrong in a Neoliberal Era*, 140–71. While the truth claims that emerge from these accounts are also mediated, Jane Schneider and Peter Schneider remind us that ethnographic "revelations" of criminalized realms can impart critical insights that are otherwise made invisible through illegalization. Jane Schneider and Peter Schneider, "Is Transparency Possible? The Political-Economic and Epistemological Implications of Cold War Conspiracies and Subterfuge in Italy," in *States and Illegal Practices*, ed. Josiah Heyman (New York: Bloomsbury Academic, 1999), 169–98. Further, the act of learning *from* illegalized actors can constitute a de-prohibitionist praxis through which we can reconstruct what sources are considered valid.

43 See also Alfred W. McCoy, "The Stimulus of Prohibition: A Critical History of the Global Narcotics Trade," in *Dangerous Harvest: Drug Plants and the Transformation of Indigenous Landscapes*, ed. Michael Steinberg, Joseph Hobbs and Kent Mathewson (New York: Oxford University Press, 2004), 24–111; Ethan Nadelmann "The Case for Legalization," *Public Interest* 92 (1988): 3–31. This logic is *not* a supply and demand logic, where limiting supply through enforcement increases prices and, in turn, reduces consumption.

44 Decorte and Potter, "The Globalisation of Cannabis Cultivation."

45 Michael Polson, "Outlaw," *Journal for the Anthropology of North America* 22, no. 2 (2019): 128–30.

46 Corva, "Neoliberal Globalization."

47 Autumn Zellers, "Drug Production, Autonomy, and Neoliberal Multiculturalism in Indigenous Colombia" (PhD diss., Temple University, 2018); Michael Steinberg, "The Marijuana Milpa: Agricultural Adaptations in a Post-subsistence Maya Landscape in Southern Belize" in Steinberg, Hobbs and Mathewson, *Dangerous Harvest*, 167–81.

48 Kenza Asfahi and Salem Darwich, "Hashish in Morocco and Lebanon: A comparative study," *International Journal of Drug Policy* 31 (2016): 190–98.

49 Julian Bloomer, "Using a Political Ecology Framework to Examine Extra-legal Livelihood Strategies: A Lesotho-Based Case Study of Cultivation of and Trade in Cannabis," *Journal of Political Ecology* 16, no. 1 (2009): 49–69; Ralph Weisheit, *Domestic Marijuana* (Westport, CT: Greenwood Press, 1992); Hekia Bodwitch, Michael Polson, Eric Biber, Gordon Hickey and Van Butsic, "Barriers to Compliance and Small Farmer Exclusion in the Formalization of Cannabis Agriculture" (unpublished manuscript, December 20, 2020).

50 Gulzat Botoeva, "The Local Drug Economy: The Case of Hashish Production in a Post-Soviet Kyrgyz Village" (PhD diss., University of Essex, 2016); Prasenjeet Tribhuvan, "Cannabis and Social Change in the Indian Himalayas," *Journal of Ethnobiology* 38, no. 4 (2018): 504–16.

51 Zellers, "Drug Production in Indigenous Colombia"; Pierre-Arnaud Chouvy and Laurent Laniel, "Agricultural Drug Economies: Cause or Alternative to Intra-state Conflicts?" *Crime, Law and Social Change* 48, no. 3–5 (2007): 133–50;

Thembela Kepe, "*Cannabis sativa* and Rural Livelihoods in South Africa: Politics of Cultivation, Trade and Value in Pondoland," *Development Southern Africa* 20, no. 5 (2003): 605–15; Ann Laudati, "Living Dangerously: Confronting Insecurity, Navigating Risk, and Negotiating Livelihoods in the Hidden Economy of Congo's Cannabis Trade," *EchoGéo* 48 (2019), https://doi.org/10.4000/echogeo.17676; Botoeva, "Hashish Production in Kyrgyz Village."

52 Chouvy and Laniel, "Agricultural Drug Economies"; Jamon Alex Halvaksz, "Cannabis and Fantasies of Development: Revaluing Relations through Land in Rural Papua New Guinea," *Australian Journal of Anthropology* 18, no. 1 (2007): 56–71; Polson, "Marketing Marijuana."

53 Dominic Corva, "Requiem for a CAMP: The Life and Death of a Domestic US Drug War Institution," *International Journal of Drug Policy* 25, no. 1 (2014): 71–80; Laudati, "Living Dangerously"; Michael Polson, "Land and Law in Marijuana Country: Clean Capital, Dirty Money, and the Drug War's Rentier Nexus," *PoLAR: Political and Legal Anthropology Review* 36, no. 2 (2013): 215–30.

54 Kepe, "Cannabis in South Africa"; Michael Polson, "Making Marijuana an Environmental Issue: Prohibition, Pollution, and Policy," *Environment and Planning E: Nature and Space* 2, no. 2 (2019): 229–51; Michael Polson and Margiana Petersen-Rockney, "Cannabis Farmers or Criminals? Enforcement-First Approaches Fuel Disparity and Hinder Regulation," *California Agriculture* 73, no. 3 (2019): 185–93.

55 Bloomer, "Using a Political Ecology Framework"; Polson, "Land and Law in Marijuana Country"; Christopher Suckling, "Chain Work: The Cultivation of Hierarchy in Sierra Leone's Cannabis Economy," *Review of African Political Economy* 43, no. 148 (2016): 206–26; Martin Bouchard and Holly Nguyen, "Professionals or Amateurs? Revisiting the Notion of Professional Crime in the Context of Cannabis Cultivation," in *World Wide Weed: Global Trends in Cannabis Cultivation and Its Control*, ed. Tom Decorte, Gary Potter and Martin Bouchard (Burlington, VT: Ashgate, 2011), 109–29; Kepe, "*Cannabis sativa* and Rural Livelihoods in South Africa"; Michael Polson, "Through the Gateway: Marijuana Production, Governance, and the Drug War Détente" (PhD diss., City University of New York, 2016).

56 Dinesh Paudel, "The Double Life of Development: Peasants, Agrarian Livelihoods, and the Prehistory of Nepal's Maoist Revolution" (PhD diss., University of Minnesota, 2012); Tribhuvan, "Cannabis in the Indian Himalayas"; Polson and Petersen-Rockney, "Farmers or Criminals?"; Michael Polson, "Buttressed And Breached: The Exurban Fortress, Cannabis Activism, and the Drug War's Shifting Political Geography," *Environment and Planning D: Society and Space* 38, no. 4 (2020): 626–45.

57 Polson, "Marketing Marijuana."; Jentri Anders, *Beyond Counterculture: The Community of Mateel* (Pullman: Washington State University Press, 1990); Helle Vibeke Dahl and V. Asmussen Frank, "Medical Marijuana–Exploring the Concept in Relation to Small-Scale Cannabis Growers in Denmark" in Decorte, Potter, and Bouchard, *World Wide Weed*, 116–41.

58 Zellers, "Drug Production in Indigenous Colombia"; Botoeva, "Hashish Production in Kyrgyz Village"; Polson, "Marketing Marijuana"; Halvaksz, "Cannabis in
   Papua New Guinea."
59 Bouchard and Nguyen, "Professionals or Amateurs?"; Xabier Arana and Virginia
   Montanes Sanchez, "Cannabis Cultivation in Spain: The Case of Cannabis Social
   Clubs," in Decorte, Potter and Bouchard, World Wide Weed, 163–77; Mafalda Par-
   dal, "An Analysis of Belgian Cannabis Social Clubs' Supply Practices: A Shapeshift-
   ing Model?" International Journal of Drug Policy 57 (2018): 32–41; Sandra Riggs
   Hafley and Richard Tewksbury, "The Rural Kentucky Marijuana Industry: Orga-
   nization and Community Involvement," Deviant Behavior 16, no. 3 (1995): 201–21;
   Eirik Hammersvik, "Four Barriers and a Set of Values that Prevent Violence among
   Cannabis Growers," International Journal of Drug Policy 26, no. 3 (2015): 290–95;
   Craig Boylstein and Scott Maggard, "Small-Scale Marijuana Growing: Deviant
   Careers as Serious Leisure," Humboldt Journal of Social Relations 35 (2013): 52–70;
   Suckling, "Cultivation of Hierarchy in Sierra Leone"; Michael Polson, "From
   Outlaw to Citizen: Police Power, Property, and the Territorial Politics of Medical
   Marijuana in California's Exurbs," Territory, Politics, Governance 3, no. 4 (2015):
   387–406. On race, sex and ethnicity, see Suckling, "Cultivation of Hierarchy in
   Sierra Leone"; Karen August, "Women in the Marijuana Industry," Humboldt
   Journal of Social Relations 35, no. 1 (2013): 89–103; Aili Malm, Rebecca Nash, and
   Samuel Vickovic, "Co-offending Networks in Cannabis Cultivation," in Decorte,
   Potter and Bouchard, World Wide Weed, 226–54; Polson and Petersen-Rockney,
   "Farmers or Criminals?"; Daniel Silverstone and Stephen Savage, "Farmers, Facto-
   ries and Funds: Organised Crime and Illicit Drugs Cultivation within the British
   Vietnamese Community," Global Crime 11, no. 1 (2010): 16–33.
60 Pierre-Arnaud Chouvy, "Cannabis Cultivation in the World: Heritages, Trends
   and Challenges," EchoGéo 48 (2019), https://doi.org/10.4000/echogeo.17591.
61 Arif Akgul and Kamil Yilmaz, "Ramifications of Recent Developments in Turkey's
   Southeast on Cannabis Cultivation," International Journal of Drug Policy 26, no. 3
   (2015): 330–31; Laudati, "Congo's Cannabis Trade"; Akeia Benard, "The Material
   Roots of Rastafarian Marijuana Symbolism," History and Anthropology 18, no. 1
   (2007): 89–99; Asfahi and Darwich, "Hashish in Morocco and Lebanon"; Bloomer,
   "Using a Political Ecology Framework"; Paudel, "Double Life of Development."
62 Anders, Beyond Counterculture; Hammersvik, "Barriers, Values, Violence"; Harvey, "Condemnation to Collaboration: A Preliminary Examination of Relationships between Canadian Governments and the Cannabis Sector" (unpublished
   manuscript, December 20, 2020); Polson, "Marketing Marijuana"; Weisheit,
   Domestic Marijuana.
63 Asfahi and Darwich, "Hashish in Morocco and Lebanon."
64 Laudati, "Congo's Cannabis Trade"; Paudel, "Double Life of Development"; James
   Bradford and David Mansfield, "Known Unknowns and Unknown Knowns: What
   We Know about the Cannabis and the Hashish Trade in Afghanistan," EchoGéo 48
   (2019), https://doi.org/10.4000/echogeo.17626.

65 Ana Maria de Souza Mello Bicalho and Scott William Hoefle, "From Family Feud to Organised Crime: The Cultural Economy of Cannabis in Northeast Brazil," *Bulletin of Latin American Research* 18, no. 3 (1999): 343–60.

66 Lina Britto, *Marijuana Boom: The Rise and Fall of Colombia's First Drug Paradise* (Berkeley: University of California Press, 2020); Bicalho and Hoefle, "Cannabis in Northeast Brazil"; Bloomer, "Using a Political Ecology Framework"; Ralph Weisheit, "Cannabis Cultivation in the United States," in Decorte, Potter, and Bouchard, *World Wide Weed*, 145–62; Botoeva, "Hashish Production in Kyrguz Village"; Polson, "Marketing Marijuana.

67 Chouvy and Laniel, "Agricultural Drug Economies"; Neil Carrier and Gernot Klantschnig, "Illicit Livelihoods: Drug Crops and Development in Africa," *Review of African Political Economy* 43, no. 148 (2016): 174–89.

68 Polson, "Marketing Marijuana."

69 Laudati, "Congo's Cannabis Trade"; Paudel, "Double Life of Development"; Polson, "Buttressed and Breached"; Asfahi and Darwich, "Hashish in Morocco and Lebanon."

70 Richani, "War System in Colombia"; Polson, "Land and Law."

71 Teo Ballvé "Narco-frontiers: A Spatial Framework for Drug-Fuelled Accumulation," *Journal of agrarian change* 19, no. 2 (2019): 211–24; Chouvy "Cannabis Cultivation in the World"; Corva, "Neoliberal Globalization"; Polson, "Marketing Marijuana."

72 Chouvy and Laniel, "Agricultural Drug Economies," 147.

73 Decorte and Potter, "Globalisation of Cannabis Cultivation"; Duvall, "Agricultural History of Cannabis in Africa." Duvall's concern with North/South relations is understandable given Northern market capture and growing dispossessions of genetic stock.

74 Lucas Richert, *Break on Through: Radical Psychiatry and the American Counterculture* (Cambridge: MIT Press, 2019), 131.

75 James McCubbrey, "Impacts of Illicit-Drug Policy on Community Cohesion: A Case Study of the Campaign Against Marijuana Planting in Southern Humboldt County California" (PhD diss., Western Institute of Social Research, 2007).

76 Gail Wells, "Restructuring the Timber Economy," Oregon History Project, 2006; updated and revised by OHP staff, 2014, www.oregonhistoryproject.org.

77 On all these points, see McCubbrey, "Impacts of Illicit-Drug Policy on Community Cohesion."

78 Peter Kraska, ed., *Militarizing the American Criminal Justice System: The Changing Roles of the Armed Forces and the Police* (Lebanon, NH: UPNE, 2001).

79 Edward Stelzer, *Military Support to Domestic Law Enforcement Agencies: A Policy with Unintended Consequences* (Carlisle, PA: Army War College, 1996).

80 Werner, "Medical Marijuana and AIDS."

81 Polson, "From Outlaw to Citizen"; Polson, "Buttressed and Breached."

82 Christopher Dillis, Eric Biber, Hekia Bodwitch, Van Butsic, Jennifer Carah, Phoebe Parker-Shames, Michael Polson, and Ted Grantham, "Shifting Geogra-

phies of Cannabis Production in California," *Land Use Policy* 105 (2021), https://doi.org/10.1016/j.landusepol.2021.105369

83 Polson, "Making Marijuana an Environmental Issue"; Polson and Petersen-Rockney, "Farmers or Criminals?"

84 Bodwitch et al., "Barriers to Compliance."

85 Zellers, "Drug Production in Indigenous Colombia"; Duvall, "Agricultural History of Cannabis in Africa"; Harvey, "Condemnation to Collaboration"; Bodwitch et al., "Barriers to Compliance."

86 Chris Dillis, Michael Polson, Hekia Bodwitch, Jennifer Carah, Mary Power, and Nathan Sayre, "Industrializing Cannabis? Socio-Ecological Implications of Legalization and Regulation in California," in *Routledge Handbook of Interdisciplinary Cannabis Studies*, ed. Josh Meisel and Dominic Corva, forthcoming.

87 Bodwitch et al., "Barriers to Compliance; Dillis et al., "Industrializing Cannabis?"; Polson, "Making Marijuana an Environmental Issue."

88 Bryon Adinoff and Amanda Reiman, "Implementing Social Justice in the Transition from Illicit to Legal Cannabis," *American Journal of Drug and Alcohol Abuse* 45, no. 6 (2019): 673–88; Robert Chlala, "Misfit Medicine and Queer Geographies: The Diverse Economy and Politics of Cannabis in Carceral Los Angeles," *Environment and Planning C: Politics and Space* 38, no. 7–8 (2019): 1180–97, https://doi.org/10.1177/2399654419884074; Beau Kilmer and Erin Kilmer Neel, "Being Thoughtful about Cannabis Legalization and Social Equity," *World Psychiatry* 19, no. 2 (2020): 194; Michael Polson and Hekia Bodwitch, "Cannabis, the Criminal Commons and Alternatives to Enclosure" (unpublished manuscript, December 20, 2020).

89 See Ryan Stoa, "Marijuana Appellations: The Case for Cannabicultural Designations of Origin," *Harvard Law & Policy Review* 11 (2017): 513–40.

PART III

The Domestic Front

5

The Local War on Drugs

PETER C. PIHOS

"The Local War on Drugs" examines how the Chicago Police Department and other law enforcement institutions and actors have managed illicit drug use since the Second World War. Until the late 1980s, drug-related arrests were only loosely connected to lengthy prison terms. Local institutions had to create punitive capacity and greater coordination in order to produce the mass incarceration of Black Chicagoans for illicit drug-related crimes. Amid conditions in which the Black poor and working class was excluded from the labor market and pushed into neighborhoods of concentrated poverty, white advocates of law and order and Black liberals seeking nuanced solutions to serious violence produced a war on gangs and drugs in the 1980s that became a critical mode for governing the city.

In 1950, the Chicago Police Department (CPD) made fewer than five hundred arrests on illicit drug–related charges; in 2000, they made fifty-eight thousand.[1] As historian Kathleen Frydl reports, during the 1960s and 1970s, "entire police departments had become vice squads with a primary interest in narcotics and, conversely, illicit drug enforcement emerged not just as something to police but as a *way* to police."[2] Yet, until the 1980s, prosecutors and courts lacked the capacity and inclination to incarcerate large numbers of people. In 1980, judges in Cook County (the territory that contains most of Chicago) sentenced half of a percent of drug-related arrestees to prison, around one hundred out of seventeen thousand. Only thereafter did Chicago's mayors and police superintendents, as well as Cook County's state's attorneys, judges, and sheriffs develop new punitive capacities within their institutions and coordinate much more closely to target and punish Black Chicagoans. Such institutional transformations were central to the War on Drugs as it was waged in Chicago and other cities.

This case study of Chicago highlights two underdeveloped aspects of scholarship on the domestic War on Drugs. The first is temporal. In James Forman Jr.'s words, "Mass incarceration wasn't created overnight; its components were assembled piecemeal over a forty-year period."[3] Chicago and Cook County institutions developed punitive capacity over time and in relationship to each other. Police tactics changed, producing different kinds of drug arrests in different locations. The actions of other law enforcement institutions changed the significance of those arrests. The second is jurisdictional: As criminologist Mona Lynch argues, "Although sentencing statutes have been toughened at the state and federal levels, thereby creating the capacity for mass incarceration, mass incarceration has not been realized without local-level criminal justice actors transforming their daily practices to send more and more offenders away to state penal institutions."[4] While both the federal and state governments acted to create the War on Drugs, this chapter focuses on the role of local actors in transforming their institutions.[5] These developments in Chicago are unique but not singular. There is a growing literature on the War on Drugs in specific urban places, which highlights specific facets of local change, such as police militarization and the development of dragnet policing in poor and working-class Black and Latino neighborhoods.[6] What distinguishes this chapter's approach, however, is a focus on the relationship of local law enforcement institutions to the policing of illicit drugs in the period since the Second World War, and the development and coordination of punitive capacity among police, prosecutors, and judges.

Over time, local action transformed the place of the policing of drugs in urban governance. By the 1980s, Chicago politicians embraced a state of war on gangs and drugs as a mode of managing inequality. Black poor and working-class people faced, as sociologist Loïc Wacquant has described it, "joblessness and economic exclusion . . . rising to extreme levels against the backdrop of rigid racial segregation and state abandonment."[7] When the liberal Black politician Harold Washington took power as mayor in 1983, he sought to address what political scientist Lisa Miller has called "racialized state failure"—government abandonment of its first-order political responsibility of providing safety from violence.[8] The political failure of Washington's multifaceted approach to violence in the face of fiscal austerity and white resistance channeled the city's response toward more intensive policing. Black political demands for greater neighborhood safety thus came to align with the punitive law-and-order ideology advanced by working-class white ethnics, led by Cook County State's Attorney Richard M. Daley. At the dawn of the crack crisis, Chicago's political leaders had already embraced governing through war on gangs and drugs, creating a local foundation for a regime to arrest, process, and imprison Black Chicagoans.

"Nobody Went to Jail"

Local law enforcement institutions created three different local drug regimes in Chicago since the Second World War. The first targeted a concentrated spike in heroin usage following the war. The second focused on a multi-drug crisis that stretched from the mid-1960s to the end of the 1970s, highlighted by the normalization of marijuana and the extension of heroin outside of historic copping areas (heroin distribution locations). The third focused on controlled substances, especially cocaine, and the rise of public drug markets in high-poverty Black neighborhoods. In each crisis, the CPD seized the dominant role—one that would grow dramatically over time.

Between 1950 and 1980, the CPD's policing of drugs went from being a specialized project of managing drug users on the margins of society to a widespread tactic for regulating urban order. In 1951, the CPD increased its Narcotics Section from four to sixty officers and the County Court opened a special Narcotics Branch.[9] These institutions centralized the processing and tracking of individuals police registered as drug addicts, three-quarters of whom were Black.[10] Once an individual was on the CPD's addict registry, police would send them downtown for booking and interrogation for all arrests, regardless of the offense.[11] The Narcotics Section used their arrest powers to regulate drug markets on Chicago's "skid row" and in the historic Black Belt that stretches between 22nd and 63rd Streets and between State Street and Cottage Grove. When Black Chicagoans demanded that something be done about illicit drugs in the Black Belt, police responded with vicious treatment.[12] One Narcotics Squad officer remembered: "[I]t was real easy just to go out on Madison or Maxwell streets and pick them up and do whatever we wanted with them. Nobody cared what we did to them niggers." Police used overtly racist forms of street justice, rather than long-term incarceration, to maintain social control.[13] Police collared most arrestees for nondrug crimes, and Narcotics Court creatively managed a massive docket—6,518 cases were heard in its first six months of operation—largely through a high dismissal rate and convictions for minor offenses.[14] Harsh mandatory penalties for drug possession, passed by the state of Illinois in 1951, did lead to increases in incarceration for drug-related crimes and overcrowding in the Cook County Jail, where sentences of up to five years were served.[15] Nonetheless, for the vast majority of people the police arrested, the punishment was a night in jail. With the aid of the County Courts, the CPD used these minor arrests as a tool to manage addicts and copping areas.

In the 1950s, the specialized Narcotics Section had engaged in spatially delimited and demographically concentrated policing, but the second drug crisis, beginning in the 1960s, led the CPD to vastly expand the people and places it policed for illicit drugs. In part, this was a response to real changes in drug use. Paul Hemphill, a Chicago corrections official, testified in 1971 to "a sudden increase in [drug] use on every socioeconomic level by our young people. What had once been a problem confined to the poor, to the chronically ill, and to various underworld subcultures has within the past five years virtually exploded out of the control of our institutions."[16] The use of drugs by white teenagers led many committed drug warriors, including the state's attorney and police superintendent, to argue in 1971 for tying penalties to their understanding of a drug's potential harmfulness. Law enforcement officials focused almost exclusively on "heroin pushers," whom William Bauer, the local US attorney, described as "more dangerous to society than murderers and armed robbers."[17] Ultimately, legal reforms and their application on the street produced a broader and looser punitive net. For example, even as the number of arrests expanded, the Cook County state's attorney created a pretrial diversion program to divert youthful offenders.[18] Nonetheless, arrest and detention remained the principal tools of control.

In the 1970s, the CPD expanded interdiction efforts targeting major traffickers within the city, vastly expanding the amount and value of drugs seized over the course of the 1960s.[19] While this would remain a key strategy—particularly for making major cases in coordination with the federal government—police leaders recognized early on that such efforts had little impact. As Deputy Superintendent Michael Spiotto lamented in 1978, "it is almost impossible to make a seizure which seriously diminishes the supply of heroin."[20] In combination with these supply reduction strategies, the department vastly expanded everyday drug policing. In 1965, police made 2,500 arrests for drug-related crimes; by 1976, this had grown sevenfold to 17,500. As Figure 5.1 illustrates, until 1976, cannabis and controlled substance arrests grew in tandem, after which controlled substances arrests declined, likely in relationship to declining heroin usage.[21]

In this everyday drug policing, the CPD followed Black Chicagoans across the new residential geography that emerged during the 1950s and 1960s. Described by historian Arnold Hirsch as a "second ghetto," it included many Chicago Housing Authority developments as well as formerly working and middle-class white neighborhoods on the South and West Sides.[22] By the 1970s, police arrested many more Black Chicagoans for illicit drug-related offenses in a much wider variety of locations than during the 1950s. Moreover, more police were engaged in anti-drug activities. By 1970, the International Association of Chiefs of Police observed, "All beat officers and district vice officers are employed

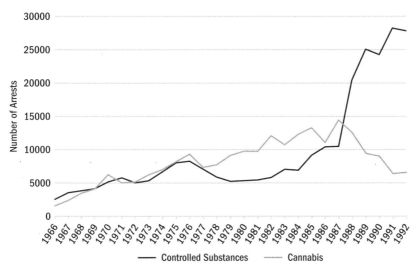

Figure 5.1. Drug-Related Arrests by the Chicago Police Department, 1966–92.
Source: Chicago Police Department, *Annual Reports*, 1966–1992, https://home.chicago police.org/statistics-data/statistical-reports/annual-reports.

in the general suppression of illegal narcotic activities."[23] These changes produced two new important patterns of arrests. First, police made more arrests of white people for drug-related offenses, doubling their rate of arrest between 1965 and 1970 from the first half of the decade. This did not mean the end of discrimination: Blacks were still arrested three times more frequently than whites per capita. Second, as historic vice districts broke down and new patterns of residential segregation emerged across the city, the geography of arrests also became racially segregated. During the 1940s and 1950s, police typically arrested white people within the same vice districts as Blacks. By the 1960s, police made drug arrests in racially homogenous spaces—Black Chicagoans were arrested in predominantly Black neighborhoods, whereas whites were mostly arrested downtown or in white residential areas.[24]

Despite this vast expansion of drug policing, the law enforcement system, particularly courts and prosecutors, had little capacity to convict and sentence arrestees to prison sentences. As the Illinois Legislative Investigating Commission concluded before the reform of marijuana laws in 1971, since most arrests were for possession, "well intentioned judges, prosecutors, and arresting officers . . . would rather issue a warning than to have to impose the severe mandatory penalties now required."[25] Judges actively managed their dockets and inquired into police work, throwing out a third of the cases for improper seizures of evidence.[26] Typically, these searches were the product of police aggressively confronting people or situations they found to be suspicious. The suspects were usually young (many of them had petty criminal records) and the searches usually took place at night, either on the street or during a car stop. Judges were most suspicious when officers tried to justify these searches with general rationales—the suspect was out late or apparently drunk, or the officer "saw" something, including the defendant throwing or dropping drugs.[27]

As a result, drug policing remained only loosely connected to imprisonment. Mike Royko, Chicago's most popular newspaper columnist, pointed out to his *Sun-Times* readers in 1980: "Of about 3,700 arrests last year for heavy drug charges—heroin, angel dust and other brain burners—about one hundred led to somebody going to jail. Of about four thousand arrests of adults in Chicago for peddling or possessing marijuana in felony quantities (not teen-age nickel bag stuff), nobody went to jail."[28] As in the 1950s, police continued to use drug arrests as a tool of control and harassment, albeit one that expanded beyond Black addicts in known copping areas to being a more generalized way to manage suspicious people and spaces. In the 1980s, this would change.

"A Drug Dealer Is More Harmful Than Any Other Criminal"

By the end of the 1970s, incarceration for drug use had hardly moved. Arrests for drug use fell over the second half of the 1970s, not eclipsing their 1976 level until 1984. By contrast, the number of prisoners in Illinois grew sharply, increasing from six thousand to seventeen thousand between 1974 and 1984.[29] Narratives explaining mass incarceration often miss the multidimensional nature of criminal justice politics during the 1970s, especially in Chicago, where Black activists organized against crime and also against repression, seeking to end the under-protection and over-policing of their communities. Nonetheless, the passage of Governor James R. Thompson's "Class X" law in 1977 to eliminate parole, fix determinate sentences, and create a new class of felonies symbolized a widespread embrace of retribution as the leading rationale for punishment.[30]

In running for Cook County state's attorney in 1980, Richard M. Daley sought to bring this retributive impulse to the handling of drugs, gangs, and youth crime. He criticized his Republican opponent because "only a couple of hundred people were sent to jail on drug charges in Cook County."[31] Daley framed his promises for more punitiveness explicitly as an appeal to Black voters, accusing his opponent of ignoring gangs, drug abuse, and other crimes committed against Black people.[32] In doing so, Daley hoped to tap into longstanding Black grievances about Police under-protection. For example, despite the disproportionate rate at which African Americans were arrested for drug crimes, Renault Robinson, the leader of the militant Chicago Afro-American Patrolmen's League, criticized the CPD's failure to stop drug traffic in Black neighborhoods. "[I]n the average neighborhood children know who sell[s] dope . . . but the police can't seem to find them."[33] Black voters and commentators remained suspicious of Daley's sincerity.[34] He prevailed in the election by just sixteen thousand votes, two-tenths of a percent, on the strength of his support from white ethnics the Southwest Side. While doing well in some middle-class Black wards, he did not perform as well as previous Democratic candidates had among Black voters.[35] Daley justified his punitive approach to gangs, drugs, and youth crime as a necessary response to the long-term crisis of serious violence in Chicago. But he did so by targeting the groups most vulnerable to that violence, primarily poor and working-class Black males. Blue-collar work declined steeply in the 1970s as Chicago lost almost a third of its manufacturing jobs. These losses hit Black males particularly hard.[36] Moreover, the losses were not distributed evenly across Black Chicago. Class stratification was embedded in space, as the number of Black neighborhoods of concentrated poverty dramatically multiplied from 1970 to 1980.[37] Many Chicago Housing Authority properties were left worse off, and they became examples of the desperate conditions produced by the combination of hyper-segregation and concentrated poverty.[38] In 1980, Chicago's most populous public housing project, the Robert Taylor Homes, which housed less than 1 percent of the city's population, was the site of 11 percent of all murders.[39] Another major public housing project, Cabrini-Green, had thirty murders between 1978 and 1981. A March 1981 killing there led Mayor Jane Byrne to take up residence in one of its high-rise apartment buildings, accompanied by a rush of services—planted grass, garbage pick-up—that only emphasized the city's routine failures.[40] Byrne's more lasting response was a new policing program, which engaged in widespread harassment of Black youth through mass arrests. In 1982, the Bureau arrested 145,000 people, more than one-third of all the arrests made in Chicago that year.[41] A lawsuit by the American Civil Liberties Union revealed that the Chicago Police made some eight hundred thousand harassment arrests overall from 1978 to 1983.[42]

As state's attorney, Daley doubled down on punitive approaches. He lauded the CPD's campaign of mass arrests, as "an example of what local police can do." He restructured his office so that his assistant district attorneys (ADAs) would turn those police arrests into prison sentences.[43] Daley required the ADAs to take many more cases to trial and to request more prison time. He required his ADAs to provide regularly updated status reports for every case in their courtrooms, as well as to compile monthly reports documenting their success in sending people to prison.[44] In his two terms as state's attorney, Daley took pride in seeking severe prison terms, even for minor offenses.[45]

Daley focused his office's attention on drug dealers. "A drug dealer," he told reporters, "is more harmful than any other criminal."[46] He created two special prosecution teams focused on gang and drug enforcement. He selected aggressive prosecutors for these units, people one admiring journalist described as having "the same them-or-us attitude that is common among the police." Kenneth Wadas, the attorney in charge, emblematized the approach: "a dealer is a 'dog.'" Wadas asserted, "'We're dealing with dogs, scum.'"[47]

A creative administrator, Daley reorganized the district attorney's office to ensure that cases stayed on track and more accused offenders ended up in prison. He set up a system of vertical prosecution that allowed for closer tracking of cases, as the same attorney oversaw the case from the preliminary hearing through sentencing. Daley, who had been raised by his father, Mayor Richard J. "Boss" Daley, to understand Chicago's inner workings, created much greater coordination between police and prosecutors. He made sure that state's attorneys were on call to supervise warrant applications, for example, to ensure that evidence was always properly admitted in court.[48] Using his insider knowledge and political savvy, Daley reorganized the district attorney's office to be a highly efficient incarceration machine.

Daley also worked closely with the CPD on "aggressive use" of the 1982 Illinois' Narcotics Forfeiture Act. The CPD loved the financial incentives the 1982 act provided them. Sergeant James O'Neill, a department leader, noted that "every dollar, every man-hour an agency invests will have a ten-fold return."[49] The extra cash the police received through the Forfeiture Act helped them improve their drug cases.[50] They used some of the forfeited drug money, ironically, in "buy-and-bust" drug transactions, which were more likely than typical "possession with intent" cases to hold up in court. By 1983, the narcotics section had not only doubled in size; it had at least twenty teams engaged in undercover buy and bust operations.[51] Daley collaborated with the CPD to ensure that forfeiture money led to more successful arrests and prosecutions.

Daley sought to transform the courts, as well, seeing them as obstacles to more punitive treatment of drugs, gangs, and youth crime. He used his bully pulpit as a prosecutor to challenge County Court judges, who oversaw gang and drug cases. Many of these judges had remained skeptical of drug prosecutions and had pushed back against the District

Attorney's zeal. Daley went after them in the court of public opinion, relentlessly bashing them in the media for their recalcitrance in the War on Drugs. Professional norms, which expected judges to stay out of public political debates, made it difficult for the judges to fight back.[52] Daley relentlessly pilloried judges who sought to avoid sending people to prison for minor drug charges[53] and backed electoral challengers against sitting judges he thought were too protective of due process and the rights of defendants.[54]

Even more lasting was Daley's role as a lawmaker. Historians seldom focus on the role local officials play in shaping state government, but Daley demands attention for his assiduous cultivation of the state legislature and governors. As state's attorney, Daley's impact on the Illinois criminal code was remarkable. His office proposed and lobbied for a wide variety of changes to Illinois substantive and procedural law.[55] Legislators in Springfield complied by passing statutes making evidence gathering easier, creating new crimes, and treating juveniles like adults.[56] Just as important, Daley fought to restrict judges' authority by successfully lobbying the state legislature to pass laws that mandated harsher, mandatory sentences for drug felonies. Although he could not get the legislature to go as far as he wished, he was also the principal promoter of reducing the amount of cocaine necessary to qualify for a Class X felony charge to just fifteen grams, a law that confirmed the near-total punitive consensus on drugs by passing both houses unanimously.[57]

"The Selling of Narcotics Is a Curbside Operation"

Political observers correctly assumed that Daley planned to challenge incumbent Jane Byrne for mayor in 1983. But liberal Black Congressman Harold Washington undercut Daley's plans. With the white ethnic vote split, Washington's rainbow coalition—Black nationalists, liberals, and conservatives, a growing number of Latino voters, and white "lakefront liberals"—prevailed with a plurality in the Democratic primary. Although Washington came up through the machine before breaking with it in 1978, he had a long record of criticizing the CPD as a political institution that over-policed and under-protected Black Chicagoans.[58] In a speech to the Afro-American Patrolmen's League following his election, Washington called for "total police reform," including civilian control, as well as an end to police brutality and poor service. At the same time, he stressed Black officers' special obligation "to confront crime and violence" facing "our poorest and most defenseless citizens," particularly stressing the need to stop drug trafficking "by every legal means at our disposal," and "to disentangle young people from the violent gangs which blight too many of our neighborhoods."[59] Nonetheless, while he had supported certain actions to criminalize gang activity, Washington broadly stood against punitiveness as the answer. In 1978, he had argued that the creation of Class X felonies, "isn't going to do a damn thing" to reduce crime.[60] Five years later, he advanced a proceduralist vision of justice, proposing that police officers treating people with "respect and dignity," rather than the building of "a dozen new state prisons," would be the best way to address crime.[61]

Washington understood the strategic importance of policing in urban politics. During the election, even the conservative *Tribune* asked whether Washington's opponents were attempting to "whip up fears of a lawless rampage if Mr. Washington is elected?"[62] The newspaper highlighted the racism behind these fears: "That a black mayor could and would fight black crime as well as a white mayor is beyond their comprehension."[63] Despite the fact that Washington won the election as a Democrat, twenty-eight white and one Latino Democratic machine regulars took control of the Council and opposed his every move. Washington treaded carefully around policing. For example, he took a historic step in appointing Fred Rice as the CPD's first Black superintendent. But Rice was also a safe choice as the Department's highest-ranking and most experienced administrator. The city council's majority bloc challenged even mild reforms undertaken by the superintendent, including his prerogative to appoint his own command staff. Rice's effort to address disparities in patrol strength and 911 call response times between Black and white neighborhoods was also met with intransigence. Alderman Roman Pucinski demanded to know why the superintendent "want[ed] to strip of us the police details and beats simply because we do not record a large number of crimes."[64] In response, the city council's majority bloc sought to strip Rice's administrative power to assign police patrols to those areas most in need of protection.

Washington confronted the dilemma of austerity that bedeviled the first generation of Black mayors in the 1970s and 1980s: how could the city manage increased social needs in the face of declining revenue? Spending on the CPD accounted for nearly a quarter of the city budget. During lean budgetary years, previous mayors reduced the size of the uniformed ranks. Between 1976 and 1984, the number of police officers shrank from 13,510 to 11,952.[65] During his campaign, Washington had promised to raise staffing levels, but when faced with deficits in the 1984 and 1985 budgets, he followed his predecessors in proposing cuts.[66] Although the majority bloc on the city council had been quiescent in the face of attrition under previous mayors, its members now declared that Washington was "soft on crime." According to the *Tribune*'s editorial board, the bloc was implying "that every new rape and mugging in the city resulted from Mr. Washington's trims in the police force. Including the crimes that haven't occurred yet."[67]

The murder of Benji Wilson, the nation's top-rated high school basketball player, on November 20, 1984—the same day as the hearing on Washington's 1985 police budget—heightened the stakes of the debate. Wilson's killing was not gang motivated. Nonetheless, once the media made a connection between the shooter, sixteen-year-old Billy Moore, and the Black Gangster Disciples, a single crude narrative dominated the headlines: "gang violence" killed Ben Wilson. Gang-motivated homicides had been on the rise since 1976, as Figure 5.2 demonstrates. While turf rivalries between Latino gangs the Latin Kings and Two Sixes produced most of the killings in the late 1970s, between 1981 and 1984 conflict among Black gangs produced at least forty homicides each year. As the artist and activist Useni Perkins argued, framing Ben Wilson's death as a case of gang violence caused "the city government, the police and other public officials" to finally listen to the community leaders, clergy and social service representatives" whose "annual denunciation of black street-gang violence . . . routinely went unanswered."[68]

Washington demonstrated his preference for an all-of-the-above response to gang violence after Wilson's death. Nonetheless, the city council majority's resistance to social spending that would only benefit Blacks and Latinos limited his options. As his aide Mike Holewinski explained, there were two choices: to "deal with just the hard-core gang members or broaden the program so as to also deal with young people in general."[69] Anti-violence professionals favored micro-social interventions targeted at actual gang beefs rather than youth delinquency programs.[70]

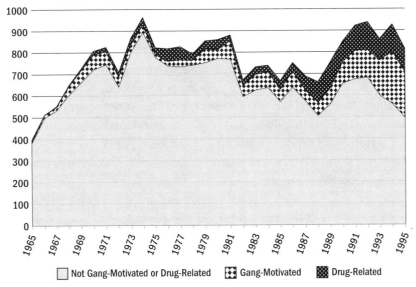

Figure 5.2. Homicides in Chicago, 1965–95. Source: Carolyn Rebecca Block and Richard L. Block, "Homicides in Chicago, 1965–1995," ICPSR 6399, July 6, 2005, https://doi.org/10.3886/ICPSR06399.v5.

Given the limited funds available, however, such a program could provide money only in Black and Latino wards, bypassing the constituents of the city council majority. Holewinski believed this would have been "a very difficult thing to sell to the Chicago City Council."[71] Unsurprisingly, the administration's program, called the Crisis Intervention Network, had goals that were far too diffuse for effective action: to "attack gang crime, prevent juvenile crime, treat delinquent behavior and nurture positive youth development." Irving Spergel, a leading scholar and practitioner of gang intervention, concluded that the program could not succeed in reducing gang violence because the majority of its time was not spent dealing "with conflict among gang members, threats by gangs, and pressure by gangs."[72]

The city council majority's willingness to fund more police, but not the targeted interruption of violence, brought Black demands for greater neighborhood safety into alignment with the ideology of punitive law and order. Even before Wilson's funeral, the Council flipped Washington's proposal to cut five hundred officers, raising the number of uniform personnel by that same number.[73] In contrast to the constant wrangling that rendered the violence-prevention program ineffective, changes in the police department were almost immediately felt on the ground. As the CPD hired new officers, it put more police in Black neighborhoods. Renewed attention was given to policing public spaces, such as housing, schools, trains, and streets. By the end of December 1984, the deputy chief of the Patrol Division had implemented periodic checks of Chicago Housing Authority buildings by uniform personnel from Public Housing, Gang Crimes, and district tactical units.[74] Increased attention brought increased arrests.

By the mid-1980s, media, politicians, and ordinary people frequently linked a variety of distinct but interrelated phenomena. As Spergel later noted, there was "tendency to mix gangs, violence, and drug trafficking into one large 'ball of wax.'"[75] Numerous Chicago gangs were selling drugs as early as the 1960s, according to gang scholar John Hagedorn. And for gangs such as El Rukns, the Latins Kings, and the Black Gangster Disciples, drug trafficking became increasingly common in the 1970s and early 1980s.[76] For example, working from a remarkable set of ledgers for a "Black Kings" (probably Gangster Disciples) set in the Robert Taylor Homes during the early 1980s, Sudhir Venkatesh and Steven Levitt found drug trafficking between 1982 and 1986 to be driven by independent entrepreneurs; regional and city leaders only loosely governed their endeavors.[77] As the cocaine trade grew, many Black males who could not secure blue-collar work found that selling drugs afforded them a form of masculine independence.[78] By 1985, Congresswoman Cardiss Collins asserted the widely held conclusion that the city had seen "a resurgence of street gang activity; and much to my alarm, we see more street gangs getting into the drug scene, not necessarily from the point of usage, but from the distribution and marketing end."[79] The specific dynamics at play were less important than the strong association between drugs and gangs that existed in the minds, not just of police and politicians, but also of residents in Black neighborhoods.[80]

News editors reinforced the police strategy. Repetitive ledes emphasized the same narrative over and over: "Indictments were announced today against twenty-five reputed members of two street gangs accused of selling heroin and cocaine to undercover investigators" and "Chicago police yesterday snapped the trap on ninety-four reputed street gang members from whom they allegedly bought drugs during the past year."[81] While Chicago newspapers had run such ledes in the past, they used them with much greater frequency after 1985. Though accurate, the ledes were also misleading. They overstated the degree to which visible drug markets were highly organized and gang-controlled, creating greater fear and reinforcing the choice of a punitive policing strategy. They also misrepresented the work that police were doing on the street by overemphasizing the extent to which police were engaged in sophisticated identification, targeting, and dismantling of high-level drug operations. By the 1980s, most drug policing targeted small-time retail-end sellers through buy-bust transactions, rather than taking down large-scale trafficking organizations.

Mayor Washington both touted and questioned police success in making arrests in retail drug markets. As he explained to NY Congressman Charles Rangel's Select Committee on Narcotics Abuse and Control, "the selling of narcotics is a curb service operation." He recognized that arrests were a futile approach to addressing the presence of public sales: "police make arrests all year long at these curb-service operations," he noted, "yet they continue to exist and to flourish." Moreover, the mayor concluded that such activity was actually a distraction from meeting the needs of "people in cities crying loudly for additional police protection, which is almost impossible to give them in light of the fact you need to use so many of them for drug prevention."[82] While the mayor pleaded with the federal government for more money for prevention and rehabilitation, the CPD turned its attention toward making drug-related arrests in Black neighborhoods, where drug markets were concentrated— not because of the residents' rates of drug use because of the spatially concentrated poverty.[83]

Such arrests satisfied bureaucratic demands at police headquarters because they could be instrumentalized numerically, allowing the police department to tout its progress without actually having to show changes in conditions on the street, as in the claim that "vice arrests for the quarter are up more than 10 percent due to increased emphasis on gang related narcotics operations."[84] Success in making more arrests itself justified further focus on policing drugs. As a result, police increasingly made drug arrests a central activity, as Figure 5.3 illustrates. In 1983, drug arrests were just 4 percent of all arrests; by 1985, 9 percent; by

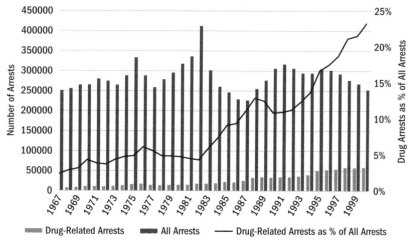

Figure 5.3. Changing Arrest Patterns in Chicago, 1967–2000. Source: Chicago Police Department, *Annual Reports*, 1967–2000, https://home.chicagopolice.org/statistics -data/statistical-reports/annual-reports.

1987, 13 percent. This ratio would continue to increase thereafter, reaching 23 percent in 1998. The unique nature of drug arrests in Chicago is highlighted by comparison with the rest of Illinois. Although there is scant evidence that people in the city used drugs at a higher rate than other Illinois residents, Chicagoans went from being 2.3 times more likely to be arrested for drug offenses in 1978 to 8.4 times more likely in 1990.

The CPD's intensive focus on retail-level drug arrests resulted in dramatic changes in the demographics of drug arrestees. Between 1985 and 1987, police arrested Black Chicagoans for drug-related crimes at a vastly higher rate—an increase of 40 percent. By contrast, police arrests of all other Chicagoans for drug-related crimes fell 11 percent. These changes were the beginning of a massive shift in the rate of drug arrests for Black Chicagoans as compared with the rate of drug arrests for all other Chicagoans. As Figure 5.4 shows, in 1985, the rate of drug-related arrests for Black Chicagoans was 3.18 times the rate for all other city residents; just two years later this ratio had risen to 4.9. This ratio would increase until it stabilized around seven to one in 1991. These growing disparities in arrest rates would be at the heart of the differential impact of mass incarceration and its attendant social consequences.

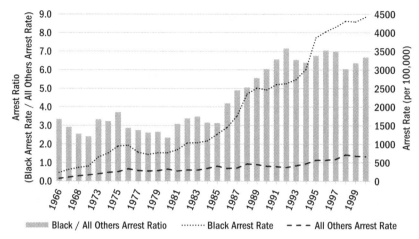

Figure 5.4. Drug Arrest Rates in Chicago, 1966–2000. Source: Chicago Police Department, *Annual Reports*, 1966–2000, https://home.chicagopolice.org/statistics-data/statistical-reports/annual-reports.

"The Toughest Gang in Town"

The arrival of crack cocaine in Chicago at the tail end of the 1980s exacerbated the punitive trends prevailing when Harold Washington died suddenly in November of 1987. The geography and structure of crack sales reinforced the conditions that led police to focus on drug arrests. Crack appeared in Chicago as early as 1986, an innovation in production, distribution, and marketing.[85] Cooking crack was much safer than freebasing cocaine, while delivering a similar high. Dealers could sell individual units, dramatically bringing down the cost and expanding the market. By reducing the amount for sale, crack also expanded turnover, leading to regular market activity. As street gangs like the Gangster Disciples entered the crack market, they had to significantly reconfigure their internal organization, a feat that not all gangs could accomplish.[86] Nonetheless, the popular understanding was, in social service provider Nancy Abate's words, that "[d]rugs are the lifeblood of gangs."[87] Open drug sales and gang control became particularly pervasive throughout Chicago Housing Authority developments.[88]

In 1988, new Police Superintendent LeRoy Martin launched the Street Narcotics Intervention Program. Martin, a straight-shooting, aggressive street cop, had been a surprise appointment. His term started off controversially: "When you talk about gangs," he noted in his first public press conference, "I've got the toughest gang in town: the Chicago Police Department."[89] He lacked Fred Rice's administrative experience but offered a more vigorous and demanding approach to street policing. His credo for fighting drug traffic was simple: "I've got to make arrest after arrest after arrest until I break the backs of the street peddlers."[90] Whereas CPD leaders had promised for years that they were targeting major dealers, Martin cut the bullshit. He admitted that his focus was on "'small-time' dealers in various Chicago communities where drug dealing is particularly rampant."[91] During Martin's first two years as superintendent, the CPD increased controlled substance arrests from 10,469 to 25,081—growth that outstripped any other period in its history. By the early 1990s, narcotics had become such a standard part of policing that that even when one supervising Gang Crimes officer put pressure on his officers not to make drug arrests, he found, "The tactical officers just can't avoid it."[92] Throughout the city, from 1987 to 1994, Black street gang members were arrested more frequently for drug offenses than for all other offenses combined.[93]

As the police and the state's attorney converged around a punitive consensus in the mid-1980s, they created more pressure on other institutions. When Daley entered the state's attorney's office in 1980, approximately 10 percent of drug cases led to convictions. By 1985, 30 percent of the nearly seven thousand drug cases he filed resulted in convictions. Despite the increase, the Tribune's editorial board decried this as proof that the courts were too easy on drug dealers. It demanded not fewer arrests, but for the courts to "develop ways to handle its huge volume of drug cases."[94] The logjam in the court docket remained unresolved until the Presiding Judge Thomas R. Fitzgerald reorganized the Criminal Division of the Cook County Courts around a two-shift system, with five dedicated nighttime narcotics courts added in October of 1989, and further expansion in 1991. While the courts did not process cases more efficiently, the increase in capacity meant that a much larger volume could be processed.[95]

Similarly, the punitive consensus put tremendous stress on the county jail, which was grossly overcrowded, so much so that the federal courts forced the sheriff to release prisoners on their own recognizance in order to meet population limits. The opening of a new five-hundred-bed division in 1985 only temporarily relieved the situation. By 1988, the average stay tripled to 140 days.[96] Reporters noted widespread agreement among legal professionals about the causes: "an increased number of arrests, particularly in drug cases; more felony charges, resulting in a backlog in the courts; and tougher mandatory sentences that make suspects more reluctant to plead guilty."[97] The response was not to reexamine these punitive policies, but to build more thousands of new beds in the early 1990s, culminating in the state-of-the-art 1,600-bed Division XI in 1995.[98]

This interlocking coordination between police, prosecutors, courts, and jails produced the devastating and disproportionate mass incarceration of Black Chicagoans for drug crimes. In 1983, Illinois prisons held 534 people for drug-related offenses, 3 percent of the total prison population; by 2000, 11,468, or 26 percent.[99] These statistics understate the punitive impact of the War on Drugs, because of the higher churn rate of prisoners sentenced in drug-related cases. For example, while people sentenced for drug offenses made up about 25 percent of prisoners by 1998, they were more than 40 percent of the twenty-five-thousand-plus new prison admissions.[100] Black people made up around 80 percent of people admitted to prison for drug crimes in Illinois during the 1990s, despite being less than 15 percent of the population.[101]

As much as militarized policing or dragnet arrests, this interlocking punitive orientation among institutions that produced racially disproportionate mass incarceration was the essence of how the War on Drugs became a mode of governance as it emerged in Chicago in the 1980s. This was true despite its failure to control gangs, drugs, or violence. Punitive action came to seem so indispensable to governing the city that regardless of whether it succeeded, politicians, police, prosecutors, and many ordinary Chicagoans continued to call for more punishment. This included Black public housing residents, a majority of whom continued to support the Chicago Housing Authority's Drug Elimination Program of comprehensive door-to-door anti-drug inspections, regardless of whether they felt safer after the CPD had previously completed sweeps of their complex.[102] More broadly, the thousands of arrests and prison terms did little to address the problems of gang-affiliated individuals dealing drugs in public spaces. By the end of the 1990s, after more than fifteen years of intense street anti-drug enforcement, police continued to estimate there were three hundred open-air drug markets, 60 to 70 percent of which involved street gangs.[103]

Most devastatingly, the crackdown on gangs and drugs did little to prevent the problem that had motivated it in the first place: the city's serious levels of lethal violence. Gang-motivated homicide, drug-related homicide, and the killing of youth (ages fifteen to nineteen) and young adults (ages twenty to twenty-four) skyrocketed beginning in 1988. Rather than addressing the problem of violence, the intensive policing of drugs provided incentives for greater vertical organization and stronger coordination, for spreading risk from more high-level managers to inexperienced youth, and for the use of increasingly high-caliber guns as a means to manage rivalries over money and turf.[104] Chicago's police and other local law enforcement institutions managed the inequality that emerged through the 1970s by excluding Black Chicagoans from the most basic of rights of liberty and safety under the guise of affording them protection.

Conclusion

While a more complete history would incorporate federal and state institutions into this story of the expansion and coordination of punitive capacity, this article's granular focus on local institutions and their relationships helps to reframe the conditions under which the full-blown War on Drugs emerged, with its racial disproportionality and its heavy reliance on prison. Mass incarceration was a product of the development and coordination of a range of punitive capacities by institutions at every jurisdictional level, including the local. Some of the changes in police behavior documented by other scholars, including militarization and the development of new techniques of dragnet policing, were essential to this process. But policing in the 1960s and 1970s in Chicago demonstrated that arrests alone did not produce high levels of felony incarceration in state prisons. Rather, harsh and racialized punishment occurred only when prosecutors, courts, and jails were able to hold, prosecute, and process large numbers of felony arrests. Because local government institutions in Chicago, as elsewhere, are loosely articulated—often coming under entirely separate municipal governments—efforts of drug warriors like Richard M. Daley to harmonize their activities were contested, cumbersome, and halting. Only by the end of the 1980s did they begin to incarcerate Black Chicagoans on a wide scale.

This process and its timing should give scholars some pause in considering the emerging consensus that seeks to push the history of mass incarceration back in time, linking its emergence to Great Society liberalism.[105] Inasmuch as the War on Drugs remains an important part of our understanding of mass incarceration, liberals' embrace of repression must be shown at work on the ground. In Chicago, such a case is difficult to make, as those most identified with civil rights liberalism in the local Democratic Party, such as Harold Washington, were among the staunchest opponents of punitive ideology. While historical continuities exist with the liberalism of the 1960s, the punitive and racialized War on Drugs of the 1980s occurred on highly distinctive historical terrain. The history recounted here shows the limited capabilities of the local state's law enforcement institutions during the 1960s and 1970s. Only during the 1980s—as the simultaneous crises of economic exclusion, increasingly limited federal social provision, and local white intransigence intersected with the rise of gang violence and public drug markets—did the conditions that supported the War on Drugs come together. In short, the vicious urban inequality of the 1980s, more than the liberalism of the 1960s, shaped the development of the War on Drugs and its role in mass incarceration.

NOTES

1 Patrick Hughes, et. al, "The Natural History of a Heroin Epidemic," *American Journal of Public Health* 62 (1972): 995–1001; Chicago Police Department, *Annual Report* (2000), Chicago Public Library, Municipal Reference Collection.

2 Kathleen J. Frydl, *The Drug Wars in America, 1940–1973* (New York: Cambridge University Press, 2013), 10.

3 James Forman Jr., *Locking Up Our Own: Crime and Punishment in Black America* (New York: Farrar, Straus and Giroux, 2017), 13.

4 Mona Lynch, "Mass Incarceration, Legal Change, and Locale: Understanding and Remediating American Penal Overindulgence," *Criminology & Public Policy* 10, no. 3 (August 2011): 676.

5 Elizabeth Hinton, *From the War on Poverty to the War on Drugs: The Making of Mass Incarceration in America* (Cambridge: Harvard University Press, 2016), 307–32.

6   Donna Murch, "Crack in Los Angeles: Crisis, Militarization, and Black Response to the Late Twentieth-Century War on Drugs," *Journal of American History* 102, no. 1 (June 2015), 162–73; Foreman, *Locking Up Our Own*; Max Felker-Kantor, *Policing Los Angeles: Race, Resistance, and the Rise of the LAPD* (Chapel Hill: University of North Carolina Press, 2018).

7   Loïc Wacquant, *Urban Outcasts: A Comparative Sociology of Advanced Marginality* (Cambridge: Polity Press, 2008), 94.

8   Lisa L. Miller, *The Myth of Mob Rule: Violent Crime and Democratic Politics* (New York: Oxford University Press, 2016).

9   Hughes, "The Natural History of a Heroin Epidemic"; James Doherty, "O'Connor Tells What He's Done to Police Force: Counts Up Progress and Is Still Ambitious," *Chicago Tribune*, February 12, 1951; "Court Opened to Try Drug Traffic Cases," *Chicago Tribune*, April 3, 1951.

10   David T. Courtwright, *Dark Paradise: A History of Opiate Addiction in America* (Cambridge: Harvard University Press, 2001), 2. During the 1950s and 1960s, less than 2 percent of the population had used any illicit drugs over their lifetimes. David F. Mhusto and Pamela Korsenmeyer, *The Quest for Drug Control: Politics and Federal Policy in a Period of Increasing Substance Abuse, 1963–1981* (New Haven: Yale University Press, 2002), 2–3.

11   Lois B. DeFluer, "Biasing Influences on Drug Arrest Records: Implications for Deviance Research," *American Sociological Review* 40 (1975): 99; Hughes, "The Natural History of a Heroin Epidemic," 996–97.

12   Simon Balto, *Occupied Territory: Policing Black Chicago from Red Summer to Black Power* (Chapel Hill: University of North Carolina Press, 2018), 137–44.

13   Quote in DeFluer, "Biasing Influences on Drug Arrest Records," 98; statistics, 98 (table 1), 100 (table 2).

14   William H. Haines and John J. McClaughlin, "Narcotics Addicts in Chicago," *American Journal of Psychiatry* 108, no. 10 (April 1952): 755.

15   Hans Mattick, "Comparison of Sentenced Prisoners by Offense Category and Length of Sentence for March 31, 1956 and March 31, 1958" (n.d.), 7, Box 159, Folder 2, Hans Mattick Papers, Chicago History Museum.

16   Testimony of Paul Hemphill, US Congress, House, Subcommittee on Alcoholism and Narcotics of the Committee on Labor and Public Welfare, *Narcotics and Alcoholism, 1971: Part 2*, Ninety-second Congress, first session, May 17 and June 25, 1971, 678.

17   Illinois Legislative Investigating Committee [ILEC], *The Drug Crisis: Report on Drug Abuse in Illinois* (Springfield, Ill.: ILEC, 1971), 222, 217.

18   See, e.g., "Program for Action: Report and Recommendations of the Commission on Administration of Criminal Justice in Cook County" (Chicago: Chicago Bar Association, June 1975), 131–33; "Draft: Evaluation of Treatment Alternatives to Street Crime (TASC) Phase 2" (Bethesda, MD: System Sciences, Inc., February 16, 1978).

19   Testimony of James Rochford, US Congress, House Select Committee on Narcotics Abuse and Control, *Investigation of Narcotics Trafficking Proceeds (Chicago,*

Illinois), Ninety-fifth Congress, first session, September 30 and October 1, 1977, 36–37.

20 Testimony of Michael Spiotto, US Congress, House Select Committee, *Investigation of Narcotics Trafficking Proceeds*, 38.

21 New heroin users and heroin-related hospital admissions declined dramatically between 1976 and 1980. National Institute on Drug Abuse, Division of Epidemiology and Statistical Analysis, *Epidemiology of Heroin: 1964–1984* (Rockville, MD: National Institute on Drug Abuse, 1985), 41 (table 14B); 54 (table 2).

22 Arnold R. Hirsch, *Making the Second Ghetto: Race and Housing in Chicago, 1940–1960* (Chicago: University of Chicago Press, 1998).

23 Field Operations Division International Association of Chiefs of Police, "A Survey of the Police Department: Chicago, Illinois" (June 1970), 442, Chicago Public Library, Municipal Reference Collection. For a personal view, see "Oral History with Commander Hubert Holton (Retired)," in *The Thin Black Line: True Stories by Black Law Enforcement Officers Policing America's Meanest Streets*, ed. Hugh Holton (New York: Tom Doherty Associates, 2008), 185.

24 DeFluer, "Biasing Influences on Drug Arrest Records," 92–97, figs. 1–6.

25 Illinois Legislative Investigating Committee, *The Drug Crisis*, 225.

26 James E. Spiotto, "Search and Seizure: An Empirical Study of the Exclusionary Rule and Its Alternatives," *Journal of Legal Studies* 2, no. 1 (January 1973): 243–78.

27 This evidence comes from the 1980s, but the rationales fit the patterns of policing in the 1970s. See Myron W. Orfield Jr., "The Exclusionary Rule and Deterrence: An Empirical Study of Chicago Narcotics Officers," *University of Chicago Law Review* 54, no. 3 (Summer 1987): 1056–65, quote from 1059.

28 Mike Royko, "Can't Carey It Off," reprinted in *Chicago Tribune*, November 2, 1980, N8.

29 Pamela L. Griset, "The Evolution of the Determinate Ideal of Sentencing," *Law & Policy* 19 (1997): 271.

30 Francis T. Cullen, Karen E. Gilbert, and John B. Cullen, "Implementing Determinate Sentencing in Illinois: Conscience and Convenience," *Criminal Justice Review* 8 (1983): 1–15.

31 Robert Benjamin, "Daley and Burke in a Slugfest," *Chicago Tribune*, March 9, 1980; "The Race for State's Attorney," *Chicago Tribune*, March 7, 1980.

32 Joseph Sjostrom, "Carey Ignores Blacks, Daley Says," *Chicago Tribune*, October 16, 1980.

33 Renault Robinson, "Resentment of Law Experience Rooted," *Chicago Defender*, May 22, 1971.

34 Vernon Jarrett, "The Prosecution Rests Its Case," *Chicago Tribune*, October 29, 1980.

35 Paul M. Green, "Daley's Victory—A Prelude to the Big Brawl," *Illinois Issues*, January 1981, 4–8.

36 Joel Rast, *Remaking Chicago: The Political Origins of Urban Industrial Change* (Dekalb, Ill.: Northern Illinois University Press, 1999), 88 (table 8); Gregory

D. Squires, Larry Bennett, and Kathleen McCourt, *Chicago: Race, Class, and the Response to Urban Decline* (Philadelphia: Temple University Press, 1987), 29–37.

37 William Julius Wilson, *The Truly Disadvantaged: The Inner City, the Underclass, and Public Policy* (Chicago: University of Chicago Press, 1987), 49–56. On cross-class racial segregation, see Douglass S. Massey and Nancy A. Denton, *American Apartheid: Segregation and the Making of the Underclass* (Cambridge: Harvard University Press, 1993), 85–87.

38 D. Bradford Hunt, *Blueprint for Disaster: The Unraveling of Chicago Public Housing* (Chicago: University of Chicago Press, 2009).

39 William Julius Wilson, *The Truly Disadvantaged*.

40 Ben Austin, *High-Risers: Cabrini–Green and the Fate of American Public Housing* (New York: Harper, 2018), 98–108.

41 Maurice Possley, "Gang Crackdowns Have Been Tried—and Found Wanting," *Chicago Tribune*, November 30, 1984.

42 Maurice Possley, "800,000 Arrests Voided: Primarily Minorities Involved," *Chicago Tribune*, March 31, 1984.

43 Testimony of Richard M. Daley, US Congress, House Select Committee on Narcotics Abuse and Control, *Abuse of Dangerous Licit and Illicit Drugs: Psychotropics, Phencyclidine, and Talwin*, Ninety-fifth Congress, second session, August 8 and 10, September 19, and October 6, 1978, 343.

44 Bonita Brodt, "Daley: He's Got a Little List," *Chicago Tribune*, October 28, 1982.

45 Rick Pearson and John Byrne, "The Mayor: The Impact of Richard M. Daley," *Chicago Tribune*, May 1, 2011.

46 Bonita Brodt, "Daley Forms New Drug Unit," *Chicago Tribune*, January 29, 1981; Bonita Brodt, "Daley Forms Team to Fight Gang Crime," *Chicago Tribune*, February 25, 1981.

47 Brian Kelly, "One Man's War: A Hardnosed Prosecutor's Tireless Battle Against Drug Traffic," *Chicago Tribune*, March 24, 1985, H33, H34.

48 Orfield, "The Exclusionary Rule and Deterrence," 1027.

49 James L. O'Neill, "Asset Forfeiture," in *International Drug Trafficking*, ed. Dennis Rowe (Chicago: Office of International Criminal Justice, University of Illinois at Chicago, 1988), 115–34.

50 Prepared statement of Frank Deboni and Kenneth Wadas, US Congress, House Select Committee on Narcotics Abuse and Control, *Drug Abuse and Drug Trafficking in Chicago*, Ninety-ninth Congress, first session, September 30 and October 1, 1985, 147.

51 Lynn Emmerman, "The Most Dangerous Game: Drugs," *Chicago Tribune*, January 9, 1983, 13.

52 E.g., Charles Mount, "Daley Hits Judge, Asks Sentence in Drug Case," *Chicago Tribune*, February 2, 1982.

53 *People ne*
rel. Daley v. Suria, 112 Ill. 2d 26 (Ill. 1986).

54 David Jackson, "The Law and Richard M. Daley," *Chicago*, September 1988, https://www.chicagomag.com/; Mark Eissman and Joseph R. Tybor, "Few Convicted of Drug Crimes Here," *Chicago Tribune*, December 22, 1985.

55 David Jackson, "The Law and Richard M. Daley."

56 Bonita Brodt, "Daley Urges Eased Eavesdropping Law," *Chicago Tribune*, April 15, 1981; Lee Strobel, "Daley Urges US to Help Crack Down on Guns," *Chicago Tribune*, May 17, 1981; Statement of Richard M. Daley, US Department of Justice, Attorney General's Task Force on Violent Crime, *Hearing*, June 18, 1981, 207; Lee Strobel, "Lenient Drug Rulings Criticized but Upheld," *Chicago Tribune*, October 1, 1981; Jane Fritsch, "Daley 'Shocked' as Judge Bars Adult Trial for Teen," *Chicago Tribune*, July 31, 1981; Daniel Engler, "Prosecutors Armed for Antidrug Fight," *Chicago Tribune*, September 25, 1986; David Axelrod, "Federal Agents Hunt Weapons at Cabrini," *Chicago Tribune*, March 23, 1981; Joseph R. Tybor, "Lawyer Group OKs Pre-Trial Detention," *Chicago Tribune*, July 11, 1985.

57 Tim Franklin, "Tough Anti-Drug Measure Clears General Assembly," *Chicago Tribune*, December 6, 1986.

58 Peter C. Pihos, "Policing, Race, and Politics in Chicago" (PhD Dissertation, Philadelphia, University of Pennsylvania, 2015), 302–7.

59 Mayor Harold Washington, "Speech Before Afro-American Police League" (August 19, 1983), Box 96, Folder 2, Harold Washington Archives and Collections, Mayoral Records, Press Office Records.

60 "Class X Passes as Part of Sentence Reform Law," *Illinois Issues*, January 1978, 27, http://www.lib.niu.edu.

61 Washington, "Speech Before Afro-American Police League."

62 "*Editorial*: Disgraceful, Mr. Brzeczek," *Chicago Tribune*, February 27, 1983, A6.

63 "The Constituency of Fear," *Chicago Tribune*, March 27, 1983, A6.

64 James Strong and Manuel Galvan, "Rice Accused of Concealing Cutback Plan," *Chicago Tribune*, November 20, 1984, A1; Phillip Wattley, "Rice Slams Aldermen on Cop Plan," *Chicago Tribune*, December 9, 1984, C11.

65 Jim Merrine, M. W. Newman, Susy Schultz, Lynn Sweet, and Lillian Williams, "'Hands Off' on Public Safety: Mayor Puts Confidence in Police, Fire Chiefs," *Chicago Sun-Times*, September 21, 1986, 6. Chicago's cuts were about average. Aaron Chalfin and Justin McCrary, "Are Cities Underpoliced?" *Review of Economics and Statistics* 100, no. 1 (March 2019): 167–86.

66 Monroe Anderson, "855 in Police Dept. Face Layoff, City Says," *Chicago Tribune*, August 13, 1983, 1; Strong and Galvan, "Rice Accused of Concealing Cutback Plan."

67 "Editorial: Budget Double Talk," *Chicago Tribune*, November 21, 1984, 12.

68 Useni Eugene Perkins, *Explosion of Chicago's Black Street Gangs: 1900 to the Present* (Chicago: Third World Press, 1987), 15.

69 Statement of Mike Holewinski, in *Gangs, Juvenile Court, and the Community: What Can Be Done*, 1985, 21.

70 Illinois Department of Children and Family Services, "Report on the Illinois Symposium on Gangs," February 28 to March 1, 1985, 17, Box 9, Folder 1, Harold Washington Archives and Collections, Mayoral Records, Public Safety Subcabinet Records.

71 Holewinski, *Gangs, Juvenile Court, and the Community*, 21.

72 Irving Spergel to Ben Kendrick, August 8, 1986, Box 8, Folder 5, Harold Washington Archives and Collections, Mayoral Records, Public Safety Subcabinet Records.

73 Thom Shanker and Jean Davidson, "Washington's Gang Strategy Still in Pieces," *Chicago Tribune*, December 2, 1984, C1; Thom Shanker, "Mayor Rewrites Budget to Fund War on Gangs," *Chicago Tribune*, December 4, 1984, 1.

74 Chicago Police Department, Patrol Division: Special Order 84–15, Dec. 28, 1984.

75 Irving Spergel, *The Youth Gang Problem: A Community Approach* (New York: Oxford University Press, 1995), 43.

76 John H. Hagedorn, *The Insane Chicago Way: The Daring Plan by Chicago Gangs to Create a Spanish Mafia* (Chicago: University of Chicago Press, 2015), chap. 3.

77 Sudhir Alladi Venkatesh and Steven D. Levitt, "'Are We a Family or a Business?' History and Disjuncture in the American Street Gang," *Theory and Society* 29, no. 4 (August 2000): 443. Cf. Malcolm W. Klein, Cheryl L. Maxson, and Lea C. Cunningham, "'Crack,' Street Gangs, and Violence," *Criminology* 29 (1991): 623–50.

78 W. Wayne Wiebel, "Substance Abuse Trend Update for Chicago and Illinois," in *Patterns and Trends in Drug Abuse: A National and International Perspective, Community Epidemiology Work Group Proceedings*, vol. 2 (Rockville, MD: National Institute on Drug Abuse, 1985), 23; Will Cooley, "The Work: Dealing and Violence in the War on Drugs Era," *Labor: Studies in Working-Class History* 15, no. 2 (2018).

79 Testimony of Representative Cardiss Collins, US Congress, House Select Committee, *Drug Abuse and Drug Trafficking in Chicago*, 114–15.

80 Perkins, *Explosion of Chicago's Black Street Gangs*, 61–67. Calls to the anonymous tip-line of the Chicago Crime Commission revealed similar conclusions. Testimony of Patrick Healy, US Congress, House Select Committee, *Drug Abuse and Drug Trafficking in Chicago*, 32–33.

81 Rosalind Rossi and Jim Casey, "Drug Indictments Hit 25," *Chicago Sun-Times*, January 22, 1986.

82 Testimony of Mayor Harold Washington, US Congress, House Select Committee, *Drug Abuse and Drug Trafficking in Chicago*, 6, 8.

83 Leonard Saxe, Charles Kadushin, Andrew Beveridge, David Livert, Elizabeth Tighe, David Rindskopf, Julie Ford, and Archie Brodsky, "The Visibility of Illicit Drugs: Implications for Community Based Drug Control Strategies," *American Journal of Public Health* 91 (2001): 1992. See also Michael H. Tonry, *Punishing Race: A Continuing American Dilemma* (New York: Oxford University Press, 2011), chap. 3.

84 Sharon Gist Gilliam, Budget Director, to Michael Holewinski, March 9, 1987, Attachment: Fourth Quarter Variance Report (1986), 2, Box 14, Folder 15,

Harold Washington Archives and Collections, Mayoral Records, Public Safety Subcabinet.

85 Steven K. Johnson, "'Crack' Puts New Pop in Cocaine Market," *Chicago Tribune*, May 21, 1986, 1. See also David Farber, *Crack: Rock Cocaine, Street Capitalism, and the Decade of Greed* (New York: Cambridge University Press, 2019), 60–65.

86 Venkatesh and Levitt, "'Are We a Family or a Business?'" 443.

87 Testimony of Nancy Abate, US Congress, Senate, Subcommittee on the Constitution of the Committee on the Judiciary, *Drugs and Crack in Illinois*, One-hundred-and-first Congress, second session, April 11, 1990, 73.

88 Sudhir Allahdi Venkatesh, *American Project: The Rise and Fall of a Modern Ghetto* (Cambridge: Harvard University Press, 2000), chaps. 3–5; Austin, *High-Risers*, chaps. 7–13. See also Alex Kotlowitz, *There Are No Children Here: The Story of Two Boys Growing Up in the Other America* (New York: Anchor Books, 1991).

89 Jim Casey, "Martin: Cops Are 'Toughest Gang,'" *Chicago Sun-Times*, November 3, 1987; Wes Smith, "Top Cop Martin Shows He's Always on Patrol," *Chicago Tribune*, November 13, 1987.

90 Art Petacque, "Martin Explains Drug War," *Chicago Sun-Times*, March 9, 1988.

91 State of Illinois, "Statewide Drug and Violent Crime Strategy" (Chicago: Illinois Criminal Justice Information Authority, 1989), 16–17.

92 Jim Weston, "The Chicago Police Department's Response to Gangs and Drugs," in *Final Report: Response to Drugs and Gangs: Studies of Police Decisionmaking*, ed. Deborah Lamm Weisel and John E. Eck (Police Executive Research Forum, 1992), 57–58.

93 C. R. Block, A. Christakos, A. Jacob, R. Przybylski, "Street Gangs and Crime: Patterns and Trends in Chicago," *Research Bulletin* (Illinois Criminal Justice Information Authority, September 1996), 14, fig. 9.

94 "Editorial: Drug Dealer's Paradise," *Chicago Tribune*, December 27, 1985.

95 Farber, *Crack*, 155–60.

96 Alf Siewers, "Chicago's Full Jail Shows Court Reform Needed," *Christian Science Monitor*, September 20, 1988.

97 Matt O'Connor, "Many Can Be Blamed for Jail Crisis," *Chicago Tribune*, September 18, 1988.

98 Melanie Newport, "Jail America: The Reformist Origins of the Carceral State" (PhD diss., Temple University, 2016), chap. 7.

99 Paul Street, "The Vicious Circle: Race, Prison, Jobs, and Community in Chicago, Illinois and the Nation" (Chicago: Urban League, 2002), 13.

100 Nancy G. La Vigne and Cynthia A. Mamlian, "A Portrait of Prisoner Reentry in Illinois," Research Report (Urban Institute Justice Policy Center, 2003), 11, figs. 3–4, www.urban.org.

101 Arthur J. Lurigio and Pamela Loose, "The Disproportionate Incarceration of African Americans for Drug Offenses: The National and Illinois Perspective," *Journal of Ethnicity in Criminal Justice* 6, no. 3 (2008): 228.

102 Susan J. Popkin, Lynn M. Olson, Arthur J. Lurigio, Victoria E. Gwiasda, and Ruth
G. Carter, "Sweeping Out Drugs and Crime: Residents View of the Chicago Housing Authority's Public Housing Drug Elimination Program," *Crime & Delinquency*
41, no. 1 (January 1995): 86–87.
103 Weston, "The Chicago Police Department's Response to Gangs and Drugs," 62.
104 Carolyn R. Block and Antigone Christakos, "Chicago Homicide from the Sixties
to the Nineties: Major Trends in Lethal Violence," in *Trends, Risks, and Interventions in Lethal Violence: Proceedings of the Third Annual Spring Symposium of the
Homicide Research Working Group*, ed. Carolyn R. Block and Richard Block, 1995,
17–50.
105 On this point, see Donna Murch, "The Color of War: Race, Neoliberalism, and
Punishment in Late Twentieth Century Los Angeles," in *Neoliberal Cities: The
Remaking of Postwar America*, ed. Andrew J. Diamond and Thomas J. Sugrue
(New York: NYU Press, 2020), 129–30.

6

Cannabis Culture Wars

EMILY DUFTON

Over the course of two decades, in the 1970s and 1980s, a new outgrowth of the "cannabis culture wars" was waged in the United States. These were battles over the role and accessibility of marijuana in America, fought not by state actors but by common citizens—concerned parents, magazine writers, and lawyers—who used elements of public discourse, like publications, conferences and lobbying groups, to convince lawmakers and voters of the safety, or danger, of cannabis use. Focusing explicitly on the threat increased access to cannabis posed to adolescents, the cannabis culture wars of late twentieth century brought debates over marijuana's safety and hazards back to the public stage for the first time since the "Reefer Madness" era of the 1930s. As the two sides wavered between earnest activism and mockery, the movement toward legalization we see today was paved by these important discussions, which ultimately framed legalization as a protective measure for the public health and safety of some of the country's most innocent and dispossessed populations.

In the United States in the 1970s and 1980s, a cannabis culture war erupted between two ideologically opposed groups: pro-cannabis advocates who wanted to increase access to marijuana, and anti-drug parent activists who wanted to ensure that their children would grow up drug-free. Given the nature of their battles, which more often took place on the pages of magazines than in the halls of Congress, the cannabis culture wars of the late twentieth century were unique in terms of America's larger War on Drugs. Drug war scholars often rightly focus on the powerful roles that law enforcement and political officials play in drug users' lives. Politicians, police officers, customs and border patrol agents, judges, and lawyers determine the social structures that directly affect drug users, and their decisions can either deprive users of their freedom or, conversely, allow their use to be legalized.

159

The cannabis culture wars that began in the 1970s were radically different, however. They weren't fought between lawmakers and lawbreakers; instead, they were waged by citizen activists across the country who had no capacity to arrest, incarcerate, or punish each other. Their skirmishes weren't waged on city streets or in prisons or courtrooms. Instead, they were waged on the battlefields activists had available to them: in the media, in social organizing, and in lobbying. Most importantly, the cultural battles over cannabis weren't fought exclusively over laws and policies that the belligerents could actively control. Instead, they were fought over how drug use—and specifically marijuana use— was understood and the role its users played in the public imagination. By seeking to control the public discourse surrounding marijuana, each group hoped it could ultimately influence either increased or decreased legal access to the drug. Controlling cannabis culture could control the cannabis war.

To accomplish these aims, activists argued for two decades over how drug users appeared in the media, how the "drug culture" surrounding cannabis was marketed, and who had the "right" to partake in, or be protected from, marijuana use. These battles, waged as marijuana became one of the most prominent drugs in American life, mirrored the larger culture wars of the era that pitted liberal activists against conservative "pro-family" organizations. But this war focused solely on one topic: the meaning of cannabis and the culture it created in an America that was renegotiating the impact of drug use nationwide.

Like the culture wars that were waged over marijuana decades earlier, during the "Reefer Madness" era of the 1930s, the battles of the 1970s and 1980s focused on the dangers the drug posed to children. But what made the cannabis culture wars of the late twentieth century different was that this argument—that drug laws needed to protect children's safety—would ultimately be coopted by legalization advocates as one of the most powerful arguments *for*, not against, legalization. In an unprecedented turn of events, the main argument of anti-marijuana advocates for nearly a hundred years—that children needed to be shielded from marijuana's effects—was convincingly used in the twenty-first century not to continue to criminalize cannabis, but to inspire some of the most liberal changes in drug laws in America's

history, an outcome that continues to resonate today, and which opponents of marijuana surely did not expect.

* * *

Children have been at the heart of debates over marijuana since the drug
was introduced to the US. In the late 1800s, cannabis was widely available as a medicine, purchased freely from any pharmacist or storekeeper
without prescription. Found mostly in tincture form in products like
Eli Lilly's Dr. Brown's Sedative Tablets and the One Day Cough Cure,
cannabis was not as popular as opiate-containing medicines (including
those specifically marketed to children, like Mrs. Winslow's Soothing
Syrup), but was nonetheless used to treat children's maladies. Some cannabis medicines even specifically appealed to children: cannabis-based
painkillers were coated with sugar to sweeten the taste and to prevent
pills from sticking together.[1]

When recreational marijuana smoking arrived in the US at the turn
of the century, however, debates shifted from the benefits the drug could
provide for children's health to the threat the drug posed to their safety.
Harry Anslinger, director of the Federal Bureau of Narcotics from 1930
to 1962, was marijuana's most forceful opponent. He launched a culture
war against the drug, writing articles like 1937's "Assassin of Youth" that
specifically detailed the dangers marijuana posed to children, which,
in Anslinger's view, were twofold. First, a marijuana user could harm
a child, like the West Virginia man Anslinger noted in his article who
raped a nine-year-old girl. More dangerously, however, marijuana could
also turn otherwise peaceful children into violent criminals. Anslinger
famously detailed the grisly acts committed by cannabis users, including the stories of a Florida youth who murdered his family with an ax
and an Ohio juvenile gang that committed thirty-eight armed robberies. Anslinger's view of marijuana as a menace to children and parents
everywhere was at the heart of his powerful culture war against pot
throughout the three decades he led the FBN. This view would hold
sway until the mid-1960s, when a new vision of marijuana emerged.[2]

As marijuana use spread nationwide in the 1960s alongside the
growing counterculture, fears about the drug's effects shifted. Sociologist Jerome Himmelstein detailed the transition marijuana underwent

from a drug purported to cause dangerous violence in the 1930s to a substance that caused users to retreat from public life in the 1960s:

> The *social* characteristics of the Counterculture, as perceived by the dominant society, were projected onto marihuana and then said to be the *psychological* effects inherent in the drug; because the Counterculture was characterized as passive and escapist, marihuana became seen as a producer of passivity and escape on the individual level.[3]

Now the danger of cannabis use was not that it turned children into ax murderers, as Anslinger had warned, but rather than it turned them into youthful rebels who dropped out of organized social life and sought to escape from reality.

But increased cannabis use by middle-class youth also transformed the characterization of the user. By the late 1960s and early 1970s, marijuana users were no longer potential ax murderers; they were "someone's children," and as arrest rates for marijuana possession rose—clocking in at about four hundred thousand a year throughout the 1970s—activists sought to challenge drug laws to reflect the drug's growing "embourgeoisement."[4] A wave of decriminalization laws were passed in a dozen states between 1973 and 1978 to reflect America's growing social comfort with cannabis use, and these laws transformed both marijuana's cultural locus as well as the nation's drug economy.

State-based decriminalization laws were first inspired by the final report from the National Commission on Marijuana and Drug Abuse, issued in 1972, which, after two years spent researching the breadth and scope of marijuana use in the US, argued that the drug was less harmful than legal intoxicants like alcohol and tobacco and that its use and possession should be decriminalized nationwide. The report was delivered to President Richard Nixon but found no traction in the federal government, which continued to consider cannabis a Schedule I drug. In the years following the report's release, however, states from Alaska to Oregon to Minnesota to North Carolina decriminalized marijuana possession between 1973 and 1978, ultimately allowing a third of the country's population to live in areas where possession of up to an ounce of marijuana was punishable by no more than a civil fine.[5]

In response to the widespread passage of decriminalization laws, a vibrant new cannabis economy flourished, not only in terms of sales of the drug itself (which generated $4 billion annually), but also in terms of goods that assisted in the enjoyment of the "marijuana lifestyle." In the summer of 1974, Tom Forçade, an entrepreneurial writer and dope smuggler, launched the first edition of *High Times* magazine, an ode to cannabis that mocked "straight America's uptight views of the drug. The magazine featured articles about everything from drug trafficking to politics and pop culture, alongside (in a nod to *Playboy*) centerfolds of lush marijuana. For Forçade, the purpose of *High Times* was twofold: to have fun at the expense of the rich, and to subvert President Richard Nixon's so-called War on Drugs. The magazine's first run of twenty-five thousand copies sold out within a week, and subsequent printings sold out quickly as well. According to Michael Kennedy, who served as its lawyer for forty-two years, the magazine's irreverence and open enjoyment of drug use tapped a vein in the American public. It was a "political farce that quickly became a political force."[6]

Like all magazines, *High Times* subsidized its publication with ad sales. But the ads in *High Times* were as remarkable as the rest of the magazine's content. Pipes, bongs, scales, rolling papers, "stash cans," toys, and games were all for sale in the pages of *High Times*, as well as at a growing number of convenience stores and "head shops" nationwide. Paraphernalia—legal goods used to consume and enjoy a still-illegal substance—was quickly becoming very big business. By 1977, paraphernalia sales grossed $250 million, more than the annual revenue generated by the original *Star Wars* film, released that year.[7]

High Times also became the mouthpiece for a new organization: NORML, the National Organization for the Reform of Marijuana Laws, a lobbying firm founded by lawyer Keith Stroup in Washington, DC in 1970. The nation's first marijuana-rights lobbying group, NORML took a consumer rights approach to challenging marijuana laws, arguing that responsible cannabis users were customers, not criminals, who deserved protection and not punishment for a drug they used in the privacy of their own homes. Almost immediately after it began a regular publication schedule, *High Times* became NORML's most visible supporter, running Keith Stroup's monthly column alongside fundraising ads, which were published at no charge to the organization. As outsiders to polite society, *High Times* and the lobbying organization were a team. Both were dedicated to increasing the acceptability, and economic potential, of decriminalized cannabis, and each promoted the other's work. As Keith Stroup put it in his 2013 memoir, "It's fair to say that during the 1970s, most people who knew about NORML had read about our work . . . in *High Times*."[8]

By the mid-1970s, in the wake of the National Commission's report, the passage of decriminalization laws, and the growing popularity of pot-related media and paraphernalia, national attitudes toward cannabis had shifted markedly from the era of Harry Anslinger and "Assassin of Youth." Marijuana was by far the most widely used illicit drug in America, and its use seemed both cool and relatively benign. Cannabis's association with youth movements, including the counterculture and anti-war activism of the late 1960s, gave the drug a young, hip feeling, while the parallel epidemic of heroin use and overdose deaths, which peaked in 1971, painted opioids, rather than marijuana, as the drug menace of the era. Cannabis was also celebrated widely. In music, movies like Cheech and Chong's 1978 comedy *Up In Smoke*, and magazines, including countless spin-offs of *High Times*, the drug was represented as fun, funny, and, most importantly, safe—especially for users who saw its use as a way to defy conventional social standards. Ozzy Osbourne of Black Sabbath summed up the feeling in 1971, in the song "Sweet Leaf," when he sang, "Straight people don't know what you're about / They put you down and shut you out / You gave me a new belief / And soon the world will love you, sweet leaf."[9]

There was one unanticipated effect of the era's embrace of cannabis, however: with decriminalization and paraphernalia spreading nationwide, rates of adolescent marijuana use began to substantially increase. Decriminalization is different from legalization in that legalization imposes a set of public health regulations on the market, such as age restrictions on sales, that decriminalization does not. When a third of the country lived in states where possession of up to an ounce of marijuana was decriminalized, reports showed it had negative effects for kids. By 1976, 56 percent of the nation's high schoolers reported that they had tried marijuana, with 26 percent reporting they smoked weekly and 6 percent reporting they smoked every day. Eighty percent of high schoolers and 60 percent of junior high schoolers reported that the drug was easy to get.[10] And, as more adolescents smoked pot, sales of paraphernalia to minors were rising, In 1978, the *New York Times* reported that "like babes in Toyland, three boys from eleven to fourteen and a thirteen-year-old girl went on a buying spree recently in 'head shops' around the metropolitan area. They came back with $300 worth of drug-culture paraphernalia that included . . . a baby bottle fitted with both a nipple and a hashish pipe and a felt-tipped pen that allows a surreptitious snort of cocaine in the classroom."[11]

Children's use of marijuana and their ease in accessing cannabis and drug paraphernalia, alongside increasing political comfort with decriminalization nationwide, prompted a new army of anti-marijuana activists—the parent movement—to form in the summer of 1976. Forty years after the era of Reefer Madness, these parents would be the strongest opponents to marijuana since Harry Anslinger, and their tactics would be similar to the leader of the FBN. In magazines, newsletters and speeches, they would highlight the dangerous effects that marijuana specifically posed to children, and argue that adolescent safety had to be at the center of the nation's drug laws. Though they lacked the political power of Anslinger, who headed a federal agency for over three decades, they nonetheless went on to influence state and federal laws over the next decade, a powerful outcome for a movement that started during a backyard birthday party.

In the summer of 1976, in Atlanta, Georgia, America's growing problems with cannabis literally followed a mother named Marsha "Keith" Manatt Schuchard home. In August of that year, after what seemed like a harmless party, Schuchard, first realized that her 13-year-old daughter Ashley and her friends were smoking pot. That night, after the other children returned home, Schuchard described what she and her husband found scattered on the family lawn: "marijuana butts, small plastic bags with dope remnants, homemade roach clips, cans of malt liquor, and pop wine bottles." She and her husband were shocked. Schuchard had tried marijuana once in the past, but it was when she was in grad school and a legal adult. She was frightened by the children's behavior, and she felt she suddenly understood her daughter's recent transformation from a "formerly model child, cheerful, thoughtful, and responsible" into someone "either irritable and restless or lethargic and withdrawn."[12]

After discovering her daughter's drug use, Schuchard, a talented researcher with a PhD in British literature from the University of Texas,

Austin, looked at all the information available about marijuana's effects on kids. What she found terrified her. Federal reports warned that cannabis was particularly harmful to adolescent bodies; it could make young boys grow breasts and render young girls infertile, permanently damaging chromosomes so that generations of Americans could be harmed by the drug. A report from the American Medical Association argued that "the group most vulnerable to the hazardous effects of marijuana are children and adolescents," noting that "marijuana is potentially damaging to health in a variety of ways, but it can be especially harmful when used by a person who is immature, unstable or already ill." She also found that cannabis damaged children's developing personalities, noting reports that argued that "heavy marijuana users" exhibited "amotivational syndrome," where "the user becomes apathetic, lethargic, passive, and withdrawn." Smokers suffering from amotivational syndrome were less likely to focus on immediate priorities like schoolwork or sports, and they also neglected to develop the resilience necessary to move from adolescence into adulthood, which could have even more damaging long-term effects. "Youngsters who do not experience and grow out of adolescence because of regular drug use," Schuchard later warned, "stand a good chance of becoming chemically dependent adults."[13]

Given the physical and psychological dangers cannabis posed to kids, Schuchard was distressed by America's embrace of the drug. Schuchard wrote a guidebook, *Parents, Peers and Pot*, released by the National Institute on Drug Abuse in 1979, which laid out the dangers of marijuana and how to form an anti-drug parent group. In the book, she decried the "drug culture," whose rituals, accessories, and effects formed what she called an "alien world"—a highly organized subculture that revolved around marijuana and which seemed bent on tearing children away from their families before they were ready for the change. "In many ways," Schuchard wrote, "the most disturbing aspect of the young people's drug culture was its apparent distance and independence from home. The rituals of drug supply and use had gradually become a lifestyle, with its own behavioral patterns and ethical values. For the kids, it had all the attractiveness of a complicated game and all the lure of adventure." But this adventure wasn't only reinforced by kids and their friends. The more she paid attention to popular culture, the more Schuchard warned that pro-drug messages were everywhere, "reinforced by rock music, popular magazines, TV, and movies . . . Regardless of what kind of parents or what kind of personality the child had, when s/he turned on the radio, went to a movie, left the house—s/he came into contact with the drug culture. As [one teenager] told his mother, 'A kid has a drug problem the minute that kid walks out the front door, because the drugs are all around.'"[14]

When Schuchard visited convenience shops and record stores and saw paraphernalia for sale that seemed expressly designed to appeal to kids—things like the BuzzBee, a Frisbee-shaped pipe, or books called *A Child's Garden of Grass*—she realized that the ubiquity of drugs and drug accessories was both precisely the problem and precisely the point. The American economy struggled in the 1970s, battered by recessions, oil embargoes, and stagflation. Paraphernalia sales were one of the few bright spots in an otherwise depressed market, and a sale was a sale, regardless of the age of the purchaser. This, Schuchard realized, was the heart of the problem. "The primary values of the drug culture were ignoble," she wrote. "First, sheer commercial greed; second, lack of concern for the younger and more vulnerable end of the 'drug market'; third, the ideal of intoxication as the highest social and experiential goal."[15] The drug culture's emphasis on selling a drug that could harm generations of kids by promoting intoxication as fun and cool: that required a response—so she launched one, from her house.

Schuchard's first reaction to the drug culture was hyper-localized and community focused. In *Parents, Peers and Pot* she recommended that parents form activist groups to work within their own families, neighborhoods, and with their schools' parent-teacher associations to recognize and prevent the symptoms of drug use. First, she encouraged parents to focus on their own families, talking with their children about marijuana and warning them of the physical and mental dangers of the drug. Then she suggested that parents organize across friend groups and neighborhoods to offer alternative drug-free activities, set uniform rules, and ban access to drug paraphernalia and magazines like *High Times*. Finally, she encouraged schools to develop drug prevention programs, not only for kids, but also for parents and teachers so that adults across the spectrum of children's lives could help kids avoid cannabis use.

Despite her firm stance against adolescent drug use, however, Schuchard was not a hardliner against all drug use. She didn't preach prohibition forever (she repeatedly says through *Parents, Peers and Pot* that people should be capable of making their own decisions about drug use when they are adults), and warned parents against coming across as overly partisan, sectarian, or puritanical, noting that children respond better to adults who seemed genuinely interested in their health and well-being. Schuchard understood why children smoked pot, but the allure of the drug culture was precisely the problem, and she genuinely wanted parents to help their kids. Schuchard also recognized that she was asking a lot of parents, and closed her book with a distinct note of caution: "Parents, remember, it is better to occasionally feel like the local crank than to often feel helpless—especially when the welfare of your children is at stake. You can make a difference. And if you don't, who will?"[16]

Despite her emphasis on community engagement, Schuchard didn't retain her hyper-local focus for long. In 1978, she met Thomas "Buddy" Gleaton, a physical education professor at Georgia State University, and the two bonded over their mutual interest in preventing adolescent drug use. Together they formed PRIDE, the Parents' Resource Institute for Drug Education, housed in Gleaton's office at Georgia State, in order to expand Schuchard's concept of "parent groups" nationwide. PRIDE's philosophy, as outlined in the group's first newsletter from June 1979, argued that "a child's parents are his best bulwark against drug involvement," and that "the universal instinct of parents to protect their young is society's best bulwark against the expansion of the commercialized drug culture." PRIDE focused on two things: educating parents about the dangers of adolescent drug use, and bringing parents together to fight the drug culture. By providing information about drugs' effects on children and instructions on how to become a parent activist via PRIDE newsletters, pamphlets, reports and Schuchard's book, PRIDE hoped not only to thwart the drug culture's negative effects on kids, but to transform the relationships between families and communities nationwide. "A child's drug use can tear a family apart," Schuchard wrote, "but a sincere parental effort to give a child a drug-free adolescence can strengthen and enrich the whole family relationship. An extended communal effort by groups of parents can strengthen and enrich the whole community relationship."[17]

Bolstered by the popularity of *Parents, Peers and Pot*, PRIDE quickly became one of the most notable anti-marijuana groups in the US.

Sympathetic media coverage nationwide, along with Schuchard's positive relationship with Dr. Robert DuPont, director of the National Institute on Drug Abuse, resulted in PRIDE-style groups forming in all fifty states. By 1982, parent groups were being celebrated in the *New York Times.* "In the war against teen-age abuse of alcohol and marijuana, one more weapon has been added to the arsenal," the newspaper reported. "It's called parent networking, the objective of which is to bring the sprawling, diverse economic and ethnic suburban neighborhoods a sense of mutual community values." Dr. Keith Schuchard, described as "a national proponent of parent networking," was cited repeatedly, telling parents that communities with activist groups were "much healthier for teenagers" because mutual enforcement among families relieved the pressure to use drugs.[18]

But PRIDE wasn't the only parent activist group forming in America at the time; it wasn't even the only one in Atlanta. In autumn of 1977, just a year after Schuchard discovered her daughter's marijuana use, her neighbor Sue Rusche had her own disturbing experience with cannabis when she went to a store to purchase a *Star Wars* record for her two young sons. She was shocked by the "sudden influx of drug paraphernalia for sale in neighborhood stores and shopping centers . . . toys, gadgets, and magazines promoting the use of illicit drugs as teaching tools which broadcast messages in sharp contrast to the teachings of most families." By November, she had formed her own parent group, called DeKalb [County] Families in Action (FIA), which, as she wrote in her 1979 guidebook *How to Form a Families in Action Group in Your Community*, was dedicated to exposing "an industry that glamorizes and promotes illicit drugs to children" through collecting information on the industry, teaching other parents what she had learned, and finding ways to "exert control over the industry's impact on youngsters." By alerting parents to this insidious field, and, most importantly, opening "lines of communication between parents and those who, in governing us, make daily decisions that affect children's lives," Rusche hoped that groups like FIA could undermine the flourishing paraphernalia industry, ultimately ending drug use by children and teenagers.[19]

Whereas Schuchard and Gleaton were educators, Rusche was an activist, with a laser-like focus on changing laws. Rusche realized that one way to attack the cannabis culture was to hit it where it would hurt most:

its money. Lacking the narrative formalities of *Parents, Peer and Pot,* Rusche's text was a workbook focused exclusively on teaching parents how to form lobbying groups that would effectively hound state lawmakers to pass legislation that would regulate the sale of drug paraphernalia to the point that the practice would no longer be economically feasible. In step-by-step guidelines, she taught readers what to discuss at meetings, how to form a board of directors, and offered sample language for an anti-paraphernalia bill.

Rusche's aim was to see FIA-style groups thwart the drug lobby nationwide, but she had higher goals, as well. For her, parent activism was akin to the civil rights movement, which Rusche had prominently supported in Atlanta. "Many people despair that society is already so saturated with the acceptance of marijuana that we shall not be able to avoid legalization," she wrote.

> We reject this argument. We must not lose sight of the fact that the widespread use of marijuana is a phenomenon of the past ten years. Many people in the US took the same position about racial segregation, which was rooted in our culture for *four hundred* years. But the civil rights movement taught us that no barrier—economic, legal, or social—can stand in the way of change once enough people decide that change must take place. As the number of America's children and teenagers who use psychoactive drugs increases, the question for parents of the 1980's is: Are we ready to work for change?[20]

By 1979, Atlanta had given birth to two prominent parent activist groups: PRIDE and FIA. The groups had differing approaches—PRIDE sought to educate parents and help them become active in their own communities, whereas FIA sought to transform parents into effective political lobbyists—but both were concerned with the effects of cannabis on adolescents, and both believed that increased parental involvement could help reduce the negative impact of marijuana in children's lives. Both also saw themselves in stark opposition to the "drug culture" they saw encroaching on children's health and well-being. The biggest challenge in thwarting the drug culture, for Schuchard and Rusche, wasn't only in educating parents or lobbying state governments; it was overthrowing a profitable capitalist enterprise. As Schuchard wrote in

Parents, Peers and Pot, "drug businessmen today do not point accusing fingers at Wall Street capitalism or American imperialism as their moral rationale for dealing; instead, they invoke the profit motive, free enterprise, and service to consumers to justify their trade." When "glossy magazines advocating multidrug use and slickly packaged drug paraphernalia appear on the shelves of neighborhood supermarkets," Schuchard lamented, "many adults feel helpless to fight 'recreation' and 'free enterprise.'"[21]

But parents didn't have to feel helpless for long. By May 1980, when parent groups had spread nationwide, the movement was powerful enough to form its own Washington-based lobbying group, the National Federation of Parents for Drug-Free Youth (NFP), which organized national protests and sent activists to Capitol Hill to testify in congressional hearings about the dangers pot posed to kids. In November, the movement got an enormous boost when Ronald Reagan was elected president. Reagan appreciated the groups' volunteer identity and their willingness to take on drug prevention without needing federal financial support. When his wife Nancy, guided by parent activists with the NFP, took on the prevention of adolescent drug abuse as her platform as first lady, the parent movement found an even more prominent patron as Reagan brought parent activism onto the international stage.[22]

In the late 1970s, when Schuchard and Rusche were writing their guidebooks, they felt that the drug culture had the upper hand, and that mass activism was necessary to stop the wave of decriminalization and save the nation's kids. But the tables were already beginning to turn, and by 1980, when Reagan was elected and parent activists ascended to the national stage, the pro-cannabis lobby had been back on its heels for years. The late 1970s were an extremely difficult time for *High Times* and NORML, and the parent movement's successes were compounded by the pro-drug community's political and internal struggles. In 1978, Nebraska became the last state to decriminalize marijuana possession and NORML lost its support in Washington. President Jimmy Carter, elected during decriminalization's heyday in 1976, had been urged by his chief drug advisor Peter Bourne to quietly support states in changing their marijuana laws. But in July 1978, Bourne was forced to resign when allegations of his cocaine use at a NORML Christmas party the year prior were leaked to the press—by Keith Stroup, who was angry at Bourne for allowing Mexico to use American equipment to spray paraquat, a powerful herbicide, on Mexican marijuana fields. In the aftermath of the scandal, Stroup, who once believed that decriminalization, and perhaps even legalization, would prevail nationwide by 1980, was ousted from the organization he founded, leaving NORML to spin through a rotating door of executive directors throughout remainder of the 1970s and the 1980s. Then, in November 1978, *High Times* founder Tom Forçade committed suicide at age thirty-three. He bequeathed trusts to benefit *High Times* and NORML, but by 1980, both groups were floundering economically, socially, and philosophically.[23]

Pro-cannabis activists grew angry that parent activism had damaged their finances. In July 1980, Michael Antonoff, editor of *Accessories Digest* magazine (formerly known as *Paraphernalia Digest*), wrote in an editorial in *High Times* that summarized the paraphernalia industry's feelings about parent activism, titled "Those Mothers are Trampling Adult Rights." The parent movement's shift to targeting legal paraphernalia rather than illegal drugs was destroying an otherwise robust industry, Antonoff complained, and the effect was the equivalent of creating a "thought police." "While penalties for pot possession have mainly been decriminalized, a whole new form of proscription is erupting around its accoutrements," Antonoff wrote. "The law is so lopsided that in places like Brookings, Oregon, if a person is carrying up to an ounce of marijuana and a packet of Zig-Zags [rolling papers], he can be fined for the pot but jailed for the paper." Targeting paraphernalia for its potential use in illegal activity was frightening, Antonoff concluded, because "the problem with laws directed against intentions is that what is really being legislated against are thoughts . . . Drug laws, as always, are a potent political weapon."

For Antonoff, the parent movement's attack on paraphernalia was nothing short of "a new kind of McCarthyism," where "the word cocaine has been substituted for communism," and where "the most basic of American institutions—free speech—has been swept away." The source of Antonoff's problems were parent activists who were as motivated in 1980 as pro-decriminalization activists had been in the 1970s: it was "mothers for a straight America" who "carry signs and harass politicians," "circulate petitions" and "commandeer the attention of the media," he warned, who were rolling back the rights pro-cannabis activists had fought for over the past decade. Antonoff also associated parent activists (if incorrectly, in the case of lifelong Democrats Schuchard and Rusche) with resurging Republicanism. "The New Right has in the last two years successfully shifted the public spotlight away from decriminalization to the plea of 'save our children,'" he wrote. "No one wants children smoking pot, but to scapegoat by stigmatizing legitimate business makes as much sense as banning swizzle sticks to prevent alcoholism." Still, cannabis consumers' general lack of reaction to the parent movement's increasing power caused Antonoff to worry. "The vast majority [of smokers] don't seem to care that a right they have taken for granted is being taken away," he complained, and then closed his article with a dire warning: "If the generation to whom pot was the symbol of causes shared does not wake up, it may soon discover that 1984 has arrived four years early."[24]

Antonoff's editorial laid the foundations for the culture war that was to play out in the pages of *High Times* over the next few years. While parent activists painted cannabis activists as unscrupulous businessmen bent on selling drugs to kids regardless of the social cost, writers at *High Times* viewed parent activists as hysterical fanatics out to destroy a legitimate industry, as well as minions of the New Right ushering in a new era of government control. The magazine also wasn't above name calling. In October 1980, *High Times* published an article condemning Sue Rusche, the "Dragon Lady of DeKalb County Families in Action," and her role in the formation of the NFP. "Anti-pot hysteria has gone nationwide with the formation of the National Federation of Parents for Drug-Free Youth," the anonymous article warned. "Claiming to represent over 370 groups in forty-eight states," the NFP was "a major accomplishment for DeKalb Families, the pioneer hate-group in the field." Literature from FIA made "pot out to be somewhat more poisonous than strontium 90," a radioactive metal that causes cancer, and the article lamented how the NFP was bringing this view to the national level, with apparent federal support. The NFP was "warmly supported by the federal Drug Enforcement Administration," and the press conference announcing the group's formation was attended by "a gaggle of US senators, congressmen and their wives, and White House drug adviser Lee Dogoloff." (Dogoloff replaced Peter Bourne after Bourne's resignation in 1978.) The group's "war against heads and head shops," the article warned, was evidence of the "anti-pot panic" gripping the nation.[25]

The article, while hyperbolic, wasn't entirely wrong. Parent activists were effective lobbyists, urging states to overturn decriminalization laws and penalize the sale of paraphernalia to kids. They urged the election of local representatives who would enforce their claims, and soon bills supporting the drug war and regulating paraphernalia were being considered before Congress. By the spring of 1981, *High Times* reported that the Senate was considering the Drug Paraphernalia Prohibitions Act, a bill that would have made possession with intent to distribute paraphernalia a misdemeanor and would have made delivery of paraphernalia to a minor a special offense, thus bringing FIA's chief concern to Capitol Hill. (The act was referred to the Subcommittee on Security and Terrorism, where it languished.) In the House of Representatives, Billy Lee Evans, a strong anti-drug advocate and parent movement-favored politician from Georgia, introduced a bill to repeal the 1978 prohibition against American funding of the spraying of paraquat on foreign marijuana fields, overturning the very act Keith Stroup had spent his political capital to pass. Most worrisome, HR 3519, the "Department of Defense Authorization Act," was being considered by the House Armed Services Committee, which *High Times* warned could allow for the limited use of military equipment (including radar planes, reconnaissance aircraft and helicopters) by "federal, state and local law enforcement officials" in their battle against drug trafficking, if they were so assigned by the Defense Department of Defense. "This is a license for a real 'war on drugs,'" *High Times* warned, one that was clearly designed to target growers and dealers.[26]

By the early 1980s, with the Reagans in the White House, anti-drug bills being considered in Congress, and decriminalization laws being repealed nationwide, it was clear that Washington was turning against drug use, and that groups like *High Times* and NORML no longer possessed the political influence they had wielded in the past. Rather than work to reinvigorate their base, however, *High Times*, counterproductively, responded with mockery. Throughout 1982, in a section called "Seeds'N'Stems," *High Times* satirized everything from conservative politics to parent activism to the federal response to drug use. In a February article titled "New Right Goes Pro-Dope!" *High Times* mocked the idea that only the counterculture was interested in profiting off of drugs. Cit-ing "Richard W. Vigorish, comptroller and guiding genius of the Con-servative Political Action Conspiracy" (a stand-in for Richard Viguerie, the pioneer of political direct mail promotion, and the Conservative Political Action Conference), *High Times* wrote that "Vigorish . . . has called for the complete opening of the narcotics industry to indepen-dent American businessmen. 'Laws against drugs do absolutely noth-ing except concentrate the drug trade into the hands of a few select syndicates, generally composed of tightly knit hereditary clans with non-American names ending in vowels,' Vigorish observed. 'This con-stitutes an outrageous, state-sponsored monopoly of an industry that would otherwise distribute scores of billions of dollars among inde-pendent American entrepreneurs.'"[27]

In June 1982, *High Times* took direct aim at parent activists, publishing a satirical newsletter, "Stop Dopes at Their Source," from "Zoo Rooch," "executrix" of the "DeFunct County Parents Up in Arms, Combatting Drug-Abuse-Type And Non-Christian Influences From Outside The Community All Across The Nation." "Rooch's" article warned parents of the newest threat to their children: URA, "Unsupervised Respiratory Activity," also known as "oxygen abuse . . . the intentional taking in of too much air into the body system by breathing in a too-deep, too-rapid way." "The children are taught by older children, or by people from out-side the community, how to breathe in special ways that give them an 'oxygen overdose,'" the article warned.

> These outside-the-community people do not care if a child blows his lungs up by too much URA, or falls victim to any of the other science-documented hazards. It is up to parents themselves, as DeFunct County Parents Up in Arms have always insisted, to both supervise their pre-cious children's breath-by-breath behavior, and to vigorously take ac-tion against disagreeable, strange, or upsetting people from outside the community.[28]

Finally, in November 1982, *High Times* published a three-page satirical version of *The American Journal of Drug, Substance and Alcohol Preven-tion, Recovery and Aftercare*, warning, alongside a picture of an infant, that "Drugs in Nursery Rears Ugly Head!" In it, "Dr. Robert Alcoa" (a satirical version of Dr. Robert DuPont, who had retired from his position as head of the National Institute on Drug Abuse by that time) responded to

> recent proof that substance-use-abuse-type behavior appears among preschool kids, many as young as three or four years old. "We're talking about babies and drugs here," Alcoa, currently head of the US Council on Marihuana Et Cetera (CMEC), told the *American Journal*. "Babies and drugs. Let no one miss the message—it's babies and drugs. Let's hear it one more time: babies and drugs. Horrendous."

At the bottom of the page, a box informed readers that *"The American Journal* is a wholly owned subsidiary of the Drug Abuse Industrial Complex (DAIC)."²⁹

Throughout 1982, as Congress considered more anti-drug legislation and President Reagan ramped up his militarized drug war, *High Times* was focused primarily on mocking the parent movement and anti-marijuana attitudes among government officials. There wasn't much else for the magazine to do, and NORML, cycling through three executive directors—Larry Schott, James N. Hall, and George L. Farnham—between 1980 and 1983, was too disorganized to effectively lead cannabis activists' response. But in the spring and summer of 1983, *High Times* suddenly began presenting a very different view, in a change brought about by its aging readership, who needed the magazine to respond to their needs as parents when it came to addressing drug use and their kids. In a move that turned parent activists' message on its head, suddenly it was pot smoking *parents* who needed advice on kids and drug use, and they looked to *High Times*, rather than PRIDE or FIA, for advice.

In a series of letters to the editor published in the spring and summer of 1983, parents discussed marijuana use—their own and by their children—and the magazine published them in an ongoing conversation about the role adolescent drug use played in families where parents were cannabis consumers and *High Times* readers. An anonymous reader from New Haven, Connecticut, opened the conversation in a letter published in April. "My husband and I have been avid readers of your magazine for the past five years and we count on *High Times* for giving us the truth about a variety of subjects," it began. "I have, however, yet to see an article directed to the many parents who read *High Times* and are confused as to what to tell their children about drug use . . . I'm not into having 'hip kids,' but they see us smoking all the time and I really don't know how to handle the situation. I don't want my kids to smoke till they're old enough to handle it intelligently, but I'd rather see them smoke weed for the buzz of their choice than anything else. At the same time, I don't want them to think that *all* drugs are okay because mom and dad smoke pot. I'm sure that there are other parents in this same position, and we all would appreciate greatly an article that concerns itself with this problem."[30]

A far cry from their mocking attitude toward parental concerns a year earlier, the editors responded with a sense of humility and openness: "Your point is well taken and we are a little chagrined at not having addressed it on our own. We will try our best to get such a piece in the magazine as soon as possible. In the meantime, we'd like to encourage our readers who are parents to write and tell us how they're handling this situation."[31]

A number of people did. In July and August *High Times* published responses from several readers, some using their own names, others choosing to remain anonymous, which ran the gamut from parents who were concerned about children's drug use and wanted their kids to stay sober, to those who wanted to share cannabis with them, preferring to ensure that their child's drug use stayed safely within the family. A reader whose name and address were withheld responded that, "It was comforting to read that *High Times* does not take lightly the serious issue concerning parental drug use and the worries of inevitable conflicts resultant in the children. I am a mother of two school-aged kids. I can attest personally to the enormous difficulties that do exist . . . in trying to merge credibly those divergent views: approval of personal drug use by the parents at home, versus the school/legal/media hype that proclaims the evil inherent in all drugs." Like Schuchard and Rusche before her, the writer then offered advice that regarded parental actions and responsibility as paramount to deflecting conflicts before they arose. "You must try to maintain respect for your child's innate intelligence, maturity and sound instincts for self-preservation," she wrote. "When your child perceives you as a parent who has integrity, who behaves in a manner appropriate to the situation, who may indulge in drugs moderately and in control, and who is there when needed, *then* you can afford the luxury of feeling confident that your child is well-armed to face whatever drug-related question and/or problem he or she may encounter."[32]

An anonymous father took a different tack. He wrote that he "never tried to hide" his smoking from his 10-year-old son. His child, he believed, "views it in very much the same way I viewed my parents' cigarette-smoking": as something quotidian and banal. Still, he continued, parents have a responsibility to help their kids lead lives that don't require getting high. "I feel a kid's life is supposed to be relatively easy and enjoyably straight," he wrote, "and if you instill in your child a basic self-esteem and security, they won't need anything to put in their bodies to make their life more pleasant (the way we adults do) . . . Just don't give your kids a reason to want to get high and it'll be okay."[33]

In a final letter published on the topic, an anonymous mother of two who had "tried every drug available" wrote that, although she was fine with her 13-year-old son's periodic marijuana use, she was firmly opposed to adolescent use of other substances, like mushrooms or cocaine, and she disapproved of kids constantly being high. Echoing Schuchard's concerns about amotivational syndrome, she wrote that, as a teacher, she saw "what can happen to children who take drugs all the time or use them to ease an intolerable life; they lose their interest in everything else." Nonetheless, she continued, she valued the honest relationship she had with her children about drugs. "So far," she wrote, "my kids trust me and believe that the information I give them is the truth. This relationship goes both ways, and they tell me when they think one of their friends is in deep water, and I try to talk to that kid." She also looked forward to sharing more drug experiences with her children "when they are full grown," she continued, "and I will make sure that they use the best, and under ceremonial conditions."[34]

These letters published over the spring and summer of 1983 were evidence that the counterculture of the 1960s had aged, and that the pro-decriminalization activists of the previous decades were parents now, with their own concerns about adolescent drug use. Now, rather than viewing parent activists as enemies, *High Times* readers shared many of their concerns, which they voiced not at NFP rallies or in parent groups, but in the very magazine Schuchard and Rusche considered the voice of the "drug culture." This was an enormous shift for a magazine that, just a few years prior, had mocked the concept of preventing adolescent drug use, and it marked the beginning of a period of détente in the cannabis culture wars, when pro-cannabis and anti-drug activists found a sense of camaraderie in their shared responsibilities as parents.

Three years later, the cannabis movement's alignment with the parent movement's key priority—the protection of children from drug abuse—was being voiced by NORML as well. In the spring of 1986, Jon Gettman, a twenty-nine-year-old academic who specialized in drug policy, took NORML's reins as executive director and ushered in a period of economic and philosophical stability for the organization, refocusing NORML on educational initiatives while promoting the full legalization, rather than decriminalization, of cannabis at the state and federal level. The mid-1980s were a period of surprising resurgence for NORML. Despite the Reagan administration's increasingly punitive and militarized War on Drugs, the country's new focus on the dangers of crack cocaine allowed cannabis activists to quietly reorganize. Kevin Zeese, who served as NORML's executive director from 1983 to 1986 and began to stabilize the organization, told the Associated Press, "Thank goodness for Ronald Reagan . . . He's making no dent in the marijuana business, but he's scaring people and some are turning to us. Reagan has improved our ability to activate marijuana users. That wouldn't have happened if we'd had Carter for four more years."[35]

Zeese focused on stabilizing NORML economically and maturing the group's lobbying tactics, and when he left to found the Drug Policy Foundation at American University in 1986, NORML's board of directors chose Gettman to succeed him. Gettman was the perfect candidate to continue NORML's evolution from a group known for its wild Christmas parties into a mature organization dedicated to the legalization of cannabis for health and economic reasons. Under Gettman's leadership, NORML refocused itself, transitioning from a 501(c)4 lobbying group into a 501(c)3 educational institution. "We realized we had to educate the public about the issue if we wanted anything to change," he recalled. "Mobilizing people was much more effective than lobbying Congress."[36]

Gettman's term as executive director also served as an olive branch to concerned parents. Because he took his aging base's concerns seriously, Gettman appealed to marijuana-smoking parents who had recently written to *High Times*, and, as a repentant former salesman who had spent eight years in the paraphernalia business, he was also helpful in bridging the divide between the legalization movement and potential parent activists—non-smoking parents of adolescents who were concerned about children's drug use. In 1987, a year into his tenure, Gettman admitted in a *High Times* editorial something parent activists never expected to hear: he knew the paraphernalia market was "free-market capitalism at its best," and the looseness of the industry's practices had caused people, including children, harm. "The problem with the free-wheeling paraphernalia market was that we were pandering to an illegal interest in the marketing of our goods," he wrote. "Much like sex is used to sell cars, we were, in retrospect, using drugs to sell knick-knacks." This retrospect then prompted something unseen in any previous issue of the magazine: recognition that "our exploitation of drugs was offensive to some, especially parents trying to keep their kids away from any drug use, illegal or otherwise."[37]

In order to secure NORML's recognition as a 501(c)4 organization, Gettman also had to produce more educational materials, so in 1986 and '87, he published *The Common Sense Series*. With titles like "Marijuana and Justice," "Marijuana and the Economy," and "Urine Testing for Marijuana and Other Drugs," these pamphlets focused on the dangers of prohibiting cannabis, framing them as attacks on liberty, at their core. Most notably, he published a pamphlet titled "Drugs and Children," which parroted the parent movement's major tenet by proclaiming that "NORML is strongly committed to the concept that growing up should be *drug-free*. NORML believes that meaningful communication within the family based on honest information on the health and social consequences related to all drugs is the best way to *prevent* drug abuse."

But he also turned parent activists' argument on its head. Prohibition wasn't the solution to prevent kids using drugs, he wrote, because "law enforcement efforts have *failed* to keep marijuana and other drugs away from America's adolescents." Instead, prohibition "has only created a widely available, unregulated forbidden fruit." If marijuana were legalized, Gettman argued, it could "eliminate the black market, reduce crime and most importantly reduce adolescents' access to drugs. A marijuana tax could raise up to $15 billion annually which could be used for credible education and discouragement programs"—programs that, like parent activists promoted a decade prior, would offer children alternatives to drug use. "To prevent marijuana abuse," Gettman concluded, we shouldn't keep the drug illegal. Instead, we should legalize cannabis and use the proceeds from taxation to "devote more resources to recreation programs to interest children in life and to help parents, schools and communities provide a better environment for our children"—precisely what Schuchard had advocated a decade earlier.[38]

Gettman's argument was powerful and poignant. By basically agreeing with the parent movement's core argument—that children shouldn't use drugs—he ended the war between parent activists and NORML. But he also made a key distinction by arguing that it was *prohibition*, and not the simple existence of the drug itself, that allowed children to access cannabis in the first place, and if parents really wanted to protect their children from the "drug culture," the country should bring marijuana aboveground. Similar to the alcohol and tobacco industries, Gettman argued, legal weed would decrease adolescent access by implementing oversights like age restrictions, and would tame the capitalist beast behind paraphernalia sales, reducing the market for products that blatantly appealed to kids. By choosing to work with, rather than against, the parent movement, Gettman helped transform NORML into an organization that worked to achieve both groups' aims: a system that encouraged a drug-free childhood while also increasing legal access to cannabis for adults.

Gettman's adaptation and reversal of the parent movement's primary argument brought the cannabis culture wars to a standstill. With Gettman's concession, there was no way for parent activists to argue against him: he agreed that it was necessary for children to be prevented from accessing pot, though he disagreed on how to achieve those ends. More importantly, by the end of the 1980s, agreeing with NORML wasn't the parent movement's only problem. The parents' own arguments were losing steam as the media's demonization of crack cocaine swept parental fears about cannabis from the headlines, and as marijuana reemerged as a useful medicine for those struggling with diseases like cancer, glaucoma, and the effects of HIV/AIDS. As fears about pot's effects on kids were replaced by cannabis's utility as a medicine, and as advocates like Gettman argued that legalization was the most effective way to prevent adolescent marijuana use, parent activism faded as a national concern. Families no longer had to prevent children from using a drug that systems of medicalization and legalization could just as readily keep out of their hands.[39]

In 1996, California passed the country's first medical marijuana initiative, setting off almost thirty years of increasingly liberalized cannabis laws. As of November 2020, medical marijuana is now legal in thirty-five states, Guam, Puerto Rico, the US Virgin Islands and the District of Columbia, and fifteen states and Washington, DC have fully legalized recreational use. This marks a century of significant shifts in the country's cannabis culture wars. From Anslinger's concerns in the 1930s that marijuana would either turn users against children or make adolescents perpetuate violent crimes, to growing social acceptance in the 1960s and 1970s that resulted in the parent movement's forceful backlash against decriminalization, to a second period of growing acceptance from the mid-1990s to outright legalization today, debates over cannabis in the public discourse have repeatedly changed minds and changed laws. But the concept of childhood in relation to drug use—the idea that children need to be kept safe from the drug's harmful effects and shielded from any negative outcomes of its wider availability—has remained at the core of all arguments for and against changing drug laws. As marijuana has shifted from a cultural menace to a useful medicine and now, as a recreational intoxicant, a means by which states can significantly increase tax revenue, the protection of childhood safety and sobriety has consistently stayed at the center of these debates.

What differentiates the cannabis culture wars of the 1970s and 1980s from the Reefer Madness era of the 1930s, however, is the lasting power of the argument that legalization protects children far better than prohibition does. In Washington State, which, with Oregon, was one of the first states to legalize recreational marijuana use in 2012, an editorial in the *Seattle Times* encouraged voters to approve ballot measure I-502 using language similar to NORML's twenty years prior, while mocking the concerns of people like Anslinger: "The question for voters is not whether marijuana is good. It is whether prohibition is good. If marijuana killed people, or if smoking it made people commit violence and mayhem, prohibition might be worth all its bad effects. But marijuana does not kill people; there is no lethal dose." "Parents may ask whether I-502 will make marijuana more available to their teenage children," the editorial continued. "The answer is to compare marijuana with beer. For teenagers, both are illegal—and available. But which is more easily available, the one that is banned or the one that is regulated? For more than forty years, the one more easily available to teenagers has been the one that is banned."[40]

A far cry from Harry Anslinger's warnings that marijuana would transform children into violent maniacs or Schuchard's fears that de-criminalization would result in generations of children harmed, in the thirty years since the most recent skirmish in the cannabis culture wars came to a close, legalization is now presented as the safer alternative to ensure the public health of America's most innocent citizens. The drug's popularity is also increasing: two-thirds—67 percent—of Americans now support some form of marijuana legalization, many because they believe it will have beneficial health and social justice-related effects.[41] This result would not have been possible without decades of debate over cannabis's role in America, especially in terms of the drug's safety and marketability. The core argument of the cannabis culture wars that both parties finally agreed on—that legal cannabis cannot be made available to children, nor can the market pander to them in any way—has consistently resulted in public health and safety concerns being put at the center of the legal-ization debate, with controls over who can access the drug and why—and has now resulted in outright recreational legalization for millions of Americans over the age of twenty-one. While it surely wasn't what Harry Anslinger argued in 1937 or Keith Schuchard envisioned in 1976, it is legalization, not prohibition, that has engendered these fiercely sought-after effects, bringing a surprising, and potentially permanent, détente to over a century of cannabis culture wars.

NOTES

1 Martin Booth, *Cannabis: A History* (New York: Picador, 2003), 116.
2 Jerome Himmelstein, "From Killer Weed to Drop-Out Drug: The Changing Ideol-ogy of Marihuana," *Contemporary Crises* 7 (January 1983): 13–38.
3 Himmelstein, "From Killer Weed to Drop-Out Drug."
4 Jerome Himmelstein, "The Continuing Career of Marijuana: Backlash . . . within Limits," *Contemporary Drug Problems* 13 (Spring 1986): 8–9.
5 Emily Dufton, *Grass Roots: The Rise and Fall and Rise of Marijuana in America* (New York: Basic Books, 2017), 57–72.
6 Michael Kennedy, "Introduction," *High Times: A 40-Year History of the World's Most Infamous Magazine* (New York: powerHouse Books, 2017), 7–8.
7 Kennedy, "Introduction," 73.
8 Keith Stroup, *It's NORML to Smoke Pot* (New York: Trans High Corporation, 2013), 48.

9 Black Sabbath, "Sweet Leaf," track 1 on *Master of Reality* (Vertigo Records, 1971).

10 Dufton, *Grass Roots*, 95.

11 Laurie Johnston, "Children, in Test, Buy Drug Trappings Freely at 'Head Shops,'" *New York Times*, March 30, 1978.

12 Marsha Manatt, *Parents, Peers and Pot* (Rockville, MD: National Institute on Drug Abuse, 1979), 3, 10–11.

13 Manatt, *Parents, Peers and Pot*, 36, 48.

14 Manatt, *Parents, Peers and Pot*, 10–11.

15 Manatt, *Parents, Peers and Pot*, 10.

16 Manatt, *Parents, Peers and Pot*, 79.

17 Marsha Schuchard, "What is PRIDE?? Parents' Resource Institute for Drug Education," *PRIDE Newsletter*, June 1979, 7.

18 Patricia Teasdale, "Parent Networks Catching On," *New York Times*, February 7, 1982, K11.

19 Sue Rusche, *How to Form a Families in Action Group in Your Community* (Atlanta, GA: DeKalb Families in Action, Inc., 1979), 1, 3–4.

20 Rusche, *How to Form a Families in Action Group*, 62.

21 Manatt, *Parents, Peers and Pot*, 26.

22 See forthcoming article by Emily Dufton, "PRIDE International and Drug War Diplomacy: The Parent Movement's Global Battle against Marijuana," in *Cannabis: Global Histories*, ed. Lucas Richert and James H. Mills (Cambridge: MIT Press, 2021).

23 Stroup, *It's NORML to Smoke Pot*, 100–103.

24 Michael Antonoff, "Those Mothers Are Trampling Adult Rights," *High Times*, July 1980, 8.

25 N. A., "Fanatics Run Wild! Anti-Pot Panic Grips Nation," *High Times*, October 1980, 23, 26.

26 Charles Winston-Levy, "Antidrug Hysteria Looms in Congress," *High Times*, September 1981, 19, 26–27.

27 N. A., "New Right Goes Pro-Dope!" *High Times*, February 1982, 79.

28 N. A., "Stop Dopes at Their Source," *High Times*, June 1982, 71.

29 All articles from *High Times*, November 1982, 71–73.

30 Name Withheld, "Pot and Parenting," *High Times*, April 1983, 7–8.

31 Name Withheld, "Pot and Parenting."

32 Anonymous, "Parents' Responsibility," *High Times*, July 1983, 7.

33 Letter published under the heading "Parents' Responsibility II," *High Times*, August 1983, 7–10.

34 Letter in "Parents' Responsibility II."

35 David Goeller, "Marijuana Lobby Says It's Thriving, Credits Reagan Administration," Associated Press, April 22, 1985, https://apnews.com.

36 Jon Gettman, interview with the author, August 17, 2020.

37 Jon Gettman, "Parity: The Drug Paraphernalia Issue," *High Times*, April 1987, 30.

38 NORML, "Drugs and Children," Common Sense Series, 1987, provided to the author by Jon Gettman.

39 Dufton, *Grass Roots*, 189–205.

40 "Approve Initiative 502 — It's Time to Legalize, Regulate and Tax Marijuana," *Seattle Times*, September 22, 2012, quoted in Clayton J. Mosher and Scott Akins, *In the Weeds: Demonization, Legalization, and the Evolution of US Marijuana Policy* (Philadelphia: Temple University Press, 2019), 171–72.

41 Andrew Daniller, "Two-thirds of Americans Support Marijuana Legalization," Pew Research Center, November 14, 2019, www.pewresearch.org.

7

Psychedelic Wars

LSD as Mental Medicine in a Battle for Hearts and Minds

LUCAS RICHERT, ERIKA DYCK, AND ALEXIS TURNER

Psychedelic drugs, particularly LSD (d-lysergic acid diethylamide), have an awkward place in the War on Drugs. Through a focus on distinct "psychedelic wars" in the historical literature, in the clinic, with one's self, and on the home front, this chapter showcases how substances were concurrently depicted as legitimate and illegitimate, as medicines or dangerous drugs. It will also illustrate how the historical actors involved (whether doctors, patients, policy makers, or users) fought their personal psychedelic wars in the field of mental medicine and beyond. Finally, in reflecting on psychedelics as part of the War on Drugs, this chapter addresses under-explored elements related to diversity and equity, criminalization, commercialization, and the messy relationship among those factors.

In 1965, David Solomon tried to shape a wider public understanding of psychedelics and drugs in the United States. Straddling laboratory and literary realms, and based in New York City, Solomon was well positioned to interact with countercultural figures at Timothy Leary's Castalia retreat in Millbrook, New York, as well as with scientists at Spring Grove State Hospital, in Maryland, a home of significant government-funded psychedelic research. The editor of *LSD–the Consciousness-Expanding Drug* (1964) and *The Marijuana Papers* (1966) and co-editor of *Drugs and Sexuality* (1973) and *The Coca Leaf and Cocaine Papers* (1975), Solomon did not have any biomedical training; instead, he communicated knowledge drawn from his experiences in the jazz community, drug subcultures, and relationships with figures such as Beat writer William Burroughs and jazz giant Dizzy Gillespie, in addition to well-respected psychedelic psychiatrists. As an editor at *Esquire* and *Playboy*, Solomon oversaw the publication of articles by countercultural luminaries Ram Dass, Timothy Leary, and Alan Watts. Solomon also noted how the Princeton-based Humphry Osmond (a "wonderful cat" and the coiner of the term psychedelic) had offered "complete cooperation" in the making of a documentary for the National Broadcasting Corporation (NBC).[1] Well-connected, a user, and *bon vivant*, Solomon believed psychedelics had value in medicine *and* wider society.[2] Solomon, in short, embodied various psychedelic ideas, cultures, and agendas that operated independently, or at other times intersected. In 1965, prior to the federal scheduling and absolute criminalization of LSD in 1968 and then 1970, he bridged the divide between recreational and medical worlds of psychedelics, as well as the wide-ranging narratives that others have told about psychedelics.

Solomon was far from alone in trying to shape how people in the United States understood psychedelics as interlocutors between medicine and cultural enhancers. Various stakeholders—doctors and day trippers, psychiatrists and psychonauts, cops and career politicians— sought to design and publicly promote psychedelic narratives. These narratives, when compared, reveal an inherent tension in the characterization of psychedelics, and particularly LSD. One set of people claimed that psychedelics might enable a more harmonious vision, and they claimed that psychedelics represented a "societal antidote" that could open hearts and minds. Yet others described psychedelics substances as having terrible destructive power, in terms of both personal risk to mental health and the social danger of infecting minds with uncivil attitudes. These characterizations competed with other perspectives, specifically that LSD allowed for mind control and was a potent "Cold War weapon." Psychedelic psychiatrists and others in the biomedical realm, meanwhile, suggested that insights gained from psychedelic experiences had therapeutic value; these drugs were considered a "breakthrough therapy" for curing alcoholism and other health problems. Solomon, as described above, was a historical actor who represented a point of convergence among these disparate LSD narratives.[3]

Battles over LSD's meaning continue to resonate. Drugs "never fully shed their past," according to Science and Technology Studies scholar Nancy D. Campbell. "At any given time, there are many discourses circulating that have overlapping historical resonance."[4] Some fifty years after the passage of the Controlled Substances Act (CSA) and the scheduling of LSD in Schedule I (meaning it had no medical purpose and possessed a serious potential for abuse), people continue to wrestle with the safety, utility, and accessibility of psychedelics. A growing number challenge the complete criminalization of LSD, calling on new scientific findings showing its therapeutic value, while others still debate the past to reveal a more complicated way of understanding what was at stake, decades ago, in the war on psychedelics.[5]

In this chapter, we reconsider psychedelics during the War on Drugs by examining some of the historical discourse surrounding their contested place within psychiatric medicine and countercultural, drug-induced recreation, self-exploration, or liberty of consciousness—concepts that themselves challenge the distinctions made between medicine and pleasure. We identify the struggles over who claimed to have authority: when it came to attempts to legitimate the use of psychedelics, either as a medicine or as a recreational substance. And we suggest that internal debates within the psychedelic community bear witness to and reveal deeper contests about identity politics and evaluations of drugs as beneficial medicines or simply as recreational forms of escape. Ultimately, the lack of consensus in the medico-scientific community over the benefits and risks associated with psychedelic drug use, coupled with a rising tide of interest in psychedelics for recreational purposes alone, proved instrumental. Scales tipped in favor of a characterization of psychedelics as recreational, or at the very least, nonmedical, and therefore subject to an assault on drugs that included a war on psychedelics and what they represented. The subsequent criminalization of psychedelics, we argue, was a byproduct both of a lack of evidence about LSD's therapeutic benefits and of the nature of the figures who championed its use as a recreational, spiritual, or hedonistic technology.[6]

Based on archival records, surveys of biomedical literature, and a deep reading of the secondary sources, this chapter examines dominant psychedelic narratives while also seeking to address under-explored elements related to diversity and equity, criminalization, commercialization, and the messy relationship among those factors. In the following pages, through a focus on distinct "psychedelic wars" in the historical literature, in the clinic, in the self, and on the home front, we provide certain insights. On the one hand, we present a view of how substances are concurrently depicted as legitimate and illegitimate. On the other hand, we illustrate how the historical actors involved (be they doctors, patients, policy makers, or users) fought their personal wars in the field of mental medicine and beyond. The result is a more complicated but also more holistic assessment of psychedelic history in the US against the backdrop of the War on Drugs. In this chapter, we chronicle competing narratives within the biomedical community. But we also reflect on whose voices have been heard in psychedelic history and those that have been ignored or silenced—and at what cost.

Historiographical Wars, or the Troubled History of Psychedelic History

The history of psychedelic history has varied widely and, in the American context at least, has rarely been as expansive as it could be. Psychedelics have been, are currently, and should be understood amid a swirling set of controversies about their utility, purpose, potential for abuse, and the state of our knowledge about them. The first generation of psychedelic scholarship found itself preoccupied with contemporary political debates and so examined psychedelics as "weapons," "antidotes" for society, "cures" for individual pathologies, and through standard "rise and fall and rise" lenses.[7] And while these diverging categories were very much products of their time, they still matter in the contemporary climate, when psychedelics, once considered medicines in the mental health marketplace prior to the CSA fifty years ago, have returned as objects of scientific study and public fascination. Just as swathes of scientific papers were published on psychedelic subjects between the 1950s and 1970s, the recent return of psychedelics into mainstream culture has prompted the growth of new studies and sparked tensions over interpretation and theoretical approaches. However, contemporary attempts to debate psychedelic legitimacy based on utility, purpose, abuse potential, and scientific knowledge frequently mirror the dynamics of historical debates. And while different contexts may mean that approaches that failed in the past could succeed in the present, failing to understand the nuances of such a context risks replicating the failures. Problematically, such studies will not sufficiently explain the scope of psychedelic history if they fall prey to the narrow disciplinary silos that some critics describe as distinctively Western.[8]

If the first generation of psychedelic scholarship that occurred in the 1970s was deep but not necessarily broad, the proliferation of scholarship on the history of drugs and alcohol laid the foundation for a second wave of psychedelic history in both biomedicine and society that has begun expanding the domains it addresses, including dealing with an international context, questions of gender and sexuality, race, and the problem of criminalization.[9] At times, this new scholarship has an uneasy relationship with other areas of contemporary discourse, particularly insider accounts. Psychedelic knowledge and, critically, its legitimacy, is frequently framed by active participants with firsthand experiences. But, as in the case of David Solomon's writing and editing in the mid-1960s, public discourse on—and the historiography about—psychedelics has long been furnished by white male, insider accounts.

Belinda Eriacho, an Indigenous scholar and healer, argues that ignoring insider accounts can also undermine certain forms of evidence, including Indigenous knowledge. Eriacho reminds us of the tremendous value of personal experience as a form of argumentation. She also shows that many of the enthusiastic claims about the benefits of psychedelic drug use rely on severing the *current* culture of psychedelics from the *past*, from archivally based interpretations, and from theories that rely on a more holistic understanding of healing that moves beyond Western models. Often, the assertion is made that the current psychedelic renaissance is superior because the science (and the researchers) are more sophisticated. Unsurprisingly, perhaps, the desire to distance the current discourse from the past has put some historians at odds with a mounting literature on psychedelics that emphasizes personal testimonies claiming that today's approaches are inherently better, or that the activities of the past were inherently less sophisticated or ethical. But both tensions—these *historiographical wars*—between progressivist testimonials and archivally grounded critical analysis, as well as "good science" and "bad science," have roots in the past, and also tap into economic motivations that have guided interpretations of good and bad, or of the medical and the criminal.

In the 1950s and the first half of the 1960s, these tensions were less clear. Many researchers were relatively comfortable publicizing their budding work on psychedelics to popular audiences in a variety of formats, including personal testimonies. They believed they had a strong case to make about their psychedelic discoveries and applications, and they felt that the public would be both interested and excited by their findings. Indeed, their work was championed by a broad selection of periodicals that published stories about psychedelics, which ultimately attracted a popular audience. One of the US public's first introductions to psychedelics was in a 1957 article published in *Life*, America's biggest circulating magazine. Gordon Wasson, a vice president at J. P. Morgan bank, gave a long and fascinating account of his adventures seeking out the "divine mushroom." The article coincided nicely with the release of *Mushrooms, Russia, and History*, a massive two-volume study he had written with his wife, Valentina.[10] Other psychedelic accounts appeared in pulp magazines with breathless article titles like "I went INSANE for science!" (in the equally virile *Man's Magazine*, no less).[11] In 1964, Sidney Cohen, a prominent research psychiatrist, published *LSD: The Beyond Within*, a fairly serious but general-audience book on the science of LSD, where he discussed his self-experimentation.[12]

By the mid-1960s, though, openly championing psychedelics in popular media became far more contested. Access to LSD and other psychedelics had become increasingly difficult following passage of the Kefauver–Harris Amendments of 1962. The legislation increased strictures on using investigational new drugs (IND), making access difficult for scientists and enthusiasts alike.[13] An underground market developed in response, and scientists responded in different ways to what many interpreted as an impending threat to their research. In doing so, they widened existing fissures within the research community about what psychedelics were good for, as well as how to legitimate their use. Some investigators promoted their findings through the scientific community exclusively. Others broke ranks with their colleagues and continued to popularize the use of psychedelics for recreational purposes, without detailing the commercial aspect of psychedelic sales. Some of the scientists argued in favor of maintaining it strictly for research purposes, categorizing it as a medicine, subject to sales as a pharmaceutically regulated product. And some simply argued for both: psychedelics as a mainstream commercial product, not restricted to medicinal use nor left to the vagaries of a black market.[14]

War in the Clinic

Even prior to the formal declaration of a War on Drugs and passage of the CSA of 1970, psychedelic researchers in hospitals and laboratories struggled with public perceptions of their work. Scientists working in this area had to confront an increasingly fearful public and powerful interests (as other chapters in this collection have shown) who viewed mind-altering drugs as dangerous and lacking any redeeming qualities beyond their possible use in government-sponsored covert psy-warfare. And, in the absence of incontrovertible findings, biomedical actors in labs and clinics struggled to craft accounts of their research that might legitimate their interest in LSD and other psychedelics.

Some researchers certainly tried to meet this challenge. Researchers at the Spring Grove State Hospital, in Maryland, for example, embraced it. Home to influential psychedelic luminaries, including Stanislav Grof, Charles Savage, Sanford Unger, and others, Spring Grove staff developed a "Policy Statement Covering Conduct of Psychedelic Research within the Department of Medical Research at Spring Grove State Hospital." They circulated their statement within the psychedelic science community and beyond. It generated considerable debate, not least because it held that LSD therapists ought to have tried the drug themselves. Johns Hopkins Professor Emeritus of Psychiatry Dr. John Whitehorn blasted the statement: "In my judgment this represents a very bad mixture of 'public relations' aims and research aims." He continued, "I do not believe that it is necessary . . . that the doctors should take the drug, any more than it was necessary when studying the therapeutic value of electroshock to have the doctors given electroshock." Whitehorn also discouraged the "temptation to exploit the public interest" and any "desire to gain favorable publicity." Working to these ends, in his opinion, constituted "dangerous diversions" that might undermine the "scientific competence and integrity" of the research.[15] The idea that scientists and researchers have to take psychedelic medicines did not gain traction, and it further divided the research community, as well as wider society. Whitehorn felt that it was not important to "win over" the public or convince them of the drug's safety. Scientists, he insisted, should not be in the public-relations business.

Scientists and clinicians, such as Whitehorn and others, sometimes clashed over the question of the appropriate and valid use of psychedelics, thus further weakening the broader case for the continued use of the psychedelics in either a therapeutic or clinical setting. Some particularly controversial approaches to psychedelic therapy further weakened the legitimacy of the enterprise. Mexican-based Salvador Roquet was a lightning rod for criticism.[16] He combined psychoanalysis, psychotherapy and psychedelics in an effort to induce negative feelings in patients that he felt would help to confront past trauma and ultimately bring about a therapeutic breakthrough.[17] The idea that therapy could induce terror, or that patients were overly vulnerable to the suggestions of therapists in a state of altered consciousness, ran counter to the contemporary social and political discourse of civil rights, patient rights, and the changing power dynamics of the therapeutic relationship.[18] A great many therapists believed his approach was simply unethical and demonstrative of the abuses psychedelic therapy could produce. Some therapists also used LSD to "treat" the "pathology" of homosexuality, in hopes of transforming the patient's same-sex desires. This approach, too, raised a good deal of controversy, especially among more politically progressive therapists.[19]

Some therapists also pushed back against colleagues who advocated for psychedelic use beyond the confines of the clinic. Psychiatrist R. D. Laing, for instance, drew criticism for his extravagant public persona and expansive views. At once therapist and scientist, guru, mystic, and cultural critic, Laing was an easy target. According to Abram Hoffer, who, along with Humphry Osmond, was a pioneer of LSD testing in Saskatchewan, Laing represented scientific regression on the one hand and overreach on the other. This unfortunate combination, Hoffer believed, gravely threatened psychedelic research in mental medicine and might lead to criminalization. "Physicians are qualified to treat diseases," Hoffer wrote Ralph Metzner, another psychedelic pioneer, and "society expects us to use a medical model and to act as physicians. We have no special training, nor competence, nor license to deal with all of man's problems." He added that Laing ought to give up his medical license and admit he was a spiritual counselor, like a priest, and not a doctor or a scientist. "I object to a masquerade (game) in which my colleagues take every advantage of their MD and comport themselves like non-doctors."[20] Even among psychiatrists who saw value in psychedelic therapy, questions of legitimacy loomed large, divided colleagues along disciplinary or training lines, and ultimately exacerbated the professional turf wars. Such internal wars, even among credentialed psychedelic therapists, over questions of whether psychedelics best nurtured a philosophical desire for meaning or a pathological need for treatment, deepened the public and scientific debates over the legitimacy of psychedelic research and treatment. These often-angry debates pitted researchers against one another, further radicalizing and marginalizing the psychedelic science of the 1960s.

War with the Self

The variety of fears about and hopes for psychedelics in the 1960s were linked as much to scientific understandings of human nature and selfhood as they were to broader political decisions and commitments. Contrary to the assertions of many anti-drug crusaders and pro-LSD researchers anxious about its freewheeling use in the public sphere, most users did not take psychedelics for hedonic purposes. Instead, most users of psychedelics, as well as researchers and their patients, treated them as a "technology of the self." Notably, even as psychedelic use entered new and sometimes illicit domains, *how* and *why* users took psychedelics tended to hew closely to existing medical knowledge. The following section of this chapter will explore patient and practitioner perspectives to illustrate that psychedelic narratives were often far more personal.

By the time the FDA began confiscating researchers' supplies of LSD in 1962, which was many years prior to the formal declaration of a War on Drugs, scientists had already explored it as a possible adjunct to psychotherapy, a truth serum, a brainwashing drug, a creativity booster, a consciousness expander, a cure for alcohol addiction, and a drug that mimicked schizophrenia and psychosis. Even before 1953, the year that CIA Director Allen Dulles advocated for a new era of "brain warfare," researchers had already identified psychedelics as a promising aid for people in the throes of addiction.[21]

Word of this promise got out to the public through friends who had tried it and through news articles, and interviews.[22] In 1969, a young woman named Alice Smith wrote the Spring Grove State Hospital in

Maryland to ask about psychedelic treatment. She explained, "I don't really understand too much about alcoholism," but "I have been in trouble
several times + each time I have been dead drunk." Not wanting to commit herself to a mental hospital, she added, "I want to do something
to help myself with this problem . . . nor am I trying to use you to get
myself out of anything."[23] So, too, James Sinclair of Berkeley, California,
who also wrote to Spring Grove to ask about enrolling himself in psychedelic therapy to help deal with "personal problems." Having read up
on LSD psychotherapy, he was intrigued by the possibility that a mix of
psychoanalysis and existentialism might help him battle alcohol.[24] Elsewhere, Bill Wilson, the founder of Alcoholics Anonymous, tried LSD
under the watchful eyes of Gerald Heard, who frequently functioned as
a trip sitter and research assistant to Sidney Cohen. Wilson was so convinced of his LSD trip's similarity to the born-again experience that had
originally led him to stop drinking that he considered introducing LSD
to AA, although it never came to pass.[25]

Numerous mental health professionals, patients, and members of the
public saw psychedelics as a useful adjunct to therapy, more generally.
By 1962, Dr. Oscar Janiger alone had administered LSD to upwards of a
thousand patients for reasons as varied as a desire to lose weight, sexual
frigidity, spiritual enlightenment, or because their therapist had recommended it. One patient wrote on his intake form that he wanted LSD so
that he could learn how "to cry," something he'd never been able to do.
The majority of Janiger's patients after 1958 indicated that they had previously heard about LSD through friends, the writings of Aldous Huxley,
or through public lectures and magazine articles, suggesting that public
knowledge of LSD was already fairly robust.[26] Actor Cary Grant gave an
interview to the writer in early 1959 and declared that "for the first time
in my life I am truly, deeply and honestly happy." Soon, Hyams's phone
started ringing off the hook with friends wanting to know where to get
LSD and doctors complaining to him about their own deluge of subsequent patient requests. "Every actor in town under analysis wanted it,"
Hyams told Bob Gaines, bemused. "In all," he noted, "I got close to eight
hundred letters."[27]

Janiger's approach is described at length in Thelma Moss' pseudon-
ymous memoir *Myself and I*, in which she describes her time in LSD
therapy with him.[28] While his therapeutic sessions took place in a

naturalistic setting where the patient took the lead, his was certainly not the only method used by psychiatrists who prescribed LSD, any more than we have a singular approach to therapy today. Despite broad agreement within the psychiatric community by the early 1960s that LSD was a useful therapeutic tool, doctors disagreed about precisely how to use it with their patients. Their debates were largely rooted in professional disagreements about the nature of the self, approaches to therapy, and the purpose of therapy, more broadly.

The divergences between Oscar Janiger and Sidney Cohen were instructive of the ways that scientific theories of mind, biology, and "self" had become hopelessly entangled with both the therapeutic relationship and political commitments. Both Janiger and Cohen worked in Los Angeles and knew one another. They were on friendly terms: Janiger even occasionally enlisted the aid of Cohen's graduate students in collecting data for his LSD research.[29] Still, people who were part of the relatively small LSD community of the time understand how differently the two men approached the use of the drug. For example, the eminent writer Aldous Huxley, mentioned above, considered collaborating with Janiger on a book project on psychedelics but believed that Janiger used "the stuff badly" and told Sidney Cohen that he disapproved of the doctor.[30] Huxley, unlike Janiger, believed that LSD was really only appropriately used by those he considered intellectual elites. He hoped intellectuals could use LSD not only to enhance their own gifts but also to envision a more spiritual, cooperative, and unified social order. Huxley laid out such a psychedelic utopia in his last novel, *Island*.[31] While Sidney Cohen did not direct his research toward the utopian, he did think, like Huxley, that Oscar Janiger was much too cavalier in the way he prescribed LSD.

Both Cohen and Huxley wanted only a chosen few to take psychedelics. Janiger prescribed LSD to a multitude of subjects. By enlisting the help of several local psychologists who were not themselves able to prescribe psychedelics, Janiger administered LSD to both his own psychologist-patients and to their patients as part of his massive research program. But while Cohen and Janiger occasionally swapped research subjects, Cohen was much less convinced of the average patient's ability to handle the psychedelic experience meaningfully or even safely. After Cohen's initial enthusiasm for psychedelic therapy wore off in 1959, he spent the next decade trying to make the case that

PSYCHEDELIC WARS | 197

psychedelics had little significant use value, good *or* bad, for "normals" (as he put it) that couldn't be attributed to the skillful abilities of their therapist.[32] Even worse, the experience could endanger particularly troubled patients or patients without adequate therapeutic oversight.[33] More to Huxley's taste, Cohen believed that patients he considered intellectually exceptional—painters, artists, politicians, writers, doctors, and scholars—*did* tend to make good candidates for the treatment.

This fundamental difference informed how the two psychiatrists approached therapy with patients, more generally, and in terms of their LSD research, specifically. LSD experiments that Cohen performed with "normals" were done in the Veterans Administration hospital where he worked. He had a nurse or graduate student assistant ask the subjects a predefined list of questions during the LSD experience. For his special patients, though, he would trip-sit personally, often with his friends and unofficial lab assistants, Gerald Heard and Michael Barrie. These trips were self-directed by the patient. His favorite patient was the famous playwright, conservative journalist, and former ambassador Clare Boothe Luce. Her LSD therapy usually took place where she was available, whether in her homes in Hawaii, New York, or Arizona, or at her California friends' estates.[34] Janiger, in contrast, treated *all* his patients to a naturalistic setting and largely allowed them to lead the course of their treatment, including allowing them to bring their own trip sitter, if desired.

Despite Janiger's belief in the average person's ability to solve their own problems with only modest intervention from a therapist, he was not a radical egalitarian. Like Cohen, he also had a special place for "exceptional" patients, many of whom he would take to his cottage in the mountains near Lake Arrowhead, California when it was time for their experiments. And, like Cohen, these patients were often artists, writers, doctors, philosophers, scholars, and the like. The key for both Cohen and Janiger—and, for that matter, Huxley—was that they believed exceptional people had a gift for *creativity* and this gift could be enhanced by LSD.[35] In this respect, they fit squarely within contemporary scholarly debates about selfhood, particularly about what type of self was necessary to be a full-fledged, productive democratic citizen. American Studies scholar Jamie Cohen-Cole has written at length about how left-leaning scholars sought during Cold War to identify the communist and fascist-accepting "totalitarian personality." In doing so, they posited an idealized, Western democratic citizen as its opposite and began work on pinpointing what was distinctive about this classical liberal subject. Creativity quickly became seen as the fundamental faculty that underpinned both the open-mindedness that was permissive of difference while also allowing for intellectual independence and the ability to self-fashion as an individual.[36]

Although post–Second World War intellectuals in the US shared a belief that creativity and individuality were vital to the future of the democratic citizen, they disagreed on what creativity even was, much less how to operationalize it for research purposes or how to foster it. Cohen, Huxley, and Janiger were no different. Having outwardly similar interests in LSD as a possible creativity booster wasn't the same as being able to prove that it could deliver such a result. Nor did it weigh in on the questions of who was capable of being creative; whether LSD might be good for other types of therapy; and what kind of therapist could get the most out of their patient.

Herman Denber captured some of these technical difficulties in an early letter to Cohen as they organized a conference together in 1959. He asked: "Is LSD therapy (or mescaline or any similar drug) really of value? Many of us say 'yes,' but somehow we lack specific analytic data to show that the result was not due to the therapist, chance, state of the moon, etc." He continued: How does the drug even produce its results? Can we control the studies? Do we need a special therapeutic procedure or just any of them? Do we even have follow-up studies at this point?[37]

Such technical debates among LSD practitioners were haunted not only by the question of what kind of person psychedelics could make you, but also how that making was achieved. Alone? With a scientist? A friend? They were also haunted by the question of who could achieve it. And so, while some researchers studying creativity, such as the eminent University of California psychology professor Frank Barron, decided to pursue their research programs into using LSD as a technology of self-improvement openly at personal growth centers like the Esalen Institute, others like Cohen decided to work within the system to legitimize LSD scientifically. Their carefully prescriptive and limited approach could put them publicly at odds with less conservative colleagues who believed psychedelic selfhood could and should be attainable by anyone. But even the sense that scientists' legitimacy was tied to their ability to be "discreet" or "dispassionate" or, as Eriacho has noted, that understanding demands isolating entities rather than treating them holistically, are normative claims with political ramifications. Science, it turns out, is never value-free.

Wars: Cold, Hot, and the Homefront

The US witnessed several wars on the home front in the mid-1960s. One of those—which of course operated in tandem with the Vietnam War—centered on the interpretation of *recreational* LSD. What were the effects? Who were the users? What did they believe? As a result of biomedical researchers' failure to make a compelling case for the legitimate use of psychedelics, in 1970, powerful anti-drug advocates lumped psychedelics in with other controversial and nonmedical substances and made them Schedule I drugs. One of these advocates, among many, was the leading Republican senator from Kansas, Robert J. Dole. His constituents fostered his enmity toward drug use, as his office mail reveals.

On December 3, 1969, Jonathan Reid of Manhattan, Kansas wrote Senator Dole about America's growing drug problem. "Drugs—LSD, Marijuana—are becoming more common each day," he began. "I recently heard of a high school student very near to my home town" who ran into "a nearby cemetery and slit his wrists. He was under the influence of a drug, possibly LSD." Reid added that the American drug problem was "developing to such proportions that an agency should be set up" to mitigate the hazards to the country and its citizens. "Appealing young people" were needed to communicate the dangers of LSD, marijuana, and other substances. Reid generously volunteered himself. Senator Dole responded eight days later, writing on December 11 that there was "little doubt that if we do not take prompt and appropriate action to halt the traffic of dangerous drugs, our health and crime problems will continue to grow."[38] Such sentiments were a winning political move in Kansas and throughout most of the US.

Senator Dole held particularly strong opinions about psychedelics, which were, for him, a broad category. In late November 1969, he wrote to Miss Barbara Nesmith, a high school newspaper reporter looking for quotes. Smoking pot had become the "in" thing, according to Dole, and most young people who tried cannabis were "really not 'criminals.'" Still, he continued, marijuana was a "hallucinogen, like LSD," since any "substance which produces distortions of time or space must be considered somewhat dangerous." Altering one's consciousness, he insisted, was to be avoided. He added that it was important to impose "lighter penalties for less serious crimes," whereas "the penalties for using LSD ought to be stiffer than those for marijuana use."[39] Bob Dole's letter to Miss Nesmith reflected his strong anti-drug sentiments and widespread notions about the growing ubiquity and harmful nature of various drugs.[40] Psychedelics, by this time, were generating broad public fears about "birth defects, brain damage and psychotic episodes," not to mention being linked to chromosomal damage and blindness caused by staring too long into the sun.[41] For a politician such as Dole, being against LSD was a no-brainer. To this political end, Senator Dole participated in the crafting of the CSA, which in 1970 placed LSD in Schedule I. A core feature of the subsequent American War on Drugs, the CSA institutionalized for many the perceived dangers of mind-altering substances.

In contrast to Senator Dole's poorly informed views on psychedelics, users themselves were often pragmatic about determining safety and risk. A 1967 university dissertation by Carol Chertkow, a graduate student in the Faculty of Medicine at the University of British Columbia, aptly captured users' underground knowledge about psychedelics, including their concerns about the drugs' inherent dangers.[42] She conducted a psychological and ethnographic study of drug use in Vancouver, Canada, a top psychedelic destination in North America, and one of the top Canadian destinations for American draft dodgers.[43] An estimated 35,000 Americans entered Canada between 1965 and 1975, which in part represented a reaction to the military draft but also tapped into a broader rejection of American values. In a master's thesis conducted by Aisling Murphy, who interviewed people who were part of this migration, their "decisions to leave the United States were in fact expressions of a deep disaffection with American society more broadly informed by their participation in the democratic struggles for change such as the civil rights movement, the New Left, and the counterculture that defined this period in American history."[44] Murphy's study shows that while many such resisters came north from California into British Columbia, their assumptions about Canada providing a more liberal culture were often naïve. Despite the realities of geo-political cultures in the Pacific Northwest, authorities continued to blame this rejection of values on psychedelic drugs. Carol Chertkow confronted the claim made by political figures such as Senator Dole that psychedelics caused users to reject mainstream authority, or incited antiauthoritarian attitudes altogether. Chertkow thus serves as a useful counterpoint to mainstream political views.

Chertkow found that "a recurrent theme among subjects in both groups [control and experimental] was the characterization of the student-user as a person who is dissatisfied with society and/or himself, and as one who is searching for something to believe in."[45] Of the students interviewed, a majority reported "that the LSD experience had changed them in some way."[46] She concluded that:

These people are responding in a particular way to the dissatisfaction and aimlessness which young people in general are feeling. They are not unique nor are they as different as they might think in asserting their independence as individuals. Their way of acting out in frustration is to turn inwards, if only for a time. The personal value or danger of this essentially introverted response to problems remains to be seen.[47]

Here, Chertkow seemed to suggest that the global pressures of the Cold War, the War in Vietnam, and civil rights struggles necessitated an uneasy response by informed people; or at the very least she was sympathetic to these perspectives. Chertkow's work indicated that she thought it was appropriate to question mainstream values, and LSD was not merely a recreational form of escape even as it was also not the *cause* of such questioning.[48] Her claims at the time also suggest that the war on psychedelics was as much a denial by political authorities and other "establishment" elites of the deeper underlying reasons behind many young people's dissident attitudes. Blaming LSD for young people's cultural and political rebellion fit neatly into these elites' claim that society's biggest challenge was irresponsible youth and their chemically altered brains, and not an expensive and unending war in Vietnam or endemic sexism, racism, and colonialism.[49]

In addition to confronting the implications of altered values, Chertkow also addressed the concern that illicit drug use led to more illicit drug use, riskier behavior, crime, and general deviancy. Combining ethnographic research, by living with "hippys" (sic) and interviewing forty-eight people aged twenty-four to forty-eight about their drug use, Chertkow tackled this issue head on. She found that contrary to assumptions, most LSD users demonstrated caution when it came to experimenting with other drugs (especially heroin, speed, methamphetamines), and most participants did not consider LSD to be dangerous (except for "freaking out," which they believed they could control).[50] Overall, Chertkow's work challenged the idea that psychedelic drug users were irresponsible risk takers, or that they took drugs that inspired them to question conventional values. Most users, including those in the control group, agreed that there were many reasons to question political values and that taking drugs did not inspire these critical views in the first place. Despite her findings, this knowledge base was discounted by authorities, including her supervisor, James Tyhurst, who was directly involved in helping to craft the Canadian response to psychedelic drug regulation. Chertkow was not alone, however. Other investigators, including those tapped by government officials who paid closer attention to users themselves, were also ignored.[51] She had no more success in shifting the public debate than did those researchers who made scientific claims in support of psychedelic drug use. Politicians like Senator Bob Dole, informed by sensationalist accounts from their constituents and their own gut feelings, were confident that drug users were too foolish to understand their own experiences. They needed protection from themselves. Empirical studies of users' attitudes were not decisive in shaping political beliefs in the 1960s.

"Beginning, Not the End"

In 1985, as crack cocaine was exploding into the public's consciousness, the noted LSD researcher Sidney Cohen wrote a short article directed to his fellow drug researchers. He contended that "history repeats itself, but nowadays it repeats incessantly."[52] He was not actually referring to either crack or LSD. Instead, he was discussing MDMA (known also as ecstasy or molly). He wrote, "one does not have to wait a century to witness a mindless repetition of what should been learned from past events. It seems we are so present-oriented that the errors of the past are ignored and must be reduplicated every decade or so." The struggle over the legitimate use of mind-altering drugs such as MDMA, he felt, would continue, often without benefit of serious research. As he sought to tamp down speculation and enthusiasm over MDMA in therapeutic settings, he cautioned his readers that LSD trips marked the "beginning, not the end, of a search for sustaining change." "The hard work of restructuring psychedelic research still had to be done," he concluded.[53] Cohen may have been correct, that it was not so much the drugs that changed, but the structures and narrators who gave meaning and value to public discourse about drugs.

In September 2019, the first US Center for Psychedelic and Consciousness Research was established at Johns Hopkins University. The Center was made possible by a $17 million donation from author and entrepreneur Tim Ferriss and others. Its establishment represented a major inflection point in the debate over the social legitimacy of psychedelic research. And the Center was a powerful institutional reminder that in the twenty-first century a psychedelic renaissance is in full swing, endorsed by a range of influential figures and wealthy benefactors. Along with the slow decriminalization of psilocybin mushrooms at the state level, the influx of interest and resources into psychedelic research is one more indicator of a growing, society-wide change in perspective on the War on Drugs.[54] Psychedelics, like many of the substances examined in this volume, have a complicated past and a fraught relationship with criminalization and punitive regulation. But we suggest that no other substance in the War on Drugs has been loaded with as many meanings as LSD. Psychedelic advocates today include those who hold libertarian views, suggesting that all drugs should be legalized. Others are evangelists, essentially psychedelic proselytizers who argue, as many did in the 1960s, that LSD and psilocybin could change minds and the world. Others still have more pragmatic perspectives, holding that such drugs should only be prescribed in medically sanctioned therapy sessions, or for end-of-life use, post-traumatic stress syndrome (PTSD), or a host of other medical issues.[55] A final group hope to capitalize—make money—on a new group of medicines. Together, these advocates are helping reorient perceptions and spark acceptance of psychedelics, which may pave the way for the legal reintroduction of psychedelics into American society.

The history of psychedelic science and its drug regulation constitutes an important chapter in the War on Drugs. Unlike cocaine or marijuana, psychedelics have acted as visible and viable therapeutic tools in the immediate run-up to the CSA in 1970 and were even studied closely in the years immediately after its passage. The psychedelic experience itself became an object of study, imbued with ideological significance and therapeutic meaning, though the objects of that study have more consistently focused on determining the right kind of subjects or consumers, rather than incorporating a more diverse set of experiences in order to diversify psychedelic science itself. Contests—psychedelic wars—over how best to interpret this meaning, or who best to articulate it, and who still should benefit from it, have long animated debates over who best embodies psychedelic authority.

It is the same as we write this. The present moment is witnessing a new set of testimonials, attempting to recalibrate the social capital of psychedelic experience in a continuing war over psychedelic authority. Just as in the past, Americans are seeking to unpack how LSD may function as a product of medicine, a recreational substance, a tool of religion, and a commodity. The field of mental medicine and the Food and Drug Administration seem more receptive to the potential efficacy of psychedelic medicines. And like David Solomon in the mid-1960s and after, we are seeing various interpreters of psychedelics in the present. In 2018, journalist and best-selling author Michael Pollan entered the conversation when he published *How to Change Your Mind* and introduced readers to his own psychedelic trips.[56] This testimonial-style intervention has shaped contemporary discourse on psychedelics, and found its place among an increasing trend of high-profile confessions or explorations, including those from Tim Ferriss, Gwyneth Paltrow, among others, and a host of Silicon Valley-based innovators who opened discussions about psychedelic microdosing as a precursor to innovation. Just as in the past, when psychedelic stories featured in major periodicals, so it is that the *New Yorker*, the *Atlantic*, and other magazines are closely reporting the revival of psychedelics. That these testimonials often come with repudiations of the past (and its failures) is particularly ironic, given that Silicon Valley is a direct heir of the counterculture being disowned.[57] As in the past, the face of the psychedelic renaissance is typically white and privileged. Top-tier institutions are getting involved, from Johns Hopkins to Berkeley. And, despite concerns about psychedelic tourism outside of the US that has caused environmental and cultural destruction disproportionately affecting people of color, the psychedelic character in mainstream discourse remains white.[58]

In the current wave of psychedelic literature, and as the basic legal architecture of the War on Drugs remains in place, the narratives about the psychedelic past have often been designed to distance the contemporary neuroscientific pursuit of psychedelics from its troubled past; yet these narratives have sometimes continued to reinforce a desire to separate psychedelics from a longer tradition of plant-based healing, Indigenous ways of knowing, and relatedly, colonial trauma. Historical interpretation—and the complexity of psychedelic wars—is in some cases tokenized to demonstrate that today's researchers have a better grasp of the ethical or methodological landscape, or connect with a noble or sacred set of traditions, rather than taking seriously the claims of the past, or working directly with scholars to interpret and contextualize historical cultures. Much of the non-historical and often non-academic literature is being generated within the field of biomedicine and neuroscience, but there are a growing number of popular accounts or first-hand narratives that are also shaping the discourse on twenty-first century psychedelics. Whether or not historians agree that the contemporary resurrection of psychedelics is better informed by science or not, or whether it has genuinely become a more diverse intellectual space, the commercial potential for psychedelics has new champions who have sought out alliances with clinical researchers who once more are confronting the value of psychedelics in modern society.

NOTES

1 David Solomon, letter, July 10, 1965, David Solomon Papers, MSP 92, Box 1, Folder 1, Psychoactive Substances Collection, Archives and Special Collections, Purdue University.

2 David Solomon, letter, July 10, 1965. One can infer from Solomon's correspondence that he believed psychedelics held mind-expanding powers that served countercultural purposes and were also viable in clinical settings. See also "David Solomon, Jazz Critic, Drug Guru, 81," *AM New York Metro*, August 7, 2007, www.amny.com.

3 Psychedelics, including LSD, stood apart from other substances in this way. Cocaine, cannabis, and opiates/opioids, for instance, did not embody these multiple meanings.

4 Nancy Campbell, interview by Rafaela Zorzanelli, "Drug Trajectories: Interviews with Researchers," *Pharmacy in History* 62, nos. 1–2 (2020): 49–51.

5   STS scholar Claudia Schwarz-Plaschg refers to "socio-psychedelic imaginaries" in her recent work. See Schwarz-Plaschg, "The Power of Analogies for Imagining and Governing Emerging Technologies," *Nanoethics* 12, no. 2 (2018): 1139–53. In the 2020 election, two more jurisdictions (Oregon and DC) decriminalized psilocybin. See also Ido Hartogsohn's *American Trips: Set, Setting, and the Psychedelic Experience in the Twentieth Century* (Cambridge: MIT Press, 2020), which references the multiple meanings of psychedelics.

6   See Erika Dyck, *Psychedelic Psychiatry: LSD from Clinic to Campus* (Baltimore: Johns Hopkins University Press, 2008) and Matthew Oram, *The Trials of Psychedelic Therapy: LSD Psychotherapy in America* (Baltimore: Johns Hopkins University Press, 2018) for a fuller understanding of this debate about biomedical and socio-cultural perspectives in influencing psychedelic criminalization. Oram built on and challenged Dyck's contentions about social unrest and the end of psychedelic research in the US. This chapter adds to that discussion.

7   The first wave of sustained historical accounts of psychedelics emerged in the mid-1970s, just when a mind-blowing report on CIA misadventures by the US Senate's Church Committee was made public. Among other things, the report revealed a long history of Agency experimentation with LSD that had begun in the 1940s. Author John Marks's exposé of CIA-funded mind control experiments and the work of other writers at that time thus tended to focus on LSD as a substance tailor-made for government abuse. In 1985, journalists Martin Lee and Bruce Shlain, in *Acid Dreams: The Complete Social History of LSD; The CIA, the Sixties, and Beyond* (New York: Grove Press, 1985), took this story one step further, linking CIA objectives with a strategic undermining of countercultural activities, loosely tied together by suppositions about LSD consumption. Jay Steven's *Storming Heaven: LSD and the American Dream* (New York: Grove Press, 1987) dug deeper into the counterculture scene, portraying the antics of LSD avatar Timothy Leary sympathetically against the backdrop of the psychedelic sixties and a generational search for meaning. John Marks, *Search for the Manchurian Candidate: The CIA and Mind Control* (New York: Times Books, 1978). See also Stephen Kinzer, *Poisoner in Chief: Sidney Gottlieb and the CIA Search for Mind Control* (New York: Henry Holt, 2019) for a new history of the CIA and its psychedelic experimentation.

8   Belinda Eriacho, "Considerations for Psychedelic Therapists When Working with Native American People and Communities," *Journal of Psychedelic Studies* 4, no. 1 (2020): 69–71

9   Erika Dyck, *Psychedelic Psychiatry: LSD from Clinic to Campus* (Baltimore: Johns Hopkins University Press, 2008); Nicolas Langlitz, *Neuropsychedelia: The Revival of Hallucinogen Research since the Decade of the Brain* (Oakland: California Press, 2012); Stephen Siff, *Acid Hype: American News Media and the Psychedelic Experience* (Champaign: University of Illinois Press, 2015); William Richards, *Sacred Knowledge: Psychedelics and Religious Experiences* (New York: Columbia University Press, 2016); Donald Osto, *Altered States: Buddhism and Psychedelic*

Spirituality in America (New York: Columbia University Press, 2016); Patrick Barber, *Psychedelic Revolutionaries: Three Medical Pioneers, the Fall of Hallucinogenic Research and the Rise of Big Pharma* (London: Zed Books, 2019); Alexander Dawson, *The Peyote Effect: From the Inquisition to the War on Drugs* (Oakland: University of California Press, 2018); Mike Jay, *Mescaline: A Global History of the First Psychedelic* (New Haven, CT: Yale University Press, 2019); Oram, *The Trials of Psychedelic Therapy*. Most recently, see Hartogsohn, *American Trip*; Sarah Shortall, "Psychedelic Drugs and the Problem of Experience," *Past & Present* 222, no. 9 (2014): 187–206. Petter Grahl Johnstad, "A Dangerous Method? Psychedelic Therapy at Modum Bad, Norway, 1961–76," *History of Psychiatry* 31, no. 2 (2020): 217–26; Sarah Marks, "Psychotherapy in Europe," *History of the Human Sciences* 31, no. 4 (2018): 3–12; Sarah Marks, "From Experimental Psychosis to Resolving Traumatic Pasts: Psychedelic Research in Communist Czechoslovakia, 1954–1974," *Cahiers du Monde Russe* 56, no. 1 (2015): 50–75; Stephen Snelders and Charles Kaplan, "LSD Therapy in Dutch Psychiatry: Changing Socio-Political Settings and Medical Sets," *Medical History* 46 (2002): 221–40.

10 R. Gordon Wasson, "Seeking the Divine Mushroom," *Life* (1957); R. Gordon Wasson to Philip Wooton Jr., March 7, 1957. Series IV, folder 120. Tina and R. Gordon Wasson Ethnomycological Collection Archives, 1798–1999, bulk 1945–1986, ecb00001, Archives of the Economic Botany Herbarium of Oakes Ames, Harvard University. See also Monnica Williams, Amy Bartlett, Tim Michaels, Jae Sevelius, and Jamilah George, "Dr. Valentina Wasson: Questioning What We Think We Know about the Foundations of Psychedelic Science," *Journal of Psychedelic Studies* 4, no. 3 (2020): 146–48, https://doi.org/10.1556/2054.2020.00140.

11 Dr. Robert H_____, "I Went Insane for Science," *Man's Magazine* 4, no. 7 (August 1956). The photos in the article are of LSD researcher Dr. Carl Pfeiffer.

12 Sidney Cohen, *LSD: The Beyond Within* (New York: Atheneum, 1965).

13 See Oram, *The Trials of Psychedelic Therapy*.

14 These perspectives are borne out in the literature on psychedelic history, and some historical actors shift their views over time, from support for psychedelics as pharmaceuticals to withdrawing support altogether, for example. See examples of these debates in Erika Dyck, "Just Say Know: Criminalising LSD and the Politics of Psychedelic Experience," in *The Real Dope: Historical and Legal Perspectives on the Regulation of Drugs in Canada*, ed. Edgar-Andre Montigny (Toronto: University of Toronto Press, 2011), 169–96.

15 John C. Whitehorn letter, September 4, 1965, MSP 70, Box 10, Folder 1, Charles Savage Papers, Psychoactive Substances Collection, Archives and Special Collections, Purdue University.

16 Alexander S. Dawson "Salvador Roquet, Maria Sabina, and the Trouble with *Jipis*," *Hispanic American Historical Review* 95, no. 1 (2015): 103–33.

17 Erika Dyck and Christian Elcock, "Reframing Bummer Trips: Scientific and Cultural Explanations to Adverse Reactions to Psychedelic Drug Use," *Social History of Alcohol and Drugs* 34, no. 2 (2020), https://doi.org/10.1086/707512.

208 | RICHERT, DYCK, AND TURNER

18 Nancy Tomes, "The Patient as a Policy Factor: A Historical Case Study of the Consumer/Survivor Movement in Mental Health," *Health Affairs* 25, no. 3 (2006): 720–29; David Rothman, *Strangers at the Bedside: A History of How Law and Bioethics Transformed Medical Decision Making* (New York: Basic Books, 1991).

19 Danielle Giffort, *The Psychedelic Renaissance and the Quest for Medical Legitimacy* (Minneapolis: University of Minnesota Press, 2020), 53, 78–79. See also Andrea Ens, "'Wish I Would be Normal': LSD and Homosexuality at Hollywood Hospital, 1955–1973" (MA thesis, University of Saskatchewan, 2019); Lucas Richert, *Break On Through: Radical Psychiatry and the American Counterculture* (Cambridge, MA: MIT Press, 2019): 95–96.

20 Abram Hoffer to Ralph Metzner, January 9, 1967, MSP 88, Folder 1, Hoffer correspondence, Psychoactive Substances Collection, Archives and Special Collections, Purdue University. See Richert, *Break On Through*, 124.

21 Kinzer, *Poisoner in Chief*, 70–71. G. Benedetti, "Beispiel einer strukturanalytischen und pharmakodynamischen Untersuchung an einem Fall von Alklholalluzinose, Charakterneurose und psychoreaktiver Halluzinose," *Zeitschrift fur Psychotherapie und Medizinische Psychologie* 1, no. 5 (1951): 177.

22 See, for instance, Joe Hyams, "How a New Shock Drug Unlocks Troubled Minds: LSD 'Explodes' Your Personality," *Los Angeles Times*, November 8, 1959.

23 Alice Smith to Spring Grove Hospital, April 23, 1969, Box 2, Folder 8, Charles Savage Papers MSP 70, Psychoactive Substances Collection, Archives and Special Collections, Purdue University. Spelling is exact. Names have been changed.

24 James Sinclair to Spring Grove Hospital, August 26, 1969, Box 2, Folder 8, Charles Savage Papers MSP 70, Psychoactive Substances Collection, Archives and Special Collections, Purdue University. Names have been changed.

25 See correspondence referring to Wilson, in Cynthia Carson Bisbee, Paul Bisbee, Erika Dyck, Patrick Farrell, James Sexton, and James W. Spisak, eds., *Psychedelic Prophets: The Letters of Aldous Huxley and Humphry Osmond* (Montreal: McGill-Queens University Press, 2018), 178, 381, 419.

26 Reasons for participating in the study, as well as existing knowledge of psychedelics and how patients were referred to the study appears on subject intake forms called "face sheets." Courtesy of the Estate of Oscar Janiger.

27 Cary Grant, quoted in Joe Hyams, "What Psychiatry Has Done for Cary Grant," *New York Herald Tribune*, April 20, 1959; Hyams quoted in Bob Gaines, "LSD: Hollywood's Status-Symbol Drug," *Cosmopolitan* 155, no. 5 (November 1963): 78–81.

28 Thelma Moss [Constance A. Newland], *My Self and I* (New York, Coward McCann, 1962).

29 See, for instance, Oscar Janiger's subject file for D. Lawrence, whose LSD session was overseen at UCLA by graduate student Len Korot. Estate of Oscar Janiger.

30 Aldous Huxley to Humphry Osmond, November 29, 1959, Box 5, Folder 2, Grover Smith Collection of Aldous Huxley Correspondence 1908–65, MS462, Woodson Research Center, Fondren Library, Rice University.

31 This image is most clearly laid out in his final novel, *Island*, where the drug "moksha" is a stand-in for psychedelics. Aldous Huxley, *Island: A Novel* (New York: Harper, 1962).

32 *Normals* was a technical term. It is roughly equivalent to what we mean today when we use the term "average." It could be applied to both people's mental health and their intellectual abilities.

33 William McGlothlin, Sidney Cohen, and Marcella McGlothlin, "Long Lasting Effects of LSD on Normals," *Archives of General Psychiatry* 17, no. 5 (November 1967): 521–32; Cohen, *The Beyond Within*.

34 This arrangement is laid out most clearly in a letter from Father John Murray to Sidney Cohen, November 20, 1960, Box 58, Folder 4, Sidney Cohen Collection (Collection 1845), University of California, Los Angeles Library Special Collections.

35 Janiger never published on creativity in his lifetime, although his research notes are filled with aborted attempts to tackle the question from the very beginning of his LSD work. A posthumous volume based on his data was published, but he and his co-author had intellectual disagreements about what conclusions to draw from the data. It's unclear to what extent the final product reflects his analysis rather than hers. See Marlene Dobkin de Rios and Oscar Janiger, *LSD, Spirituality, and the Creative Process* (Rochester, VT: Park Street Press, 2003).

36 Jamie Cohen-Cole, *The Open Mind: Cold War Politics and the Sciences of Human Nature* (Chicago: University of Chicago Press, 2014).

37 Herman Denber to Sidney Cohen, June 27, 1959, Box 55, Folder 2, Sidney Cohen Collection (Collection 1845), University of California, Los Angeles Library Special Collections.

38 "Correspondence," Robert J. Dole Senate Papers–Constituent Relations, 1969–96, Series 6, Box 196, Folder 13: Legislation—Drugs, 1969, Robert J. Dole Archive and Special Collections, University of Kansas, Lawrence. The names have been changed to protect identities.

39 "Correspondence with high school student," Robert J. Dole Senate Papers—Constituent Relations, 1969–96, Series 6, Box 196, Folder 13: Legislation—Drugs, 1969, Robert J. Dole Archives.

40 According to Jennifer Robison, "Decades of Drug Use: Data From the '60s and '70s," Gallup, July 2, 2002. In her view, "surveys show that drug abuse was comparably rare, as was accurate information about the effects of illegal drugs. One 1969 Gallup poll reported that 84 percent were opposed to legalization of marijuana and 88 percent had not tried pot. See "Illegal Drugs," Gallup, accessed March 21, 2021, www.news.gallup.com.

41 Richard Ashley, "The Other Side of LSD," *New York Times*, October 19, 1975, www.nytimes.com.

42 Carol Chertkow, "LSD in Vancouver: A Study of Users" (PhD diss., University of British Columbia, 1968), 13. The survey was conducted in 1967, and submitted as a thesis in 1968. Chertkow's supervisor for the topic was J. S. Tyhurst, head of psychiatry at the Faculty of Medicine at UCB, and outspoken critic of psychedelic

drug use, including medical experimentation. Although Tyhurst's influence was not explicit in this study, Chertkow embarked on an interview-based study testing the claims that psychedelic drug users were disproportionately drawn to antiestablishment and antiauthoritarian ideas.

43 Aisling Murphy, "Journeys to the 'North Country Fair': Exploring the American Vietnam War Migration to Vancouver" (MA thesis, Simon Fraser University, 2001).

44 Murphy, "Journeys to the 'North Country Fair,'" 2.

45 Chertkow, "LSD in Vancouver," 29.

46 Chertkow, "LSD in Vancouver," 25.

47 Chertkow, "LSD in Vancouver," 55.

48 See more on this topic in Andrea Tone, *The Age of Anxiety: A History of America's Turbulent Affair with Tranquilizers* (New York: New York University Press, 2008).

49 Henry John, "American Exiles beyond the Politics of the Draft: Nudity, Feminism, and Third World Decolonization in Vancouver, 1968–71," *BC Studies* 133, no. 205 (2020): 33–56.

50 Chertkow, "LSD in Vancouver," 32. When asked directly about suicides, the participants in her study denied that LSD or mescaline caused suicides but admitted that people already planning to commit suicide may not be dissuaded from that objective by taking psychedelics. As for side effects, users did not report any side effects. Chertkow prompted them by asking about acid flashes (later described as "flashbacks"), to which a minority (4/48) reported that they had experienced un-triggered hallucinations but felt that they were too pleasant to be categorized as acid flashes, which had a negative connotation.

51 See Gerald LeDain, chairman, *Commission of Inquiry into the Non-Medical Use of Drugs: Final Report* (Ottawa: Queen's Printer, 1973); for a more in-depth examination of how Canadian police forces were directed to investigate drug use in support of the LeDain Commission, see Marcel Martel, "'They Smell Bad, Have Diseases, and Are Lazy': RCMP Officers Reporting on Hippies in the Late Sixties," *Canadian Historical Review* (2009) 90(2), 215–45. A similar situation is true in the US; see Shafer Commission, National Commission on Marihuana and Drug Abuse, *The Report of the National Commission on Marihuana and Drug Abuse; Marihuana: A Signal of Misunderstanding* (1972), Schaffer Library of Drug Policy, accessed March 21, 2021, www.druglibrary.org.

52 Sidney Cohen, "They Call It Ecstacy [*sic*]," *Drug Abuse & Alcoholism Newsletter* 19, no. 6 (September 1985): 1, https://maps.org. See also Richert, *Break On Through*, 140–47. On crack, see David Farber, *Crack: Rock Cocaine, Street Capitalism, and the Decade of Greed* (New York: Cambridge University Press, 2019).

53 Cohen, "They Call it Ecstacy."

54 Chris Robert, "Oregon Legalizes Psilocybin Mushrooms and Decriminalizes All Drugs," *Forbes*, November 4, 2020, www.forbes.com.

55 Marks, *Search*, 1978; Lee and Shlain, *Acid Dreams*, 1994; Anne Collins, *In the Sleep Room: The Story of the CIA Brainwashing Experiments in Canada* (Toronto: Key Porter Books, 1988); Stevens, *Storming Heaven*, 1987.

56 Michael Pollan, *How to Change Your Mind: What the New Science of Psychedelics Teaches Us About Consciousness, Dying, Addiction, Depression, and Transcendence* (New York: Penguin Press, 2017); see also Don Lattin, *The Harvard Psychedelic Club: How Timothy Leary, Ram Dass, Huston Smith, and Andrew Weil Killed the Fifties and Ushered in a New Age for America* (New York: HarperCollins, 2009); Tom Schroder, *Acid Test: LSD, Ecstasy, and the Power to Heal* (New York: Plume, 2014). See also Casey Schwartz, *Attention: A Love Story* (New York: Pantheon, 2020).

57 James Fadiman, *Psychedelic Explorer's Guide: Safe, Therapeutic and Sacred Journeys* (New York: Simon and Schuster, 2011); Fred Turner, *From Counterculture to Cyberculture: Stewart Brand, the Whole Earth Network, and the Rise of Digital Utopianism* (Chicago: University of Chicago Press, 2006).

58 Leia Friedman, "It's 2020 and White Men Still Dominate Psychedelic Conferences," *Lucid News*, July 15, 2020, www.lucid.news.

.

PART IV

The International Front

8

The War on Drugs in Mexico

AILEEN TEAGUE

Mexico quickly came into the crosshairs of external interdiction efforts during the US War on Drugs, beginning in the 1960s. Though scholars have often focused on US actions and resources in Mexican drug control, particularly the US Drug Enforcement Administration (DEA), this essay examines how this aspect of the US drug war was shaped by Mexico's internal politics. This transnational and international analysis of America's War on Drugs helps to explain the limits of US anti-drug interventions in production countries such as Mexico.

For decades, the fiercest proponents of the War on Drugs in the United States have insisted that stopping the flow of drugs into the US is the only way to truly win the war. As a result, US drug warriors have placed Latin American supply countries in the crosshairs of their grand drug war strategy.[1] One Reagan-era study cited seven Latin American or Caribbean countries as producing the bulk of marijuana, cocaine, and heroin illegally smuggled into the US each year.[2] US leaders so focused their drug enforcement efforts in Latin America that by the 1980s the War on Drugs had been "Hispanicized," at least in the American popular imagination.[3] "The bloodshed produced by Latin American [drug] mobs," wrote one astute observer in a 1985 *New York Times* editorial, "makes the gangs of [Al] Capone's era seem by comparison like gentlemen of the old school."[4] But while this US-centered perspective is useful in explaining how the war looked from Washington, DC, it tells us little about how and why targeted nation states cooperated in the war.

From the perspective of government leaders in nations targeted by the US for drug suppression measures, the history of the War on Drugs provided both opportunities and challenges. These leaders saw the US War on Drugs less as the imposition of a greater power's anti-drug measures onto weaker nations and more as a dialectic between partners with their own, varying interests. Governments of production and trafficking societies singularly experienced and interpreted, and even exploited, Washington's increasingly militarized policies against the drug trade. Securitization around drugs gave not only Americans, but their counterparts in other countries an advantage both in their internal affairs and in their relations with Washington.[5] Washington's partners in the War on Drugs may have waged war, but it was not always on drugs. Mexico is case in point, though similar dynamics occurred in Washington's relations with other countries.[6]

As a producer of both cannabis and the opium poppy, Mexico has fit neatly into the US-centered interpretation of the drug war, even as its nearly two-thousand-mile-long shared border with the US makes it an exceptional case study. Official discourse on the Mexican drug trade— colored by violence, failures in policy execution, and the pervasiveness of corrupt and irrational figures—has produced a distorted image of drug control south of the border. At the same time, it has served a policy purpose of providing American agents with the rationales for continuing their work there. We are perhaps all too familiar with these "push" factors of intensified drug control, but less familiar with the "pull" factors, including how local actors played an equally important if not greater role in the militarized execution of drug enforcement in Mexico over the past six decades. The US designed the more intensive anti-drug policies, but, as the following pages illustrate, Mexican leaders welcomed and at times even spearheaded the militarization of its drug enforcement.

During the late 1960s and 1970s, the Mexican government used US anti-drug aid for internal security measures. Initially motivated by a desire to protect its sovereignty from the US, the Mexican government escalated its drug control program during the 1970s, discovering in the process its utility for tightening the grip on power held by the country's authoritarian ruling party, the *Partido Revolucionario Institucional* (PRI). Drug enforcement intensified as a result of the PRI's concurrent campaign of political repression and counterinsurgency, a period that scholars and activists have begun calling *la guerra sucia* (the Dirty War), which lasted from the late 1950s to the early 1980s. Mexico appears to have successfully kept US anti-drug actors at bay during the 1970s. The PRI prevailed over the Mexican Left by decade's end and Mexico's ruling party co-opted many of the demands made by leftist radicals in previous years. However, during the 1980s the emergence of the cocaine industry and intensified US anti-drug policies in Latin America made drug control even more violent. That Mexico developed into an important trafficking route for South American cocaine brought with it new security imperatives for both Mexico and the US, as well as additional threats to Mexico's sovereignty. With leftist insurgencies largely defeated, enforcement in Mexico became more complicated, and the question of how the Mexican government used the increasing American anti-drug dollars flowing south under the administration of Ronald Reagan is fair game for speculation. While sources are less abundant for the 1980s, evidence suggests that the Mexican state continued to wage a drug war to maintain control over dissent and public safety.

* * *

Scholars have examined the relationship between American state power and the emerging function of drug control.[7] Less work has been done, however, on the developing Mexican anti-drug program and its own relationship to state power. In particular, Mexican state actors took advantage of American resources and knowledge to modernize their enforcement capabilities. The increased importance of drug control was unique because it was not a grand strategic objective of the Mexican state in a traditional sense, but a social responsibility that would keep low- and mid-level policing actors in an almost constant state of low-intensity conflict. During the 1960s, when this story begins, drug enforcement was less significant to Mexican government agencies than it would become. Yet Mexican drug control and its relationship to state power underwent a transformation in the ensuing three decades and became fundamentally shaped by the concept of war. By 1985, to give a stark example, anti-drug campaigns counted toward a soldier's combat experience.[8] This work is concerned with parsing out the factors that caused US drug war partner states, in general, and Mexico, in particular, to rationalize the use of force in drug enforcement.

First of all, for some major Mexican state actors, drug control was not always primarily aimed at eliminating illegal drugs. They used a drug war, instead, as a convenient rationale for a host of other state functions. Violence—a tool that actors on both sides of the border were all too ready to employ—was not the only, nor the best means for reducing drug consumption. Yet Mexican officials rationalized, even encouraged violence in their efforts to eliminate the Mexican drug supply, as a product of the distinct political, social, and cultural factors that Mexico faced in the late twentieth century.[9] Secondly, a focus on Mexican motives demonstrates how limited, even improvised, America's earliest anti-drug efforts in Mexico actually were. For its part, the US wanted to eliminate drugs outside its borders, and it was willing to encroach on Mexican sovereignty in the process. However, US actors often lacked the conceptual tools and local knowledge to rationalize "fighting" narcotics in Mexico, given the very different situation on the ground there. As a result, complicated alliance politics developed between US and Mexican agencies that at times worked against the ostensible mission of drug control.[10] Tracing this relationship between drug enforcement and security imperatives offers one way to understand how governments, certainly in Mexico, but elsewhere too, used violence against domestic rivals and internal threats with and without the threat of drugs present.

Origins of the US Presence in Mexico's Drug War

The US established its first organized anti-drug presence in Mexico during the 1960s, a period when American travelers would acquire negligible amounts of Mexican marijuana. In 1963, the Federal Bureau of Narcotics, grandfather organization to the Drug Enforcement Administration (DEA) established a small office in Mexico City to monitor operations of the Turkish-French heroin smuggling ring, which used Mexico as a transit country. Stereotypes of drug-seeking beatniks or hippies traveling to Mexico to get high had permeated American popular culture in the works of figures such as Allen Ginsberg and Jack Kerouac. The Kennedy and Johnson administrations portrayed US–Mexico anti-drug relations as a cooperative effort, embraced by the upper echelons of Mexican policy makers, containing criticism of Mexican efforts in specific agencies and regions. Actually, the Mexican anti-drug program was drastically underdeveloped, and it remained low on Mexican policy makers' list of priorities. Because the US government at the time was focused on interdicting European heroin, it provided little in the way of financial incentives to encourage more robust Mexican anti-drug efforts.[11] It was not until the presidency of Richard Nixon

(1969–74)—when brown heroin, derived from Mexican poppies, began appearing in large quantities on US city streets—that the US government focused more attention on its southern neighbor as a major drug supplier. However, the earliest bilateral anti-drug efforts were more political theater than a response to increasing Mexican drugs in the US. Mexico did not surpass the Turkish-French smuggling ring as the primary heroin supplier to the US until 1975.[12]

Yet in September 1969, with little warning, Nixon all but closed the border with Mexico in a bid to search every vehicle transiting into the US for illegal drugs, an action known as Operation Intercept. The exercise debilitated Mexican border commerce. The Nixon administration hoped that this draconian measure would pressure Mexico to enact its own drug-crop destruction program in remote producing areas using herbicides, some of whose infrastructure can be traced to the American herbicidal spraying operations in Vietnam.[13] It worked, at least to a degree. Mexican leaders had little choice but to cooperate with US drug control policies following the border shutdown. But the prospect of spraying Mexican communities with herbicides was highly unpalatable to Mexican leaders. US involvement in Vietnam played a role in Mexican conceptions of counterinsurgency and in the Mexican government's willingness to use herbicides. Mexican leaders paid sufficient lip service to the US so that the border was reopened after three weeks, while they delayed implementing the herbicidal program for years. While Mexico held fast on the program in the years following Intercept, it did sign on to establishing a more intensive anti-drug program using other forms of US aid (aircraft, weaponry, etc.) furnished to them under the "War on Drugs" campaign proclaimed by Nixon in 1971.[14] Translated into policy, the ubiquitous metaphor in the history of US anti-drug issues provided Nixon with the political capital, as well as the legal and fiscal resources, for carrying out more extensive drug control domestically and beyond its borders, especially in Mexico.

In the years following Intercept, US pressure, resources, and conceptions of drug control profoundly changed Mexico's anti-drug program. But Mexican actors were already predisposed to militarized enforcement, especially in rural, drug-producing areas already prone to antigovernment sentiment and violence against federal government agents. Although the PRI's repressive efforts against the Left emerged in the postwar era, the seeds of the conflict were planted decades earlier. A popular spirit of revolutionary nationalism inspired the Mexican Revolution (1910–20) and the Constitution of 1917 that emerged from the conflict declared Mexico's government to be democratic and representative. But the PRI, the proclaimed party of the revolution, ruled Mexico as a one-party state from 1929 to 2000. The modernization of Mexican cities and economic growth established under PRI rule gave the country the image of a stable partner in Cold War Latin America. By midcentury, however, citizens began to contest the lack of democracy through peaceful protest. Obsessed with threats to its power, the party of the revolution began constructing its own security state, at times with American assistance.[15]

Though 1968 is often cited as a landmark year in countercultural protest in Mexico, with the Tlatelolco massacre, myriad popular protests against the government—demonstrations of workers, teachers, and peasants—had already emerged in the decade prior.[16] In silencing opposition and consolidating political power, the administration of Miguel Alemán (1946–52) embraced a strategy of using government agencies to repress cycles of peaceful demonstration. The strategy was continued by many of his successors, including Adolfo López Mateos (1958–64), Gustavo Díaz Ordaz (1964–70), Luis Echeverría (1970–76), and José López Portillo (1976–82). Alemán also increased the military's role in domestic policing, combining military and police functions for internal security measures, measures defined by the president and those in his inner circle. Despite these authoritarian characteristics, the Mexican state did not rule by complete force alone and has been described as a "hybrid regime" that combined democratic and authoritarian elements.[17] In some ways, this description made Mexico the ideal candidate to display force in its drug enforcement measures while cloaked under the facade of being a democratic partner. The government also needed support, both within and outside the country, which it attained through economic growth, distribution of resources, and by continuing to pay symbolic homage to the revolution even as it ruled with an iron fist.

Mexican government agencies, dedicated to squashing political instability, were drawn into the expanding national security apparatus and the US's broader internationalization of crime control. Still, this developing partnership was a rocky one. The US and Mexico had long clashed in the area of policy. With Customs and the Border Patrol operating at the border, US agents sometimes worked with Mexican policing agencies to apprehend criminals or drug smugglers. Often, however, US agents did not follow the formal rules of international diplomacy and crossed the southern border with impunity, reflecting an inclination toward jurisdictional overreach that would be seen in agencies such as the DEA in later years. Mexican officials, as well as the Mexican public, resented this kind of imperial arrogance, which had long characterized US–Mexico relations.[18]

Still, in the postwar era, as the Mexican government embraced anticommunism and created its own security state, the US delivered resources to aid in policing dissent, and PRI officials welcomed this kind of support. As dissent mounted, the Mexican government employed anticommunist rhetoric against the internal Left.[19] But whereas the Mexican Left was a remnant of the unfulfilled promises of the Mexican Revolution—those who criticized an enduring dictatorship—the PRI successfully cast the Left as a segment of international communism, which led US actors to enable, even support, the PRI's repression. Moreover, in the US, the reach of agencies such as the CIA and the FBI depended on their ability to gather intelligence overseas and work productively with foreign counterparts. American security and law enforcement agencies' need for this kind of cooperation strengthened state-to-state ties, especially as partner nations, very much including Mexico, began assembling their own intelligence capabilities during the period.

In the late 1940s, President Alemán modeled Mexico's political and criminal surveillance state apparatus on US intelligence agencies, which had the double aim of appeasing American Cold War aims and, in exchange, receiving aid and training in the years to come, as well as achieving the domestic policing needs of the PRI. The Federal Security Directorate (DFS), Mexico's most powerful intelligence agency, was formed in 1947. While US officials tended to view Mexican intelligence as uncoordinated and disorganized, the Mexican Interior Ministry, which housed intelligence functions, found that mundane intelligence could be useful as a bellwether for potential political unrest.[20] Unlike authorities in urban areas, intelligence agents had extensive knowledge of the inherent violence existing in areas disconnected from the capital. Eventually, Mexican intelligence agencies and the military became entrenched in the "dirty work" of social control, which included the use of violence to intimidate.[21] Later, the same organizations would play an important role in drug control. Moreover, following the Revolution, Mexican leaders conceptualized the army's role such that it supported the PRI's vision for the country. This civil-military arrangement, where the military was subordinate to civilian leadership, was starkly different from that of other Latin American countries. The largest sector of the military, the army, carried out a number of the government's reform-minded "civic action" responsibilities, especially in spaces disconnected from that capital, which included public health initiatives like vaccination, as well as drug-crop destruction.[22] Divided between posts in provincial towns and the countryside, the army's infantry and cavalry sometimes participated in dangerous policing tasks in the countryside.

US security policies, of which drug control would become a part, stoked an already precarious political situation on the ground in Mexico. By the late 1960s, vocal radical left activists challenged the legitimacy of the PRI-led Mexican state. While many of the disparate leftist groups in Mexico represented different political stances, they were united in their belief that the government had betrayed the promises of the constitution. Demonstrations climaxed at the country's largest and best-known counterhegemonic movement at the *Plaza de las tres culturas* at Tlatelolco in Mexico City on October 2, 1968. With snipers posted in the modernist buildings surrounding the plaza, the Mexican army fired on student protestors as they tried frantically to escape, resulting in as many as three hundred casualties.[23] No single event did more to color the military's role in the government's domestic policing initiatives. Nor did any single event do more to galvanize the Left and the various armed guerilla groups, many whom flocked to rural, drug-producing areas to organize. A similarly intensive demonstration occurred on June 10, 1971, when a US-trained covert operations group called *los halcones* (the falcons) attacked a group of more than ten thousand students in Mexico City on the day of the Corpus Christi festival. Although the US officially downplayed or perhaps underestimated the threat leftist insurgencies posed to the Mexican government, some US officials were supporting their Mexican counterparts' suppression of leftist dissidents. In his oral histories, US ambassador to Mexico Joseph Jova has repeatedly referenced President Luis Echeverría's working relationship with the CIA, both during the Tlatelolco massacre when he served as the Interior Minister, and then more discreetly during his presidency.[24]

* * *

When the Nixon administration began practicing more intensive drug control measures in the late 1960s, enforcement capabilities of the Mexican state were based more on party loyalty and the repressive state apparatus than they were on eliminating drugs. As such, the intensified enforcement then advocated by the US reinforced the level of infiltration the Mexican government desired in spaces remote from the capital. The US-sponsored War on Drugs allowed the Mexican armed forces to further extend its presence into hundreds of Mexican cities and towns as intelligence agents spied on its population in the name of national security. According to one account, military officers retained a considerable amount of power to "lobby, graft, and politic in the provinces through a combination of informal pacts and bold assertions of power."[25]

Prior to the late 1960s, the Mexican government's drug control efforts had been minimal. The attorney general's office facilitated drug control agreements at the higher echelons of policy, and drug crop destruction was a part of the PRI's reform-minded duties carried out by the army and at times by underdeveloped municipal and state police forces. Tactically, the army was better equipped for these tasks than other government agencies, but the army also played a critical role in protecting the PRI's one-party rule in areas disconnected from the capital. Even so, lack of organization, lack of resources, and a decided lack of political will made drug enforcement a difficult task. In previous decades, Mexican army and police forces had destroyed poppy and marijuana crops using machetes or by burning fields, especially in Mexico's Golden Triangle, the mountainous drug-producing region located in the country's northwest, comprised of the states of Sinaloa, Chihuahua, and Durango. These were also largely rural states with long histories of resistance to federal control. But enforcement efforts were complicated by officials who condoned drug production as part of the local economy.[26]

This relative indifference changed following 1969's Operation Intercept. The Mexican government took ownership of its anti-drug program largely to prevent more intensive US anti-drug interference inside Mexico. The government's decision to escalate Mexico's anti-drug efforts on its own terms—and not those of the US—reflected the decades-long distaste held by Mexicans across political lines for Yankee imperialism. Not only did President Gustavo Díaz Ordaz want to prevent American interference inside Mexico; he also wanted to control and manipulate how American power and resources would be used for his own purposes. In the execution of enforcement, the government retained much leeway in how it used the aid and policies inside Mexico. Díaz Ordaz authorized the use of US materiel in Mexico's anti-drug program, but he was adamant that US personnel could not be involved in Mexican enforcement operations. "If a Mexican soldier killed a Mexican peasant, it was unfortunate," he said, "but if an American agent did so, it would cause a national uproar."[27] Mexican leadership was initially wary of using certain forms of aid, such as remote sensor technology, even as it agreed to accept aircraft assistance.

By late 1970, however, US aid to Mexico was ramped up.[28] One of the first estimates of US aid to Mexico included Cessna-185 aircrafts, multiple platforms of helicopters, and Department of Defense (DOD)–trained pilots and mechanics on hand to administer initial sorties and training. The aid included defoliants such as Tordon 101, also known as Agent White and 2,4-D, one of the ingredients in the notorious Agent Orange that had been used to ill effect in Vietnam.[29] Despite an initial reluctance to accept US aid, it did not take the Mexican government long to realize the utility of drug-control resources for increasing the Mexican army's overall capabilities. By late 1971, Mexico requested the following items in support of its anti-drug program: three hundred Uzi submachine guns, twenty gas grenade launchers for use with 12-gauge riot shotguns, and two thousand gas grenades.[30] At the same time, Mexican records indicate a mobilization of military resources directed toward the country's Golden Triangle, as well as the states of Sonora, Michoacán, and Guerrero.[31] Mexican leaders used Nixon's War on Drugs in much the same way they used the Cold War, as a means for acquiring the material support necessary to bolster Mexico's internal security apparatus and US acquiescence around intensified enforcement in order to utilize violent tactics against the Left and assert control in peripheral areas. Framing drug control around the concept of war allowed local and mid-level Mexican enforcement actors to expand the definition of who was considered the enemy. It also gave guerrillas access to resources that could be used to bolster their power. In essence, then, Mexico's War on Drugs was more about securing the Mexican state from political tumult of the previous two decades than about Mexican interest in eradicating drugs.

The Mexican government feared that as drug production and trafficking increased in rural guerilla hotbeds, such as the state of Guerrero, anti-government actors would gain the resources they needed to escalate their challenge to state power. They were right in the state of Guerrero, for example, where guerrillas did use drug profits to acquire US arms. With more than twenty thousand weapons, including grenades and explosives, smuggled into Mexico annually—some by drug traffickers who were closely linked to anti-PRI activists—the government faced a formidable foe.[32] Mexican army and police forces were hesitant or ill equipped to enter these violent, anti-PRI, drug-producing spaces. Even before drug profits shifted the balance of power, they had suffered high casualties in Guerrero.[33] While outsiders believed that Mexican guerrillas were little more than a nuisance to the Mexican government, PRI leaders saw the matter differently. The believed that the guerrillas exposed the precarious state of the PRI's grip on Mexico. As a result, PRI leaders used American resources to station increasing numbers of DFS agents on the border to monitor the drugs and arms being smuggled between Mexico and the US.[34] The Mexican government was significantly more concerned with the weapons than it was the narcotics.[35]

In 1975, the US Domestic Council Drug Abuse Task Force's "White Paper on Drug Abuse" called for a more comprehensive strategy for overseas drug control. With studies showing that US heroin use had increased and that Mexico was the primary heroin supplier, the white paper shifted the US focus to more intensive supply-control measures against hard drugs.[36] American drug-control administrators insisted that Mexico begin a massive drug crop destruction campaign. A similar, though less-developed US program known as Operation Buccaneer had been developed in Jamaica in 1974 to eradicate marijuana. With Mexico's Operation Condor, which commenced in early 1976, newly elected president José López Portillo (1976–82) finally relented to US pressure for the full-scale use of defoliants.[37]

US drug officials closely observed this aerial herbicide campaign. Peter Bensinger, DEA administrator at the time, recalled that his agents "would send up single engine aircraft to observe the spray operations, and to make sure that the actual fields were getting sprayed and that the herbicides didn't end up in the Pacific Ocean."[38] American officials paid considerably less attention to the Mexican army's massive ten-thousand-man effort to police the countryside for both drugs and dissent. For PRI officials, Operation Condor provided an excellent opportunity to use American resources to serve its dual interest in stopping some drug production while repressing anti-government guerrillas. Many of those targeted as drug producers tended to be part of groups historically opposed to PRI rule. The Mexican state, justified by Operation Condor, committed multiple human rights violations and abuses of power against suspected drug producers who just so happened to be suspected anti-government activists.

In Sinaloa, soldiers seized homes in search for drugs, often stealing food and cash and committing other unlawful abuses in the process.[39] The governor reported unlawfully seized *campesino* livestock located near the drug plants they found as payment for their drug enforcement efforts. Mexican government officials—including local and federal police forces and prison officials—as well as US agents, were accused of participating in physical and mental torture to coerce confessions, colluding with corrupt law enforcement, extortion, and other such violations of the law.[40] The PRI's social control efforts were in the hands of the same military forces charged with policing drugs in rural spaces disconnected from the capital. This full-scale militarization of Mexican drug control served the capital's broader political interests.

US agents, aware of the claims of human rights violations, largely distanced themselves from future iterations of Condor even as the Mexican government conducted multiple similar operations in the years that followed. One 1979 report suggested that the US International Narcotics Assistance Program subsidized a program of the Mexican Federal Judicial Police—with DEA acquiescence and occasional involvement—that used systematic torture on narcotics suspects. It suggested that 90 percent of the traffickers apprehended during Operation Condor were peasants and juveniles forced by authorities to sign confessions.[41] With the initial influx of US anti-drug involvement in Mexico during a turbulent period in the country's history, there seemed to be a developing consensus inside Mexico of the use of force around enforcement issues.

The particulars of who or what the force was directed at seemed to grow less significant, while larger drug trafficking organizations were left largely unaffected. One such group was the Herrera organization, which ran a heroin operation connecting a village in the state of Durango to the streets of Chicago, dating back as early as 1957. During the 1970s, the DEA estimates that the Herrera family controlled as much as 90 percent of the heroin in Chicago, as Elaine Carey explains in her essay in this volume. The heroin was then distributed to other US cities.[42]

On the Mexican side, mid- and low-level government actors, from mayors and governors to military, police, and intelligence agents, repurposed social control energies into Mexico's drug enforcement. One December 1983 report from the CIA cheerfully acknowledged that the Mexican army took "advantage of the eradication campaign" to "uncover arms trafficking *and* guerrilla activities." The report continued: "army eradication may devote as much effort to internal security as to eradication."[43] Sometimes drugs were planted on activists or leftist propaganda was planted on rural people who were detained. While the American DEA might not have found this use of anti-drug resources in Mexico to be ideal, the CIA saw no problem with it.

The War Continues, but for What Purpose?

Mexican officials appear to have successfully kept control over the implementation of US anti-drug policy in Mexican hands during the 1970s. By the end of that decade, with the assistance of US "drug eradication" policies and resources, the PRI had prevailed over the Mexican Left. The attorney general's office, at this point, had more than five hundred anti-drug agents stationed throughout the country, making as many as thirty-six thousand arrests between 1950 and 1979.[44] But the PRI-led Mexican government had far less success prevailing over the illegal drug business. Mexico continued to be a major producer and exporter of heroin and marijuana; it also became a major cocaine trafficking country. By 1980, Mexican heroin confiscated in the US had purportedly decreased by 40 percent thanks to Operation Condor. The Mexican government—which prioritized destroying marijuana over poppy due to a longstanding cultural stigma against the weed—reported a 90-percent decline in marijuana production.[45] At the same time

American enforcement personnel confiscated nearly ten times as much cocaine, approximately a third of it trafficked through Mexico.[46] Despite the relative levels of cooperation reached between the US and Mexico in stemming the flow of heroin and marijuana via herbicidal programs, the surging popularity of illegal cocaine in the US made moot any progress in the joint US–Mexico War on Drugs. The American government responded to the rise of cocaine trafficking in Mexico by demanding that the PRI escalate its War on Drugs.

The perceived threat of cocaine in the US and President Ronald Reagan's campaign promise to wage a more aggressive War on Drugs put new pressure on the Mexican government's drug eradication efforts.[47] Frustrated over Mexican inaction, Reagan's drug warriors called out Mexican corruption in the PRI's War on Drugs and insisted that US personnel were needed "in country" to police Mexican efforts since Mexican officials seemed incapable or unwilling to do it themselves. The coercive demands by Reagan officials were part of a larger US strategy in Latin American that hinged on an ambiguous link between developmentalism and a desire to police. This heavy-handled approach emerged even as the CIA was linked to the drug trade in its operations with the Contras in Nicaragua. In Mexico, the sovereignty issue was still important both to the Mexican government and to the way subsequent bilateral anti-drug efforts were sold to the Mexican public, but in a different way from the past. US agents increasingly implicated their Mexican counterparts in corruption and official complicity in the drug trade, but they did so in direct relation to the escalation of the US anti-drug presence in Mexico. Mexico's insistence on protecting its right to prosecute its own drug traffickers deepened distrust between the two countries.

That Mexico developed into an important trafficking route for South American cocaine brought with it new security imperatives for both Mexico and the US. The South Florida Task Force, initiated in 1982 and directed by Vice President George H. W. Bush, had been relatively successful in shutting down Caribbean cocaine smuggling routes, but this had only increased the power and profits of Mexican drug trafficking organizations.[48] By 1985, according to the DEA, Mexico trafficked more than one-third of the cocaine consumed in the US. The Guadalajara Cartel, grandfather to many of today's cartels, oversaw the traffic of fifteen thousand to thirty thousand kilograms of cocaine into the US yearly.[49] The cartels' profits, and thus their power, soared. High-level traffickers began to pose a threat to the Mexican government's authority, and in some cases enjoyed considerable political influence at the state and national levels. One example is Miguel Ángel Félix Gallardo, who cofounded the Guadalajara Cartel that was predominant in the 1980s. Félix Gallardo had originally worked as a federal police officer, and during the 1960s as a bodyguard for Sinaloa's governor, Leopoldo Sánchez Celis, whose connections helped his trafficking organization flourish.[50]

Drug traffickers and their expansive organizations were increasingly entangled in the Mexican state. These traffickers did not merely corrupt government officials; they played a role in controlling how the government implemented drug policy at all levels of governance, from the local to the national. On the one hand, Mexican political leaders aligned government policy publicly with America's War on Drugs. On the other, in practice, at all levels of the Mexican government, some officials used their authority to safeguard the massive economic power and opportunities created by the traffickers. In other words, myriad state actors supported the drug trade and undermined proclaimed state interests. Bluntly stated, the drug trade often supported the livelihoods of the same municipal and state police officers who were charged with enforcing drug laws.

The increase in violence and crime resulting from the expansion of the Mexican drug trade, as well as the obvious, rampant government corruption it produced, resulted in a legitimacy crisis for the PRI-led state. According to Mexican sociologist Luis Astorga, Mexican drug traffickers' infiltration and influence over the PRI-led government in the 1980s exposed the "deterioration of the old [political] structures."[51] Mexican officials who sought to bring order to Mexican society, whether corrupt or not, understood that they had a problem: drug enforcement and security were dependent on a delicate balance between respecting the power of the drug trade and maintaining a certain degree of control over it. This balance was increasingly set off kilter.

Two well-publicized incidents in the 1980s highlighted the Mexican government's inability to manage drug trafficking organizations' increasing power and disregard for any semblance of social order. On May 30, 1984, unknown assailants murdered Mexican investigative reporter Manuel Buendía outside of his office in Mexico City. Buendía had spent a career exposing political corruption, organized crime and the drug trade, as well as CIA operations in Mexico. Buendía had allegedly acquired a videotape showing high-level government officials meeting with drug traffickers. Drug traffickers and the local police were the primary suspects in the murder, which was left unsolved for nearly five years, affirming how criminal networks protected by the government silenced those threatening to expose them. Top DFS officials were eventually implicated in 1989, but it is doubtful that they were Buendía's actual killers.[52]

The second incident, the murder of DEA Agent Enrique "Kiki" Camarena in 1985, illustrates the complications of US interference in already delicate anti-drug efforts by the Mexican state. In order to preserve PRI rule, Mexican drug enforcement agents sometimes condoned aspects of the drug trade. In November 1984, as a result of intelligence provided by Camarena, which had come from an extensive period of undercover work with the Guadalajara Cartel, Mexican forces seized the massive El Búfalo marijuana plantation. The two-square mile plantation, located in the northern border state of Chihuahua, was a highly sophisticated operation, complete with mechanized farming techniques, commercial fertilizers, a state-of-the-art drip irrigation system, drying sheds, an airstrip, and armed guards. The plantation employed ten thousand workers. At the time it was the largest marijuana seizure anywhere, ever. With drugs there valued at more than $150 million, the Mexican daily newspaper El Nacional called it the "most important" marijuana interdiction in Mexico's history, and US Assistant Secretary for International Narcotics Matters Jon R. Thomas called it "the bust of the century."[53] According to multiple accounts, El Búfalo had flourished with the protection of federal and local police, as well as the complicity of Mexican Secretary of Defense Juan Arévalo Gardoqui.[54] Rafael Caro Quintero, a major drug trafficker and co-founder of the Guadalajara Cartel, owned El Búfalo, and he was furious. He wanted Camarena dead.[55]

Camarena was abducted in February 1985, three months after the El Búfalo bust. The Mexican government told the American government that they had no idea what had happened to Camarena. US officials blamed their Mexican counterparts both for Camarena's abduction and for their failure to control the narcotraffickers who were behind it. To leverage Mexican government action, the US partially closed the border

and instigated Operation Intercept II. This US-led and mandated operation reflected a public, official repudiation of the Mexican government's
prosecution of the War on Drugs. In addition, the DEA launched Operation *Leyenda*, its own investigation into Camarena's disappearance.
This investigation exposed close links between the Mexican government
and the Guadalajara Cartel. The Mexican government responded to this
immense US pressure by convicting low- and mid-level officials and
traffickers involved in the Camarena murder. They did not, however, do
much to prosecute higher-level traffickers and refused to extradite those
they did arrest. By the end of March, arrest warrants were finally issued
for Caro Quintero, whom the DEA—not Mexican investigators—found
hiding in Costa Rica.[56] Mexican forces then did arrest Caro Quintero
and Guadalajara Cartel leader Ernesto Fonseca Carrillo. Miguel Ángel
Félix Gallardo, the cartel's most prominent cocaine trafficker, would not
be arrested for another four years; his arrest signaled the end of *Leyenda*.
    Camarena's murder and Operation *Leyenda* intensified US efforts to
investigate ties between Mexican drug traffickers and authorities. These
efforts deepened following the detention and torture of DEA Agent
Victor Cortez in Guadalajara by state police officers. Under American
pressure, President Miguel de la Madrid (1982–88) conducted major
shakeups of the Mexican government's intelligence and police forces,
which resulted in the 1985 disbanding of the DFS, the semi-secret PRI-run
agency that had a long history of productive relations with the CIA. A
number of DFS agents, including its former director, José Antonio Zor-
rilla Pérez, were linked to the drug trade and were either arrested or
fled the country. While these actions indicate that the Mexican government had stepped up its drug war, the actions were only undertaken
under immense American pressure. Mexico was still wrestling with the
delicate balance between its own interests in using the War on Drugs to
maintain social order and the economic power and violent reach of the
traffickers.
    By the mid-1980s, the Mexican government's attention had been
diverted from leftist insurgencies to the drug trade. The influence of
the drug traffickers revealed the weakness of Mexican leadership and the
state far more than small bands of guerrillas. The profitability of the cocaine trade fueled a substantial growth in crime in Mexico. Although
many crimes go unreported in the country, yearly homicide rates rose by

almost 35 percent between the early 1980s and early 1990s.[57] In producing states, the illicit drug industry fueled reports of "narco-terrorism." Reports cite violence growing from competition between rival traffickers or peasant farmers quarreling over cultivation rights. Meanwhile, the Mexican government's enforcement efforts were hindered by high foreign debt, inflation, unemployment, and rebuilding necessitated by the 1986 earthquake. The government's inability to address domestic economic problems also drove poor farmers to the financial rewards of cultivating illicit drug crops. For those in poverty, traffickers served as an economic buffer and even provided credit to peasant growers, who paid in full after the harvest.[58] As a result of both the increasing drug trafficking-related violence and the Mexican government's limited resources, Mexican officials were increasingly vulnerable to US pressure for a more militarized, American-backed War on Drugs. And by the mid-1980s, the US was pushing hard for such a war.

The Camarena murder and Operation *Leyenda* had paved the way for US policies that intensified the War on Drugs in Mexico. The Reagan administration's April 1986 drug war declaration, National Security Decision Directive (NSDD) 221, was one of these policies. NSDD 221 stated that the international drug trade constituted a legitimate threat to US national security and so sanctioned the use of force in the fight against drugs internationally. It also increased the US anti-drug presence abroad. The directive further declaimed that Third World governments could not squash the illegal drug trade on their own; they needed US direct support. NSDD 221 was a critical marker in the Americanization of drug policing on an international scale.

This American-led War on Drugs was hardly welcomed by all in Mexico. A history of local, state, and national governments' use of the police as a measure of social control fostered citizen resentment against militarized anti-drug law enforcement measures. Mexican government officials were particularly incensed by the increased surveillance at the border. In October 1986, Reagan approved the Anti-Drug Abuse Act. In the US, this law was best known for establishing draconian mandatory minimum drug sentences. Mexicans were far more focused on the massive military resources the act provided for US agents to police their border. The law directed nearly $1.7 billion to arm the border with modern radar equipment, aircraft, and other types of surveillance intended to interdict narcotics coming into the US.[59]

The Mexican government, caught between the power of the drug cartels and the need to curtail the violence and corruption the cartels and their allies were unleashing on Mexican society, generally accepted US-led militarization. This acceptance, however, was mired in political, economic, and cultural conflict. Direct US agencies' active involvement in policing drugs in Mexico created bureaucratic infighting within the Mexican state. In addition, many Mexicans rightfully complained about the lack of transparency US activities produced in Mexico's internal affairs.

American bureaucratic infighting added an additional layer of complexity to Mexico's War on Drugs. While the DEA tended to be more aligned with the federal police and the Mexican attorney general's office, other agencies, such as the CIA, cultivated their own alliances with the DFS. Although the DEA and State Department led enforcement efforts in Mexico, the CIA also played a covert role in intelligence gathering. The CIA, not surprisingly, operated in secret and often refused to coordinate its work, even with other US agencies, let alone the Mexican government. An inherent mistrust between the DEA and the CIA, in particular, resulted in a lack of intelligence sharing. The two agencies also struggled to resolve differences over the use of CIA evidence, often obtained through informants or wiretaps of Mexican officials. If CIA information was not admissible in court, what purpose did it serve the Justice Department?[60] Other US agencies also often felt stymied by each other. Customs Commissioner William von Raab said his organization had all but been "pushed out of the drug business" by the DEA.[61]

Camarena's murder demonstrated that making strides in drug control involved extensive undercover work and cultivating relationships with counterparts willing to flirt to a certain degree with the criminal underworld. FBI Director William H. Webster admitted that "corrupt public officials were absolutely necessary to the success of those [drug enforcement] enterprises," where such individuals serve as "facilitators or provide an early warning system."[62] In his study, based on hundreds of interviews with DEA agents who worked in Latin America, political scientist Ethan Nadelmann found that the most seemingly corrupt counterparts were also the ones with whom DEA agents could work most productively; they were the better, more knowledgeable law enforcement officials.[63]

Such positive personal linkages in drug enforcement did not always align with the realities of Mexican government policy at the upper echelons. The location of Reagan's final meeting with President Miguel de la Madrid in February 1988, held at Mazatlán in the drug production state of Sinaloa, was significant because it signaled at least some American approval of the Mexican government's anti-drug efforts. But even alliances cultivated at the highest levels were caught in the contradictions produced by many Mexican government officials' complicity in the drug trade. For example, despite Sinaloa's governor Francisco Labastida's well-publicized links to the drug trade, US officials continued to work closely with him, recognizing his utility in the broader fight against traffickers.[64]

Despite these complications, both the US and the Mexican government, for overlapping but not identical reasons, embraced militarized drug enforcement. Entering the presidency in 1988, Carlos Salinas de Gortari (1988–94) made defeating narco-trafficking a national priority. He restructured the deputy attorney general's office that oversaw drug trafficking, created specialized units devoted to fighting drug traffickers, and doubled anti-drug personnel and resources. The attorney general's office increased the size of its eradication air fleet and sought to improve the efficiency of its narcotics operations, growing the agency's budget from $18 million in 1987 to $23 million in 1988. While this is not an insignificant figure, it bears emphasizing that this was less than the $26 million in aid Mexico received from the US.[65] Moreover, while Mexico's willingness to wage war against drugs aligned with the state's broader interest in maintaining control over traffickers, taking this stance also necessitated additional US security assistance. The Mexican attorney general's office enjoyed a budget of nearly $2 million a year to maintain Mexico's 212 aircraft, which the US believed, incorrectly, were being used solely for fumigation. Mexican enforcement agents also received fully subsidized training opportunities in the US.[66]

Mexican military forces also increased their direct participation in the country's anti-drug effort. As had always been the case, under-resourced state and municipal police forces at the peripheries were more likely to be influenced by criminal networks. With the dismantling of the DFS, the army took on even more responsibility in drug enforcement. By the mid-1980s, the country's anti-drug program was marshalling up to fifty thousand troops, nearly half of the country's military.[67] The Mexican navy also increased its role in drug control. In a television interview with Mexico City's *Red Nacional*, Navy Secretary Miguel Ángel Gómez Ortega stressed that, "using Mexican technology and manpower," the Navy had modernized and increased its surveillance capabilities along Mexico's coasts by 70 percent.[68] Moreover, with NSDD 221 clearing the path for American military involvement in the global fight against narcotics, joint training ventures in drug control between the US military and Coast Guard and Mexican military forces increased in the late 1980s. These military efforts were all subsidized by the US. Such incentives provided the US with a drug war ally while enhancing Mexico's national security capacity.

The notion that internal factors in supply countries such as Mexico play an equal if not greater role in bilateral drug policy execution is crucial for understanding Mexico's War on Drugs. It also highlights some of the fundamental flaws of US supply-control policies. The Mexican government had its own interests at stake when the US began pressuring Mexico to cooperate in the War on Drugs. With the ostensible mutual goal of eliminating illegal drugs, the US helped Mexico create enforcement machinery that rationalized state-sponsored violence, ostensibly directed at drug growers and traffickers. During the 1970s, Mexico's PRI-led state controlled that machinery and used it not only against the illegal drug industry but also against its political enemies. The threat of leftist insurgencies was short lived—although one could argue that some of those energies were reflected in the Zapatista Movement of 1994—but the Mexican government's drug enforcement arrangements, supported by the US, endured as drug control replaced anticommunism as the primary enforcement paradigm in Latin America during the 1980s. These arrangements employed a broad definition of who could be targeted by a selective enforcement system based on corrupt economic alliances and other political factors.

The contestation of drug policy implementation in Mexico, a developing country confronted with a lucrative illicit industry, is also significant to the story. On one level, Mexico benefitted from showing the US it could effectively control drugs so that it could protect its sovereignty, a long running theme in US–Mexican relations. But Mexican officials' ties to the drug trade often undermined the state's anti-drug efforts even as the Mexican government reaffirmed its desire to wage war on drugs so that it could maintain control amid the growing power of traffickers and criminal groups. Yet, contrary to some US discourse, Mexico has not been an irrational actor, incapacitated or overrun by drug cartels and criminal organizations. Segments of the state made conscious, rational choices based on internal threats and external pressures. At times Mexico tailored, even exploited, American drug policies. Alliance politics made bilateral exchanges that much more opaque. Over the course of nearly fifty years, these factors produced a number of unintended consequences that have sometimes run counter to the very objective of controlling the flow of drugs. As the drug trade in Mexico continues to expand in new and innovative ways to meet American demand, scholars and informed citizens must understand the complicated, sometimes misguided trajectory of drug policy execution in Mexico if there is any hope of creating more thoughtful, less violent policies in the future.

NOTES

1 Conventional drug control narratives have detailed much about the "externalization" of US anti-drug policies, and Latin American supply countries have often been at the center of these studies. Until the late 1990s, the primary historian focused on the history of drugs in Latin America was William Walker III, whose works include *Drug Control in the Americas*, rev. ed. (Albuquerque: University of New Mexico, Press, 1989). Other important scholarship includes Luis Alejandro Astorga Almanza, *Drogas sin fronteras* (México, D.F.: Grijalbo Mondadori, 2003); Astorga Almanza, *El siglo de las drogas: El narcotráfico, del Porfiriato al nuevo milenio* (México, D.F.: Plaza y Janes, 2005); William B. McAllister, *Drug Diplomacy in the Twentieth Century: An International History* (New York: Routledge, 2000); David Musto, *American Disease: Origins of Narcotics Control*, rev. ed. (1973; repr., New York: Oxford University Press, 1999); María Celia Toro, "The Internationalization of Police: The DEA in Mexico," *Journal of American History* 86, no. 2 (September 1999): 623–40; María Celia Toro, *Mexico's "War" on Drugs: Causes and Consequences* (Boulder: L. Rienner Publishers, 1995); Guillermo Valdéz, *Historia del narcotráfico en México* (México, D.F.: Aguilar, 2013).

2 Bruce M. Bagley, "The New Hundred Years War? US National Security and the War on Drugs in Latin America," *Journal of Interamerican Studies and World Affairs* 20, no. 1 (1988): 163.

3 I use the term "American" to describe actors from the United States.

4 Russell Baker, "Gringos Awake at Last," *New York Times*, April 6, 1985, www.ny times.com.

5 Securitization is a widely developed term in international relations. It describes the process of states transforming issues or subjects into matters of security. I find it useful because it places much-needed emphasis on drug control as part of the larger strategic interests—beyond the battlefield and beyond diplomacy—in regions such as Latin America. I have written about the securitization of drug control in the US context elsewhere. See Aileen Teague, "The United States, Mexico, and the Mutual Securitization of Drug Enforcement 1969–1985," *Diplomatic History* 43, no. 5 (2019): 785–812.

6 See, for example, James T. Bradford, *Poppies, Politics, and Power: Afghanistan and the Global History of Drugs and Diplomacy* (Ithaca: Cornell University Press, 2019); Lina Britto, *Marijuana Boom: The Rise and Fall of Colombia's First Drug Paradise* (Berkeley: University of California Press, 2020).

7 Kathleen Frydl, *The Drug Wars in America, 1940–1973* (New York: Cambridge University Press, 2013).

8 Rodric Camp, *Generals in the Palacio: The Military in Modern Mexico* (New York: Oxford University Press, 1992), 191.

9 To tell this story, I draw from records from the Federal Security Directorate (DFS) and the General Directorate of Political and Social Investigations, two intelligence organizations of the PRI. The DFS was an agency that reached the height of its power in the 1970s and early 1980s. It played an active role in drug enforcement until the Mexican government dismantled the agency in 1985 due to its leadership's involvement in the drug trade. Media sources and interviews are also useful in highlighting the ways Mexican agents conceptualized the relationship between drug enforcement and state formation. This article builds on recent work done on the history of the PRI's repression at midcentury, especially as a result of the opening of intelligence archives following the PRI's fall from power in 2000. Restrictions were again placed on access to DFS archives following the PRI's return to power in 2012. As of the writing of this article, these files are still undergoing redaction, leaving a number of questions unanswered about the Mexican government's prolonged period of terror in the context of its relations with the United States.

10 This essay also points to the need for further exploration of Mexican militarization, in a historiography often dominated by US concerns, and how this complicated process shaped state formation and everyday governance both within and outside the scope of bilateral anti-drug issues.

11 Matthew Pembleton, *Containing Addiction: The Federal Bureau of Narcotics and the Origins of America's Global Drug War* (Amherst: University of Massachusetts Press, 2017).

12 "Post Article on Heroin from Mexico," October 30, 1975, Mexico-US Counternarcotics Policy, 1969–2013, Digital National Security Archive (hereinafter, DNSA).

13 Crop destruction has always fallen under the military's definition of biological warfare since its initial employment in the Second World War. This constitutes

an important link between the military and nonmilitary functions undergirding more intensive drug control. Peter Sills, *Toxic War: The Story of Agent Orange* (Nashville: Vanderbilt University Press, 2014), 16.

14 Though the "War on Drugs" employed a war metaphor, it actually directed unparalleled resources to reducing domestic drug addiction, eventually prioritizing control of overseas supply over domestic demand reduction in later presidential administrations.

15 Aaron Navarro, *Political Intelligence and the Creation of Modern Mexico, 1938–1954* (University Park: Pennsylvania State University Press, 2010), 11.

16 Renata Keller, *Mexico's Cold War: Cuba, the United States, and the Legacy of the Mexican Revolution* (New York: Cambridge University Press, 2015).

17 Paul Gillingham and Benjamin T. Smith, eds., *Dictablanda: Politics, Work, and Culture in Mexico, 1938–1968* (Durham: Duke University Press, 2014), vii-xiv.

18 Marc Becker, *The FBI in Latin America: The Ecuador Files* (Durham, NC: Duke University Press, 2017); Katherine Unterman, *Uncle Sam's Policemen: The Pursuit of Fugitives across Borders* (Cambridge, MA: Harvard University Press, 2015).

19 Barry Carr, *Marxism and Communism in Twentieth-Century Mexico* (Lincoln: University of Nebraska Press, 1992), 146–47.

20 Navarro, *Political Intelligence and the Creation of Modern Mexico*, 11, 170.

21 Navarro, *Political Intelligence and the Creation of Modern Mexico*, 185.

22 Camp, *Generals in the Palacio*, 22–23.

23 "DIA Intelligence Information Report," October 18, 1968, Document 23, National Security Archive.

24 *Reminiscences of Joseph John Jova: Oral History*, 1978, November 20, 1974, Columbia Center for Oral History, Columbia University, New York, NY. Echeverría rode a fine line between public condemnation of the United States and less public cooperation with a number of US agencies.

25 Thomas Rath, *Myths of Demilitarization in Postrevolutionary Mexico, 1920–1960* (Chapel Hill: University of North Carolina Press, 2013), 2, 82.

26 Peter R. Kann, "The Heroin Patrol: How Mexican Soldiers Traipse through Hill Pulling Opium Poppies," *Wall Street Journal*, May 3, 1967; Benjamin T. Smith, "The Rise and Fall of Narcopopulism in Sinaloa, 1940–1980," *Journal for the Study of Radicalism*, 7 (2013): 125–67.

27 "US Treasury Secretary's Meeting with President Díaz Ordaz," November 24, 1969, DNSA

28 "Narcotics, Marihuana, and Dangerous Drugs: Working Group Report No. 5," November 11, 1969, DNSA; "US Department of State, Bureau of Inter-American Affairs Action Memorandum," February 26, 1970, DNSA.

29 "Technical Assistance and Equipment for Marihuana Eradication," December 17, 1969, DNSA; Richard Craig, "La Campaña Permanente," *Journal of Interamerican Studies and World Affairs* 20, no. 2 (1978): 127.

30 "'Equipment Requested by Mexico," August 3, 1971, DNSA.

31 "Plan de apoyo aereo a las zonas militaries que Participan en la campaña contra enervantes," 6 de septiembre 1971, *Excelsior*, Secretaria de la Defensa Nacional, Conspraciones Políticas, c. 224, exp. 301–1974.

32 "The Potential of a Forward Strategy against Heroin in Mexico," August 15, 1975, DNSA.

33 "The Potential of a Forward Strategy against Heroin in Mexico." Note: Alexander Aviña's *Specters of Revolution: Peasant Guerillas in the Cold War Mexican Countryside* (New York: Oxford University Press, 2014) shows how the Mexican government played an active role in putting down local resistance in Guerrero. The level of violence PRI agents encountered in Guerrero influenced some of their reluctance to establish a stronger anti-drug presence there.

34 "Estado de Baja California," exp. 19-36-76; L-; H-268–269, 25 de Mayo 1976, Dirección Federal de la Seguridad, Archivo General de la Nación.

35 "The Potential of a Forward Strategy against Heroin in Mexico."

36 Drug Abuse Task Force, *White Paper on Drug Abuse*; Daniel Weimer, *Seeing Drugs: Modernization, Counterinsurgency, and US Narcotics Control in the Third World, 1969–1975* (Kent, OH: Kent State University Press, 2011).

37 Mexico's Operation Condor, the country's herbicidal drug crop eradication campaign, is not to be confused with the campaign of state terror in the Southern Cone of South America.

38 Peter Bensinger (DEA Administrator, 1976–81), personal communication, August 2018.

39 "Son diversas las quejas que se han presentado por el atropello . . . ," c. 1711-C, exp. 13, 22 de febrero 1977, Dirección General de Investigaciones Políticas y Sociales.

40 "Algunos Oficiales del ejercito de la campaña contra el narcotrafico, despojan del ganado a los campesinos," 11 de marzo 1977, Box 1709-B, Folder 9, Dirección General de Investigaciones Políticas y Sociales; Richard B. Craig, "Human Rights and Mexico's Antidrug Campaign," *Social Science Quarterly* 60, no. 4 (1980): 691–701.

41 Secretary of State, "Press Guidance Regarding Village Voice Article of June 4, 1979," June 7, 1979, Central Foreign Policy Files, 1973–79, RG59, Access to Archival Databases.

42 "Drug Enforcement Administration, 1975–1980," accessed March 22, 2021, www.dea.gov.

43 "CIA Intelligence Summary," December 2, 1983, DNSA.

44 Cited in *El Sol de Sinaloa*, July 14, 1979 in Freedom of Information Act Electronic Reading Room, Central Intelligence Agency, www.cia.gov.

45 Cited in *Excelsior*, June 19, 1979 in Freedom of Information Act Electronic Reading Room, Central Intelligence Agency, www.cia.gov.

46 "Heroin Deaths in US Cut by 40%," *Los Angeles Times*, February 11, 1978.

47 Reagan worked hard to change popular attitudes toward drugs, with his wife Nancy championing her infamous "Just Say No" campaign. Conservative discourse touted a laxity in American drug policies as the cause for increased drug

consumption, arguing that drug use had become more permissive during the Carter years.

48 "Reagan Names Task Force on South Florida Crime," *Washington Post,* January 29, 1982; Peter Andreas, *Border Games: Policing the US-Mexico Divide* (Ithaca: Cornell University Press: 2000), 43.

49 "International Narcotics Control Strategy Report, Mexico," December 30, 1985, DNSA.

50 Luis Astorga, "Organized Crime and the Organization of Crime" in *Organized Crime and Democratic Governability: Mexico and the US-Mexican Borderlands,* ed. John Bailey and Roy Godson (Pittsburgh: University of Pittsburg Press, 2000), 74.

51 Astorga, "Organized Crime and the Organization of Crime," 61.

52 Stanley A. Pimentel, "The Nexus of Organized Crime and Politics in Mexico," in Bailey and Godson, *Organized Crime and Democratic Governability,* 45–46.

53 Joel Brinkley, "Vast, Undreamed-of Drug Use Feared," November 23, 1984, *New York Times*; "Mexico Says 5,000 Workers Rescued from Pot Planters," November 14, 1984, *Philadelphia Inquirer.*

54 George Grayson, *The Cartels: The Story of Mexico's Most Dangerous Criminal Organizations and Their Impact on US Security* (Santa Barbara, CA: Praeger, 2014), 32–34; Astorga, *El siglo de las drogas,* 116; Brinkley, "Vast, Undreamed-of Drug Use Feared"; "Mexico Says 5,000 Workers Rescued from Pot Planters."

55 Grayson, *The Cartels,* 32–34; Astorga, *El siglo de las drogas,* 116; Brinkley, "Vast, Undreamed-of Drug Use Feared"; "Mexico Says 5,000 Workers Rescued from Pot Planters."

56 "Drug Enforcement Administration, 1985–1990."

57 It should be noted that Mexico was also experiencing extreme economic hardship. The rise in the homicide rate cannot solely be attributable to drug issues. Pablo Piccato, "Estadísticas del crimen en México: Series históricas, 1901–2001"; Instituto Nacional de Estadística y Geografía, *Estadísticas históricas de México CD-ROM* (Mexico City, 2000); Wil Pansters, "Zones of State-Making," in *Violence, Coercion, and State-Making in Twentieth-Century Mexico,* ed. Will Pansters (Stanford, CA: Stanford University Press, 2012), 11.

58 United States Agency for International Development, Foreign Aid Explorer, *US Overseas Loans and Grants (Greenbook),* accessed March 22, 2021, https://explorer .usaid.gov; "Revised International Narcotics Control Strategy Report (INCSR), Mexico," January 15, 1988, DNSA.

59 Cited in *Notimex,* October 30, 1986 in Freedom of Information Act Electronic Reading Room, Central Intelligence Agency, www.cia.gov.

60 J. Standefer and J. S. Meyer, "CIA Zeroes in on Mexico Corruption," November 1986, *San Diego Union,* in Freedom of Information Act Electronic Reading Room, Central Intelligence Agency, www.cia.gov.

61 William von Raab (Customs Commissioner, 1981–88), personal communication, October 2018.

62 Walter Pincus, "Hazards of Profession Ensnare DEA Agent," *Washington Post*, November 4, 1982.

63 Ethan A. Nadelmann, *Cops across Borders: The Internationalization of US Criminal Law Enforcement* (University Park: Pennsylvania State University Press, 1993), 288.

64 "ARA Guidances, Department of State," February 12, 1998, DNSA; William Orme, "Reagan Visit Backs Mexican Antidrug Effort," *Washington Post*, February 11, 1988.

65 "International Narcotics Control Strategy Report," March 1989, DNSA.

66 "Funding for Mexico's Counternarcotics Program," August 14, 1989, DNSA.

67 "Revised International Narcotics Control Strategy Report (INCSR), Mexico," January 15, 1988, DNSA.

68 "Navy Increases Surveillance by 70 Percent," *Red Nacional 13 Imevision Television*, Mexico City, December 18, 1986, in Freedom of Information Act Electronic Reading Room, Central Intelligence Agency, www.cia.gov.

9

The War on Drugs in Afghanistan

JAMES BRADFORD

For much of the first half of the twentieth century, opium and hashish from Afghanistan were used by consumers throughout South and Central Asia. But in the 1960s and 1970s, the demand for Afghan drugs grew beyond regional markets, and the Afghan government, under pressure from the United States and the international community, implemented a series of drug-control policies attempting to curb the illicit drug trade and its globalization. This chapter explores why Afghanistan emerged as a global drug hotspot, what the Afghan government did to try to stop it, and ultimately, why attempts to stop the drug trade failed.

Little has been written about the history of drugs in Afghanistan, nor about how it fits into the broader histories of the global drug trade or of international drug control policies. Unearthing the history of drugs and drug control in Afghanistan reveals how, in the 1970s, more stringent anti-drug policies were implemented largely as a vehicle for the expansion of state power, which parallels what happened in other countries' drug wars. This chapter also calls into question the notion that drugs thrive in undeveloped economies. Indeed, it explores the ways economic development, rather than serving as a deterrent, proved critical in helping to build and shape the illicit drug trade.

In October of 1971, Terry Burke, a decorated Marine and former CIA officer, flew to Kabul, Afghanistan with his family to fulfill the mandate of then-President Richard Nixon to expand the war against the supply and distribution of illicit drugs.[1] As the first agent for the Bureau of Narcotics and Dangerous Drugs to be stationed exclusively in Afghanistan, Burke's mandate to stem the tide of drugs that flowed increasingly from Kabul to destinations west was both ambitious and daunting. Burke was not there to bust the travelers who flocked to Afghanistan to find cheap drugs, but rather to stop the growing threat of the Brotherhood of Eternal Love. Unlike the usual rag-tag, drug-using American sojourners, members of the Brotherhood were a different breed of Westerner. They went to Afghanistan to buy large quantities of Afghan hashish, some of the best in the world, to smuggle back to the United States and Canada. Over the course of the two years he was stationed in Kabul, however, Burke's fears that the Brotherhood would create a sophisticated smuggling operation bringing hashish from the isolated mountain kingdom of Afghanistan to the shores of sunny California would be subsumed by a larger and more pressing problem. He watched as Afghanistan transformed from a major supplier of hash to one the world's major suppliers of opium.

Like the many other US drug agents stationed in drug hotspots around the world, Burke did not foresee the changes that would occur to the international illicit drug trade. At the time, many governments where drug production and distribution thrived were quite content to cooperate with the US to expand drug control measures. For these governments, coopting the War on Drugs meant a major infusion of money, resources, and manpower to bolster such drug suppression efforts as crop eradications, alternative development programs, and, overall, a greater exertion of political pressures to reduce supply and limit distribution. And yet, despite such cooperative efforts, a tragic game of cat-and-mouse ensued over the course of the following decades, a game that disrupted much of the flow of the illicit drug trade. Under pressure from the Nixon administration, drug laws in numerous nations increasingly emphasized the criminalization of use and users. In addition, users adapted to shortages in long-standing drug supplies by shifting to new methods of consumption or even new drugs, often more dangerous ones than what they had been using before. Producers and distributors, meanwhile, adapted to the seemingly endless demand for drugs by finding new sources of supplies and new routes and methods of distribution. Unbeknownst to Burke, or the countless others like him, in the first years of the War on Drugs those agents were coming face to face with a global illicit drug trade that was proving to be far more dynamic than anticipated. It is this organizational and entrepreneurial dynamism that has come define the illicit drug trade over the past fifty years.

The drug trade in Afghanistan exemplifies this dynamic historical process. It has changed significantly since Burke first arrived in Kabul.

Afghanistan is now the world's largest producer of illicit opium,[2] and still a major producer of hashish in Asia,[3] this despite massive amounts of money, resources, and people sent to stop it.[4] But it wasn't always the case. How, and why, Afghanistan came to be such a massive producer of illicit drugs is a history that is often overshadowed by the overwhelming attention paid to the current drug trade in Afghanistan.[5]

Contrary to more popular depictions of Afghanistan's drug trade in recent decades,[6] Afghanistan emerged as a major supplier not simply a result of the past four decades of war, marked by the Taliban insurgency, or decades of domestic corruption, political chaos and instability.[7] There is far more to this story. Through the examination of recently declassified and unexplored US and Afghan documents, I will demonstrate how, beginning in the early 1970s, Afghanistan increased efforts to curb the production and trafficking of illicit drugs, largely under pressure from the US.

Looking at the history of the US War on Drugs and its impact on Afghanistan's society and economy necessitates an analysis of the role the Afghan government played in that process.[8] Afghanistan has a long, complicated, and sometimes divisive history of state formation and growth and this history directly affected how effective the Afghan government was—and chose to be—in partnering with the US in drug control.[9] The US-led War on Drugs marked a significant change in how the Afghan government approached the issue of drug production, use, and trade. The Afghan government had tried to implement more stringent forms of drug control before American pressures were applied, including a ban of opium in 1944–45 and the eradication of opium in Badakhshan, a mountainous province in the north of the country, in 1958. But by the 1970s the contours of drug control and the drug trade in Afghanistan were increasingly shaped by American anti-drug efforts.[10]

In the late 1960s, Afghanistan was already a source for hashish and opium. But as Afghan suppliers of illegal drugs, hashish especially, became more and more critical to the US market, American counternarcotics agents began to pay greater attention to Afghanistan. Burke's arrival in 1971 marked Afghanistan's entry into the newly minted US War on Drugs. Burke worked closely with Afghan officials to ramp up suppression efforts, as the Afghan government created new police units with expanded interdiction capabilities, and also authorized increased crop eradication programs. As Kathleen Frydl has convincingly shown for the US, the drug war "served as a modality" for the expansion of muscular state power in the US. Similarly, the War on Drugs was exported to Afghanistan, where it likewise provided the fragile Afghan government with greater resources to expand its reach and power.[11] While the efforts to stop drugs were significant, they were largely unsuccessful; anti-drug crusaders were also contending with historical features that primed Afghanistan's emergence into the global illicit drug trade.

Afghanistan's transformation from a regional to a global epicenter for drugs was felt most acutely in the shifts in agricultural production in the Helmand Valley. From 1946 to the 1970s, Helmand, an arid region in the southwest of the country, was the site of a massive US-sponsored agro-industrial project. The US intended to teach Afghan farmers to use new techniques and technology toward the production of crops in hopes of improving agricultural exports. The project worked, but in unexpected ways. As Helmand farmers adjusted their crops to respond to changes in global pricing, they were also exposed to the growing demand for opium, and in turn, started to grow larger and larger quantities of opium throughout the 1970s.

The timing of the War on Drugs in Afghanistan proved critical. Successful—or, at least relatively successful—American-led drug interdiction efforts in several long-standing drug-supplying nations such as Thailand, Turkey, and Mexico, had opened up channels for Afghan drugs to fill the void. This profitable opportunity had a tremendous impact on certain regions of Afghanistan, such as Helmand, transforming it from a small producer and user of opium and cannabis to the world's largest source of illicit opium. Maybe more important was the fact that the globalizing dimensions of the drug trade in Afghanistan coincided with increasing political and social tumult in Afghanistan. The Afghan War on Drugs, the success of which hinged on the cooperation of the state, would eventually be dependent on a state with a decreasing willingness and capacity to fight this war. By the end of the 1970s, Afghanistan would be producing more drugs than it ever had in its history, just as the Afghan government and society was descending into chaos and, eventually, war.

Terry Burke could not, of course, foresee the unfolding of such events when he was stationed in Afghanistan. But as Burke's tenure in

Afghanistan drew to a close in 1973, he became increasingly pessimistic about the ability to stop the emerging drug trade in Afghanistan.[12] What had once started as a mission to catch hashish traffickers was evolving into something far more dynamic, dangerous, and potentially more intractable to the Afghan situation—the production and trafficking of heroin.

The World and the War on Drugs

Although the US had been battling illegal drug use and trafficking for much of the twentieth century,[13] when President Richard Nixon officially launched the War on Drugs in June 1971, it symbolized the growing nexus between domestic drug issues in the US and the supply and traffic in drugs from abroad. Countries whose drug supply affected the American population in some manner were now under greater scrutiny from the US government. As Frydl has noted, the global expanse of the War on Drugs transformed drug policy "from a discrete foreign policy objective into a valued collection of tools to manage relations with the developing world."[14]

The timing of Nixon's War on Drugs reflected an attempt to transform American political power in the waning days of the war in Vietnam, a conflict that had revealed the limits of American military might and had severely damaged the US's international legitimacy. In addition, the presence of heroin addiction among GIs in Vietnam shocked the American public as to the extent and reach of the drug trade in that embattled region.

Few Americans were aware of how deeply entangled the drug trade was in the conflict in Southeast Asia.[15] Over the course of the twentieth century, the rough mountainous terrain connecting Burma (now Myanmar), Thailand, and Laos had developed into one of the world's major sources of heroin. In 1971, US Assistant Secretary of State Marshall Green dubbed the region the "Golden Triangle."[16]

To stop the looming threat of the drug trade in both Southeast Asia and the US, the Nixon administration required the cooperation of states to successfully curb drug supplies. Some countries proved more willing, if not able, than others. Thailand, under the direction of King Bhumibol Adulyadej, had already started programs in the 1960s to curb opium production among the hill tribes in the north of the country by increasing economic development and political engagement. When Nixon declared the war in 1971, Americans found a ready and able partner in the king.[17] In 1972, the Burmese, too, emerged as a recipient of counter-narcotics resources from the US.[18]

The impact of Nixon's War on Drugs abroad was even more acute just south of the American border. In 1969, in an effort to curb the heavy flow of marijuana and increasingly brown heroin from Mexico, Nixon launched Operation Intercept and closed the Mexican-American border.[19] Although the border closing lasted only three weeks, it ultimately forced the leaders of the Mexican government to comply with American demands for more stringent efforts to curb the drug trade. By 1971, the US had increased aid to Mexico, and by the end of the decade, Mexico was a willing partner in the War on Drugs, with the ruling PRI co-opting much of the drug war to further entrench its political control over the country.[20]

Turkey, much like Mexico, also faced the wrath of the Americans. It was a popular assumption during the 1960s that much of the heroin that flooded the streets of New York came via the infamous "French Connection," and was sourced from Turkey. In 1971, the US offered $35 million in aid to convince the Turkish government to ban the production of opium.[21] Although the ban was relatively unpopular among farmers and drug traffickers (obviously), some involved in the illicit drug trade in Turkey anticipated the backlash to their "business." They had already sought out new sources of supply and safer trafficking routes prior to the ban in 1971.[22]

Whether through pressure or due to sincere efforts to stop drugs in their own countries, many drug-producing states cooperated to some degree with the American War on Drugs. The access to resources, money, and training were an attractive incentive for states looking to expand their own political power within their borders. The question of whether those programs actually curbed the illicit drug trade was another matter. As countries like Thailand and Mexico achieved temporary "success" in reducing the production of drugs in the own country, the global dimensions of the drug trade largely evolved. Consequently, the pressures of the War on Drugs merely shifted the contours by which the drug trade operated.[23] These seismic shifts in suppliers would ultimately ensnare Afghanistan as a primary source of opium for the global illicit drug trade.

Afghanistan

Afghanistan has a long history of cultivation, trade, and use of both opium and cannabis. Cannabis, in particular, has been used widely by Afghans for centuries, generating a unique cannabis culture that continues to this day.[24] Opium, on the other hand, has not been as widespread, but thrives in certain regions of the country ideally suited for opium production and trade. In Badakhshan, farmers have grown opium for centuries, and in the past century it has become the primary cash crop for farmers in the region. Opium in Badakhshan is also considered some of the very best in the world. Similarly, both opium and cannabis have been grown around Herat (in the west) and in Nangarhar (southeast of Kabul and bordering Pakistan). Nonetheless, despite a long history of drug production and trade, Afghanistan was never a significant player in the global drug trade until the twentieth century.

In 1924, the colonial government of British India announced the prohibition of all opium and cannabis products that made their way into British India from countries along the frontier. Although the prohibition did not mention Afghanistan specifically, it was enacted largely in response to the growing threat of opium and hashish smuggled from Afghanistan.[25] The law, in many ways, marked one of the earliest indications that the drug trade in Afghanistan was expanding beyond domestic markets. This 1924 law was the culmination of a decades-long development that began under the rule of Abdur Rahman Khan (r. 1880–1901), whereby the state expanded opium and hashish[26] exports into British India as part of a broader effort to grow the Afghan economy and the power of the state through the export trade.[27]

In the following decades, various Afghan rulers tread a delicate balance between encouraging drug production for export and trying to deter drug use and addiction among the local Afghan population. Amanullah Khan, who ruled Afghanistan from 1919 to 1928, and is considered by most historians to be the most aggressive modernizer of early twentieth-century Afghan society,[28] launched a series of new laws, also in 1924, intended to discourage domestic drug use all the while encouraging and expanding drug exports. Amanullah reduced excise duties on opium and hashish exports, but imposed strict taxes (many with steep and draconian penalties) on those drugs destined for use within Afghanistan.[29] Although there is little evidence of the impact and success of Amanullah's drug policies (especially domestically), his foray into drug control signified the growing influence of the drug trade in shaping the future of Afghanistan. But it also presented a paradox, as opium and hashish provided new opportunities for both the growth of markets (legal and/or illicit) and the growth of the Afghan state (through drug control and capital from trade).

Afghan rulers would never fully resolve this paradox. Bans on opium in 1944 and 1957 signaled that opium exports were increasingly impor- tant to the state, but so too were diplomatic relationships that could accelerate Afghanistan's economic growth and the state's political power. In 1944, Afghanistan announced a total ban on government run opium production and sale.[30] The decision to launch the ban was largely a result of the Afghan government's failed attempts to become a legal producer and exporter of opium for the global pharmaceutical market.[31] But it proved fruitful in other ways. On condition of banning opium, the US government agreed to formalize its diplomatic relationship with the Afghan government, paving the way for increased economic develop- ment, including the start of a major development project in the Hel- mand Valley.[32]

Ultimately, the 1944 ban did very little to alter the drug trade, as many Afghan companies simply stopped selling to the US. And not more than a few years later, the Afghan government began pressing the United Nations for recognition as an internationally sanctioned producer of opium. As a result, the ban of opium in 1957 was largely a continuation of the unresolved issues brought about by the previous prohibition. The difference between 1957 and 1944, however, was that the ruler of Afghan- istan in 1957, Mohammad Daud Khan, actually enforced a prohibition of opium, albeit only in the opium-dependent province of Badakhshan.[33]

These bans reflected how both the drug trade and drug control were increasingly shaped by international forces. On the one hand, Afghan opium was increasingly in demand in Europe and elsewhere as both a legal and illicit good, one on which farmers and traders were growing more reliant, especially in lieu of shrinking exports for "legal" goods.[34]

On the other hand, the need for international recognition required Afghan rulers to implement policies to curb the drug trade, despite the fact that such policies were at odds with the economic realities on the ground. In this way, the opium bans were launched largely to appease the international community, especially the US, even as opium consumers outside Afghanistan provided a lucrative market for domestic producers.

More importantly, the deeper conflicts over banning opium exhibited an enduring issue that would shape Afghanistan's future drug trade. The government's anti-drug approach, while good for diplomacy, was hard to enforce on the ground, as political issues between the state and rural tribal authorities often went unresolved. In addition, cultural norms, in which opium and hashish wee integral parts of rural livelihoods, endured. Finally, the recognition that drugs, even if illegal, were potentially lucrative goods for Afghans, ultimately made imposing drug restrictions difficult for any state, let alone one with such unstable footing as Afghanistan.[35]

Afghanistan Delivers

During the "Sixties" era, drug historians Mike Ritter and Peter Maguire recount, "Afghanistan lived up to the wildest fantasies of the hippies." As the counterculture movement gripped the West, thousands of young Americans and Europeans hit the road to Asia in search of spiritual truth, love, and, most importantly, cheap drugs. But Afghanistan was different from other stops along the infamous "hippie trail." Not only did it have an ancient culture and some of the most beautiful and stark landscapes in Asia; it also produced some of the world's best hashish. Hashish was to Afghanistan, Ritter and Maguire explain, "what wine was to France."[36]

Many young travelers in the 1960s and early 1970s acted as if Afghanistan existed to cater to their demands for drugs. In Kabul, Chicken Street, in the Shahre-Naw district, was famous for easily accessible hashish, opium, and even beer (alcoholic beverages were harder to come by in the predominately Islamic nation than were the drugs). The Noor and Mustafa Hotels were popular hangouts for drug-seeking travelers. The political and cultural climate was ideal for Afghanistan's role as a source for hashish. Although opium and hashish were technically illegal, drugs laws were rarely enforced.[37] Throughout the country, travelers would find special teahouses (*saqikhana*) dedicated to hashish use.[38] Moreover, Afghan hashish was among the best in the world; one could purchase up to twenty-five variations, much of which contained extraordinarily high percentages of THC.[39] Not only was the quality top-notch, but both opium and hashish were cheap; opium could be purchased in Kabul for $45 per kilogram; high-quality hash would go for less than $20 per kilogram. The ease of access to cheap and powerful drugs made Afghanistan one of the most important stops on the "hippie trail." In 1971 alone, almost sixty thousand "hippie" tourists from Europe and North America flocked to Kabul, many to take advantage of the drug trade.[40]

Similar to the manner in which cannabis helped prime Colombia's emergence as the global epicenter for the cocaine trade,[41] hashish proved a critical commodity in bridging the gaps between Western demand and Afghan producers. As the 1960s progressed, a noticeable change occurred in the hashish trade, which indicated that Afghan hashish was being produced for export illicitly. The British writer Peter Levi, in his travels to Afghanistan in the late 1960s, noted that in "Kandahar it was a big industry and even small children tried to sell us hash in its various forms . . . Every kind of smuggling device was for sale, strings of hash beads, hash belts, hash-heeled shoes and for all I know hash codpieces."[42] Producers began altering their methods to ensure they could supply larger volumes of hashish, often at the expense of quality. Traffickers also began mixing lower-quality resins with those of higher quality, reducing the potency of the hashish. Oils, too, were added to mimic the texture and consistency of higher quality hashish, mainly to make it feel sticky, thereby masking the deficiencies in the product.[43]

The growing demand for cannabis products was too large to ignore, even for the Afghan government. Although, the production and sale of drugs were illegal under Afghan law, the government saw economic opportunity in the trade, particularly in light of the largely stagnant national economy. As a result, in 1969 and 1970, King Zahir Shah issued an official edict to encourage farmers to use fertilizers to increase cannabis cultivation.[44] Not surprisingly, cannabis cultivation flourished around Herat, Kandahar, and Mazar-e-Sharif, and cannabis plants were seen lining many of the major roadways around the country.[45] For Afghan farmers, the growing demand for hashish provided more than just

much-needed income, it provided the capital they needed to modernize. They used their hashish money to purchase agricultural equipment,
such as tractors and the like, that normally would have been unattain-
able.[46] As the 1960s came to a close, Afghan hashish was emerging as a
global commodity. It would also prove critical in shaping Afghanistan's
future opium trade and the coming US War on Drugs.

The War on Drugs Comes to Afghanistan

As Afghan hashish flowed to markets west, opium production was
increasingly also making its way into Iran. The fact that hashish and
opium were both growing more prevalent in southwest Asian countries was ringing alarm bells for those nations that sought to stamp out
the illicit drug trade, especially the US. For Terry Burke, the Bureau of
Dangerous Drugs and Narcotics agent who arrived in 1971, policing this
growing trade would be a monumental task. For the past century, drugs
had served as a lucrative, albeit small, source of trade for Afghan farmers
and traders; the government, too, largely tolerated opium and hashish markets. The brief forays into stricter drug control policies (1944
and 1957) were either limited by the reach of the state, or enacted to
manipulate diplomatic relationships in their favor. But as the War on
Drugs expanded globally in the 1970s, Afghanistan, too, would be influenced by the growing pressure to crack down on illicit drugs, marking
a significant change in the relationship between the government and
the drug trade. For some figures in the Afghan government, especially
Mohammad Daud Khan, the increased access to resources to curb drug
production would be advantageous for the expansion of state power. But
even then, the limitations of state power in rural Afghanistan would do
little more than change the dimensions by which the government could
control or influence the drug trade.

When Burke arrived in 1971, the hippies buying small amounts of
hash on Chicken Street were largely irrelevant to his mandate. He was
there to track and bust the American drug traffickers who were import-
ing cheap Afghan hashish to the US. Burke noted in 1972:

> While of somewhat secondary significance relative to opium, hashish
> has been important in our enforcement efforts because of the smuggling

systems that have spawned. The drug seeking hippie who came to Afghanistan a few years ago and spent his last few travelers check to take home a
kilo or so of Afghan hashish has been replaced by the well-heeled young
entrepreneur from the US.[47]

Burke was particularly focused on the Brotherhood of Eternal Love. As
David Farber recounts in his chapter in this volume, the Brotherhood
emerged amid the counterculture movement in the 1960s in Southern
California and its members were, at first, true believers in the sacra-
mental and spiritual use of hallucinogens. The Brotherhood rose to
prominence by distributing massive amounts of LSD, most famously
Orange Sunshine. Under the leadership of John Griggs, himself an aco-
lyte of the infamous Timothy Leary, the Brotherhood evolved into some
of the largest distributors of the LSD and hashish in the US.[48] The presence of the Brotherhood in Afghanistan was seen by Burke as a key link
in the emerging connection between Afghan sources and Western markets. In particular, the Brotherhood specialized in buying hash oil in
Afghanistan. Hash oil was much easier for them to smuggle than bricks
of hashish. The oil was also far more potent and thus more profitable.[49]
Despite their preference for hashish oil, hashish itself was lucrative
enough. According to Terry Burke, the Brotherhood could net $80,000
for every fifty kilos of Afghan hashish sold in Montreal or New York.[50]
    The Afghan government was entirely unprepared to deal with the
globalizing dimensions of the drug trade. Afghan police, especially, appeared to be either indifferent to or corrupted by the Western traffickers. As early as 1958, a cadre of West German police officers were sent to
Kabul to train Afghan police in a wide array of enforcement techniques
and strategies. Success was minimal. The failure of policing was due in
part to the fact that police officers were often the least qualified public
servants, being drawn from the bottom 10 percent of army conscripts.
Moreover, they were woefully underpaid, and overwhelmingly illiterate
to boot. When police officers did show effort in trying to crack down on
drug traffickers, they were often placed on leave.[51] As one German police officer noted, the West German police trainers were essentially turning the Afghan police into the "most highly organized criminal element
in Afghanistan."[52] The gendarmerie was no better. Structured as a paramilitary force under the Ministry of Interior Affairs, the mission was

primarily to maintain internal security and to supplement the police. Although a large force, most gendarmes were located in key provinces just outside of Kabul, with only a few border posts on the Afghan–Pakistan and Afghan–Iranian borders. As a result, the majority of seizures from the police and gendarmerie were near Kabul, while the majority of drug smuggling continued unabated on Afghanistan's southern and western borders.[53]

Prior to Nixon's War on Drugs, the US had applied pressure to curb the growing threat of drug smuggling. In 1969, the US and its allies in the region, Iran and Pakistan, pressured the Afghan government to pass an anti-smuggling law.[54] The law centralized police and judicial efforts against drugs, placing greater power in an expanded Kabul police force. While the centralization of Afghanistan's police force to wage a war against drugs was ideal in theory, it was flawed in practice. State authority in Kabul was vastly different than in rural Afghanistan. One of the major reasons why state authority was limited was because of the role of *qawm* in shaping state–society relations. *Qawm* in Afghanistan, according to historian Olivier Roy, describes a fluctuating sense of identity, which places communal, tribal, or ethnic identity over national identity. For police and gendarmes, decisions were often dictated by their *qawm*, as they would put the needs of their tribe or community over national drug control policies.[55] In this way, *qawm* undermined the ability of the government to impose nationwide policies on drug control. More simply put: would lower-level state officials in border regions arrest smugglers, many of whom they had more in common with than people in Kabul, for the sake of the state, whose legitimacy was always in question, particularly the further one got from Kabul?[56]

American officials became increasingly aware that the size and influence of the drug trade in Afghanistan was so large and widespread that narcotics matters could not be handled under the traditional legal and police constructs. In 1971, when the War on Drugs commenced and American pressure increased, it seemed the Afghan government took a more concerted approach to fighting the drug trade. Prime Minister Abdul Zahir created a separate narcotics commission tasked with expanding customs police and border patrols. The commission increased funding and technical assistance as a means of expanding the crackdown on the production of opium and hash. By 1972, Zahir's successor,

Musa Shafiq, consolidated narcotics matters under two ministries. The Ministry of Interior Affairs was tasked with countering smuggling, including the creation of new anti-smuggling units (ASUs), while the Ministry of Agriculture dealt with issues related to drug cultivation.[57] Between 1971 and 1972, there was a noticeable increase in drug seizures from the ASUs and police. According to official Afghan statistics, the number of arrests of smugglers increased from seventy-two in 1971 (the year 1350, according to the Afghan calendar) to 221 in 1972 (1351), before skyrocketing to 584 in 1973 (1352).[58] The consolidation of the police and ASUs was starting to pay dividends for the US, especially in regard to the Brotherhood of Eternal Love, as a joint raid by the Bureau of Dangerous Drugs and Narcotics and Kabul police in 1972 confiscated almost twenty-five gallons of liquid hashish, estimated to be worth $6 million in the US.[59]

Despite such increased efforts by the Afghan government, Afghan officials readily admitted they could not stop the drug trade on their own. They appealed to the international community for help. The success of drug control programs, they insisted, ultimately rested on the willingness of the international community to fund such development. International organizations agreed, but they insisted that Afghanistan would also have undergo greater institutional transformations to fulfill international expectations for drug control. The UN Food and Agricultural Organization advocated a sweeping reform to Afghanistan's anti-smuggling and anti-opium laws to help it comply with the 1961 UN Single Convention. If the Afghan government complied, the UN proposed a three-year support program valued at around $2.5 million, with an additional $2 million per year following the initial term. Of that grant, $790,000 of UN Fund for Drug Abuse Control funds would be used for agricultural development, while $255,000 would be used for enforcement. Burke, of the Bureau of Narcotics and Dangerous Drugs, with the help of US Ambassador Alfred Neumann, piggybacked on that international effort by creating an Afghan Narcotics Control Action Plan, with a heavy emphasis on enforcement.[60] By 1972, the money started pouring into Afghanistan.

Despite money and resources from both the UN and the US, little changed. In 1973, however, when Mohammad Daud Khan ended the Musahiban Dynasty of King Zahir Shah and established the Republic of

Afghanistan, the implementation of a new, more effective drug policy seemed possible.[61] Although Daud was apparently leaning toward the Soviet Union, he embraced stricter drug control as a way to increase foreign aid for economic development and also to bolster the strength of the police and paramilitary units. Daud made significant moves to curb the production and smuggling of opium and hash. The head of the Ministry of Interior Affairs, Faiz Mohammad, was put in charge of a new ASU. Unlike previous units, which were part of local police jurisdiction, the new ASUs were given national jurisdiction and charged primarily with stopping the drug trade. Mohammad's ASU was made up of twelve "eager" men, trained by UN Fund for Drug Abuse Control and US experts, and would collect information and intelligence and launch covert sting operations against high-level traffickers. In many ways, the ASUs were an ideal manifestation of the US's War on Drugs in Afghanistan.[62] Even then, however, Daud, in an effort to maintain Cold War neutrality, seemed to push back against outright cooperation with the US, and mainly carried out drug control through the UN.

By 1975, the ASUs seemed to be producing dividends, as evidenced by several large drug busts, including a seizure of one ton of opium.[63] But there were other developments that hinted at the evolving nature of the drug trade in Afghanistan and the limits of the state's ability to stop it. First, heroin was increasingly prevalent in domestic drug seizures, indicating that demand for Afghan opium was moving beyond its regional market in Iran, as Iran was not a major consumer of heroin.[64] Terry Burke had noted in 1973 that while Afghanistan did not possess the capability then to process opium to morphine base, various Afghan drug traffickers were endeavoring to do so. Furthermore, Kurdish groups were buying Afghan opium and processing it into morphine base in Eastern Turkey.[65] Moreover, the state still remained limited in its overall impact on the drug trade; most seizures happened closer to Kabul and trafficking continued virtually unabated in border regions.[66] To make matters worse, cultivation seemed to be spreading, as well. The growing demand for Afghan opium, in large part a consequence of the dwindling supply in Southeast Asia and Turkey, was fundamentally changing rural Afghanistan.[67] In the Helmand Valley, where the US had poured hundreds of millions of dollars into transforming the agricultural economy, opium was emerging as farmers' preferred cash crop. The consequences of this agricultural transformation would profoundly shape Afghanistan's history.

The Changing Landscape of the Afghan Drug Trade

The growth of the opium trade in Helmand is indicative of the multidimensional manner in which the War on Drugs converged with market forces, as well as other policy objectives in Afghanistan. As efforts to curb the drug trade increased in the 1970s, so too did demand for Afghan opium (not just hashish). But Afghanistan, and Helmand especially, were undergoing a dramatic transformation in other ways that amplify this convergence of forces. For Helmand was the site of the largest American development project in the country, a project which sought to make Afghanistan a contributor to the global economy but also to make it a bulwark against the Soviet Union to the north.[68]

Helmand is the largest province in Afghanistan. Between the foothills to the north and the dry arid desert to the south runs the most important geographic feature of the Helmand Valley, the Helmand River. For centuries, Afghans had tried to harness the power of the river for economic development but it wasn't until the Americans arrived that Helmand province began to change significantly. In 1945, after the US and Afghan governments formalized their diplomatic relationship, the Afghan government negotiated with the famed Morrison–Knudsen company, builders of the Hoover Dam and Golden Gate Bridge, to build a dam in Helmand.[69] A few years later, $63.7 million would be spent to expand the project, including the building of the Kajakai and Arghandab Dams, a highway, canals, a power facility, with trained technicians.[70] By the 1950s, the project reached unprecedented proportions, even as poor management, corruption, and a wide array of political issues plagued it. For Afghans, the Helmand project was symbolic of the future of Afghanistan: for the nation to succeed, the Helmand project needed to succeed.

Mohammad Daud Khan, who governed from 1953 to 1963 (and would eventually overthrow the King in 1973), kept the Helmand project afloat by playing the Americans and Soviets against each other.[71] Nonetheless, even when the United States Agency for International Development (USAID) took over many of the agricultural projects in Helmand in the early-60s, problems with the program persisted. However, both the US and Afghan governments had too much at stake to let the Helmand project fail. As the scholars Antonio Giustozzi and Artemy Kalinovsky have noted, "the political significance of it was too great for the Afghan modernizers and for the US cold warriors" to abandon Helmand.[72]

By the late 1960s and early 1970s, political issues aside, the project started to show promise.[73] In the past, farmers in Helmand grew crops mainly for subsistence. But varieties of high-yield wheat and cotton were introduced that incentivized farmers to utilize American technology and resources to grow surplus crops, in turn creating a market-based agricultural economy.[74] Both cotton and wheat were the primary cash crops and proved to fetch a high market price for both farmers and the government.[75] The overarching impact of introducing varieties of high-yield wheat and the expansion of cash cropping and double-cropping was a profound shift in the agricultural practices of the valley, as farmers became more astute at understanding the global market and adapting their land to grow crops to maximize their profits. More important, this new profit-minded approach also meant that market-savvy farmers were increasingly aware of the value of all crops, including opium.

Historically, Afghan farmers grew opium for individual needs or as a minor source of income, but it was rarely a major cash crop. In the 1960s, poppy prices were low, ranging anywhere from 1,400 to 3,600 afghanis per kilogram, depending on the quality. Low prices were largely explained by the fact that there was a limited demand for Helmand opium, as most went not to more lucrative Western markets but to neighboring Iran, which had its own competing domestic opium supply.[76] Even by 1970, Helmand opium, and Afghan opium in general, faced stiff competition in the regional market.[77] Furthermore, many poppy farmers sold their opium short, essentially accepting payments before harvest, and selling for a much lower but guaranteed price. Furthermore, decent profits for farmers were rare because they had to pay out labor costs, as well as bribes to government officials. Bribes often constituted the largest cost for poppy farmers and in many cases were the biggest impediment to growing more poppies. However, by the early 1970s, opium was transforming into a viable cash crop for farmers and traders in Helmand. To farmers involved in the USAID project or those who resided in close proximity, opium poppies were well suited for double-cropping schemes that were a foundation of the USAID Helmand project. Farmers planted poppy seeds in the fall to harvest in the spring, and then would plant cotton or vegetables and harvest them in the fall.[78] Despite these changes, even up to 1972, for many farmers, the cost of growing opium was too high to make it a profitable business.

Things changed in 1973, as opium began emerging as an important cash crop in the valley. In May, Bernard Weinraub of the *New York Times* reported that "Afghan farmers are harvesting a bumper crop of opium poppies on newly irrigated land that has been developed with foreign aid. American officials are furious and embarrassed because the land was developed by the aid mission here to spur food production. Instead, farmers have grown opium because of the fast and easy profits."[79] Weinraub's article shook the DEA, the State Department, and USAID to their core; the political optics were potentially devastating. In essence, the USAID was providing Afghan farmers with the knowledge and resources they needed to grow opium; that opium, in turn, would be manufactured into heroin; and that heroin would find its way into the arms of young Americans. America was not supposed to be helping drug producers, it was supposed to be destroying drug producers. Despite the fact that most opium being grown in the valley was grown outside of the USAID zone, the impact of the American aid project was undeniable. Knowledge and resources did not sit idly within the USAID project zone; Afghan farmers shared tech, knowledge, and know-how.

Overall, the timing of the US War on Drugs could not have been more opportune for the drug trade in Afghanistan. By 1973, the global dimensions of the drug trade were changing and the US and European demand for sources of opium outside Southeast Asia, Turkey, and Mexico from drug trafficking groups was drawing the attention of Afghan farmers. Supplies from Turkey were already dwindling, even prior to the ban of opium in 1971, and many Kurdish-Turkish groups had transitioned to refining morphine base into heroin.[80] The opium for their heroin operations was largely coming from Afghanistan.[81] In Thailand, police efforts to stop production and trafficking pushed opium production into the Shan and Kachin regions of Myanmar, and much of the Southeast Asian opium supply was diverted into European and Australian markets.[82] The disruptions in the global supply of opium as a consequence of crop displacement, often referred to as the "balloon effect," were instrumental in catalyzing the growing demand for Afghan opium. As a result, opium production increased dramatically in 1973. Some US–Afghan officials, after conducting aerial surveillance of the region, estimated that there was a seven-fold increase in land devoted to opium in Afghanistan, to the point that they could easily identify poppy fields from an elevation of eight hundred feet.[83]

As opium production surged in Helmand, both US drug agents and Afghan officials made new efforts to stop the province's escalating drug trade. In 1973, fearing a cessation of US aid, Mohammad Daud Khan banned opium in the Helmand–Arghandab Valley Authority (HAVA) area, as well as in the rest of the country. Although Daud was preparing to mobilize the ASUs to crack down on opium producers, he was reluctant to curb the trade too forcefully. The situation was complex for Daud; a successful drug control intervention was ultimately dependent on the willingness and capability of local officials and community leaders to comply with national drug control policy. But for local officials, enforcing a national ban could cause significant economic hardship for local farmers, in turn straining the already tenuous political relationship between the Afghan government and local peoples.[84] Nonetheless, by July, Afghan officials proclaimed that opium cultivation had declined dramatically in the HAVA area and in the rest of Helmand. It is important to note that evidence for this claimed crop eradication is relatively scarce. In fact, the "ban" seemed to play into the hands of farmers and traders eyeing even greater payouts in the future. USAID researchers noted that opium traders believed that the opium shortage caused by the ban would lead to an increase of two hundred to three hundred afghanis per seer (equivalent to about seven kilos), once government attention moved away from the region.[85] In essence, opium farmers and traders hedged their bets, taking a loss in 1974 in hopes of a greater payout in 1975.

In 1975, opium cultivation once again sprouted up in the Helmand Valley. UN narcotics advisers noted a significant increase in opium that year, with roughly 106 fields identified near Lashkar Gah and surrounding areas (although not in the USAID area). Daud scrambled to get minsters and provincial governors to reimpose the ban, even taking US money to fund a propaganda campaign against the growing of opium. By 1976, however, it seemed that the Afghan government's ability, or willingness, to stop drug trafficking was on the decline as well, as the country descended into political tumult. In fact, with bigger political conflicts embroiling much of the country, counter-narcotics efforts decreased rapidly, as border patrol agents and anti-drug police were no longer on the state payroll.[86] Trying to impose a ban on opium was relatively meaningless as well, largely because local officials, whose cooperation and compliance would be necessary to ban opium, simply lacked the capacity to implement policies that challenged powerful local interests.[87] In other words, the illicit drug trade was flourishing, and the state was largely losing any ability to stop it. In 1977, the CIA estimated that the Helmand Valley produced nearly 51 tons of opium, a significant portion of the estimated total 200 to 250 tons produced throughout Afghanistan. The following year, the CIA estimated that Afghanistan and Pakistan together produced roughly 1,000 tons of opium, double the 500 tons UN officials had predicted.[88] The War on Drugs, for all of its global ambitions, could not stop Afghan opium from entering the global illicit drug market, and the consequences continue to reverberate today.

Conclusion

Since the late 1970s, Afghanistan has become the largest source of illicit drugs in the world. Even so, the war on Afghan drugs is still unfolding; between 2002 and March 2018, the US provided a total of $8.78 billion to combat drug production and trafficking throughout the country.[89] Yet many questions remain unanswered. Given the early history of the War on Drugs in Afghanistan, how do we understand this critical period in Afghanistan, and how does it fit into our broader understanding of the history of the drug trade and the War on Drugs? Understanding this period requires a better understanding of the multiplicity of ways in which the War on Drugs shaped Afghanistan, of the ways in which Afghanistan shaped it, and even the limitations of the War on Drugs amid broader historical processes in Afghanistan.

First, and most visibly, when Nixon launched the drug war, American efforts to suppress drugs globally were internalized in Afghanistan, largely as a means to bolster the power of the Afghan state.[90] Throughout the twentieth century, Afghan rulers created a political culture that recognized that aggressive expansion of state power would result in political upheaval from powerful rural tribal leaders, and thus opted to grow the state gradually.[91] In turn, the Afghan government became dependent on foreign aid and international investment to grow the state.[92] This dependence on foreign aid and investment led Afghanistan to adopt drug control laws, which were often in contradiction with local customs or realities, as a vehicle of maintaining access to foreign money and resources, and more important, to maintain the culture by which the Afghan state formed. In this way, the success of the American-led War on Drugs hinged on a state confined by its own political design; as the Afghan central government tried to enforce prohibitions and anti-smuggling laws to maintain access to American aid, the lack of that government's integration into its own society and the increasing resistance to centralized governance by the mid-1970s prevented any meaningful or effective form of drug control.

This analysis also reveals the limitations of the War on Drugs, given issues inherent in Afghan society—in particular, the impact of *qawm* in perpetuating the conflict between state and local governance, which often dictated the effectiveness of drug control policies. The design of Afghan political culture reinforced the government's lack of integration into society, often elevating the importance of *qawm* in determining outcomes. In effect, it was *qawm*, not adherence to national policy directives, that determined outcomes. As Afghan historian Olivier Roy notes, "the state was no more than a stake in a larger game and the strategy of a *qawm* consisted in establishing an advantageous relationship with the institutions of the state."[93] As result, to invoke political theorist James Scott, false compliance, smuggling, aversion, and corruption were forms of both peasant and police resistance and support for local and individual concerns and interests.[94]

Lastly, this analysis elucidates the ways in which internationally funded economic development served, not as a means of preventing the illicit drug trade, but rather of catalyzing it. Underlying much of our understanding of illicit drugs, especially that of the Global South, is the notion that drugs thrive in places where development is lacking. But in Afghanistan, especially in the Helmand, development projects helped shaped the future success of the illicit drug trade. There are parallels here to another drug producer state, Peru. In the 1960s, massive development projects were implemented throughout Peru, but by the late 1970s, as was true in Afghanistan, the state largely failed, and in the following decades cocaine production thrived.[95] The convergence of these different policy objectives highlights the messy and convoluted ways in which drugs, development, and the War on Drugs became increasingly interwoven. Certainly, in Afghanistan, two hallmarks of the modern American international development machine—-free market capitalism and drug suppression—collided to produce a multifaceted catastrophe.

When Terry Burke left Afghanistan in 1973, he had little to show for his time there. But no one should blame Mr. Burke. The forces at play were far too big for the generally misguided and often counterproductive efforts of the entire US government—let alone a lone drug agent—to stop.

NOTES

1 Terry Burke, *Stalking the Caravan: A Drug Agent in Afghanistan 1971–1973* (Durango, CO: La Plata Books, 2014), 5.

2 The UN estimates that, in the past decade, 84 percent of the global illicit opium supply has come from Afghanistan. United Nations Office on Drugs and Crime, *World Drug Report 2020* (Vienna: United Nations 2020), https://wdr.unodc.org.

3 Jelena Bjelica and Farbizio Foschini, "The Myth of Afghan Black: A Cultural History of Cannabis Cultivation and Hashish Production in Afghanistan," Afghan-Analysts Network, January 7, 2019, https://afghanistan-analysts.org.

4 It is estimated by the Special Inspector General of Afghanistan's Reconstruction that the US has spent $8.78 billion in counter-narcotics effort from 2002 to March 2018. Special Inspector General of Afghanistan Reconstruction, *Quarterly Report to the United States Congress,* April 30, 2018, 182, www.sigar.mil.

5 My book *Poppies, Politics, and Power* is the first to explore the history of drugs and drug policy in Afghanistan prior to the Afghan-Soviet War in 1979. James Bradford, *Poppies, Politics, and Power: Afghanistan and the Global History of Drugs and Diplomacy* (Ithaca, NY: Cornell University Press, 2019).

6 See, e.g., Gretchen Peters, *Seeds of Terror: How Heroin is Bankrolling the Taliban and al-Qaeda* (New York: Thomas Dunnes Books, 2009).

7 For the most important, and clear, analyses of the contemporary drug trade in Afghanistan, see David Mansfield, *A State Built on Sand: How Opium Undermined Afghanistan* (New York: Oxford University Press, 2016).

8 Charles Tilly, "War Making and State Making as Organized Crime," in *Bringing the State Back In*, ed. Peter Evans, Dietrich Rueschemeyer, and Theda Skocpol (Cambridge: Cambridge University Press, 1985), 169–91.

9 Some of the best examples are Barnett Rubin, *The Fragmentation of Afghanistan: State Formation and Collapse in the International System*, 2nd ed. (New Haven: Yale University Press, 2002) and Vartan Gregorian, *The Emergence of Modern*

Afghanistan: Politics of Reform and Modernization, 1880-1946 (Stanford, CA: Stanford University Press, 1969).

10 Both events are covered in Bradford, *Poppies, Politics, and Power.*

11 Kathleen Frydl, *The Drug Wars in America, 1940-1973* (Cambridge: Cambridge University Press, 2013). In Frydl's exquisite work, she analyzes why the US transitioned from a regulatory model to a prohibition model emphasizing punitive action. Her work demonstrates that much of this shift was rooted in the transformation of state power. In this way, the war on drugs was merely another tool with which the US government could exercise control over the American population, and, by the 1970s, increasingly over other parts of the world as well.

12 Burke, *Stalking the Caravan*, 229.

13 For more on the century-long war on drugs, see Frydl, *The Drug Wars in America.*

14 Frydl, *The Drug Wars in America*, 369.

15 For more on the role of the US, especially the CIA, in facilitating the production of opium to help fund anti-communist groups in the region, see Alfred McCoy, *The Politics of Heroin: CIA Complicity in the Global Drug Trade* (New York: Lawrence Hill Books, 1991).

16 Ronald Renard, *Opium Reduction in Thailand, 1970-2000: A Thirty-Year Journey* (Chiang Mai, Thailand: Silkworm Books, 2001), 8.

17 For more, see Renard, *Opium Reduction in Thailand.*

18 Ko-Lin Chin, *The Golden Triangle: Inside Southeast Asia's Drug Trade* (Ithaca, NY: Cornell University Press, 2009), 213.

19 Carmen Boullosa and Mike Wallace, *A Narco History: How the United States and Mexico Jointly Created the "Mexican Drug War"* (New York: OR Books, 2015), 27.

20 Aileen Teague, "The United States, Mexico, and the Mutual Securitization of Drug Enforcement, 1969-1985," *Diplomatic History* 43, no. 5 (2019): 8. See also her chapter in this volume.

21 James Windle, *Suppressing Illicit Opium Production: Successful Intervention in Asia and the Middle East* (New York: I. B. Taurus, 2016), 56.

22 Ryan Gingeras, *Heroin, Organized Crime, and the Making of Modern Turkey* (Oxford: Oxford University Press, 2014), 233.

23 The issue of crop displacement is often referred to as the "balloon effect," whereby the crop reduction strategies in one region merely displace it to a region more conducive for illicit crop growth. For more, see Graham Farrell, "A Global Empirical Review of Crop Eradication, Crop Substitution and Alternative Development Policy," *Journal of Drug Issues* 28, no. 2 (1998): 395–436; Cornelius Friesendorf, "Squeezing the Balloon?: United States Air Interdiction and the Restructuring of the American Drug Industry in the 1990s," *Crime, Law, and Social Change* 44 (2005): 35–78, and Peter Reuter, "The Mobility of Drug Trafficking," in *Ending the Drug Wars: Report of the LSE Expert Group on the Economics of Drug Policy*, ed. John Collins (London: London School of Economics, 2014), 33–40.

24 For more on the history of the cannabis trade and its continuing legacy, see James Bradford and David Mansfield, "The Known Unknowns and the Unknown

Knowns: The Hashish Trade in Afghanistan," *EchoGeo*, 48 (May 2019), https://doi .org/10.4000/echogeo.17626.

25 Bradford, *Poppies, Politics, and Power*, 40. British authorities were primarily concerned about the impact of smuggled Afghan drugs because they were eating into the legal colonial drug trade, especially the excise taxes derived from this trade.

26 The local form of hashish in Afghanistan is called *charse*.

27 Bradford, *Poppies, Politics, and Power*, 27–30. For more on the broader connections between South Asian markets and the development of the Afghan economy and state in the nineteenth century, see Shah Mahmoud Hanifi, *Connecting Histories in Afghanistan: Market Relations and State Formation on a Colonial Frontier* (Stanford, CA: Stanford University Press, 2011).

28 For more on Amanullah Khan and his policies, see Gregorian, *The Emergence of Modern Afghanistan*, and Thomas Barfield, *Afghanistan: A Political and Cultural History* (Princeton, NJ: Princeton University Press, 2010).

29 For more on drug laws under the Amanullah regime, see Bradford, *Poppies, Politics, and Power*, 32–41.

30 There were three main government-run opium companies: *Shirkat-e Saderat-e Taryak* (Opium Exporting Company), *Shirkat-e Sahami-e Taryak* (Opium Joint Stock Company), and *Shirkat-e Taryak* (Afghan Opium Company).

31 By the Second World War, the US emerged as the biggest buyer of Afghan opium. US pharmaceutical firms were quite fond of Afghan opium, not only because it was high in morphine content, but because it was cheap. The Afghans were notoriously unprofessional, however. Weights on their shipments were often wrong, paperwork was slow, government advisors (*alaqadars*) were dogged by allegations of corruption, but maybe most critically, most opium was grown by independent growers outside of government control. This lack of "government control" proved critical in preventing Afghanistan from gaining international recognition as a legal producer and trader.

32 For more on the 1944–45 ban of opium, see Bradford, *Poppies, Politics, and Power*, 44–84.

33 The government eradicated opium in 1958, under the condition that farmers and traders involved in the opium trade (who numbered in the tens of thousands) would be provided economic opportunities elsewhere, such as in the building of roads, schools, and hospitals. None of those were built in response to the eradication. Not more than a year later, opium returned to Badakhshan. For more, see James Bradford, "Drug Control in Afghanistan: Culture, Politics, and Power during the 1958 Prohibition of Opium in Badakhshan," *Journal of Iranian Studies* 48, no. 2 (2015): 223–48. There were four major growing regions of Afghanistan (Herat, Nangarhar, Kandahar, and Badakhshan), although opium was widespread, and likely grown throughout the country. More importantly, Daud launched the ban because Badakhshan opium was world renowned for its exceptionally high morphine content, and because banning opium would garner sympathy that could be used for diplomatic negotiations. Domestically, Daud chose Badakhshan because

it was inhabited largely by ethnic-minority Tajiks, and enforcing the ban there would generate less resistance than it would in areas inhabited by ethnic-majority Pashtuns, who had a long history of resistance to state interventions.

34 For example, lamb-skins (*karakul*) was one of Afghanistan's largest exports during the late nineteenth and early twentieth centuries. The trade for *karakul* largely evaporated by mid-century.

35 The tenuous nature of Afghan politics, particularly between the Afghan state and rural tribal authorities, has been dissected thoroughly. Most important for this study is Rubin, *The Fragmentation of Afghanistan*. Rubin notes that Afghanistan became increasingly reliant on foreign aid in the mid–twentieth century, becoming a rentier-state, and this led to an increasing disconnect between state and society that shaped the conflict that would unfold in the 1970s. For other examinations of the history of Afghan politics, see Louis Dupree, *Afghanistan* (Princeton, NJ: Princeton University Press, 1980); Barfield, *Afghanistan: A Political and Cultural History*; Olivier Roy, *Islam and Resistance in Afghanistan* (Cambridge: Cambridge University Press, 1990); and M. Nazif Shahrani, "State-Building and Social Fragmentation in Afghanistan," in *The State, Religion, and Ethnic Politics: Afghanistan, Iran, and Pakistan*, ed. Ali Banuazzi and Myron Weiner (Syracuse, NY: Syracuse University Press, 1986), 23–74.

36 Peter Maguire and Mike Ritter, *Thai Stick: Surfers, Summers, and the Untold Story of the Marijuana Trade* (New York: Columbia University Press, 2014), 27–29.

37 C. J. Charpentier, "The Use of Haschish and Opium in Afghanistan," *Anthropos* 68, no. 3/4 (1973): 484.

38 Charpentier, "The Use of Hashish," 484.

39 David Avery, Consular Department. May 19, 1970. Trafficking of Drugs in Afghanistan 1970. FCO 47/ 428. National Archives at Kew, UK. THC (*tetrahydrocannabinol*) being the psychoactive chemical that gets people high.

40 Catherine Lamour and Michael Lamberti, *Les grandes manouevres de l'opium* (Paris: Seuill, 1972), 208.

41 Lina Britto, *Marijuana Boom: The Rise and Fall of Colombia's First Drug Paradise* (Berkeley, CA: University of California Press, 2020).

42 Peter Levi, *The Light Garden of the Angel King* (London: Collins, 1972), 113.

43 Robert Connell Clarke, *Hashish* (Los Angeles: Red Eye Press, 1998), 127–29. For example, some producers abandoned the cloth sieves that took longer to extract the cannabis resins in exchange for metal sieves, which could sieve more material but would often reduce the potency because excess plant material would remain throughout the powdered resin.

44 David Macdonald, *Drugs in Afghanistan* (London: Pluto Press, 2007).

45 Clarke, *Hashish*, 117.

46 Clarke, *Hashish*, 127.

47 Bureau of Dangerous Drugs and Narcotics, "July 1972 Brief: Trafficking and Enforcement," pp. 1–2, file from former Bureau of Dangerous Drugs and Narcotics/DEA agent Terry Burke. Cited in Bradford, *Poppies, Politics, and Power*, 140.

48 For one of the more comprehensive narratives of the Brotherhood, see Nic Schou, *Orange Sunshine: The Brotherhood of Eternal Love and Its Quest to Spread Peace, Love, and Acid to the World* (New York: St. Martin's Griffin, 2011).

49 Clarke, *Hashish*, 116. Clarke notes that the demand for hash oil also spurred a change in pricing schemes between traffickers and farmers.

50 Bureau of Dangerous Drugs and Narcotics, "July 1972 Brief: Trafficking and Enforcement," p. 2, file from former Bureau of Dangerous Drugs and Narcotics/DEA agent Terry Burke.

51 This was largely a consequence of rampant corruption within the government in general.

52 Bureau of Dangerous Drugs and Narcotics, "July 1972 Brief: Trafficking and Enforcement," p. 2, file from former BNDD/DEA agent Terry Burke.

53 Bradford, *Poppies, Politics, and Power*, 170.

54 Bradford, *Poppies, Politics, and Power*, 163–64.

55 Olivier Roy has argued that *qawm* is one of the powerful political forces at play in Afghanistan. For more on *qawm*, see Roy, *Islam and Resistance in Afghanistan*.

56 Bradford, *Poppies, Politics, and Power*, 164–65.

57 Bradford, *Poppies, Politics, and Power*, 165.

58 *Ma'lumat-I ihsa'ivi-i Afghanistan* [Economic Statistics of Afghanistan] (Kabul, 1974), 211.

59 Bureau of Dangerous Drugs and Narcotics, "July 1972 Brief: Trafficking and Enforcement," p. 2, file from former Bureau of Dangerous Drugs and Narcotics/ DEA agent Terry Burke.

60 Bradford, *Poppies, Politics, and Power*, 171. The United States recommended to the UN a program worth $9.5 million over three years, with the United States paying $3.5 million, and roughly $654,000 for enforcement every year. The United States believed that the UN had undervalued the role of the gendarmerie and customs police in enforcing narcotics laws, and as a result, recommended far greater funding for enforcement.

61 Daud broke the traditional political culture that the Musahiban Dynasty had had for nearly forty-five years by allying with urban leftists rather than the ulema and tribal authorities. Although Daud placed himself on the left side of the spectrum with the coup, he initially faced little resistance from the tribal and religious authorities that had historically played such an important role in resisting the incursions of the Afghan state. Many within Afghanistan viewed his coup as little more than a family dispute, and in some ways, saw the royal dynasty (despite its new socialist tint) as infallible. For more, see Barfield, *Afghanistan*, 214.

62 Bradford, *Poppies, Politics, and Power*, 174.

63 Some of the success of the ASUs was due in part to a financial incentive program that rewarded officers for intelligence and involvement in drug busts. The morale of ASU officers was much higher than in the police.

64 Bradford, *Poppies, Politics, and Power*, 175.

65 Burke, *Stalking the Caravan*, 179–80.

66 Bradford, *Poppies, Politics, and Power*, 175.

67 It is interesting to note that Mexico, too, saw an increase in the amount of heroin flowing into the American market following the crackdown on the French Connection. See Boullosa and Wallace, *A Narco History*, 25.

68 For a history of the project, see Nick Cullather, "Damming Afghanistan: Modernization in a Buffer State," *Journal of American History* 89, no. 2 (September 2002): 512–37. Much of the impetus for the US in launching a massive project like this was to keep Afghanistan as a buffer state, and prevent Soviet encroachment into South Asia. Afghan rulers were fine with this. The policy, *bi-tarafi* (without sides) was part of the general approach of Afghan foreign policy to remain neutral.

69 Cullather, "Damming Afghanistan: Modernization in a Buffer State," 520–22.

70 Dupree, *Afghanistan*, 483. After years of problems, sky-rocketing costs, and poor management, the project was reorganized as the Helmand–Arghandab Valley Authority (HAVA).

71 Cullather, "Damming Afghanistan," 528.

72 Antonio Giustozzi and Artemy Kalinovsky, *Missionaries of Modernity: Advisory Missions and the Struggle for Hegemony in Afghanistan and Beyond* (London: Hurst, 2016), 176.

73 There were many political issues. Corruption was arguably the most consistent issue among HAVA officials. But the relocation program may have been more critical. The Afghan government relocated thousands of nomads (*kuchis*) promising jobs and quick agricultural returns. But many nomadic groups were deeply upset about their lifestyle, if not identity, being uprooted by the project. Furthermore, the promised agricultural returns didn't materialize until the late 1960s at best—a long time for many. For more, see Cullather, "Damming Afghanistan," and Giustozzi and Kalinovsky, *Missionaries of Modernity*.

74 Richard Scott, Frydoon Shairzai, and Ghulam Farouq, *1975: Farm Economic Survey of the Helmand Valley* (Kabul: US Agency for International Development, 1975), 46.

75 Cynthia Clapp-Wincek, and Emily Baldwin, *The Helmand Valley Project in Afghanistan* (Washington, DC: USAID, 1983), 13. But growing cotton and wheat also yielded unexpected costs, particularly for fertilizer, as cotton and wheat depleted the soil of much needed nutrients.

76 G. P. Owens and J. H. Clifton, *Poppies in Afghanistan* (Kabul: USAID, 1972). Taken from Bradford, *Poppies, Politics, and Power*, 197.

77 The Shah of Iran restarted domestic opium production in 1969, Turkey produced significant amounts until 1972, Pakistan was also a major producer, and other areas of the country, particularly Badakhshan, continued to produce opium.

78 Owens and Clifton, *Poppies*.

79 Bernard Weinraub, "Afghans Use US Aid Project for Opium," *New York Times*, May 26, 1973. Found in Bradford, *Poppies, Politics, and Power*, 198.

80 James Windle, "A Very Gradual Suppression: A History of Turkish Opium Controls, 1933–1974," *European Journal of Criminology* 11, no. 2 (2013): 207–9.

81 Burke, *Stalking the Caravan*, 179–80.
82 Alfred McCoy, "Heroin as a Global Commodity: A History of Southeast Asia's Opium Trade," in *War on Drugs: Study in the Failure of US Narcotics Policy*, ed. Alfred McCoy and Alan A. Block (San Francisco: Westview Press, 1992), 262–63.
83 Bradford, *Poppies, Politics, and Power*, 200.
84 Bradford, *Poppies, Politics, and Power*, 203.
85 Bradford, *Poppies, Politics, and Power*, 205–6.
86 Bradford, *Poppies, Politics, and Power*, 207–8.
87 Barfield, *Afghanistan*, 224.
88 Bradford, *Poppies, Politics, and Power*, 208.
89 Special Inspector General of Afghanistan Reconstruction, *Quarterly Report to the United States Congress*, 182.
90 See Isaac Campos and Paul Gootenberg, "Toward a New Drug History of Latin America: A Research Frontier at the Center of Debates," *Hispanic American Historical Review* 95, no. 1 (2015): 1–35.
91 Gregorian, *The Emergence of Modern Afghanistan*, 343
92 For more, see Rubin, *Fragmentation of Afghanistan*.
93 Roy, *Islam and Resistance in Afghanistan*, 24.
94 James Scott, *Weapons of the Weak: Everyday Forms of Peasant Resistance* (New Haven, CT: Yale University Press, 1985), 29.
95 Paul Gootenberg, "Orphans of Development: the Unanticipated Rise of Illicit Coca in the Amazon Andes, 1950–1990," in *The Origins of Cocaine: Colonization and Failed Development in the Amazon Andes*, ed. Paul Gootenberg and Liliana Dávalos (New York: Routledge, 2018), 1–15.

PART V

The Alternative to War

10

Between the Free Market and the Drug War

DAVID HERZBERG

This chapter explores a little-noticed aspect of American drug policy during the 1970s: a push for consumer protection in an era remembered primarily for its War on Drugs. The Controlled Substances Act of 1970 was not (just) a drug-war law. It was also designed to give regulators the power to rein in the overpromotion of sedatives and stimulants by the pharmaceutical industry and to reform medical practices warped by that overpromotion. Its passage was driven, in part, by consumer advocates who used anti-drug rhetoric to build the political coalitions needed to pass, and then to enforce, new controls on economically and politically powerful industries and professions. It was not a prohibition law; instead, its robust regulation reduced risks in markets for pharmaceutical sedatives and stimulants that remained large—a remarkable success when compared to the catastrophic failure of the twentieth century's punitive prohibition policies. The racism built into anti-drug rhetoric limited and ultimately doomed this experiment in drug-policy pragmatism. But it still worth studying as a rare and largely forgotten example of an effort to govern addictive drugs that was separated, at least partially, from the racialized moral crusades to which such efforts have so consistently and destructively been harnessed.

Introduction

In 1973, the most commonly used drug in America was not heroin or marijuana but Valium—it was prescribed over one hundred million times that year alone.[1] Valium made a fortune for its manufacturer, Roche Pharmaceuticals. Its impact on consumers was more mixed: it undoubtedly eased a great deal of anxiety and related suffering, but it was also associated with more emergency room visits and overdoses than any other drug. Thanks to Roche's lobbying, Valium was prescription-only but faced few other sales restrictions, and thanks to Roche's marketing, prescriptions were relatively easy to come by. The boom times did not last forever, though; new restrictions were imposed in 1975 and by the end of the decade Valium sales had declined by 50 percent. Emergency room visits and overdoses plummeted as well.[2]

Valium's fall was far from unique. A host of other pharmaceutical sedatives and stimulants that had dominated best-seller and overdose rankings for decades also faced new restrictions in the 1970s, accompanied by declines in drug-related harms. For some drugs like the sedative methaqualone (best known as the "love drug" Quaalude), the declines were particularly steep: it was ultimately withdrawn from the market altogether.[3]

Valium's decline and Quaalude's disappearance highlight a little-noticed aspect of American drug policy during the 1970s "war" against drugs. As a number of historians have noticed, for all its warlike rhetoric, the set of policies launched by the Nixon administration at least initially included more funding for treatment than for policing and punishment.[4] Few observers, however, have paid attention to a second complicating element of Nixon's drug war: it was waged, at least in part, against an out-of-control drug industry whose over-promotion of sedatives and stimulants had been producing a slow-motion public health crisis in the nation's legal pharmaceutical "white markets" for more than thirty years. It also took unprecedented aim at an asleep-at-the-wheel medical profession whose careless prescribing was central to the long-running psychoactive bull market. The Nixon administration's center-piece drug law, the 1970 Controlled Substances Act (CSA), gave federal regulators a raft of new powers over one of America's most powerful industries and most powerful professions, curbing the party and creating, in effect, a command economy for some of the nation's most profitable products. Importantly, in this context the CSA was not a prohibition law. White markets remained very widely accessible to consumers; they were just smaller and safer.

This remarkable accomplishment makes little sense when considered only in the context of America's punitive drug wars, which, as many observers have noted, have had little positive impact on patterns of drug use or drug harms. Instead, this aspect of the CSA is best understood as belonging to the history of consumer advocacy, inheritor of a tradition of pioneering food and drug safety laws that began with the 1906 Food and Drug Act, and emerging along with other "third wave" consumer legislation in the 1970s, such as the National Traffic and Motor Vehicle Safety Act and the Truth in Lending Act. The CSA thus highlights the way anti-drug rhetoric has been deployed for more purposes than racist prohibition: consumer advocates have also used it to build the political coalitions needed to pass, and then to enforce, new controls on economically and politically powerful industries and professions. The period of regulated white markets ushered in by the CSA had serious flaws, but considered against the backdrop of drug policy failures, they may well represent the closest approximation of effective drug policy America has seen for the circulation of potentially addictive substances.

Yet the racism built into anti-drug rhetoric left an indelible mark on the contours of consumer protection in the 1970s. The safer drug markets reformers built were envisioned as serving the predominantly white consumers known as "patients," and actually strengthened the barriers preventing other consumers from accessing white market drugs. This racialized regulatory regime was nothing new; since the late nineteenth century, consumer protections for psychoactive drugs in America had been consistently predicated on their status as "medicines." Good—or at least, better—drug policy is one of the many racial privileges white drug consumers have enjoyed, at least occasionally, in a history dominated by prohibition and too-free markets.

This chapter surveys this mostly forgotten, limited, yet effective side of 1970s drug policy. It explores battles between Big Pharma and a range of federal and state agencies tasked with restraining it. These battles took place everywhere from the intensely local, where physicians and pharmacists navigated between drug marketers and suddenly zealous Medical and Pharmacy Boards, to the national level where the new DEA confronted industry resistance as it "up-scheduled" what it considered to be the most dangerous drugs.

Such efforts provide an important historical example of a path not taken for drug policy more generally: regulation and safer markets rather than prohibition. Exploring them requires bringing questions of race into pharmaceutical history, an area of scholarship where—unlike "drug" history—it has not traditionally been a central area of focus. We know more about how drug policy has been used to police racialized, marginalized populations than we do about how pharmaceutical policy has (sometimes) been used to protect privileged populations. Examining the drug policies possible within white markets provides a real-world, practical model to aspire to as we attempt to disentangle the urgent need to regulate highly desirable, highly profitable, and highly dangerous products from the multifarious social hierarchies to which that need has been unnecessarily, and destructively, harnessed.

Consumer Advocacy and the Passage of the CSA

Pharmaceuticals and Third Wave Consumer Advocacy

As they had been in the Progressive Era and the New Deal, pharmaceuticals were an important area of focus during the "third wave" of consumer advocacy in the 1960s and 1970s. Big Pharma made a tempting target. Despite the introduction of miracle drugs like antibiotics, the pharmaceutical industry found itself on the defensive by the mid-1950s as a series of scandals revealed astonishing profits, price fixing, hidden drug risks, and questionable marketing tactics.[5] Hoping to capitalize on the situation, anti-monopolist crusader Tennessee Senator Estes Kefauver convened high-profile hearings on pharmaceuticals that produced a new wave of media exposés of high prices and dubious benefits.[6] Kefauver's success did not go unnoticed by newly elected President John F. Kennedy, eager for ways to deliver on his campaign promises of dynamic and muscular government; his Consumers' Bill of Rights included prescription drugs among the poorly regulated products needing new protections.[7] Soon enough, the Kefauver–Harris Amendments, passed in 1962 in the wake of the thalidomide crisis, gave consumer advocates one of their first federal victories. The new law gave the FDA authority to require proof of effectiveness before drugs could be marketed and, for the first time, authority to regulate the content of advertising to physicians.[8]

These consumerist victories breathed new life into a longstanding, largely fruitless federal quest to rein in barbiturate "goof balls" and amphetamine "thrill pills." Potentially addictive drugs had long been among the best-selling and most profitable products of a mighty pharmaceutical industry. In the late nineteenth century, sellers of so-called patent medicines had competed with "ethical" pharmaceutical companies in their eagerness to sell opioids and cocaine.[9] As sales of that first generation of addictive blockbusters drugs receded in the early twentieth century, reputable pharmaceutical houses fueled a boom in barbiturate sedatives starting in the 1920s and amphetamine in the 1940s and 1950s.[10] Even as the sedative and stimulant craze crested in the 1950s, new "minor tranquilizers" like Miltown and eventually Librium and Valium pushed sales even higher, well into the 1960s.[11]

The incredible popularity of sedatives and stimulants (and of opioids before them) was no pharmaceutical industry conspiracy. Humans, across cultures and times, have sought and used psychoactive drugs to relieve suffering and pursue pleasure. But like other potentially harmful products, drugs can be sold in ways that increase or decrease risk to consumers. By 1970, drug companies had been overpromoting benefits while downplaying risks (including addiction) for a solid fifty years, delivering colossal profits but making it difficult for physicians and patients to make informed choices.[12]

Despite the many public health consequences of that fifty-year boondoggle, efforts to rein in white markets for sedatives and stimulants had largely failed. By the 1950s, pharmaceuticals were one of America's most powerful industries; its lobbyists rarely lost battles in Washington, DC (or in most statehouses). It was often difficult to persuade legislators to impose new restraints on profitable industries, and never more so than during the pro-business 1950s. Increased controls over "narcotics," including medical opioids as well as illegal "dope," were an exception to this rule; in that case, the reform agenda had been supported by moral crusaders' simultaneous campaign against "dope fiends."[13] But such racialized drug panics, with their dark criminals terrorizing (or worse, enslaving) white women, were a poor fit with white markets. Reformers' more nuanced stories of badly needed medicines that could, in some circumstances, be misused by respectable, innocent consumers, were not enough, on their own, to overcome the pharmaceutical lobby.[14]

The emergence of third-wave consumer advocacy, however, gave new power to stories of innocents wronged by ruthless, profit-mad corporations. Drug companies, it turned out, made an excellent boogeyman in the eyes of the public and their political representatives. Drug reformers hammered home drug companies' amoral avarice in the testimony they gave before Congress. As one testified, "There is no limit to the efforts they [drug companies] will expend to suppress information concerning the addiction liability or misuse of dangerous drugs."[15]

Thanks to liberal victories in the 1964 elections, this consumerist argument was quite effective—even without much help from anti-drug moral crusaders. In 1965, Congress passed a Drug Abuse Control Act designed primarily to protect consumers by regulating major commercial actors, rather than to punish "dope fiends."[16] Sellers were now required to keep records of all transactions; pharmacists could not refill a prescription without a physician's written permission; and refills were limited to a maximum of five. The FDA was empowered to add new drugs to the law without congressional approval. Companies could protest and force formal hearings on such a determination, but the final decision lay with the FDA and its chosen pharmacological experts, not with Congress.[17]

One should not oversell the Drug Abuse Control Act. The new market regulations were relatively weak. Perhaps more importantly, the Act was the product of a political coalition that also included traditional anti-drug crusaders—not in the driver's seat as they traditionally had been when it came to psychoactive substances, but still a crucial ally needed to overcome pharmaceutical industry lobbying. This coalition was possible because consumer advocates were perfectly willing to criminalize informal (i.e., nonmedical) markets, whose customers they did not recognize as "consumers." As a result, one of the law's main provisions created a new agency within the FDA, the Bureau of Drug Abuse Control, which could field armed agents to investigate and shut down illicit traffic.[18]

The Controlled Substances Act

The consumer advocacy movement was still building momentum in the later 1960s and early 1970s, and pharmaceutical companies continued to be an important area of focus. A new generation of investigative reporters published a steady stream of damning reports on pharmaceutical industry misconduct. New advocacy groups like the Ralph Nader–affiliated Health Research Group and (more specifically) the Task Force on Prescription Drugs provided research data and expert witnesses. Grassroots activist groups, especially among second-wave feminists, grabbed headlines with investigations like Barbara Seaman's birth-control pill exposé, *The Doctors' Case against the Pill* (1970).[19] This drug reform work was taken up at the federal level by politicians eager to burnish their consumer-advocate bona fides. Senators Birch Bayh, Gaylord Nelson, and Edward Kennedy, for example, convened a series of congressional hearings into pharmaceutical company behavior throughout the 1970s. Sedatives and stimulants featured prominently in these hearings, in part because they were one place where liberal consumer advocates could garner support from conservative drug warriors. Amphetamines were on the docket in 1971 and again in 1972 and 1976; barbiturates in 1971, 1972, and 1973; Quaalude sedatives in 1973; "psychotropics" in 1978; Valium and Darvon in 1979. All were interspersed with a range of more targeted congressional investigations of pharmaceutical advertising, pricing, and other issues.

Drug reformers depended on the CSA to implement their agenda. Congress passed this law in 1970, using the 1965 Drug Abuse Control Act, in part, as a template. While the CSA is best known as the centerpiece of America's drug wars, it actually served two major purposes by repealing America's welter of existing drug laws and rewriting them into a single, unified law that controlled both "narcotics" (previously covered by the 1914 Harrison Narcotics Tax Act) and "dangerous drugs" (previously covered by the Drug Abuse Control Act). The law also unified enforcement by moving it into a single location in the Justice Department.[20]

Congress passed the unification bill at a moment of unprecedented turmoil in American drug policy. Traditionally, moral crusaders had dominated drug policy in the United States. They supported laws to contain threats they perceived as emanating from racialized or immigrant urban communities.[21] Other reformers, such as public health professionals, actively pursued drug regulation, but they were passengers on the train, not the engineers. In the 1970s, however, the politics of drug reform and drug regulation had grown more complex. Moralistic drug warriors had certainly not gone away, but they were no longer in complete control of the train. A relatively new group, linked to health professionals who specialized in the treatment of drug addiction, had joined the drug debate. This group, which I call addiction medicalizers, overwhelmingly rejected criminal justice approaches to addiction.[22]

Addiction medicalizers found an unexpected ally in pharmaceutical industry lobbyists, who discovered their own sudden opposition to warlike, prohibitionist drug policy.[23]

The pharmaceutical industry's sudden alliance with addiction medicalizers was motivated by outspoken consumer advocates, whose influence and anti-corporate posture had only grown stronger since the 1965
Drug Abuse Control Act. These consumer advocates had ripped into
the pharmaceutical industry at the congressional hearings on the bill
that ultimately became the CSA. They pinpointed instance after instance
of corporate greed, putting the pharmaceutical industry witnesses on
the defensive. They made a clear and compelling call for more robust
regulation of the industry. A majority of congress was moved by their
testimony. "It seems to me," mused Connecticut Senator Thomas Dodd,
"every once in a while I am reading in the paper about some drug that
has been peddled to the public, and a year or two later somebody comes
along and says it is a very bad thing." Sedatives and stimulants were
"obviously dangerous drugs," he continued; "why in the world can we
allow producers to make them by the millions and peddle them wher-
ever they want to?"[24] "Frankly," joined in one representative, "I'm weary
of watching good kids suspended from high schools—and even junior
high schools—in my district, because Government cannot or will not
crack down on the big drug houses."[25] Legislators were asked by the
consumer activists to consider such aggressive reforms as eliminating
all advertising for addictive drugs and placing restrictions on physicians' therapeutic decision-making.[26] "If doctors will not control their
colleagues' misuse of prescribing powers," Dodd argued, "someone else
should."[27] Even industry allies warned that the writing was on the wall.
"This is the year of the consumer legislation," one corporate-friendly
legislator warned a reluctant witness from Eli Lilly (one of a parade of
industry figures hauled before the committees during the hearings). "I
am a great believer in private enterprise and I want to keep it that way,
but public demand works its nefarious ways sometimes . . . so I suggest
that you cooperate with the committee."[28]

When the dust settled and Congress passed the CSA in 1970, American drug policy moved in a new and unprecedented direction. Thanks
to addiction medicalizers (and, in part, their pharmaceutical industry
backers), the new law weakened criminal punishments and expanded

treatment options for informal market consumers. Thanks to consumer advocates (and, in part, their drug warrior allies), it introduced robust oversight of all addictive white-market pharmaceuticals. Much has been written about the former—the all-too-brief easing of the punitive drug war. The remainder of this chapter examines the latter: a remarkable, if flawed and limited, experiment in regulating addictive drugs to allow safe consumption.

Federal Story: Reining in Big Pharma Profits

The 1970 CSA imposed unparalleled control over psychoactive pharmaceuticals. It created a closed system, offering manufacturers, distributors, prescribers, and pharmacists access to a highly profitable market in return for their adherence to a strict set of rules based on the public good that would place real limits on that profitability. Traditionally, drug companies had circumvented restrictions by discovering new products that, they claimed, did not suffer from older problems of addiction and overdose. But the new CSA shut down this option, requiring that new sedatives and stimulants be screened for addiction potential by a committee of the National Research Council before, not after, they went on the market.[29]

Anyone involved in the newly regulated white markets had to register with federal authorities (first the Bureau of Narcotics and Dangerous Drugs, then the DEA) and keep records of all transactions. They also had to ensure that their sales were intended to benefit consumers, that is (according to the logic of the day) that they were for "legitimate medical purposes."[30] Importantly, companies' self-policing was supplemented by federal surveillance, as the DEA, taking a page from the drug industry's own increasingly sophisticated market analysis tools,[31] began to make effective use of the vast troves of data produced by its recordkeeping requirements. The central innovation was a new program called ARCOS (Automation of Reports and Consolidated Order Systems). Sales records from manufacturers, distributors, pharmacies, hospitals, and dispensing physicians, including information about the purchaser and the amount purchased, were fed into computers, which then cross-referenced them to provide overall snapshots of the market.[32] These snapshots could identify potential new drug "fads" as they developed, drawing attention to a product earlier in its life cycle. They also identified physicians and pharmacists who purchased in unusually high volumes, allowing authorities to investigate the situation at an earlier stage.

Participating in this closed, highly surveilled market meant accepting a range of profit-dampening constraints. Pharmaceutical companies and distributors had to implement a variety of costly safeguards measures to protect their supply chains. Restricting sales to "legitimate medical purposes" meant more than selling only to other properly registered parties. It also meant a legal obligation to be skeptical of, report, and perhaps even refuse what, in other kinds of commerce, would be cause for celebration: unusually large or frequent sales.[33] This was a particularly bitter pill, since it is a rule of thumb that holds particularly true for addictive substances that 80 percent of sales come from 20 percent of the customers. Meanwhile, the FDA pushed against advertising of both stimulants and sedatives for "everyday or minor life stresses,"[34] diminishing access to one of the most profitable strategies pharmaceutical companies used to grow their customer base.[35]

Pharmaceutical companies also suffered from the simple fact that physicians had to register for a special DEA license. This registration requirement might not seem like much of a problem; the DEA had no power to refuse any licensed physician. Pharmaceutical marketing departments were acutely aware, however, that even relatively minor obstacles meant steep declines in sales—because of the inconvenience, because they signaled a need for extra caution, and because they reminded prescribers that authorities were watching over their behavior.

The limits imposed on drugs in stricter Schedules were even more stringent. Prescriptions for Schedule II drugs—which included all the stronger opioids—could not be refilled at all; every new sale required a new prescription. Even more importantly, the CSA modernized and expanded a practice that had previously been applied only to opioids and cocaine: limiting the overall volume of production to the nation's legitimate medical need, as determined by a federal control board. This federally determined limit placed a powerful brake on sales growth while also giving federal authorities important leverage: they decided how much of the total market each company would be allotted, based, among other things, on their track record of good behavior.

The government-mandated production quota system had a real impact on sales. Federal authorities reduced the annual quota for amphetamine by 80 percent from 1969 to 1971, for example.[36] Three of the most dangerous barbiturates and methaqualone, a nonbarbiturate sedative whose brand name Quaalude had gained a passionate following and a reputation as the "love drug" among counterculture youth, went into Schedule II in 1973.[37] As manufacturing quotas dropped for these up-scheduled sedatives, sales fell by nearly half for the three barbiturates and by 80 percent for methaqualone.[38]

Because of the CSA's hybrid status as both regulatory and criminal law, pharmaceutical companies faced real punishments for transgressions, including jail time for "willful and knowing" avoidance of record-keeping responsibilities or failure to take steps to prevent diversion.[39] This criminal culpability was particularly notable because, due to the influence of addiction medicalizers, the CSA actually decreased criminal penalties for most informal-market drug infractions. Here was a different kind of drug war: the CSA trained more of its firepower on regulating industry than it did on policing "dope fiends."

State Story: Regulating the Health Professions

In addition to new rules hemming in pharmaceutical industry practices, the CSA also served as the centerpiece for a new system regulating physicians and pharmacists—the retail level of psychoactive white markets. This regulatory regime was particularly remarkable for the restrictions it placed on physicians, who had long enjoyed unparalleled professional self-governance and therapeutic autonomy. The federal government had, it is true, long regulated opioid prescribing, but these restrictions were only spottily enforced. And other psychoactive medicines were governed only by prescription-only rules, established in the late 1930s, which placed no limits on physicians' decision making. Moreover, the rules were primarily enforced by state medical and pharmacy boards, who tended to see little benefit in overzealous policing of their members. Thus, physicians were left with few alternative sources of guidance other than pharmaceutical company marketing campaigns. It was a wonderfully efficient setup for pharmaceutical companies, who could reach a consumer base of millions by concentrating their attention on the much smaller number of physician-prescribers who made the real decisions. The result was a seemingly never-ending rise in sedative and stimulant prescriptions.

The CSA ushered in new constraints on this marketing-driven medical bonanza. For one thing, it imposed limits on the purposes for which Schedule II drugs could be legitimately prescribed. Opioids had long faced such limits (for example, they were mostly not allowed to treat chronic pain). Starting in the 1970s, amphetamines faced similar restrictions. In 1970, the FDA announced that amphetamines could only be properly labeled for use to treat narcolepsy, hyperkinesis ("minimal brain dysfunction"), and obesity (short term only).[40] These limits became more robust after 1971, when the Bureau of Narcotics and Dangerous Drugs "up-scheduled" amphetamine and amphetamine-like stimulants from Schedule III to Schedule II.[41] In 1973, the FDA held hearings to consider eliminating obesity as a legitimate use, and in 1979 they actually did so.[42]

Of course, these new restraints would mean little if they were not enforced. But in the wake of the CSA, and driven by the new political passion for consumer advocacy, state authorities finally began to regulate physicians and pharmacists. Forty-two states passed Uniform Controlled Substances acts, which, among other things, required dedicated agencies for drug control.[43] Many states created their own interagency Controlled Substances Board (CSB) or a Diversion Investigation Unit. Often funded by federal grants from the Law Enforcement Assistance Administration, state Diversion Investigation Units were designed to consolidate what had been "scattered and uncoordinated" and "in some instances non-existent" oversight of addictive pharmaceuticals.[44] The first units were established in 1972 in Texas, Michigan, and Alabama; ten more states had followed their lead by 1977.[45]

Wisconsin's state authorities kept unusually good records, allowing us to take a closer look at how these new tactics worked in practice. This state passed its Uniform Controlled Substances Act in 1972 and appointed a new agency, a CSB, to administer it. This CSB included representatives from the pharmacy and medical boards as well the Department of Justice, the Bureau of Alcohol and Other Drug Abuse, a range of other state agencies, as well as area DEA agents.[46]

A good example of the CSB in action came in the spring of 1976, when, after consulting with the state medical and pharmacy boards, the Board requested ARCOS data on purchases of Wisconsin's most popular amphetamine, Pennwalt's Biphetamine-20.[47] The result more than justified the inquiry. ARCOS statistics revealed that just twenty-six of the state's 9,500 licensed physicians had bought 71 percent of all Biphetamine-20 in 1975—and just four individual practitioners were responsible for the vast majority of that 71 percent.[48] The numbers were similar for pharmacies: less than 5 percent of the state's pharmacies bought nearly one-half of all Biphetamine.[49] When pharmacy sales were traced back to the prescribing physicians, it revealed the same pattern. In Milwaukee County, for example, just eight physicians had prescribed 82 percent of all Biphetamine doses sold.[50]

Based on these and other data, the CSB convened all relevant state agencies for a symposium on drug diversion, setting the stage for a dramatic change in policy by the state medical board. The most common use of amphetamines or other stimulants, weight loss, was banned. The drug could only be prescribed for narcolepsy, hyperkinesis, drug-induced brain dysfunction, epilepsy, or (in rare cases) depression.[51] The changes were immediately followed by a dragnet operation to investigate physicians who dispensed or prescribed unusually large volumes of stimulants. Within three years, the CSB had opened over thirty investigations, each of which began with a form letter asking for detailed information about, and justification for, unusual orders of scheduled substances.[52]

The most common type of investigation involved older physicians whose prescribing practices had been forged during white-market boom decades, and who, for a variety of reasons, resisted new constraints. Some insisted on their professional autonomy, like the small-town doctor who, claiming to have "ladies who need these pills for pep," raged that "I'll go underground or you'll see a big jump in the narcolepsy cases around here" and even threatened to stymie authorities by burning his own office to destroy his records.[53] Others were simply "naïve," and had "a difficult time saying no when the patients request drugs."[54]

What these old-fashioned prescribers had in common was that they sold without safeguards to protect consumers from the risks associated with sedatives and stimulants. The would-be arsonist doctor, for example, defended prescribing Dexedrine (amphetamine) for a case of tinnitus (ringing in the ears): "I can't see any danger," he said; "I doubt that anybody can get addicted to it. They get addicted to aspirin much more than they do that."[55] He was quite open about prescribing stimulants for "tired housewife syndrome," or for women who are "slightly tired in the morning":

> you would be surprised how this works with some of the housewives with four kids, and it also keeps them from eating between meals, and they get mad at their kids . . . I think they used them as a crutch once in a while, too. They get their weight down to level, but they got to like the drug and they will probably use it to keep the weight down, but they also do feel better and they get their work done.[56]

He also prescribed and dispensed a range of sedatives and opioids with similar lack of concern—or even awareness—of their potential risks. Such sales transformed the CSA's flawed system of consumer protection into a monopolistic free market: physicians had a monopoly on legal sales, but faced no requirement to inform their patients of risks or advise them on how to use safely.

Another physician, distraught after a chronic pain patient he had weaned off narcotics committed suicide, decided to treat patients with "chemical dependency," even though he had no training to do so.[57] With no training and having become a "soft touch," in practice this meant prescribing whatever sedatives, stimulants, and opioids were requested by a rapidly growing group of addicted patients. He wrote five prescriptions for stimulants and Quaalude to an undercover agent, including one for her "boyfriend," a bartender who, she admitted, "sold pills, dispensed them over the bar and took them." The doctor responded by advising them that "I wouldn't take the Ritalin and the Quaalude to the same pharmacy. They are like uppers and downers." "Now, don't get reckless and sell it to some of the wrong persons," he continued; "I'd be upset if you sold to someone you didn't know." Needless to say, no medical examination, or medical advice, was involved in the transaction.[58] In another case, he prescribed both Percodan and Valium, "probably fifty or sixty at a time every two or three weeks," for a patient with heroin addiction. That drug combination is particularly dangerous, but there is little sign that the physician warned the patient—or was even aware of the danger.[59]

However unhappy these physicians may have been to be subjected to Medical Board discipline, neither of them faced the kind punishment endemic to American drug wars. The Board initially let off the self-proclaimed housewife's friend with a warning, for example, and when, as promised, he refused to change his practice, the Board revoked his Controlled Substances license, to be returned if he stayed out of trouble for five years. He continued to practice medicine.[60] The "soft touch" came out worse. At first, his Controlled Substances license was revoked, but after he continued to prescribe, using a false DEA registration number, he was convicted in federal court, served ninety days in county jail, was put on probation for two years, and had his medical license revoked by the Board.[61] Such punishments were an outlier: most cases were dropped either when the physician provided an adequate explanation for their unusual prescribing patterns or agreed to change their habits.

Undergirding these free prescribers, and the relatively rational response they could expect from state authorities, was a racial logic that interpreted patients' whiteness as a proxy for safety. White physicians, in other words, tended to assume that addiction was primarily a problem of racial minorities and, thus, gave the benefit of a doubt to their white patients. One physician deemed a "naïve, easy touch" by the Board, for example, refused to prescribe amphetamine for dieters "on welfare"—a highly recognizable racist stereotype at the time. For them, he said, "I recommend cutting their welfare benefits to force them to reduce weight."[62] The housewife's friend reassured the Board that there was no "black market for pills" in his tiny town; "there are some drugs but nothing like the city."[63] State authorities tended to sympathize with these doctors' racist rhetoric and prescribing patterns; they gave the same race-bound benefit of a doubt to these white physicians as the physicians gave to their white patients.

This racial logic can be seen most directly in a case that is an "exception that proves the rule." In this case, a white physician had moved from a small town to set up a practice in a predominantly Black neighborhood in Milwaukee. When his too-free prescribing attracted the attention of the Medical Board and the local media, he was frank in laying the blame: "God bless the Democratic Party, the addict's friend," he said,

before proceeding to explain that he was too scared to refuse to prescribe for his Black patients because he might "get hit with some kind of
thing about not treating all people equally, etc., etc., etc. . . . you know,
civil rights and all that business . . . [but] not all people are equal. You
know, some of them are really out to con you." As if trying to make sure
his questioner recognized the racial logic, he became even more explicit:
"I've never seen anything like I've seen in Milwaukee. This used to be a
nice quiet German–Polish town. You had your beer and your kraut and
everything went smoothly. Well, walk down Walnut St. with that idea in
your mind and blow it. This town has really gone wild . . . you know, the
amount of drug addiction . . . is just incredible."[64] In his view, physicians
were the victim in the situation; all he had done was acknowledge racial reality and act accordingly. The Board was relatively sympathetic to
his complaints, eventually imposing a limited license suspension for six
months: he could still see existing patients, but could prescribe only for
in-patient care and could not prescribe Schedule II substances at all.[65]

While these light punishments of physicians might seem outrageous
in comparison to the heavy sentences meted out to informal market
"pushers," it is important to recognize that it was the drug war, not the
Medical Board, that was out of line. A license to sell psychoactive drugs
is a valuable commodity, and the Medical Board was not wrong to see
it as leverage to force sellers to be responsible. With few exceptions,
the new policies had the intended effect: not ruining mis-prescribers'
lives, but guiding them toward safer prescribing. For amphetamine, this
meant drastic declines in overall sales: a 97 percent drop in just two
years.[66] Only those tiny few physicians who repeatedly refused to accept
guidance faced criminal penalties. Meanwhile, consumers themselves
faced no new penalties, and those with addiction had expanded options
for treatment.

Other States

Many other states took steps similar to Wisconsin's. Illinois, for example, took action after the state medical society warned in 1973 that a
"what's the use" attitude among regulatory agencies had led to a plague
of "quasi-legitimate drug markets" for "weight control, the 'nervous
housewife,' the 'insomniac' businessman."[67] In 1975, Illinois legislators

amended the state Medical Practice Act to create a new medical coordinator, supported by six full-time investigators and adequate funding.[68] A Diversion Investigation Unit was established two years later.[69] State agencies began to computerize triplicate prescription records so that they could identify and contact high-volume prescribers. In 1975 alone, this led to thirteen high-profile disciplinary actions.[70] As one official noted proudly, the state boards were no longer just "a conduit for licenses" but a true "consumer oriented regulatory agency."[71] The state also implemented new safeguards, such as requiring triplicate prescriptions for Schedule II barbiturates.[72]

Many other states set up similar regulatory safeguards. Utah's state medical board acted against amphetamine in 1970. Maryland ended amphetamine use for obesity in 1972. Ten other states joined them by the end of the decade.[73] Many state medical boards began to comply for the first time with American Medical Association requests for information about disciplinary actions.[74] In 1970, thirty-five state pharmacy boards had formal arrangements to share information with federal drug surveillance networks.[75] California, long among the most cooperative of states when it came to drug enforcement, set up its own Diversion Investigation Teams and computerized prescription and sales surveillance in 1971.[76] New Jersey formed a Diversion Investigation Unit in 1974 and sharply increased its oversight of physician prescribing.[77] "Doctors are recognizing that the board is not here to protect them," *Medical Economics* reported; "its responsibility is to protect the consumers, and it is showing that it takes that responsibility seriously."[78] Virginia was proud enough of its own stepped-up enforcement actions that it began to circulate a newsletter, *Board Briefs*, which devoted most of its front page to disciplinary actions and investigations.[79] Many other states circulated notices of their recent actions, as did the Federation of State Medical Boards in its monthly "Board Action Report."[80]

Evaluating the CSA Regime
CSA Worked for White Markets—Why?

Stepped-up federal restrictions and state enforcement led to real changes in white markets for sedatives and stimulants. For the first time since the late nineteenth century, the overall volume of white market sedative and stimulant sales declined. Amphetamine plummeted by a factor of ten, from four billion pills in 1969 to four hundred million in 1972, and then fell even further when new restrictions were imposed later in the decade.[81] Sedative sales dropped by half between 1973 and 1983.[82] Notably, this white market contraction was accompanied by a decline in fatal overdoses and other drug-related harms. In the decade after 1976, for example, emergency room visits involving sedatives fell by a remarkable two-thirds. Stimulant-related ER visits, already low by 1976, dropped an additional 20 percent. Even pharmaceutical opioids were affected, with ER visits dropping by half or in some cases two-thirds.[83]

Given the long and almost entirely discouraging history of "supply-side" drug policies, these data are a marvelous mystery. When legal supplies are cut off, people who want to use drugs, especially people with addiction, turn to more dangerous illegal (unregulated) supplies. Why did this not happen when authorities restricted white market supplies in the 1970s?

The answer is that not all supply-side policies are created equal. The best-known supply-side policy is punitive prohibition: the criminalization of a substance, its sellers, and its consumers. This approach has given supply-side policies their bad name. It is ineffective for any imaginable goal of drug policy, but all too brutally effective in policing racialized and marginalized groups. The CSA's pharmaceutical controls, however, featured a different sort of supply-side policy, one based at least partly on principles of consumer protection quite different from prohibition.

The first and most important feature of the consumer protection approach was that it did not prohibit sales and use. Sedatives and stimulants remained available to a much greater extent than, say, morphine had in the aftermath of the Harrison Narcotics Tax Act. So-called pill mills and dope doctors were part of this continued availability, providing consumers with quality-assured, brand-name products (if few other consumer protections).[84] But such pharmaceutical gray markets were a last resort that most white market consumers found unnecessary. All sedatives, for example, remained medically available in the 1970s, and despite new regulatory pressures, no legal limit existed on how long a physician could prescribe for a patient. Unlike under the Harrison

Narcotics Tax Act, in other words, it was not illegal for physicians to "maintain" a person addicted to sedatives.

Instead, 1970s reforms made sedative white markets safer in two other ways. First, new red tape and new professional norms helped reduce casual prescribing that unnecessarily exposed patients to the risk of addiction. Refill limits, for example, meant that deliberate decisions had to be made before allowing long-term use (they did not make such use illegal). Second, federal and state controls shifted markets toward the safest sedatives by imposing stricter controls over more dangerous drugs. Thus, for example, short-acting barbiturates and Quaaludes were placed in Schedule II in the early 1970s, helping to shift markets toward safer benzodiazepines such as Valium that remained in Schedule IV. Valium was not free of risk, of course, and as it came to dominate sedative markets it had its turn atop lists of ER visits and fatal overdoses. Nonetheless, benzodiazepines were the safest of the sedatives, and their dominance could be considered a real, if imperfect, public health success.

Intriguing, but speculative, evidence that drug availability was an important part of policy successes in the 1970s can be found in the counterexample of amphetamine. At first, amphetamine's story was similar to that of sedatives: new controls restricted but did not prohibit sales and use. By the mid-1970s, however, when authorities became both dissatisfied with the rate of decline in prescribing and concerned about growing informal use among counterculture youth, stricter federal and state controls were imposed that came much closer to outright prohibition. As it happens, that moment coincided almost precisely with the return of a fully criminalized drug that had long been marginal in American society: cocaine. Granted, first-time cocaine users tended to be fairly young (the average age being in the early twenties), but otherwise their demographics matched those of pharmaceutical white markets.[85] It is important not to overstate this link; the return of transnational cocaine commodity chains to US informal markets occurred for many reasons and can be more than adequately explained without reference to amphetamine restrictions.[86] It nonetheless remains a suggestive development worth further exploration.

Finally, in evaluating the success of 1970s reforms, it is important not to forget one central aspect of the era's broader drug policy: a massive investment in addiction treatment that dramatically expanded its availability. The work of addiction medicalizers succeeded, in the late 1960s and early 1970s, in prompting the federal government and many states to shift emphasis (and funding) from punishing drug consumers to providing them with addiction treatment programs.[87] True, treatment during these years was problematic in any number of ways, from the predominance of ineffective or even punitive abstinence-only approaches to unequal accessibility along lines of class and race.[88] Even so, it is significant that the absolute scale of increased treatment capacity— especially for relatively privileged white-market consumers—was probably larger than the total contraction of white-market drug availability. And in at least one way, the treatment surge actually *expanded* white markets: methadone maintenance became accessible to at least some poorer, nonwhite, and addicted consumers who had never had access to legal opioids before.

The CSA Also Reinforced the Harmful Architecture of the Drug War

However well it worked for white markets, the CSA regime remained a sharply limited and deeply flawed policy. These limits and flaws stemmed from a common source: the continued importance of drug warriors in the political coalition that developed and helped lobby for the CSA. Their influence had diminished from earlier decades, but they were still useful allies, and consumer advocates were glad for their help in facing down the pharmaceutical industry.[89] For their part, drug warriors were happy to find at least one place where their policing-and-punishment approach had not fallen out of favor. Beyond this tactical alliance, however, lay a deeper affinity: consumer advocates (and addiction medicalizers, for that matter) still shared moral crusaders' complete opposition to nonmedical drug use. Other than the relatively meager, and punitively regulated, expansion of white-market methadone, the CSA regime was designed to shrink access to safe drug markets for all consumers other than "patients"—an exclusion fraught with race and class implications. Rational and compassionate drug policy was something imagined relevant only for the presumptively white consumers who supposedly desired health, not pleasure.

The impact of this restricted imagination can be seen in two nearly unanimous compromises built into the CSA: the continued criminalization of even small-scale drug "pushers," and the premise that all nonmedical drug use was "drug abuse."

President Nixon set the anti-"pusher" tone when he introduced the bill. "However far the addict himself may fall," Nixon told Congress, "his offenses against himself and society do not compare with the inhumanity of these who make a living exploiting the weakness and desperation of their fellow men." For them, Nixon continued, "society has few judgments too severe, few penalties too harsh."[90] Here, unlike in other areas, Nixon met with no opposition; "pushers" had no defenders in Congress. As a result, the federal law's penalties were built around a simple divide between sellers and consumers. As noted earlier, consumers fared relatively well under the CSA. "Simple possession" was illegal if "knowing or intentional," but penalties had been reduced from their 1950s-era peak: a maximum of one year imprisonment and a $5,000 fine for a first offense, which courts could replace with probation; youths under twenty-one could then have their records expunged. For "pushers," however, penalties were much more severe. Even a first offense could bring up to fifteen years imprisonment and a fine of $25,000.[91]

The distinction between sellers and consumers, however, made practical sense only in white markets, where sellers were easily identifiable corporations, physicians, and pharmacists. In informal markets, the line was far harder to draw because people with addiction so often also sold drugs to support their habits. Moreover, a white market consumer could legitimately keep a month's supply of a drug, while possession of even a relatively small amount of illicit drugs was evidence of "intent to sell." Finally, even "simple possession" did not mean the same thing in both markets. To be illegal, "simple possession" had to be "knowing and intentional"; as we have seen, white market consumers had long been able to claim ignorance and argue that they were just following physicians' orders. Informal market consumers could make no such claims; possession itself was evidence of a crime. In multiple ways, then, this key compromise (protecting consumers but punishing "pushers") undermined the Controlled Substance Act's challenge to the "bad" drug–"good" medicine divide.

Congress's second key decision, to define all nonmedical use of controlled substances as "abuse," had similar consequences. This definition was no minor element of the law. Indeed, the schedule was almost entirely structured around the assumed desirability of medical use and the assumed undesirability of nonmedical use. The criteria for determining where to schedule a drug included the potential for "dependence" and "abuse," but also whether the drug had "a currently accepted medical use in treatment in the United States." The public health catastrophe in white markets had seriously weakened the case for such criteria.

Conclusion

The CSA was a complex achievement that contained the tools to pursue contradictory agendas. We are familiar with one of those agendas: a punitive campaign to police and control urban racial minorities carried out under the aegis of a "war" against drugs and addiction. This chapter has highlighted a lesser-known agenda: a regulatory campaign to make psychoactive drugs more safely available to white market consumers by limiting corporate profit. Historically, in the 1970s, these two agendas were different sides of the same coin. Racialized fears of addiction were an important political tool in achieving sensible white market safeguards. Creating safer white markets so that "patients" could enjoy access meant further penalizing nonmedical sales to "junkies."

Initially, the dominance of consumer advocacy and addiction medicalization kept the two agendas in some sort of uneasy balance. Moral crusaders, however, had the greater victory, continually building up the law's punitive elements and chipping away at corporate regulations until, by the early 2000s, both medical and informal markets were in the midst of their deepest crises yet: a prescription-drug-driven opioid crisis and a racialized mass incarceration driven in part by drug arrests. This crisis does not invalidate the original 1970s reforms. Quite the opposite: it was a terrible consequence of having slowly abandoned them.

That the two agendas were inextricable in the 1970s does not mean that we can never disentangle them. If we reject the racial logic that separated largely white patients, seen as health-seeking innocents, from other, less socially favored consumers, seen as thrill-seeking "junkies," we can catch a glimpse of a different kind of drug policy. The CSA of

1970 accepted widespread use of potentially addictive drugs, but robustly regulated sales to limit the malign influence of corporate profit and to protect and fully inform consumers. Consumers who developed addiction despite protections faced not punishment but expanded treatment options, including, for many, the option to continue using the drug to which they had become addicted. Distracted by culturally loaded terms like "patients" and "addicts," we have been slow to recognize that this approach worked and reluctant to even imagine applying it broadly for all drug consumers. Given the disastrous failure of the alternatives, it is time to start imagining.

NOTES

1 Significant portions of this chapter are drawn from David Herzberg, *White Market Drugs: Big Pharma and the Hidden History of Addiction in America* (University of Chicago Press, 2020). Thanks are due to of Chicago Press for permission to use and reprint this material.

2 David Herzberg, *Happy Pills in America: From Miltown to Prozac* (Baltimore: Johns Hopkins University Press, 2009), chap. 4.

3 Herzberg, *White Market Drugs*, 212–32.

4 See Claire Clark, *The Recovery Revolution: The Battle over Addiction Treatment in the United States* (New York: Columbia University Press, 2017); David Courtwright, "The Controlled Substances Act: How a 'Big Tent' Reform Became a Punitive Drug Law," *Drug and Alcohol Dependence* 76 (2004): 9–15; Michael Massing, *The Fix* (University of California Press, 2000); Matthew June persuasively argues that Nixon himself did not want these treatment elements and tried to divert or undermine them; see Matthew June, "Protecting Some and Policing Others: Federal Pharmaceutical Regulation and the Foundations of the War on Drugs" (PhD diss., Northwestern University, 2018).

5 Nancy Tomes, *Remaking the American Patient: How Madison Avenue and Modern Medicine Turned Patients into Consumers* (Chapel Hill: University of North Carolina Press, 2016), 231–42; Scott Podolsky, *The Antibiotic Era: Reform, Resistance, and the Pursuit of a Rational Therapeutics* (Baltimore: Johns Hopkins University Press, 2015); Dominique A. Tobbell, *Pills, Power, and Policy: The Struggle for Drug Reform in Cold War America and Its Consequences* (Berkeley: University of California Press, 2011); Herzberg, *Happy Pills*; Andrea Tone, *The Age of Anxiety: A History of America's Turbulent Affair with Tranquilizers* (New York: Basic, 2008).

6 Podolsky, *Antibiotic Era*.

7 John F. Kennedy, "Special Message to Congress on Protecting Consumer Interest," March 15, 1962, John F. Kennedy Presidential Library, Digital Identifier JFKPOF-037-028-p0002, pp. 2, 6, www.jfklibrary.org.

8 June, "Protecting Some and Policing Others"; Daniel Carpenter, *Reputation and Power: Organizational Image and Pharmaceutical Regulation at the FDA* (Princeton, NJ: Princeton University Press, 2010); Jeremy A. Greene and Scott H. Podolsky, "Reform, Regulation, and Pharmaceuticals: The Kefauver–Harris Amendments at 50," *New England Journal of Medicine* 367, no. 16 (2012): 1481–83.

9 Joseph Spillane, *Cocaine: From Medical Marvel to Modern Menace in the United States, 1884–1920* (Baltimore: Johns Hopkins University Press, 2000); David Courtwright, *Dark Paradise: A History of Opiate Addiction in America*, enlarged ed. (Cambridge, MA: Harvard University Press, 2001; first published 1982).

10 Herzberg, *White Market Drugs*, chaps. 4 and 5.

11 Herzberg, *Happy Pills in America*, chaps. 1–4.

12 Herzberg, *White Market Drugs*

13 See Lisa McGirr, *The War on Alcohol: Prohibition and the Rise of the American State* (W. W. Norton, 2015), who argues that the "moral state" grew even during fallow periods for regulatory reform.

14 See Herzbeg, *White Market Drugs*; Tobbell, *Pills, Power, and Policy*.

15 Bernard Casselman testifying in *Illegal Narcotics Traffic and Its Effect on Juvenile and Young Adult Criminality, Part 12: Hearings Before the Subcomm. to Investigate Juvenile Delinquency of S. Comm. on the Judiciary*, Eighty-seventh Congress (1962), 3040.

16 For more about the buildup to the law, see Kathleen Frydl, *The Drug Wars in America, 1940–1973* (New York: Cambridge University Press, 2013), 243–70, and June, "Protecting Some and Policing Others."

17 "An Act to . . . Establish Special Controls for Depressant and Stimulant Drugs and Counterfeit Drugs . . . ," Pub. L. No. 89–74, 79 Stat. 226 (1965). The FDA quickly contracted with the National Research Council's Committee on the Problems of Drug Dependence to evaluate new sedatives and stimulants just as they did opioids; the screening program was in place by 1975. See Herzberg, *White Market Drugs*, 190.

18 For an excellent history of the Bureau of Drug Abuse Control, see June, "Protecting Some and Policing Others."

19 Elizabeth Watkins, *On the Pill: A Social History of Oral Contraceptives, 1950–1970* (Baltimore: Johns Hopkins University Press, 2001); Lizabeth Cohen, *A Consumers' Republic: The Politics of Mass Consumption* (New York: Vintage, 2008); Lawrence Glickman, *Buying Power: A History of Consumer Activism in America* (Chicago: University of Chicago Press, 2009).

20 To be fair, its origins lay not in a consumerist campaign but in a classic law-and-order push by President Lyndon Johnson playing up his anti-crime bona fides as the 1968 election approached. Congress followed the president's plan and merged the FDA's Bureau of Drug Abuse Control and the Federal Bureau of Narcotics into a new, tougher Bureau of Narcotics and Dangerous Drugs in the Department of Justice. The new Bureau immediately ran into both practical and political problems, however, and after his election Richard Nixon proposed a fix—the CSA.

See Herzberg, *White Market Drugs*, chap. 5; June, "Protecting Some and Policing Others"; and Frydl, *The Drug Wars in America*.

21 See, e.g., David Musto, *American Disease: Origins of Narcotics Control*, rev. ed. (1973; repr., New York: Oxford University Press, 1999); Caroline Jean Acker, *Creating the American Junkie: Addiction Research in the Classic Era of Narcotic Control* (Baltimore: Johns Hopkins University Press, 2002); Lisa McGirr, *The War on Alcohol: Prohibition and the Rise of the American State* (New York: W. W. Norton, 2016).

22 Addiction medicalizers were a complex group. They agreed that all nonmedical use of addictive drugs was bad and favored disciplinary tactics to essentially force people to stop using, but in practical terms they opposed arrests and jailings. See Herzberg, *White Market Drugs*, chap. 5.

23 See, e.g., American Pharmaceutical Association; Smith, Kline & French; and Roche Pharmaceuticals in *Drug Abuse Control Amendments—1970: Hearings on H.R. 11701 and H.R. 13743, Parts 1 and 2, Before the Subcomm. on Public Health and Welfare of the H. Comm. on Interstate and Foreign Commerce*, Ninety-first Congress (1970), 256, 265, 640.

24 *Narcotics Legislation: Hearings on S. Res. 48, S. 1895, S. 2590, and S. 2637 Before the Subcomm. to Investigate Juvenile Delinquency of the S. Comm. on the Judiciary*, 91st Congress (1969), 638–39.

25 *Drug Abuse Control Amendments—1970: Hearings on H.R. 11701 and H.R. 13743, Parts 1 and 2, Before the Subcomm. on Public Health and Welfare of the H. Comm. on Interstate and Foreign Commerce*, Ninety-first Congress (1970), 62–63.

26 Joel Fort in *Crime in America—Illicit and Dangerous Drugs: Hearings Before the H. Select Comm. on Crime*, Ninety-first Congress (1965), 45; see also 41–42, 53.

27 *Narcotics Legislation*, 317–18, 325.

28 *Crime in America*, 330.

29 John Ingersoll to Dr. Charles L. Dunham, June 15, 1970, Folder "D. Med: CPDD: U. of Michigan Screening Program Contract Correspondence, 1970–1972," Records of the Committees on Drug Addiction, Drug Addiction (Advisory), and Drug Addiction and Narcotics, 1928–65, National Academy of Sciences, Washington, DC.

30 There are significant problems with using therapeutic benefit as the opposite of "harm," as we will see. The purpose of this chapter is not to endorse the particular framework of the CSA, but rather, to explore one of the few examples of a drug policy oriented around safe consumption rather than prohibition—as a departure point for policy consideration rather than an end point.

31 Jeremy A. Greene, "The Afterlife of the Prescription: The Sciences of Therapeutic Surveillance," in *Prescribed: Writing, Filling, Using, and Abusing the Prescription in Modern America*, ed. Jeremy A. Greene and Elizabeth Siegel Watkins (Baltimore: Johns Hopkins University Press, 2012), 232–56.

32 US Department of Justice, Drug Enforcement Administration, "Automation of Reports and Consolidated Orders System (ARCOS)," accessed March 22, 2021, www.deadiversion.usdoj.gov.

33 Controlled Substances Act, Public Law 91–513, 84 Stat. 1236 (October 27, 1970); see Brian T. Yeh, "The Controlled Substances Act: Regulatory Requirements," Congressional Research Service, December 13, 2012.

34 *Investigation of Juvenile Delinquency in the United States; Investigative and Legislative Hearings on Barbiturate Abuse, Pursuant to S. Res. 32, Section 12, and S. Res. 256 Before the Subcomm. to Investigate Juvenile Delinquency of the S. Comm. on the Judiciary*, Ninety-second Congress (1971–72), 200.

35 Herzberg, *Happy Pills*.

36 Food and Drug Administration, Notice, "Amphetamines: Drugs for Human Use; Drug Efficacy Study Implementation; Amendment or Previous Notice and Opportunity for Hearing," 44 *Federal Register* 41,552 (July 17, 1979), https://cdn .loc.gov.

37 On barbiturates: Drug Enforcement Administration, "Title 21—Food and Drugs, Chapter II—Drug Enforcement Administration, Department of Justice, Part 1308—Schedules of Controlled Substances," 38 *Federal Register* 31,310 (November 13, 1973), https://cdn.loc.gov. On methaqualone: American Medical Association, "For A.M. Release Monday, June 11, 1973: Strict Control Urged for 'Love Drug' Pills," Box 221, AMA, Dept. of Investigation, Records, Drugless Healing, Ryan, Edmund Joseph—Drugs, Corr., 1951, Folder 08, "Drugs, Special Data, 1967–1974," Historical Health Fraud and Alternative Medicine Collection, Department of Investigations Records, American Medical Association Archives, Chicago.

38 Annual quotas posted in *Federal Register*.

39 *Drug Abuse Control Amendments—1970*, 121–22; see also 84–86, 134.

40 Nicolas Rasmussen, *On Speed: The Many Lives of Amphetamine* (New York: New York University Press, 2008), 217–19; Public Health Service, "For Release: Immediate," *HEW News*, August 5, 1970, Box 4528, Folder 511.07–511.09, 1971, Records of the Food and Drug Administration, Record Group 88, National Archives II, College Park, MD.

41 Food and Drug Administration, Notice, "Amphetamines: Drugs for Human Use; Drug Efficacy Study Implementation; Amendment or Previous Notice and Opportunity for Hearing," 44 *Federal Register* 41,552 (July 17, 1979), https://cdn .loc.gov.

42 Food and Drug Administration, Notice, "Amphetamines: Drugs for Human Use; Drug Efficacy Study Implementation; Amendment or Previous Notice and Opportunity for Hearing," 44 *Federal Register* 41,552 (July 17, 1979), https://cdn .loc.gov.

43 For the Uniform Controlled Substances Act, see *Handbook of the National Conference of Commissioners on Uniform State Laws and Proceedings of the Annual Conference Meeting in its Seventy-Ninth Year* (Baltimore: Port City Press, 1970), 223–63; for state adoption statistics, see *Competitive Problems in the Drug Industry, Part 31: Hearings Before the Subcomm. on Monopoly of the S. Select Comm. on Small Business*, Ninety-fourth Congress (1976), 14, 903.

44 Controlled Substances Board, "Draft: Diversion Investigation Unit Proposal," April 27, 1977, Box 1, Folder 39 "Diversion Investigation Unit 1977," Wisconsin, Pharmacy Examining Board, Correspondence and Subject Files, 1927–88. Series 2638 MAD 3/16/F5-7, Wisconsin Historical Society, Division of Library, Archives, and Museum Collections, Madison (hereinafter, "PEB Correspondence").

45 Controlled Substances Board, "Diversion Investigation Unit (DIU)," n.d., Box 1, Folder 39 "Diversion Investigation Unit 1977," PEB Correspondence. For an example of closer cooperation, see "Memorandum of Agreement [between Wisconsin and federal controlled substances agencies]," May 23, 1979, Box 4, Folder 6 "Controlled Substances Board 1979," Wisconsin, Medical Examining Board, Correspondence and Subject Files, 1938–89, Series 1610 MAD 3/41/C2-5, Wisconsin Historical Society, Division of Library, Archives, and Museum Collections, Madison (hereinafter, "SBME Correspondence").

46 See, e.g., "Controlled Substances Board, Minutes of Meeting, 15 August 1979," Box 4, Folder 6 "Controlled Substances Board 1979," SBME Correspondence.

47 David E. Joranson to Controlled Substances Board Members, "A Preliminary View of Amphetamines in Wisconsin: Review and Recommendations," February 2, 1977, Box 2, Folder 4, "Amphetamines—Legislative Documents 1976–1978," SBME Correspondence.

48 Joranson to Controlled Substances Board Members, "Preliminary View of Amphetamines in Wisconsin."

49 David Joranson, "Reducing Licit Amphetamine Supply: Results in Wisconsin," Box 1, Folder 6 "Amphetamine Rule 1978–1983," SBME Correspondence.

50 Joranson, "Reducing Licit Amphetamine Supply."

51 Joranson, "Reducing Licit Amphetamine Supply."

52 Dennis E. Curran, Chief Investigator, to John W. Rupel, November 15, 1977, enclosing "Summary of investigations into amphetamine practice of Wisconsin physicians," Box 1, Folder 5, "Amphetamine Rule 1977," SBME Correspondence; Jerome A. Flynn, Investigator to Donald Ausman, MD, 11 August 1977, Box 8, Folder 13 "Ausman, Donald/MEB 1976," Wisconsin. Medical Examining Board. Investigations, 1929–2005; Series 1616, MAD 2m/9/G3-H3, K6-7; additional accessions, Wisconsin Historical Society, Division of Library, Archives, and Museum Collections, Madison (hereinafter, "SBME Investigations").

53 Jerome Flynn to Medical Examining Board, September 6, 1977, Box 23, Folder 2, "Theiler, Alvin 1976," SBME Investigations.

54 "Memo from Wayne Rusch," February 17, 1976, Box 8, Folder 16, "Balcunias, Vitoldas/MEB," SBME Investigations. See also the Ben Davis Kohne case for the inability to say no, even to dangerous requests, Box 18, Folder 13, "Kohne-DEA Investigations, 1977," SBME Investigation.

55 "In the Matter of: Alvin Theiler, MD," January 11, 1978, p. 24–26; Box 23, Folder 2, "Theiler, Alvin 1976," SBME Investigations.

56 "In the Matter of: Alvin Theiler," 36, 28, 26–27, Box 23, Folder 2, "Theiler, Alvin 1976," SBME Investigations.
57 U.S. v. James R. Couch, MD, Case 80-CR-72, Milwaukee, WI, August 20, 1980, "Change of Please Held in the Above-Entitled Matter," Box 10, Folder 25, "Couch—Circuit Court," SBME Investigations.
58 U.S. v. James R. Couch.
59 U.S. v. James R. Couch.
60 Mary Reddin, State of Wisconsin Medical Examining Board to Alvin Theiler, June 15, 1978; Jerry Flynn to Mary Reddin, July 1, 1977, "Current Status of the Following Investigations"; both Box 23, Folder 2, "Theiler, Alvin 1976," SBME Investigations.
61 "In the Matter of Disciplinary Proceedings against James R. Couch, MD, Respondent: Findings of Fact, Conclusions of Law and Order," Box 10, Folder 25, "Couch—Circuit Court," SBME Investigations.
62 "On welfare": Timothy N. Fast to Dennis Curran, Investigator for Division of Consumer Complaints, "Interview with Vitoloas Balciunas," January 12, 1977; "cutting welfare benefits" from "In the matter of disciplinary proceedings against Vitoldas Balciunas, MD; Order," January 21, 1982; both in Box 8, Folder 16, "Balciunas, Vitaldas/MEB," SBME Investigations.
63 "In the matter of Alvin Theiler, MD," January 11, 1978, 24–28, 36, 43, 46–47, 77, Box 23, Folder 2, "Theiler, Alvin 1976," SBME Investigations.
64 Joel McNally, "Medicaid, Welfare Hist as Addict's Friends," *Milwaukee Journal*, March 6, 1978, Box 14, Folder 9, "Haavik—Prescription Research," SBME Investigations.
65 "In the Matter of the Revocation or Suspension of the License of Arne G. Haavik, MD, Respondent: Proposed Decision," Box 14, Folder 8, "Haavik, Arne/Medical Board 8/9/77," SBME Investigations.
66 Joranson, "Reducing Licit Amphetamine Supply."
67 Albert W. Ray Jr., MD, Illinois State Medical Society, December 7, 1973, "Statement to the Illinois Legislative Investigating Commission Regarding Misuse of Medical Prescriptions in response to House Resolution 285," Folder "Controlled Substances Section," Department of Professional Regulation, "Administrative Files," Record Series 208.045, Illinois State Archives, Springfield (hereinafter, "DPR Admin").
68 Illinois State Medical Society memo to Illinois General Assembly, October 30, 1975. The Controlled Substances Act was also amended to close several loopholes; see Louis R. Fine to Thomas F. Howard, February 20, 1975, Folder "Controlled Substances Act—Enforcement," in DPR Admin.
69 For DIU, see David B. Selig to David Fogel, Director of IL Law Enforcement Commission, July 12, 1974, and "Testimony of Thomas B. Kirkpatrick, Jr., Executive Director of IL Dangerous Drug Commission, before the House Select Committee on Narcotics Abuse and Control, Oct 1, 1977," both in Folder "IDAP Task Force," DASA Admin. For state-level data, see "Task Force on Prescription Drug

Abuse," September 6, 1979, in File "Medical marijuana—1979: hearings, responses to inquiries; amphetamines, re: weight reduction; #1," Department of Alcoholism and Substance Abuse, "Prevention and Education Division Administrative Files," Record Series 223.006, Illinois State Archives, Springfield (hereinafter, "DASA Admin").

70 Illinois Dangerous Drugs Advisory Council Meeting, September 26, 1977, Department of Alcoholism and Substance Abuse, "Commission Meeting Minutes," Record Series 223.004, Illinois State Archives, Springfield (hereinafter, "DASA Minutes").

71 Ronald E. Stackler, DPR Director, "For immediate release," November 5, 1975, Folder "Discipline imposed upon licensees, File II," DASA Minutes.

72 Dangerous Drugs Advisory Council Meeting Minutes, March 23, 1976 and June 29, 1976, DASA Minutes.

73 Food and Drug Administration, Notice, "Amphetamines," 41567.

74 See, e.g., dozens of letters filed in Box 222, "AMA, Dept. of Investigation, Records, Drugs, Correspondence, 1952—Drugs, Non-Prescribed, Patent Medicines, Correspondence, 1947," Folder 4 "Drugs, Illegal Prescribing and Selling, Correspondence," Historical Health Fraud and Alternative Medicine Collection, Department of Investigations Records, American Medical Association Archives, Chicago.

75 *Drug Abuse Control Amendments—1970*, 666.

76 Administrative Narcotics Division, "Six Month Report, January—June, 1976," Folder "Criminal Justice Council (Folder 2) 1973–1976," Correctional Agencies Records. Dept. of Corrections Records, Director's Office Records, Director's Subject Files, Los Angeles County Narcotics and Dangerous Drugs Commission Files, F3717:322, F3717:1558–59, California State Archives, Office of the Secretary of State, Sacramento. For the computerized system, see *Drug Abuse Control Amendments—1970*, 592.

77 Alfonso A. Narvez, "Task Force Seeks Power to Study Theft of Drugs and Makers' Level," *New York Times*, June 29, 1977, www.nytimes.com.

78 John H. Lavin, "What Happens When a State Licensing Board Gets Tough," *Medical Economics*, June 14, 1976, 101.

79 See, e.g., Board Briefs, October 1975, in "Discipline imposed upon licensees, File II," DASA Minutes. This was issue 11, suggesting recent origins.

80 See, e.g., Jackson W. Riddle, Exec Secretary of New York's Medical Board, to Secretaries of all State Medical Boards, February 17, 1976, Folder "Medical Disciplinary Board," DASA Minutes; Raymond Reed, Executive Secretary of California Board of Medical Examiners to All medical examining boards, October 22, 1975, and Federation of State Medical Boards of the United States, Inc., "Board Action Report for October 1975," both in Folder "Discipline imposed upon licensees, File II," DASA Minutes.

81 Rasmussen, *On Speed*, 220.

82 Herzberg, *Happy Pills*, app. 2.

83 See Drug Abuse Warning Network, *Trends in Drug Abuse Related Hospital Emergency Room Episodes and Medical Examiner Cases for Selected Drugs, 1976–1985* (Bethesda, MD: National Institute on Drug Abuse, 1986).

84 Herzberg, *White Market Drugs*, chap. 6.

85 Joseph Gfroerer and Marc Brodsky, "The Incidence of Illicit Drug Use in the United States, 1962–1989," *British Journal of Addiction* 87 (1992): 1345–51.

86 See, e.g., Gootenberg, *Andean Cocaine: The Making of a Global Drug* (Chapel Hill: University of North Carolina Press, 2008).

87 Courtwright, "'Big Tent' Reform"; Massing, *The Fix*.

88 Clark, *Recovery Revolution*; Julilly Kohler-Hausmann, *Getting Tough: Welfare and Imprisonment in 1970s America* (Princeton, NJ: Princeton University Press, 2017), chap. 1.

89 See, e.g., *Drug Abuse Control Amendments—1970*, 233–38, 268–69, 386–7, 466, 681–82; *Narcotics Legislation*, 317, 354, 621, 953.

90 *Controlled Dangerous Substances, Narcotics and Drug Control Laws: Hearings Before the H. Comm. on Ways and Means*, Ninety-first Congress (1970), 195.

91 Less-strict schedules still carried significant punishments for "pushers": five years and $15,000 for non-narcotics in Schedule I or II, or any Schedule III drug; three years and $10,000 for Schedule IV; and even for lowly Schedule V, one year and $5,000, Pub. L. No. 91-513, § 404, 84 Stat. 1264 (1970); § 401, 84 Stat. 1260–61.

11

The Pharma Cartel

KATHLEEN FRYDL

Even as the United States government waged a fierce and punitive War on Drugs, a catastrophic epidemic of opioid addiction ravaged the nation. This epidemic resulted from a systemic failure in US government regulation of the pharmaceutical industry, particularly by the US Food and Drug Administration. Under both Democratic and Republican administrations, a failed neoliberal approach to drug regulation oversight produced a national tragedy.

"Neoliberalism has undermined democracy for forty years."[1]
—Joseph Stiglitz, 2019

Most Americans blame Purdue Pharma, makers of the oxycodone pain-killer OxyContin, for the opioid crisis in the United States.

They have good reason. Since 2012, illegal drugs like heroin have driven the rate of increase in opioid overdose deaths, but this surge in illegal drug use was the successor to—and was in many ways dependent on—the initial phase of the opioid crisis: the oversupply and over-prescribing of legal opioids. In 2019, researchers conducting statistical analysis found that those states more exposed to OxyContin when it was first released suffered higher rates of drug overdose deaths than those with less exposure, effects that persisted for many years.[2] Meanwhile, thousands of Americans still fatally overdose on legal opioids—and do so at five times the rate they did in 1999, before what is typically regarded as the opioid crisis began in earnest.[3] Whether considered from the perspective of initiating illegal opioid use, or from one of driving the oversupply and overprescribing of legal ones, OxyContin is the most compelling point of origin for the worst drug crisis in US history.

This is in part because the drug's original formulation presented an attractive target for misuse. As a single-entity drug, unadulterated with other active components that make snorting or injection less attractive, OxyContin offered illicit users a superior option, resulting in heavy diversion to underground markets. Purdue Pharma primed the pump for this illicit channel with an unprecedented marketing campaign for Oxy-Contin, targeting physicians and other prescribers with well-calibrated and often misleading pitches regarding the drug's safety, including the ability of the drug's "extended release" technology to work on anyone, and for the advertised length of time.[4]

In fact, officials at Purdue Pharma did more, and much worse, than that. When submitting OxyContin for Food and Drug Administration (FDA) approval, the company minimized or withheld data that cast doubt on its extended-release technology. Before and after the drug's release, Purdue ignored reports of abuse of OxyContin, discarding its legal obligation to report "adverse effects" to the FDA. As officials from Purdue hid damaging information necessary to safeguard public health, they simultaneously worked to influence public opinion through "unbranded advocacy," channeling payments via several nonprofit groups in order to retain ostensibly disinterested experts to speak on the company's behalf, or in its interest. Purdue is also a recidivist offender: facing the threat of criminal charges from the federal government, corporate executives and the company paid a modest amount in damages, then reverted to their characteristic posture of pushing sales while disregarding danger. Purdue's corporate board, and especially its owners, the Sackler family, purchased powerful defenders from Washington, DC's political establishment—people like Rudolph Giuliani, former mayor of New York City and personal lawyer to Donald Trump; former New York City police chief Bernard Kerik; former US Attorney General Eric Holder; and former chair of the US Securities and Exchange Commission, Mary Jo White.[5] Though well-connected insiders have so far managed to shield the Sacklers from criminal charges, the damaging information released in civil suits have coalesced into a de facto public indictment, with a verdict already certain: Purdue Pharma is guilty, and the only remaining question is the scope of crime, and how to count the bodies.

But there is a great deal more that should figure into an account of who is responsible for the opioid crisis. To our detriment, the vilification of Purdue Pharma substitutes for an analysis and understanding of the opioid crisis itself, much in the same way that law enforcement officials

invite Americans to view traffic in illegal drugs as the result of a powerful cadre of criminal cartels, as opposed to the cold calculations made by
all manner of people, supplying all sorts of demand.[6]

This is not to suggest that any given perpetrator is innocent or unfairly
maligned. Rather, it is to point out that others could be found equally
culpable—and, more importantly, that concentrating blame on one group
or person often entails a behind-the-scenes absolution of several others,
perhaps even an entire policy regime or political approach. Convicting
the notorious gangster "El Chapo" Guzman on drug trafficking charges,
for example, means figuratively "acquitting" drug prohibition, the cor-
nerstone of the War on Drugs, of the perverse incentives that made his
business possible, his profits rewarding, and his succession inevitable.
Likewise, condemning the Sackler family to disgrace means character-
izing them as aberrational, possessed of some peculiar malevolence. This
neglects the precursors to their conduct; it obscures their many enablers
and fellow travelers; and it exonerates the context and choices that facilitated OxyContin's approval and subsequent misuse. These distortions
do more than oversimplify. They undermine our understanding and risk
perpetuating the mechanisms driving overdose deaths in the first place.

So far, public awareness of the opioid crisis has been shaped by our
adversarial legal process, which puts people on trial, not policies. But
any serious review of the origins of the opioid crisis draws attention
to policies—specifically to neoliberal policies. Neoliberalism is the conservative philosophy of governance that provided the impetus toward
the deregulation and privatization that proved critical in expanding the
supplying and prescribing of opioids. This point bears special emphasis
since to speak in terms of a "pharma cartel"—or a nexus of business
enterprises that sometimes work together to advance industry-wide
goals—raises the same set of concerns as exist on the illicit side: namely,
what policies enabled the cartel's business model? Moving from the
question of culpability to an examination of power, we can see that the
American opioid crisis is a drug epidemic made, and made catastrophi-
cally worse, by neoliberalism.

What follows is a narrative of the origins of the opioid crisis that min-
imizes the role played by a company named Purdue Pharma marketing a drug called OxyContin—a deliberate move made in order to cast
light on a larger story. First and foremost, the drug's approval should be

placed within the changing institutional culture of the FDA; one drug approved among many in an atmosphere of lighter regulation. Second, the fixation on OxyContin leaves an impression that its approval by the FDA was tantamount to an endorsement of opioid use for chronic pain treatment. In reality, the cultivation and legal sanction of that new market for opioid prescribing predates that decision by several years, and features a diverse cast of powerful sponsors, particularly a small activist community of nonprofits funded by several opioid manufacturers (Purdue Pharma among them). A government agency might properly recognize and expose this kind of orchestrated campaign of influence; instead, in the case of opioids, the FDA and Drug Enforcement Administration (DEA) not only turned a blind eye; it saw high-ranking officials leave their ranks to take positions in the very industries they once regulated, a so-called revolving door—a recurring theme of the opioid crisis, and a neglected feature of neoliberalism in general. Most noteworthy, the raw materials necessary to the scale of expanded opioid prescribing were secured by a concerted campaign by the two largest narcotic importers, Johnson & Johnson and Mallinckrodt.

Taking cognizance of these other corporations and developments brings some overlooked features of the early years of the opioid crisis to the fore: the other partners to OxyContin's production and prescribing; and the damage wrought by opioids other than OxyContin, including immediate-release formulations and generic drugs. In connecting these threads, we deepen our understanding of neoliberalism, moving beyond its veneer and rhetoric to its actual operation. Contrary to its professed disdain for government bureaucracy, neoliberalism actually depends on it, capitalizing on the impression of adherence to regulation, while relying on insiders who know its processes intimately in order to circumvent its substance. In practice, deregulation is less of a critique of liberalism and more of a "free rider" on it.

To miss this story in favor of jeering the Sacklers on their public gibbet is to substitute a vendetta for justice.

The Adoption and Influence of Neoliberalism

When New Deal liberalism reached a highwater mark in the early 1970s, its core building blocks of union power, the black freedom movement, and women's rights faced entrenched adversaries and daunting prospects. Still, opponents smarted from their gains. Liberalism's statecraft—progressive social policy and institution-building, particularly the rise of a regulatory state—built resentment throughout corporate America, despite broadly distributed benefits. Yet, though unimpressive in its grasp of power, liberalism was without serious rival as a governing paradigm. Few questioned its foundational bedrock, a merger of those who wanted more from government: the countercyclical economic spending of Keynesian economics, especially deficit spending, and social democracy, or the recognition of citizenship in new ways, and in more people.

But some did. Collecting liberalism's critics, conservatives launched an era of infrastructural investment, funding new institutions like the Heritage Foundation, and reinvigorating old ones like the American Enterprise Institute. The task that fell to them was essentially the mirror opposite of liberalism: forge an alliance between economic conservatives who wanted the government to do less, and the forces of cultural backlash who wanted the same, but in different respects. Their shared impulse to constrain government coalesced into a new governing paradigm of *neo*liberalism, so called because its proponents positioned themselves as followers of the classical liberal tradition of economics, particularly that of Alfred Marshall, who placed private property rights above public obligations.[7]

Neoliberalism consisted of discrete but overlapping objectives: removing government-imposed impediments to the free flow of capital and labor; curbs on deficit spending, often including the sale of entities or privatization of functions previously belonging to government; and a substantial overall limit on government debt. In general, neoliberals sought to return businesses to their former position as the preeminent clients and beneficiaries of government action—and, if corporate America had never really been dislodged from this position of privilege, then neoliberalism's advocates supported the elimination of political commitments that interfered with a more straightforward form of patronage.

In the US, neoliberals shaped the presidency of Ronald Reagan, lending intellectual stature and organizational support to calls to privatize executive operations[8] and core components of social policy.[9] But their influence hardly stopped there. Elsewhere in the developed world, Prime

Minister Margaret Thatcher of the United Kingdom privatized government entities on a scale unthinkable since before the Second World War,
when the Beveridge Report delineated the architecture of the modern
social welfare state. Following Thatcher, the European Union replicated
many neoliberal policy objectives, especially in the Maastricht criteria used to determine eligibility for the Eurozone, or shared currency,
which limited the debt obligations of member states. Arguably, neoliberal thinking reached an apex at global institutions of finance like
the World Bank and the International Monetary Fund, where its policy
prescriptions, unalloyed by the opposition of organized labor, exerted
force throughout the developing world. According to one contemporary
appraisal, by the end of the 1980s, "sales of state enterprises worldwide
had reached a total of over $185 billion—with no signs of a slowdown. In
1990 alone, the world's governments sold off $25 billion in state-owned
enterprises—with continents vying to see who could claim the privatization title."[10] A report from the World Bank in 1992 boasted of knowing
"virtually no limits on what can be privatized."[11]

Though we live in a world dramatically altered by neoliberalism, we
have yet to reckon adequately with its legacy, including identifying precisely what was "*neo*" in approaches long advocated by segregationists,
rightwing ideologues, and businessmen of various sorts, or why the synergistic connection between and among them gained traction when it
did. Much of its significance rests on the breadth of its influence, gaining
unlikely support from across mainstream politics. President Bill Clinton, like his Republican predecessors, championed neoliberal policies,
despite relying on an electoral coalition traditionally regarded as liberalism's stronghold. Clinton joined conservatives in attacks on New
Deal social policy, most notably in curtailing Aid to Families with Dependent Children; he also finalized negotiations and secured passage
of the North American Free Trade Agreement (NAFTA), establishing
a trade corridor stretching from Mexico to Canada defined by progres-
sively lower tariffs and the removal of many quantitative quotas. In addition to these widely discussed trade and social policy policies, President
Clinton embarked on a comparatively less contentious (and far less
noted) neoliberal initiative to privatize government executive functions under the guise of "Reinventing Government." Few post–Second
World War executive reorganization efforts rival its scale; none match

its success in transforming the executive branch. If Ronald Reagan established privatization of government as an aspirational goal, then Bill Clinton's "Reinventing Government" secured it as operational reality; a rarely questioned objective against which agency performance would be judged.

That being said, deregulation and privatization did not spring fully formed from executive orders issued during the Clinton presidency; nor did it derive from manifestos issued by well-funded nonprofits poised to look earnest while professing "no limits" to what could be privatized. At least in regard to the FDA's handling of opioid regulation, several of the agency's fateful moves echo decisions made before the agency matured in power. For this reason, a review of the agency's history helps to pinpoint what marks neoliberalism as distinct from other, similar approaches to governance, and how the opioid crisis became an inextricable part of its modern legacy.

The FDA and the Opioid Crisis

The origin of the Food and Drug Administration dates back to the Bureau of Chemistry of the Department of Agriculture, and in particular to the post–Civil War leadership of Harvey Wiley, whose advocacy for an uncontaminated supply of food and medicine led to the Pure Food and Drug Act of 1906.[12] Although Wiley's success in securing groundbreaking legislation to establish a role for new forms of federal regulation lent the impression of vigorous government power, the Bureau of Chemistry struggled for resources and relevance throughout the Progressive Era. Surprisingly, the Bureau—renamed the Food and Drug Administration in 1930—also did not enjoy favor in the early days of the New Deal, despite repeated and well-publicized problems of danger lurking in the food and drugs sold to Americans. That changed years later, following a particularly dramatic episode of medicinal poisoning that killed over one hundred people. In response, Congress passed the Food, Drug, and Cosmetic Act of 1938, granting the FDA the power to review drugs prior to market release in order to ensure safety, and the regulatory authority to ensure that such drugs advertised only the claims supported by evidence.[13]

Though these regulatory powers sound natural to us now, their original appointment was remarkable—and, for many years following, an innovation emulated elsewhere. The FDA earned more than just admirers and imitators, however; they made enemies as well. Set against a long and eclectic tradition of self-medication, many Americans, including many pharmacists, felt the FDA impinged on prerogatives properly belonging to an individual—an unjust preemption, in their eyes, and possibly an injurious one as well. The budding American pharmaceutical industry gradually adopted a different view, however, as the most powerful among them realized that the agency's regime of pre-market approval enhanced the prestige of the drugs they marketed, setting them apart from formulations never subjected to scientific review. Drug makers also benefited by placing many products behind an access wall of "prescription only," since marketing for those drugs needed only to target prescribers, as opposed to the general public. Always there was some pharmaceutical company or drug classification that proved thorny or vexatious. But in the main, throughout the 1950s, the industry partnered with the FDA to stunning effect. In the decade following the 1938 Act, Americans shifted away from older, clinically unevaluated tinctures or tablets in favor of medicine engineered in a laboratory, tested by a parent pharmaceutical conglomerate, and placed before the FDA for review and approval. "More new and truly effective drugs were invented between 1935 and 1955 than in all of previous human history," observes Philip Hilts, author of a comprehensive history of the FDA.[14]

As the US pharmaceutical industry developed into an undisputed global leader, the FDA's long-serving Commissioner George Larrick, known for a congenial approach, avoided potential points of confrontation, including those raised by widespread overprescribing, lethal misuse, and possible mislabeling of amphetamines and barbiturates.[15] Perhaps Larrick dismissed concerns by noting that such medicines came to any user only by way of a doctor's prescription pad, and an attending physician was in the best position to judge what medicine, in what amount, suited any given patient.

If so, then Larrick did not much understand the evolution in the industry over which he presided. Once a family doctor would consult entries in the long-running "seal of acceptance" program of the American Medical Association (AMA) to inform his or her professional judgment. By the 1950, the FDA rendered the AMA's program obsolete; in fact, it fell into disuse.[16] In the place of the AMA's imprimatur, the FDA emerged as de facto advisor to physicians, a role that took on greater importance as advertising targeting them grew exponentially. "In 1930 about 95 percent of drug company advertising was aimed at the public," Philip Hilts observes, but by 1972, "perhaps as much as 90 percent was aimed at doctors."[17]

As the opioid and other drug crises reveal, to rely on a physician's judgment to make sense of an exploding market in prescription drugs was, in effect, to delegate medical decision-making to Madison Avenue advertising budgets. Even when the FDA had evaluated the drug's basic safety profile in a reliable fashion, this still left more fine-grained judgments without guidance. For example, a drug might not be lethal in any given dose, but it might prove dangerous when taken for an extended period or in combination with other commonly used substances. Not surprisingly, insiders identified such problems in oversupply and over-prescribing as potential pitfalls of the FDA's laissez-faire posture; even in the face of congressional investigation of barbiturate and amphetamine abuse, Commissioner Larrick chased down small-time traffic, but sought no accountability from manufacturers.[18] One medical examiner working at the FDA in the 1950s recounted that, after expressing reservations regarding the safe use of a tranquilizer, her superior walked into her meeting with the company's representatives and announced approval of the drug, without "any proof of safety over longtime use."[19]

In spite of warnings and risks, Larrick's FDA maintained a restrained approach to regulation, preferring good relations with pharmaceutical companies. Grievances with the agency grew after his departure, and especially after the Kefauver–Harris Amendments of 1962, which required drug manufacturers to satisfy a more stringent criterion of drug efficacy, established by "well-controlled studies" (construed as randomized clinical trials), as a condition for drug approval. Before long, corporate executives echoed many of the complaints voiced by proponents of self-medication, accusing the FDA of spurning valuable drugs in favor of complying with onerous bureaucratic procedures. After the Kefauver–Harris Amendments became law, the arch-conservative John Birch Society openly advocated the repeal of its efficacy provisions.[20]

Though far from ascendant, deregulation of the FDA was given a dress rehearsal of sorts when Richard Nixon was elected president—albeit with a bizarre personal twist, characteristic of Nixon's vindictive temperament.[21] In the main, Nixon administration officials resorted to hectoring civil servants with proposed relocations, or some other form of nuisance, to thin the ranks at the FDA. Only with election of Ronald Reagan, the crowning achievement of a coalition of anti-government conservatives, did officials pursue deregulation of the FDA on a more systematic basis, including regular editorializing against the agency's authority in the pages of the *Wall Street Journal*; the platforming of those affiliated with the new the Tufts Center for the Study of Drug Development, an institution dedicated to deregulation[22]; and a "broke on purpose" approach to the FDA budget that, by depriving the agency of medical examiners, added evidentiary weight to accusations of slow approval times. Although new drug applications grew substantially, climbing from 4,200 in 1970 to 12,800 in 1989, the FDA workforce actually contracted over the same period, from 7,960 employees in the mid-Seventies to 6,960 by the mid-Eighties.[23]

Reagan-era budgets proved so crippling for the FDA that the need for new personnel grew urgent. With the help of allies in Congress like conservative Utah Senator Orrin Hatch,[24] a key ally of the pharmaceutical industry, the administration of George H. W. Bush supported legislation called the Prescription Drug User Fee Act, which was presented to the public as a way to supply a beleaguered agency with a new source of funds. For any new drug application, a sponsor paid a fee; the collection of all such revenue went toward hiring new medical examiners, and with this new workforce came a promise to bring down the time it took for the FDA to review a new drug application. While some voiced concern about turning a portion of the budget of the federal agency over to the industry it regulates—today, the User Fee Act accounts for roughly half of the FDA budget—a decade of prominent deregulation advocacy allowed supporters to position "user fees" as a reasonable approach, designed to stave off further encroachment.[25] Conservatives depicted the fee act as modest reform, while many liberals declared it an urgent matter of necessity. Activists dedicated to expedited approval for experimental drugs to test against the HIV virus focused attention on the dangerous cost of a drug approval system that lumbered along, indifferent to patients dying by the thousands. In reality, the poor incentives provided by commercial drug research slowed progress.[26] When it came to HIV treatment trials, in cases like that of the drug azidothymidine

(AZT), FDA officials acted expeditiously; in others, their caution proved circumspect. Though some AIDS activists later recanted their criticism of the FDA, there was little question that, in the early 1990s, the agency was in political crisis.[27] The Prescription Drug User Fee Act passed the House by unanimous consent, and subsequently passed in the Senate by voice vote.

During this time, David Kessler, a young medical professional who served on Orrin Hatch's staff, assumed leadership of the FDA. Best known to the public for his campaign to classify cigarettes as drugs, Kessler will also be remembered to history for his support and implementation of the User Fee Act. The new FDA Director received support from the newly elected president, Bill Clinton, who vowed to "get rid of yesterday's government" and urged the FDA to regard the pharmaceutical industry as "partners, not adversaries," an approach familiar to the agency via Larrick's leadership, and one that presaged overprescribing and oversupply.

At first, the User Fee Act was judged an unqualified success in that approval times for drugs went down demonstrably, meeting the timetables stipulated in the legislation.[28] One congressional staff lawyer noted that such targets could be met "by either approving the drug or denying the approval"—but, over time, he acknowledged that "what Congress really wanted was not just decisions, but approvals." "That is what really gets dangerous," he added.[29] Some dangers manifested quickly: shortly after Kessler announced his departure in late 1996, the *Los Angeles Times* reported on dangerous drugs recently approved by the FDA, eventually culminating in a Pulitzer Prize being awarded to the reporter, David Willman, for a series collected under a title that alluded to the User Fee Act: "The New FDA: How a New Policy Led to Seven Deadly Drugs."[30] "Either you play games or you're going to be put off limits," a medical review officer told Willman; "The people in charge don't say, 'Should we approve this drug?' They say, 'Hey, how can we get this drug approved?'" Meta-analyses spanning decades of approval decisions since the User Fee Act was implemented confirm that the FDA now approves new drugs based on less, and less rigorous, evidence.[31] Yet, regardless of early warning signs, the User Fee Act was reauthorized in the "FDA Modernization Act" of 1997, a key component of Clinton's "Reinventing Government" initiative, and has been reauthorized ever since.[32]

Understanding the institutional history of the FDA supplies context to its decision to approve Purdue Pharma's application for OxyContin in 1995.[33] In documents submitted to the FDA reviewers, Purdue claimed that its slow-release technology worked for at least half of the patients prescribed the medication for experimental purposes. Several of the studies furnished to the FDA showed nothing of the kind: in one trial of eighty-seven cancer patients, "rescue medication," or a pain reliever administered in between doses, "was used frequently in most of the patients," and "95 percent resorted to it at some point in the study." On the other hand, one clinical trial that Purdue furnished in its application did show a 12-hour effect for at least half of the patients. Purdue relied on that experiment to support its claims for innovation, key to its pending patent. The FDA approved the slow-release technology on the strength of that lone citation; this approval then provided the basis for Purdue's marketing claim that OxyContin presented less of a risk of cultivating opioid dependence, as the drug was (theoretically) released on a steady basis over a longer period, meting out its narcotic payload over time. As part of its aggressive marketing campaign launched in 1996, Purdue claimed OxyContin "spares patients from anxious 'clock-watching.'" In fact, many patients found themselves in agony awaiting their next dose. As the *Los Angeles Times* subsequently reported, Dr. Curtis Wright, who led the FDA's medical review of the drug, left the FDA shortly after Oxy-Contin was approved and, "within two years, was working for Purdue in new product development."[34]

On the basis of very little, Purdue won quite a lot from the FDA. Journalist Sam Quinones pointed out that Purdue's first-in-class warning label enabled the company to claim "that OxyContin had a lower potential for abuse than other oxycodone products because its timed-release formula allowed for a delay in absorbing the drug."[35] *New York Times* reporter Barry Meier was among the first to expose how little scientific evidence actually backed this claim, in his 2003 book *Painkiller: A 'Wonder' Drug's Tale of Addiction and Death*. Yet, in spite of faulty evidence, the FDA granted approval for a claim that enabled a marketing plan of staggering ambition. OxyContin soon became America's best-selling painkiller,[36] earning $31 billion in revenue for Purdue Pharma and vaulting its owners, the Sackler family, to the upper reaches of the *Forbes* list of America's wealthiest families.[37]

The review of OxyContin on the basis of drug extension rather than new drug approval is especially noteworthy because it spared Purdue Pharma of the obligation to demonstrate the efficacy of opioids when used to treat chronic pain. Based on prior FDA approvals of oxycodone formulations, the drug was presumed to be safe and effective; the only question was whether the slow-release technology presented—and could be marketed—as a competitive advantage over other similar drugs. Lost in the discussion of "extended release" was the larger issue of whether opioids could treat chronic pain effectively at all, a proposition that science has yet to vindicate.[38] Previously, prescription opioids for patient use were confined to two different situations: palliative care, especially cancer-related pain; and acute pain care, typically lasting seven to ten days, most often for postoperative recovery. Prescribers of various sorts looked to expand that ambit of prescribing to include more ordinary circumstances, like back pain or tooth extraction. OxyContin's particular promise of safety, anchored in extended release, fit remarkably well into this campaign to enlarge the market of opioid prescribing. Naturally, the FDA could have asked how well opioids work over an extended period of use. Instead, just as was the case in the FDA of the 1950s, when regulators friendly to business approved a tranquilizer without requiring any assessment of risks versus benefits for long-term use, the FDA chose to say "yes" to OxyContin when the application before them ought to have prompted them to say, "show us more." A provocative historical parallel, these two regulatory encounters separated by four decades raise the question of whether neoliberal deregulation simply marks a return to the business clientelism of 1950s America, when it could be said openly, "what was good for our country was good for General Motors, and vice versa."[39]

Yet this comparison, premised on similarity, also brings out some key differences. Following the emergence of a rigorous regulatory state—in the FDA's case, following the Kefauver–Harris Amendments—pharmaceutical companies were obliged to remain in compliance with fairly elaborate procedures, including furnishing specialized data to public agencies. Detecting diligence or its absence in these data is a job for the regulators themselves (although others may eventually gain awareness of problems with particular drugs, and this may in turn expose vulnerabilities in the original submission to the FDA). A bustling "revolving door" between industry and government suggests not only that agency regulators may not execute their public function with the public foremost in mind, but that their specialized, insider knowledge is highly prized by industry.[40] In the days of Larrick, only Larrick was needed to perform favors for industry. Following the User Fee Act, a cadre of medical examiners could steer regulatory decisions in favor of drug companies, using their inside knowledge of bureaucracy, rather than their personal political capital, to pursue their goal.

This made regulatory lapses harder to detect, or even name. It is a distinguishing feature of neoliberalism that, in contrast to previous agency failures, there is no learning curve. Following one tragic episode of drug poisoning, Congress passed the 1938 Food, Drug, and Cosmetic Act; the FDA collaborated with the National Academies of Sciences, Engineering, and Medicine to review *every drug* on the market.[41] Likewise, following the revelation that birth defects caused by one particular drug, Congress augmented FDA regulatory power with the Kefauver–Harris Amendments; a review of the FDA's clearance process for experimental drugs followed. In the case of the opioid crisis, there has been no comparable infusion of regulatory power in the FDA; if anything, Obama's Twenty-First Century Cures Act stripped the agency of power.[42] In similar fashion, FDA officials refuse to account for previous mistakes—a willful blindness that points to something more. Thus far, the agency has refused to implement the public-health approach to opioid approval—including retroactive review—recommended by a consensus panel of experts convened by the National Academies, a startling rejection that prompted a prominent activist to call for the replacement of the FDA's director of drug evaluation.[43] Instead of resigning, she has responded to congressional inquiries by claiming the agency properly enforced its regulations. As Dr. Andrew Kolodny points out, though faced with "mounting criticism," FDA "policies for approving and labeling opioids remain largely unchanged," while the institution remains "defensive."[44]

Though clearly a factor, the User Fee Act does not, by itself, account for the fate of Purdue Pharma's OxyContin application before the FDA, or its subsequent marketing coup. In fact, some additional circumstances that facilitated approval and the ready adoption of OxyContin have nothing whatsoever to do with reigning political philosophies. For example, the long-running problem of a medical profession poorly

prepared to receive the onslaught of well-financed public relations campaigns gave Purdue's marketing an outsized influence. Regardless of era,
the FDA's approval processes do not seem adequate for consideration
of a drug proposed for long-term, habitual use, which may require a
substantially different safety review than if the same drug were used only
occasionally or for a short period of time. Finally, in his stellar book on
the origin of the opioid crisis, Sam Quinones highlights pressures within
the business of medicine that asked physicians to become more profitable by spending less time with each patient, and consequently to find it
much simpler to prescribe a pill than take an exhaustive case history and
seek an integrated approach to pain management.[45]

Bearing those concerns in mind, it is still remarkable how little the
FDA has done to respond to the opioid crisis. Based on their own internal reviews, agency officials know that post-release labeling changes
amount to little; they also know that a hasty drug approval process ought
to go hand in hand with strengthening the FDA's post-market power to
review, and if necessary to recall, a drug.[46] Yet, to date, labeling changes
and a voluntary training program on safe opioid prescribing (funded by
manufacturers) is all that the FDA has managed to offer to help ameliorate the opioid crisis.

Creating the Market: Expanding Demand

Another hallmark of neoliberal advocacy is the proliferation of both
industry and corporate-specific messaging through ostensibly independent agents—usually nonprofit groups and professional associations,
but often esteemed professionals as well. So-called "unbranded" advocates appear not as mere accessories, but as necessary mechanisms for
a neoliberal agenda, since their funders, forced to comply with elaborate regulation, require the appearance of a public consensus among
stakeholders, both real and invented. Whereas a company sponsoring a
tranquilizer in the 1950s need only rely on a pliant director of the FDA,
the more ambitious goal of expanded opioid prescribing, launched in
earnest in the late 1980s, required a chorus of approval from trusted
sources.

This point raises what is by far the most remarkable aspect of the first
stage of the opioid crisis: no pharmaceutical company has ever been

asked by any government regulator to subject opioids to a clinical trial for the treatment of chronic pain. Instead of demonstrating efficacy, opioid manufacturers gained access to that sizable market by aggressive use of unbranded advocacy, targeting individual state medical boards, lawmakers, and outlets of influence within the medical profession, like professional conferences and medical schools.

Other accounts regarding the early stages of the opioid crisis date the campaign to expand prescribing to a 1995 address to the American Pain Society, declaring pain the "fifth vital sign" that must be attended to by primary care physicians in everyday medical settings.[47] In reality, the address marked a new stage of assertiveness for a movement that had already attracted momentum and resources. Its origin can be traced to the palliative care research conducted in the 1980s by Drs. Kathleen Foley and Russell Portenoy, who gained a following when they decried the lack of adequate prescribing of opioids to treat cancer pain.[48] Though uncaring and often cruel, the under-treatment in palliative care persisted (and persists to this day) in part because doctors feared "addicting" patients when prescribing opioids. From this rally point emerged an understanding that pain was, in general, under-treated by the medical profession— not just in end-of-life settings, but in all ways. Both Sam Quinones and Barry Meier trace how these concerns coalesced into a movement to prescribe opioids for chronic pain, much of which hinged on a critical citation—often referred to in shorthand as "Porter and Jick"—that proponents advanced in order to argue that, when prescribed to treat pain, opioids presented a remarkably low risk of addiction in users.[49] For example, Russell Portenoy cited Porter and Jick in this way, and his work became a standard citation in itself.[50] But, as Quinones and Meier also note, "Porter and Jick" actually refers to a letter published in the *New England Journal of Medicine* describing an impressively small percentage of cases of addiction in an analysis of opioids administered to patients in a hospital setting for a short period of time. Though the drug companies used this citation to promote their new opioids as nonaddictive, Dr. Hershel Jick adamantly stated: "that's not in any shape or form what we suggested in our letter."[51]

Despite its lack of direct bearing, "Porter and Jick" became a frequently invoked source of authority for an emerging community of opioid-prescribing activists, many of whom intersected with nonprofits

funded by opioid manufacturers.[52] (Since many of these nonprofits benefit from a tax status that allows them to keep funders private, it is likely
that, even after several investigations, our knowledge of the pharmaceutical corporation–funded apparatus is only partial.) What is known
about the links between unbranded advocates and their corporate
funders derives from seminal work by the *Milwaukee Sentinel Journal/
Medpage Today*[53]; a 2012 US Senate Finance Committee investigation,
led by chair Max Baucus and ranking member Charles Grassley (some
portions of which were publicly released in late 2020)[54]; an important
2018 inquiry conducted by then-ranking member Senator Claire Mc-
Caskill[55]; and the 2019 investigation of the global campaign to expand
opioid prescribing led by Congresswoman Katherine Clark.[56] From
these various sources, we learn that important actors in unbranded advocacy for opioid prescribing include the American Pain Foundation,
which ceased operations after receiving the funding inquiry letter from
Baucus and Grassley[57]; the Soros Foundation's Open Society Project on
Death in America, where Kathleen Foley worked; the American Academy of Pain Medicine; the American Pain Society; the US Pain Foundation; the American Chronic Pain Association; the Washington Legal
Foundation; the Mayday Fund; and the University of Wisconsin Pain
and Policy Studies Group.[58] The *Milwaukee Journal Sentinel/Medpage*
investigation also named an advisory committee of the Robert Wood
Johnson Foundation for failing to disclose ties to opioid manufacturers, essentially operating as a front to fund projects without raising any
conflict-of-interest questions.[59] Early investigations identified the drug
makers Johnson & Johnson, Endo Pharmaceuticals, and Purdue Pharma
as funders of these organizations; later, McCaskill added Insys and
Mylan to the list, and the 2020 release of material by Senators Grassley and
Ron Wyden includes several other major pharmaceutical companies,
like AstraZeneca, GlaxoSmithKline, and Mallinckrodt Pharmaceuticals.

One relatively neglected aspect of the hive of activity generated by
the early efforts of unbranded advocacy is their push to pass state laws
or push for the adoption of rules to explicitly sanction the use of opioids
to treat chronic pain. In 1998, one supporter remarked on the number
of states that had "enacted laws . . . adopted administrative rules, and/
or established guidelines for the use of narcotic analgesics for the treatment of chronic pain."[60] As she noted, many of those guidelines seemed

to have no real target, as few administrative proceedings were directed against chronic pain prescribing.[61] But clearly opioid-prescription activists wanted to send an affirmative message to doctors; some resorted to filing professional complaints against doctors who did not prescribe opioids to treat chronic pain. Still, doctors proved reluctant to prescribe opioids to the degree envisioned by activists. Soon advocates extended their approach to include the formation of state "pain commissions." Writing in the *American Pain Society Bulletin* in 1996, David E. Joranson, a researcher affiliated with the University of Wisconsin Pain and Policy Studies Group, lauded the example of such boards at work in Florida, Michigan, Ohio, and Massachusetts.[62] In fact, the Pain and Policy Studies Group conducted workshops for state medical boards between 1994 and 1997 to survey the prevailing views on opioid prescribing among members of state medical boards. In 1998, the Federation of State Medical Boards of the United States (FSMB), in collaboration with the American Society of Law, Medicine, and Ethics (working through the support of the Mayday Fund),[63] published a "model" guideline for chronic pain prescribing.[64] Another study funded by the Mayday Foundation found that years later, "twelve states had adopted the FSMB's Model Guidelines in full, and nine in part," and that the "attitudes and practices of medical boards toward physicians' prescribing of opioids have changed for the better"—by which the authors meant that there was greater recognition of the value of opioid prescribing for chronic pain.[65] In systematic fashion, tucked away in mostly quiet corners of government, a tightly woven nexus of nonprofit and other interest groups worked to overhaul the disposition of the medical profession toward prescribing opioids for chronic pain. By such methods, they accomplished in concert what drug manufacturers would never have been able manage on their own, working under their corporate banners.

Although researchers and advocacy groups did not disclose their financial ties to opioid manufacturers, their work appeared in public with no alarming or sinister cast. To the contrary, their campaigns carried the blessing of the establishment and the imprimatur of scientific authority. In 1998, the same year the Federation published its model guidelines, former FDA Commissioner David Kessler agreed to serve as honorary chair of the Mayday Fund's National Advisory Committee. "We know from various surveys that Americans are sometimes reluctant to take over-the-counter and prescription pain medications because they fear becoming addicted to them," Kessler said in a press release, "even though addiction is, in fact, extraordinarily rare."[66] Years later, Kessler would again be quoted on the subject of opioid prescribing, this time in the *Los Angeles Times* ground-breaking series on Purdue Pharma.[67] The failure to recognize the addictive potential of opioid painkillers is "one of the greatest mistakes of modern medicine," Kessler offered, adding that the pharmaceutical ambition to export opioids globally after its domestic market came under scrutiny was "right out of the playbook of Big Tobacco," his old nemesis. The article omitted any mention of the Mayday Fund as a pivotal player in that project, or that Kessler was serving as FDA commissioner when OxyContin received approval, and as a key advisor to the Mayday Fund shortly thereafter.[68]

Bearing endorsements from respected authorities, the orchestrated campaign of unbranded advocacy required a closer look into the data in order to detect a false note. The "Porter and Jick" fiasco stands out as a failure to do just that, but others deserve mention. In the mid-1990s, opioid-prescribing advocates seized on certain administrative decisions penalizing physicians for prescribing opioids to treat chronic pain in order to perpetuate a sense of grievance and justify their fixation on state medical boards. One typical example is the citation of *Hoover v. Agency for Health Care Administration* in the Hoffman and Tarzian article (cited above) published in the *Journal of Law, Medicine & Ethics*.[69] The text reads: "some state boards [have] disciplin[ed] physicians for 'overprescribing' opioids, including physicians who were treating pain patients." The case in question involved Dr. Katherine Anne Hoover, who soon found herself before the medical board again for soliciting a seventeen-year-old patient to have sex with her son. She has since earned infamy in West Virginia: prescribing more pain pills than any other doctor in that state, she ultimately fled for the Bahamas after her offices were raided by federal officials.[70] The other citation offered by Hoffman and Tarzian is a Louisiana case: "In re DiLeo, 661 So. 2d 162 (La. Ct. App. 1995)," involving Dr. Lucas DiLeo, a doctor in St. Bernard Parish who was once interviewed by the House Select Committee on Assassinations in connection with the murder of Martin Luther King Jr. (The committee declined to make much of DiLeo's reported connection to the New Orleans mob or a rumored meeting between DiLeo and

James Earl Ray, but did seem to voice a general skepticism by noting his "record for such minor offenses as disturbing the peace, resisting arrest, and assault." DiLeo's interview remains sealed.) The 1993 case against his prescribing practices stipulates that in 1990 DiLeo "voluntarily surrendered his license to prescribe Schedule II and III drugs to the DEA, for reasons which are not altogether clear"; later proceedings revealed this move came after two federal agents appeared in his office, presumably as the result of suspicious prescribing.[71]

What's most puzzling about the citation of both of these cases is that in each instance, the state board's initial decision to penalize the prescribing physician was later reversed, in part or in full, in such a way as to affirm precisely the principle which the articles present as under threat: opioid prescribing for chronic pain. To calamitous misfortune, Dr. Katherine Hoover went on to prescribe many, many more pills. Louisiana ultimately sustained the deprivation of DiLeo's medical license, but only on the grounds that he prescribed controlled substances without a license.[72]

With no one digging into footnotes, advocates successfully perpetuated an atmosphere of persecution, perhaps most of all because of one notorious case: Dr. Frank Fisher, arrested by California state officials in 1999. His story was no footnote buried in an academic journal, but a cause célèbre[73]—and little wonder, given that the initial filing against Dr. Fisher included murder charges for three of Fisher's patients found with high levels of oxycodone in their system when they died.[74] Other charges included improper prescribing of controlled substances, and (filed the previous year) fraud charges involving a pharmacy kick-back scheme based on alleged overcharging of the state Medicaid system. But, in the eyes of prosecutors, the true crime—the reason Fisher came to the attention of authorities in the first place—must have been the fact that Fisher, a Harvard-trained physician, was the largest prescriber of Oxy-Contin in the state. Throughout his ordeal, a defiant Dr. Fisher maintained that he prescribed according to a standard of care that increased the dose in patients accustomed to opioids to levels that would be lethal for the uninitiated, but tolerated in pain patients.

When Fisher could not make bail, he was sent to jail for five months. A group of patients rallied to his defense.[75] At a preliminary hearing, the judge reduced the charges to manslaughter, including those filed against his alleged co-conspirator, Stephen Miller, owner of the only pharmacy in Redding that would fill Fisher's prescriptions. Over time, the criminal case against Fisher faltered, then fell apart. Even civil suits filed by relatives of patients who overdosed were dismissed. In the end, it was the state medical board that imposed the only official penalty on Fisher: a period of probation—meaning, subject to professional monitoring—and a requirement to keep a list of controlled substances he prescribed.[76] After enduring a public and humiliating ordeal, the damage to his life and reputation hardly seemed proportionate or justified.

The criminal complaint against Fisher would seem to be a classic case of overreach; a blunt and chilling effect on opioid prescribing for chronic pain. Fisher's subsequent speaking engagements and public testimony suggest that his story was certainly understood and received in this way. Yet investigators' 1999 filing before the state medical board—the one that served as the basis for the penalties ultimately imposed on Fisher—alters the conventional impression of the state's action against Fisher, including how Fisher (and others) went on to present his story.

Dr. Fisher came before the board as a result of an investigation that cited numerous infractions: failing to prescribe long-acting (extended release) opioids for chronic pain, instead relying on short-acting ones; failing to explain to patients that short-acting opioids used in conjunction with extended-release formulations were to be used for "breakthrough pain"; prescribing dangerous levels of acetaminophen to patients, rendering them vulnerable to liver damage; failing to document functional improvement with opioids before increasing the dose; prescribing potentially dangerous combinations of drugs, including benzodiazepines, without performing any psychiatric evaluation, or referring a patient to another medical provider to perform one; failing to take previous substance use disorders into account when prescribing potentially addictive drugs, and failing to follow-up on any such patient's recovery efforts while under his care.

The violations were numerous, depicting a pattern of extreme carelessness. Contrary to Fisher's claim that he became a target of state attention because he prescribed opioids at too high a dose, the actual complaint discloses that he increased dose without ascertaining whether opioids worked for a particular patient in the first place. A number of the charges cited by the Board violate "responsible care" guidelines set forth by opioid manufacturers in their own promotional literature. Rather than a poster child for chronic pain opioid prescribing, Dr. Fisher's documented infractions ought to have been regarded by his many defenders as an example of what *not* to do. All told, a reasonable person reading the document might well conclude that Fisher ran a "pill mill" by any other name, and was spared criminal sanction by a combination of aggressive and misguided handling by the state attorney general, the incredible protection offered by professional status, and the usefulness of his story, including its inarguably excessive components, in presenting a picture of a medical profession as under siege.

Such a sweeping effort derived support from more than just Purdue Pharma, and worked to the benefit of more than just OxyContin. Certainly, Purdue's new drug experienced a boon: according to the Department of Justice Inspector General, OxyContin prescriptions for non-cancer related pain increased "from about 670,000 in 1997 to about 6.2 million in 2002."[77] It is also very likely that the timing of Purdue's massive public relations campaign for OxyContin lent authority to the opioid prescribing movement, and vice versa, forging a new consensus in symbiotic fashion. For example, Purdue disseminated the Federation's revised prescribing guidelines at its own cost.

Be that as it may, according to researchers, most people prescribed an opioid analgesic, whether for short or for long term use, take immediate release—not extended release—formulations.[78] In 2017, the National Academies confirmed this in their report.[79] Recent data from the FDA also make clear that, even after generic versions of oxycodone extended-release formulations came to market, the number of prescriptions for all such pills, including OxyContin, did not compare to other opioids. Definitely OxyContin sparked heavy diversion to illicit markets; it also clearly established the viability of opioid prescribing for chronic pain, with adoption rates in white-working-class communities on a scale that would one day usher in new heroin markets. But, on the other hand, given the amount of other opioid drugs circulating, it is not surprising that a *New York Times* exposé on illicit pharmaceutical use on college campuses, published in 2000, does not mention OxyContin, but does discuss Vicodin (hydrocodone with acetaminophen) and Percocet (oxycodone with acetaminophen).[80] This is not to diminish in any way the spectacular effect of OxyContin. It is rather to suggest, as a different *New*

York Times article disclosed in 2001, that other drugs laid the ground-work for its ascendance in illicit markets: "there were plenty of oxyco-done users in Appalachia before OxyContin came along," Paul Tough has written. "Many of the OxyContin addicts I spoke to in Kentucky and West Virginia used to snort or chew a mild oxycodone-based painkiller called Tylox."[81]

Expanding Supply: Privatizing Poppy Fields

Unbeknownst to most, the narcotic raw material needed to make legal opioids appears in the US only as an import, never as a domestic com-modity. These imports arrive according to another set of regulations promulgated by the DEA, presenting another target for neoliberal-minded deregulation: performative compliance, accompanied by an insider's understanding of how to negotiate the desired result or, in this case, change the rules entirely.

Without supply, drug companies would be unable to serve the ex-panded market they worked to create. In this particular case, the de-regulation came about as a quiet "exception" to an arcane rule familiar only to drug importers and devoted readers of the *Federal Register*. In fact, it was an audacious stroke, spearheaded by Johnson & Johnson, one of two certified importers of narcotic raw material, whose officials came to view this particular regulatory obstacle as a business advantage—that is, a unique opportunity to privatize their production chain from seed to sale.

Probably nothing enhanced Johnson & Johnson's chances for success more than the obscurity of the regulation they sought to change. Its his-tory belongs to the struggle many governments face when confronting the global traffic in pharmaceutical drugs. First the League of Nations, then the United Nations, grappled with the illegal diversion of licit drug supply by adopting protocols designed to monitor the production and importation of raw or refined materials. The final version of this global system of bookkeeping, the 1961 Single Convention Treaty, was imple-mented in the US as one component of the Controlled Substances Act of 1970. One condition of participation in the treaty required the des-ignation of a single government agency to determine a country's medi-cal needs for certain drugs, and set importation and production quotas accordingly. The US assigned the DEA to this task[82]—an odd delegation that raised some small questions at the time, but one that rested on the institutional legacy of the DEA, comprised in part by the former Bureau of Narcotics, once located in the Department of Treasury, with drug imports as a major focus of its work.[83]

The settled intricacies of the legal drug trade left a lot to be desired. Given that morphine is an essential conversion stage on the path to producing heroin, signatories to the treaty hoped that limiting the legal morphine supply would in turn limit (now contraband) heroin. In reality, legal producers of narcotic raw materials—mainly Turkey and India—had not supplied the bulk of the illegal market for years. Instead, heroin derived from an illegal, underground supply chain, all the way from poppy to powder. Still the diplomatic corps of the US reasoned that awarding legal supply to Turkey for concentrated poppy straw and India for opium gum kept both countries invested in treaty compliance; it also served as an acknowledgment of the difficulty in inducing poppy farmers to convert to another crop.

Soon after the US passed the Controlled Substances Act, trouble between the Nixon administration and the government of Turkey interrupted the supply of Turkish opium imports, resulting in a medical shortage of critical drugs. While the US eventually restored good relations with Turkey, the countries that had supplied the raw material for America's needs in the interval asked to continue their opioid trade with the US. To broker a sensitive compromise, US policy makers devised the so called "80–20" rule, published in the *Federal Register* in 1981, stipulating that "at least eighty (80) percent of the narcotic raw material imported into the US shall have as its original source Turkey and India," and the remaining 20 percent would be divided among Yugoslavia, France, Poland, Hungary, and Australia.[84] The rule was not a quantitative quota, but for the 20-percent countries, it operated as a qualitative one, compelling them to march at quite a distance behind what India and Turkey could produce in any given year.

For this reason, had this rule remained intact, the US never would have received the raw materials necessary to launch OxyContin from Australia. Consequently, the effort to undermine it, kicked off by an undiscussed amendment to the 1988 Anti-Drug Abuse Act calling for an executive review of the 80–20 provision, tells us a lot about the forces at work to expand the opioid supply.[85] When the report commissioned by Congress recommended preserving the rule for three more years, Democratic Congressman William Hughes of New Jersey, chair of the House Judiciary Committee's Subcommittee on Crime, convened a hearing on the "Licit Importation of Opium," the only public forum to feature a lengthy discussion of the 80–20 rule.[86] Testimony provided at the 1990 hearing clearly established Johnson & Johnson's intent to rework narcotic raw material importation rules in favor of greater amounts sourced in Australia. They initially did so by underscoring or inflating concerns of diversion in the Indian supply—over the objections of the State Department, which sent delegates to Congress to attest to the success and importance of 80–20, and minimize concerns regarding illicit diversion from Indian stockpiles.

Interestingly, the other major importer of narcotic raw material, Mallinckrodt, did not join Johnson & Johnson corporate executives in their depictions of an unruly Indian supply of opium gum. Undoubtedly this was because, at the time, Mallinckrodt valued the Indian supply for its rich alkaloid content, including the presence of thebaine, the base for synthesizing oxycodone (the active ingredient in drugs like OxyContin and Percocet). In contrast, representatives from Johnson & Johnson—specifically, its international office of Noramco—pledged that Australian poppy straw promised a more professional approach, with a product easier to process, subject to high productivity per hectare (and therefore less diversion), and isolated on the island of Tasmania to boot. No one raised a concern regarding diversion of concentrated poppy straw (CPS) from Turkey—which was not surprising, given that the method of producing straw was engineered in order to avoid lancing the poppy flower for opium gum, the easiest path to heroin. DEA official Gene Haislip noted that "diversion of narcotic materials in Turkey for the production of heroin virtually disappeared" as a result of the CPS method.[87] The Noramco president agreed, adding that "Turkey has not been the source of illicit narcotics since, at US urging, it banned opium production," by which he meant the extraction of opium gum.[88] But he disputed the stability of the Turkish supply, arguing that fluctuations resulted in higher prices. The DEA disagreed, noting that the "price for [narcotic raw material] has decreased over the past decade, has not increased, although the price for virtually every other commodity has increased in the world."[89]

Adding weight to the DEA's testimony was Mallinckrodt's insistence that the company had "relied on the countries, traditional countries, for over one hundred years, and we have never been unhappy with price or availability."[90] In the main, those at the hearing avoided discussion of the obvious market dynamics in play. That is, both Turkey and India supplied narcotic raw material using state-owned enterprises, while Australian poppy fields were owned and operated by Glaxo, a French company, and Tasmanian Alkaloids, a subsidiary of Johnson & Johnson. But the Mallinckrodt representative alluded to this when he offered a parting and prophetic shot, warning that "placing the US supply of this regulated specialty in the hands of a very few foreign corporations will invite abuse and trouble."[91]

Years later, when Oklahoma sued Johnson & Johnson for its role in fomenting the opioid crisis, the role of Tasmanian Alkaloids became a focus of the prosecution's case. Internal documents obtained in discovery and revealed during the trial disclosed the boasts of Johnson & Johnson executives when, in 1998, they brought "Norman" to market, a poppy variety bred to be particularly high in thebaine. But gains in the poppy field would mean little unless the company found a way to import the CPS-thebaine into the American market, where 80–20 effectively capped their imports based on what Turkey and India produced. Recognizing this, since 1990 (if not before), Johnson & Johnson dedicated itself to circumventing the rule. Yet, despite support from allies in Congress, the State Department held firm in defending 80–20. The crucial turning point came when, at some point, Mallinckrodt became convinced that it, too, would benefit from the proliferation of CPS-thebaine sources. According to the *Wall Street Journal*, in April of 2000, months before a buyout from corporate giant Tyco, Mallinckrodt joined Noramco in lobbying "for the DEA to change the 80/20 rule to 60/40 over three years," or, alternatively, "exempting thebaine altogether."[92]

Remarkably, the DEA chose the latter option. Frank Sapienza, in charge of the DEA office tasked with raw material import and production quotas and therefore responsible for this decision, later founded the private consulting firm The Drug and Chemical Advisory Group, LLC. His name is cited in an email released as part of the multi-jurisdiction opioid lawsuit as someone "on retainer" who would work with the (now defunct) American Pain Foundation (APF) to "get 'people who know the DEA, how they work, who they answer to, their vulnerabilities, etc.' in a room to help APF devise a plan to successfully change DEA policy/ actions regarding prescription pain medicines." In a different document in this same case he is identified as an "outside contractor" who works for Mallinckrodt, one of the main beneficiaries of the 80–20 exception.[93]

Officials from the DEA would later hint to journalists that CPS-thebaine had always been exempt from 80–20. As a result, it is sometimes reported as such, on the basis that 80–20 targeted only morphine, a necessary conversion stage to heroin. But this is not the case. CPS of any sort, including that which came from Turkey, was extraordinarily difficult to convert to heroin, as the president of Noramco acknowledged himself in testimony before Congress in 1990 (and so too did the DEA). Nor do any of these *ex post facto* rationalizations account for Johnson & Johnson's decade-long fight to end 80–20. Most importantly, the entire logic of 80–20 rested on the "80" portion; that is, preserving the bulk of market access for Turkey and India in order to preempt any temptation for diversion of *their* product. Following the logic behind the rule, the appropriate question was whether any Indian opium gum would be displaced by CPS-thebaine, not whether the Tasmanian product itself was likely to be diverted.

But international statecraft was the least of the concerns of corporate executives at Noramco. Instead, as internal documents provided at trial reveal, Johnson & Johnson was interested in a "vertically integrated" supply chain for oxycodone, one in which they could reap benefits from seed to sale. The real inducement to Tasmanian product was that it was privately held; in fact, in many ways, the thebaine exception is an unheralded privatization scheme. In both India and Turkey, pharmaceutical corporations contended with state-operated enterprises for narcotic raw material, entities that they could not control or purchase. Accordingly, led by Johnson & Johnson, they opted to obviate the necessity of dealing with them at all—first by disparaging Indian supply, and later, by lobbying the DEA directly to change the 80–20 rule.[94] From this seemingly small concession involving an obscure portion of an opaque system of drug regulation, Noramco grew into a giant, supplanting Turkish and Indian supply.[95] "By 2015," according to the *Washington Post*, "Noramco supplied 65 percent of the oxycodone, 54 percent of the hydrocodone and 60 percent of the morphine and codeine used by drug makers in the

US market." The same report also notes that, as the opioid crisis came to the attention of lawmakers in 2016, Johnson & Johnson sold off both Noramco and Tasmanian Alkaloids.⁹⁶

From this one regulatory encounter, different threads of the neoliberal project are laid bare: a revolving door, this time at the DEA; unbranded advocacy of the American Pain Foundation; a technical, insider-based ploy designed to convey adherence to an important regulatory rule, but in reality undertaken in order to vitiate it; and privatization of the opioid supply chain. The 80–20 exception, essential to launching the opioid crisis, is also a quintessential distillation of the forces that drove it.

When Mallinckrodt and Johnson & Johnson successfully joined forces to target 80–20, they removed a de facto, qualitative quota, but did nothing to overturn the power of the DEA to set a quantitative one. Though they no longer needed to trail behind India and Turkey, they still had to comply with whatever quota on CPS-thebaine the DEA imposed. But this never worried them. As a recent Inspector General's report from the Department of Justice details, the DEA allowed import and production quotas to skyrocket for the years spanning the opioid crisis, a decision abetted by the arbitrary process involved in setting the quotas in the first place. The DEA's procedure—essentially a solicitation of manufacturers regarding how much narcotic raw material they would like to acquire and refine—involved publishing proposed numbers in the *Federal Register*, then incorporating feedback however they deemed appropriate. As one observer remarked, "The joke was that they called it a 'quota.' To be more accurate, the DEA should have simply called it 'demand.'"⁹⁷ Surprisingly, the quota-setting process still does not rest on any sort of formal scientific footing, a fact that raises a number of questions, including whether quotas might be revised downward in a way that jeopardizes the health of legacy chronic pain patients still treated with opioids.⁹⁸

The Opioid Crisis in History

It does little to redeem the reputation of Purdue Pharma to observe that the opioid crisis in the US has its roots in more than one company, and more than one drug. Purdue compiled a scandalous record, but it is not clear that its decisions were more brazen—or profitable—than others. Generic versions of OxyContin vied for market share once the basis of Purdue's patent—extended release—was found wanting. Actavis sales of oxycodone products went from "559 million in 2006 to more than 1.1 billion in 2012," according to *Washington Post* analysis of DEA data obtained via court order. More telling, its hydrocodone sales went "from 2.2 billion to nearly 3 billion," a figure that dwarfed the peak of oxycodone sales. Vicodin was always more widely prescribed than Percocet; and Percocet was always more widely prescribed than OxyContin. Mallinckrodt, makers of a generic version of Vicodin, sold the most of all. The *Post* analysis quotes one former DEA official who, after analyzing the agency's own data, professed to be "shocked." "I couldn't believe it," he told the reporter; "Mallinckrodt was the biggest, and then there was Actavis. Everyone had been talking about Purdue, but they weren't even close."[99]

What relation does legal prescribing bear to the illicit market for legally produced opioids, or opioid overdose deaths more generally? For many experts, the question is not a simple one. Physicians could prescribe OxyContin less, but dealers might traffic in it more. Likewise, if doctors prefer Vicodin but illicit users don't, then what would the prescribing of Vicodin really tell us about the early stage of the opioid crisis? These finer distinctions, not without merit or interest, kept the engine of the opioid crisis churning long after the correlation between total opioid sales and steep rise in opioid deaths—apparent in the now-famous Centers for Disease Control graph of 2011[100]—could no longer be denied.

One former official from the DEA, hired by the nation's most powerful drug distributors as an expert witness, carried an intellectual intransigence to linking licit prescribing with the illicit market into America's courtrooms, as state and local prosecutors searched for answers in the midst of communities inundated with opioids.[101] "Independent drug-trafficking organizations accounted for the most significant volumes of painkillers diverted across West Virginia," she told a West Virginia court, an out-of-state supply operation that led to the state's tragic opioid overdose death total. The prosecutor responded by quoting the staggering number of hydrocodone and oxycodone pills that one drug distributor,

AmerisourceBergen, drove to the state's pharmacies (119 million doses from 2007 to 2012), and then asked the witness if she believed drug dealers transacted in comparable amounts. (They don't.) Reporter Eric Eyre of the *Charleston Gazette-Mail* of West Virginia spent many years trying to dig deeper into the relationship between counties with the most opioid prescribing and those with most opioid deaths. The result, a Pulitzer Prize–winning series, opened with an unequivocal assertion intended to shatter a decade of denial: "Follow the pills and you'll find the overdose deaths," he wrote in 2016.[102] At long last, the blunt and bigger fact of oversupply and overprescribing trumped the caveats distracting from this structuring truth.

That no tidy division exists between the illicit market and legal prescribing implicates an array of interests and actors—and a chronology. The peak of opioid prescribing came in 2012, five years after Purdue Pharma's corporate executives paid a fine for misbranding OxyContin. As I argue above, the opioid crisis points to a record of government agencies incentivized to "look the other way" when making decisions— but, in a related and equally important fashion, it also shows those same agencies incapable of introspection and hostile to change, long after mounting death tolls should have prompted review and revision. In its origin as well as the ongoing refusal to reckon with it, the opioid crisis is fundamentally a failure of our political system: a regulatory system for hire; the ability of motivated interests to exploit poorly supervised processes tucked away in little-known regions of government; and the corporate leverage made possible by austerity policies and politics. If liberalism bequeathed a fragile administrative state, then it proved no match for neoliberalism, its revolving door.

Such would be obvious to many on the ground in opioid-ravaged communities, who find little solace in the niceties typical of mainstream political discourse. Take the observations of Sergeant Mike Smith of the West Virginia State Police—according to Eric Eyre, one of the foremost authorities on opioid traffic in the state. Questioned under oath by a lawyer representing the drug distributors who ferried legal prescriptions to pharmacies throughout West Virginia, Smith recounted a conversation in which he likened pharmaceutical companies to Mexican drug cartels. Many people do; the provocative analogy underscores the greed driving the oversupply and overprescribing of opioids. But Smith actually drew the comparison for a slightly more elaborate reason:

> When I'm talking about a cartel, I'm referring to the ones, say, the Medellín with Pablo Escobar, where you have multiple people involved in the same conspiracy. And the ultimate goal is to sell drugs and produce as much money as you can. And then you branch out into corruption. And then eventually the cartel becomes so strong that it actually starts to rival the state and the federal government. And then the cartel actually becomes part of the government.[103]

For Smith, the pharmaceutical industry resembled the most notorious networks of illegal drug traffickers not just for the money its most powerful members made, but for the control they wielded over the political decisions that most affected them; their infiltration of the state itself.

Surveying the origins of the opioid crisis in the US with the equally unsparing eyes of history, who can dispute that view? It is a crude perspective for a cruel story, one that casts light on the extraordinary power the "pharma cartel" holds over the regulatory state, and the ways in which the adoption of neoliberalism facilitates access to government authorities who, though tasked with the protection of ordinary Americans, choose instead to serve corporate masters indifferent to catastrophic loss.

In the past, corporate interference on this scale, though not unheard of, would prompt some sort of reckoning for the public agencies involved, and ultimately some sort of course correction. Nothing similar, certainly nothing commensurate to its scale, has happened in the case of the opioid crisis. Instead, opioid importers and manufacturers followed regulatory procedures, creating an impression of compliance, while quietly supplanting its rigor with self-serving calculations. This insidious erosion or subtle sabotage of important rules and procedures designed to safeguard public health creates a dangerous disconnect between injurious action and provable malfeasance. What does "wrong" mean in the context of a legally approved, legally prescribed drug? Some grapple with this difficult question by personifying wrongdoing in the Sacklers, or concentrating blame on Purdue Pharma. But, as Sergeant

Smith knows, a government under such heavy influence from industry must answer for itself. When it comes to opioid crisis, neoliberal governance stands "guilty," and the only question remaining is how to count the bodies.

NOTES

1 Joseph Stiglitz, "The End of Neoliberalism and the Rebirth of History," Project-Syndicate, November 4, 2019. https://www.project-syndicate.org.

2 Abby Alpert, William N. Evans, Ethan M. J. Lieber, and David Powell, "Origins of the Opioid Crisis and Its Enduring Impacts," National Bureau of Economic Research, Working Paper 26500, November 2019, www.nber.org.

3 There were 2,749 natural and synthetic opioid overdose deaths in 1999; in 2017 there were 14,495. See "Opioid Overdose Deaths by Type of Opioid," Kaiser Family Foundation, accessed March 23, 2021, www.kff.org.

4 Harriet Ryan, Lisa Girion, and Scott Glover, "You Want a Description of Hell? OxyContin's 12-Hour Problem," Los Angeles Times, May 5, 2016, www.latimes.com.

5 On Holder, see Ryan, Girion, and Glover, "You Want a Description of Hell?"; on Kerik and Giuliani, see Barry Meier and Eric Lipton, "Under Attack, Drug Maker Turned to Giuliani For Help," New York Times, December 28, 2007, www.nytimes.com; on Mary Jo White's representation of the Sackler family, see, for example, Allison Frankel, "Purdue's Sackler Family Wants Global Opioids Settlement: Sackler Lawyer Mary Jo White," Reuters, April 22, 2019, www.reuters.com.

6 See Michael Kenney, From Pablo to Osama: Trafficking and Terrorist Networks, Government Bureaucracies, and Competitive Adaptation (University Park, Pennsylvania: Pennsylvania State University Press, 2007).

7 Alfred Marshall, Principles of Economics (London: Macmillan Co., 1890), www.econlib.org.

8 See "President's Private Sector Commission on Cost Control (the Grace Commission)," Reagan Library, accessed March 23, 2021, www.reaganlibrary.gov.

9 In 1964, in a nominating speech for Barry Goldwater, Reagan proposed making Social Security purely voluntary. As a 1976 primary candidate, he discussed the possibility of privatizing it. As president, confronting the resilient popularity of the program in the face of Health and Human Services–led proposals to cut benefits, he appointed the "Greenspan Commission," and managed only to raise the retirement age from 65 to 67 and raise the regressive payroll tax.

10 John Gary Loveman Goodman, "Does Privatization Serve the Public Interest?" Harvard Business Review (November–December 1991), www.hbr.org.

11 See the Bretton Woods Project, "IMF and World Bank's Support for Privatization Condemned by Expert," December 6, 2018, www.brettonwoodsproject.org.

12 Important scholarly treatments of the FDA include Daniel Carpenter, Reputation and Power: Organizational Image and Pharmaceutical Regulation at the FDA

(Princeton, N.J.: Princeton University Press, 2010); Philip J. Hilts, *Protecting America's Health: The FDA, Business, and 100 Years of Regulation* (Chapel Hill and London: University of North Carolina Press, 2003).

13 Though often cited as simultaneously establishing a class of "prescription" drugs for dispensation only by a doctor's script, the Harrison Narcotics Tax Act of 1914 was the first to determine that a certain class of medicines could only be obtained by prescription from a doctor; subsequent classification evolved over time, partly in response to industry lobbying. See Kathleen J. Frydl, *The Drug Wars in America, 1940–1973* (New York: Cambridge University Press, 2013).

14 Hilts, *Protecting America's Health*, 105.

15 See Frydl, *The Drug Wars in America*, chap. 3.

16 See Hilts, *Protecting America's Health*, especially 126–27.

17 On Purdue's early mastery of direct-to-physician marketing, see Sam Quinones, *Dreamland: The True Tale of America's Opiate Epidemic* (New York: Bloomsbury Press, 2015): 28–29.

18 See Frydl, *The Drug Wars in America*, chap. 3.

19 Hilts, *Protecting America's Health*, 139.

20 Carpenter, *Reputation and Power*, 418.

21 When FDA Director Herbert Ley asked his superiors to authorize a ban of an unsafe antibiotic, they refused. Ley turned to Congress, informing the chair of a congressional investigating committee that the FDA's safety files concerning the drug could be sent to him within the hour. Although the Nixon administration ultimately acceded to furnish the records, and ban the drug in question, Ley was subsequently fired, only to later appear on the master version of Nixon's infamous "enemies" list. See Hilts, *Protecting America's Health*, 176.

22 Tufts is also home to the Arthur M. Sackler Center for Medical Education, which has recently removed the Sackler name, but kept the Sackler money. Evan Gerstmann, "Hypocrisy: Tufts Scrubs the Sackler Name From Its Buildings While Keeping All Its Sackler Money," *Forbes*, December 7, 2019, www.forbes.com.

23 Hilts, *Protecting America's Health*, 255.

24 See Erin Mershon, "In Orrin Hatch's Retirement, Pharma Loses Chief Congressional Ally," *StatNews*, January 2, 2018, www.statnews.com.

25 See, for example, the extreme proposals offered by the "Council on Competitiveness" run by Vice President Dan Quayle; Carpenter, *Reputation and Power*, 458.

26 See Hilts, *Protecting America's Health*, chap. 19.

27 Mark Harrington, founder of AIDS Treatment Action Group: "We were wrong. We learned. But even by the time of our big demonstration at FDA, despite the rhetoric, we didn't see ourselves as against the FDA or as against regulation." Hilts, *Protecting America's Health*, 304.

28 "The user fees have enabled the FDA to hire more medical reviewers. Last year, 236 medical officers examined new drugs compared with 162 officers on duty in 1992, the year before the user fees took effect." David Willman, "The New FDA:

How a New Policy Led to Seven Deadly Drugs," *Los Angeles Times*, December 20, 2000, www.latimes.com.

29 Willman, "The New FDA."

30 See "The Pulitzer Prizes," Pulitzer Foundation, accessed March 23, 2021, www .pulitzer.org.

31 See, for example, Audrey D. Zhang, Jeremy Puthumana, Nicholas S. Downing, Nilay D. Shah, Harlan M. Krumholz, and Joseph S. Ross, "Assessment of Clinical Trials Supporting US Food and Drug Administration Approval of Novel Therapeutic Agents, 1995–2017," *Journal of the American Medical Association* 3, no. 4 (April 21, 2020), https://jamanetwork.com.

32 For the latest FDA pitch on renewal, see "Prescription Drug User Fee Act Reauthorization Statement," Food and Drug Administration, accessed June 23, 2020, www.fda.gov.

33 This summary draws from another *Los Angeles Times* series: Ryan, Girion, and Glover, "You Want a Description of Hell?" which in turn relies on unreleased court documents involving a West Virginia lawsuit.

34 Ryan, Girion, and Glover, "You Want a Description of Hell?"

35 Quinones, *Dreamland*, 126.

36 Ryan, Girion, and Glover, "You Want a Description of Hell?"

37 Forbes, "America's Richest Families," accessed June 23, 2020, www.forbes.com.

38 Meier drew attention to this startling revelation through the activism of Art Van Zee: see Meier, *Painkiller: A 'Wonder' Drug's Trail of Addiction and Death* (Philadelphia: Rodale, 2003), 172–75; also Art Van Zee, "The Promotion and Marketing of OxyContin: Commercial Triumph, Public Health Tragedy," *American Journal of Public Health* 99, no. 2 (February 2009): 221–27.

39 A famous quote from GM President Charles Wilson, who made it before the Senate committee reviewing his nomination for the position of Secretary of Defense in the Eisenhower administration.

40 Cf. Carpenter, who does not find much of a revolving door, an idea he dismisses repeatedly (Carpenter, *Reputation and Power*, 40, 664). Rather, he suggests that public officials may be motivated by status and esteem (43). The evidence, including what can be gleaned from the opioid crisis, suggests the contrary: in 2018, *Science* magazine published a study which found that 11 of 16 FDA medical examiners who worked on 28 drug approvals and then left the agency for new jobs are now employed by or consult for the companies they recently regulated." See Charles Piller, "Is FDA's Revolving Door Open Too Wide," *Science* 361, no. 6397 (July 6, 2018): 21.

41 See Carpenter, *Reputation and Power*, chap. 5.

42 Adam Gaffney, "Congress Just Quietly Handed Drug Companies a Dangerous Victory," *The New Republic*, December 14, 2016, https://newrepublic.com.

43 See discussion of Janet Woodcock in Joyce Frieden, "Group Calls for Moratorium on FDA approvals," *MedPage Today*, March 21, 2019, www.medpagetoday.com. Woodcock led the White House vaccination efforts under President Trump and then served as Acting Commissioner of the US Food and Drug Administration.

44 Kolodny, "How FDA Failures Contributed to the Opioid Crisis," *American Medical Association Journal of Ethics* 22, no. 8 (August 2020): 743–50.

45 See Sam Quinones, *Dreamland*, 98–99. My thanks to the anonymous reviewer of this essay who reminded me of this important point.

46 According to Carpenter, FDA has revised labeling twenty-five thousand times since 1970 (*Reputation and Power*, 612); "Labeling has been shown repeatedly to be at best a weak factor in shaping physician and patient behavior" (*Reputation and Power*, 617). On page 626, he describes his conclusion that labeling changes tend to be less severe if the initial investigator who approved the drug enjoyed long tenure at the FDA.

47 Address of Dr. James Campbell, as discussed in Clara Scher, Lauren Meador, Janet H. Van Cleave, and M. Carrington Reid, "Moving Beyond Pain as the Fifth Vital Sign and Patient Satisfaction Scores to Improve Pain Care in the 21st Century," *Pain Management Nursing* 19, no. 2 (2018): 125–29.

48 R. K. Portenoy and K. M. Foley, "Chronic Use of Opioid Analgesics in Nonmalignant Pain: Report of 38 Cases," *Pain Symptom Management* 25, no. 2 (1986): 171–86 is a seminal piece on the opioid crisis. It is mentioned as being instrumental in this shift in Andrew Kolodny, David T. Courtwright, Catherine S. Hwang, Peter Kreiner, John L. Eadie, Thomas W. Clark, G. Caleb Alexander, "The Prescription Opioid and Heroin Crisis: A Public Health Approach to an Epidemic of Addiction," *Annual Review of Public Health* 36, no. 1 (2015): 559–74.

49 See Meier, *Painkiller* and Quinones, *Dreamland*.

50 See especially Portenoy, "Opioid Therapy for Chronic Nonmalignant Pain: A Review of Critical Issues," *Journal of Pain and Symptom Management* 11, no. 4 (April 1996): 203–17.

51 Taylor Haney and Andrea Hsu, "Doctor Who Wrote 1980 Letter on Painkillers Regrets That It Fed the Opioid Crisis," *All Things Considered*, NPR, June 16, 2017, www.npr.org.

52 Juurlink's letter had been cited more than six hundred times in the thirty-seven years since its publication. "It's difficult to overstate the role of this letter," David Juurlink, a doctor of internal medicine at of Toronto, who led the analysis, told the Associated Press at the time." Sari Horwitz, Scott Higham, Dalton Bennett, and Meryl Kornfield, "The Opioid Files: Inside the Industry's Marketing Machine," *Washington Post*, December 6, 2019, www.washingtonpost.com.

53 John Fauber, "Follow the Money: Pain, Policy, and Profit," *Milwaukee Journal Sentinel/MedPage Today*, February 19, 2012, www.medpagetoday.com.

54 For a long time, few documents were issued from the 2012 investigation, only a page of letters that the Baucus and Grassley sent out. In December of 2020, Senators Grassley and Wyden released more material.

55 : US Senate Homeland Committee, Ranking Member, "Fueling an Epidemic: Report 2," accessed June 23, 2020, www.hsgac.senate.gov. See especially p. 4 for chart of funding of unbranded advocacy organizations, including Washington Legal Foundation.

56 Report disclosing ties between opioid funders and the Mayday Fund, Open Society (among others): US House of Representatives Offices of Katherine Clark and Hal Rogers, "Corrupting Influence: Purdue and the WHO," May 22, 2019, https:// katherineclark.house.gov.

57 Charles Ornstein and Tracy Weber, "American Pain Foundation Shuts Down as Senators Launch Investigation of Prescription Narcotics," *Pro Publica*, May 8, 2012, www.propublica.org.

58 "The article did not disclose that their UW Pain and Policy Studies Group already had pocketed most of the $2.5 million it would be paid over the years by the very companies that made the dangerous drugs—firms that stood to lose if prescribing rules were tightened, a *Journal Sentinel* investigation found." John Fauber, "UW a Force in Pain Drug Growth," *Milwaukee Journal Sentinel*, April 2, 2011, http:// archive.jsonline.com. "In 2011, the WHO Collaborating Centre for Policy and Communications in Cancer Care at the University of Wisconsin Pain and Policy Studies Group revealed that from 1999 to 2010, it had accepted over $1.6 million from Purdue." US House of Representatives Offices of Katherine Clark and Hal Rogers, "Corrupting Influence."

59 See Fauber, "UW a Force in Pain Drug Growth."

60 Martino counts thirty-three, but using the same data I count twenty-two. See Ann M. Martino, "In Search of a New Ethic For Treating Patients with Chronic Pain: What Can Medical Boards Do?" *Journal of Law, Medicine & Ethics* 26, no. 4 (1998): 332–49. Marino marks 1988 as the first year, but data in the article she cites for this information indicates that Utah formulated the first-in-nation guideline in 1987. NB: the authors of the article she cites were, at the time of writing, affiliated with the UW Pain and Policy Studies Group discussed above.

61 "A review of the available data on state medical board actions nationwide for the period from 1990 to 1996 reveals that the perception of regulatory risk far exceeds the reality. Indeed, relatively few (less than 5 percent) of the disciplinary actions taken for overprescribing by state medical boards in any given year directly concern the treatment of chronic pain-malignant or nonmalignant-in patients." Martino, "In Search of a New Ethic For Treating Patients with Chronic Pain."

62 D. E. Joranson, "State Pain Commissions: New Vehicles for Progress?" *American Pain Society Bulletin* 6, no. 1 (1996): 7–9.

63 I learned of the support of the Mayday Fund in Diane E. Hoffmann and Anita J. Tarzian, "Achieving the Right Balance in Oversight of Physician Opioid Prescribing for Pain: The Role of State Medical Boards," *Journal of Law, Medicine & Ethics*, 31 (2003): 21–40.

64 The introduction thanks the Robert Wood Johnson Foundation for original funding, and the American Academy of Pain Medicine, the American Pain Society, the American Society of Law, Medicine, and Ethics, and the University of Wisconsin Pain and Policy Studies Group "for their contributions."

65 Diane E. Hoffmann and Anita J. Tarzian, "Achieving the Right Balance in Oversight of Physician Opioid Prescribing for Pain: The Role of State Medical Boards," *Journal of Law, Medicine & Ethics*, 31 (2003): 21–40.

66 Kessler seems to be referring to a survey, funded by Mayday, in which people reported an unwillingness to become "dependent" on over-the-counter relief like Tylenol; it's hard for me personally—let alone for a medical professional—to clinically regard that as equivalent to a fear of becoming addicted to narcotic painkillers. For Kessler's statement, see http://archive.news.yale.edu.

67 Harriet Ryan, Lisa Girion, and Scott Glover, "OxyContin Goes Global: 'We're Only Just Getting Started,'" *Los Angeles Times*, December 18, 2016, www.latimes.com.

68 Kessler currently serves as an expert witness to governments suing opioid manufacturers and distributors.

69 Hoover v. Agency for Health Care Administration, 676 So. 2d 1380 (Fla. Dist. Ct. App. 1996).

70 Corky Siemaszko, "Dr. Katherine Hoover, Accused of Fueling WV Opioid Crisis, Still Thinks She Did Nothing Wrong," NBC News, September 25, 2018, www.nbcnews.com.

71 "In the Matter of Lucas Anthony DiLeo," Court of Appeal of Louisiana, Fourth Circuit, September 28, 1995, https://casetext.com/case/matter-of-dileo.

72 More cases should be examined as part of this effort to distort the nature and degree of punishment for prescribing. See the discussion of *Hollabough v. Arkansas State Medical Board*, https://casetext.com, in C. S. Hyman, "Pain Management and Disciplinary Action: How Medical Boards Can Remove the Barriers to Effective Treatment," *Journal of Law, Medicine & Ethics*, 24 (1996): 338–43. Ultimately, the Arkansas State Medical Board suspended Denise Hollabough's license to prescribe controlled substances several times; she repeatedly violated those orders ("Pill Doctor's' License Suspended," May 26, 2010, www.areawidenews.com). The same situation applied to *Williams v. Tennessee Board of Medical Examiners*, where the court found in favor of the appellant for the same reason. Years later, in 2015, Dr. William Williams was named in the state of Tennessee's filing against drug distributor AmerisourceBergen, where he was cited for discipline from the Tennessee state board for failing to keep adequate medical records when prescribing controlled substances. In response, he voluntarily surrendered his license to manage his pain clinic, as shown in *State of Tennessee ex rel. Herbert H. Slatery III, Attorney General and Reporter v. AmerisourceBergen Drug Corporation*, https://www.tn.gov/content/dam/tn/attorneygeneral/documents/pr/2019/pr19-50-complaint.pdf. Finally, see *Sneij v. Department of Professional Regulation, Board of Medical Examiners*, https://casetext.com, cited in S. H. Johnson, "Disciplinary Actions and Pain Relief: An Analysis of the Pain Relief Act," *Journal of Law, Medicine & Ethics*, 24 (1996): 319–27. The court again demanded that the state board adduce a standard of care if its members wanted to charge a violation—though it also conceded that Dr. Sneij kept inadequate records and that his memory of the individual cases

in question was "somewhat shaky." Taken together, these proceedings demonstrate that, far from an atmosphere of persecution, state boards managed to locate what appear to be appropriate targets for investigation; and that, if and when a board failed to articulate a standard of medical care that the physician violated as part of that review, the courts stood ready to seize upon that error to reverse some or all of the board's decision.

73 Sally Satel wrote a 2004 piece in the *New York Times* devoted to Fisher: "Doctors Behind Bars: Treating Pain is Now Risky Business," *New York Times*, October 19, 2004, www.nytimes.com. Dr. Satel herself later became the subject of one installment in journalist David Armstrong's work to unmask unbranded advocacy: Armstrong, "Inside Purdue Pharma's Media Playbook: How it Planted the Opioid Anti-story," *Pro Publica*, November 19, 2019, www.propublica.org.

74 "Shasta County Physician, Two Pharmacy Operators Arrested for Felony Medi-Cal Fraud," State of California Department of Justice, February 18, 1999, https://oag.ca.gov.

75 Holcomb B. Noble, "A Shift in the Treatment of Chronic Pain," *New York Times*, August 9, 1999, www.nytimes.com.

76 *Medical Board of California vs. Fisher*, File No. 02-1999-95522, http://4pqtientsafety.org.

77 Office of the Inspector General, US Department of Justice, "Review of the Drug Enforcement Administration's Regulatory and Enforcement Efforts to Control the Diversion of Opioids," (2019), https://oig.justice.gov. Overall opiate prescribing in Medicaid increases 309 percent from 1996 to 2002; see Judy Zerzan, Nancy E. Morden, Stephen Soumerai, Dennis Ross-Degnan, Elizabeth Roughead, Fang Zhang, Linda Simoni-Wastila, and Sean D. Sullivan, "Trends and Geographic Variation of Opiate Medication Use in State Medicaid Fee-for-Service Programs, 1996 to 2002," *Medical Care* 44, no. 11 (November 2006):1005–10, https://pubmed.ncbi.nlm.nih.gov.

78 Catherine S. Hwang, Elizabeth M. Kang, Yulan Ding, Josephine Ocran-Appiah, Jana K. McAninch, Judy A. Staffa, Cynthia J. Kornegay, and Tamra E. Meyer, "Patterns of Immediate-Release and Extended-Release Opioid Analgesic Use in the Management of Chronic Pain, 2003–2014," *Journal of the American Medical Association Network Open* 1, no. 2 (June 1, 2018): e180216, https://doi.org/10.1001/jamanetworkopen.2018.0216.

79 Jonathan K. Phillips, Morgan A. Ford, and Richard J. Bonnie, eds., *Pain Management and the Opioid Epidemic* (Washington, DC: National Academies Press, 2017). Link to graph: www.nap.edu.

80 Paul Zielbauer, "New Campus High: Illicit Prescription Drugs," *New York Times*, March 24, 2000, www.nytimes.com.

81 Paul Tough, "The Alchemy of OxyContin," *New York Times*, July 29, 2001, www.nytimes.com.

82 At the time, the office was known as the Bureau of Narcotics and Dangerous Drugs; later it became the Drug Enforcement Agency; and still later, the Drug

Enforcement Administration. I have chosen to refer to the office by its current name to avoid confusion.

83 See Frydl, *The Drug Wars in America*.
84 Found in *Federal Register* 46, no. 159, August 18, 1981, www.govinfo.gov.
85 Public Law 100–690, www.govinfo.gov.
86 "The Licit Importation of Opium," Hearing before the Subcommittee on Crime of the Committee on the Judiciary, House of Representatives, One hundred-and-first Congress, Second Session, February 27, 1990—United States Congress, House Committee on the Judiciary, Subcommittee on Crime.
87 "The Licit Importation of Opium," 31.
88 Comments of Mr. Raymond Stratmeyer, vice president of Johnson & Johnson International, of New Brunswick, NJ. Mr. Stratmeyer also served as president of Noramco, Inc. J & J. in "The Licit Importation of Opium," 46.
89 Haislip in "The Licit Importation of Opium," 41.
90 "The Licit Importation of Opium," 103.
91 "The Licit Importation of Opium," 73.
92 Steve Stecklow and Jonathan Karp, "Opium Importers Assail Rule that Favors India and Turkey," *Wall Street Journal*, April 3, 2000.
93 See the following documents filed in the multi-jurisdictional lawsuit against opioid manufacturers and distributors: *In re: National Prescription Opiate Litigation, Northern District of Ohio*, ohnd-1:2017-md-02804, exhibit 504, www.docketbird.com; and *In re: National Prescription Opiate Litigation, Northern District of Ohio*, ohnd-1:2017-md-02804, Gillies, John (Mallinckrodt) 02-07-19 Redacted, www.docketbird.com.
94 For the influence campaign on the DEA, see minute 3:37 of "Opioid Trial, Day 2 – Afternoon Session," The Oklahoman, streamed live on May 29, 2019, YouTube video, 8:29:38, www.youtube.com/watch?v=8e5nSPIQGgE. See also Peter Whoriskey, "How Johnson & Johnson Companies Used a 'Super Poppy' to Make Narcotics for America's Most Abused Opioid Pills," *Washington Post*, March 26, 2020, www.washingtonpost.com.
95 Changes to the source and formulation of legal opioid supply deserve to be paired with similar transformations in the illegal market—see, Frydl, "White Powder Heroin" (forthcoming)—as essential drivers of the opioid crisis. Both market transformations can be traced to US policy decisions.
96 Whoriskey, "How Johnson & Johnson Companies Used a 'Super Poppy.'"
97 Bono quoted in Whoriskey, "How Johnson & Johnson Companies Used a 'Super Poppy.'"
98 Kathleen Frydl, presentation to the National Academies' Committee On Rising Midlife Mortality, October 21, 2019, www.nationalacademies.org.
99 Aaron C. Davis, Shawn Boburg, and Robert O'Harrow Jr., "Little-known Makers of Generic Drugs Played Central Role in Opioid Crisis, Records Show," *Washington Post*, July 27, 2019, www.washingtonpost.com.

100 Centers for Disease Control and Prevention, "Morbidity and Mortality Weekly Report," November 4, 2011, accessed October 1, 2020, www.cdc.gov.

101 Mary Roche, as reported in Eric Eyre, *Death in Mud Lick: A Coal Country Fight against the Drug Companies that Delivered the Opioid Epidemic* (New York: Scribner, 2020), 145–47.

102 Eric Eyre, "Drug Firms Poured 780M Painkillers in WV Amid Rise of Overdoses," *Charleston Gazette Mail*, December 17, 2016, www.wvgazettemail.com.

103 Smith quoted in Eyre, *Death in Mud Lick*, 141.

ACKNOWLEDGMENTS

This book was crafted and completed during the Great Pandemic of 2020–21. As a result, nothing went as planned. The University of Kansas Center for the Military, War, and Society Studies, directed by Beth Bailey, had offered generous support for a series of workshops that would have brought our War on Drugs crew together in Lawrence in the spring of 2020 for collaborative conversations and public presentations. With additional institutional support from KU, including assistance from Richard Godbeer at the Hall Center for the Humanities, we would have "met in person" over lovely meals and generous libations. Instead, we all learned to love Zoom.

In the midst of childcare crises, closed archives, professional disruptions, and every other sort of shutdown exigency, we carried on the work. With speed and precision, we crafted our individual essays, passed them around for comment, and got this book done. My utmost thanks to all of the book's contributors, who soldiered on in the midst of it all.

Thanks, as well, to NYU Press editor Clara Platter, who championed this book from its earliest days. She has been a stalwart supporter of our collective effort, solving problems when they arose, finding superb readers for both the project proposal and the book manuscript, and making sure that we would have a book that would make us all proud. We are grateful to everyone at NYU Press for their extraordinary efforts on the book's behalf.

The manuscript readers, Isaac Campos and Peter Andreas, made this book smarter, more accurate, and more engaged with the burgeoning scholarship on drugs in modern history. Working with these brilliant scholars was an honor. Thanks, too, for the strong support and assistance from two of the doyens of drug history, David Courtwright and Paul Gootenberg.

Final thanks to Beth Bailey, who helped me conceptualize this project from soup to nuts and whose Center for Military, War, and Society Studies provided needed support, even if it was not the support we had originally planned. Without that assistance and Beth's partnership, this project would never have gotten off the ground.

ABOUT THE EDITOR

DAVID FARBER is the Roy A. Roberts Distinguished Professor at the University of Kansas. He has published numerous books on recent United States history, including Chicago '68, *The Age of Great Dreams*, *Sloan Rules*, *Everybody Ought to be Rich*, *Crack*, *The Rise and Fall of Modern American Conservatism*, and *Taken Hostage*. He has lectured on drug policy, American politics, and modern US history in France, Germany, Portugal, the United Kingdom, the Netherlands, Ireland, Canada, Australia, Japan, China, Russia, Indonesia, Israel, Lebanon, and throughout the United States.

JAMES BRADFORD is Assistant Professor of History at Berklee College of Music, and Adjunct Lecturer at Babson College. His book, *Poppies, Politics, and Power: Afghanistan and the Global History of Drugs and Diplomacy* (2019), is the only substantive history of the Afghan drug trade. He has published in the *Journal of Iranian Studies, Illegal Cannabis Cultivation in the World*, and the *Oxford University Handbook of Drug History*. He teaches on the history of the global illicit drug trade and addiction, with an emphasis on Afghanistan and US drug policy.

ELAINE CAREY is the Dean of the College of Arts and Social Sciences at Oakland University Northwest. Formerly, she was Chair of the Department of History at St. John's University in Queens, New York, and the Lloyd Sealy Research Fellow at CUNY's John Jay College of Criminal Justice. She is the author of *Plaza of Sacrifices: Gender, Power, and Terror in 1968 Mexico* (2005) and the award-winning *Women Drug Traffickers: Mules, Bosses, and Organized Crime* (2014). She is also co-editor with Andrae Marak of *Smugglers, Brothels, and Twine: Transnational Flows of Contraband and Vice in North America* (2011) and the editor/author of the textbook *Protests in the Streets: 1968 Across the Globe* (2016). Currently, she is working on a book-length manuscript: "Trains, Planes, Automobiles, and Narcotanks: A Dope History."

EMILY DUFTON is a drug historian and writer based near Washington, DC. She is the author of *Grass Roots: The Rise and Fall and Rise of Marijuana in America* (2017). The University of Chicago Press will publish her second book, on the history of medication-assisted treatment for opioid addiction, in 2022.

ERIKA DYCK is a Professor and a Tier 1 Canada Research Chair in the History of Health and Social Justice at the University of Saskatchewan.

She is the author or co-author of: *Psychedelic Psychiatry* (2008); *Facing Eugenics* (2013); *Managing Madness* (2017); and *Challenging Choices* (2020). She is the co-editor of *Psychedelic Prophets: The Letters of Aldous Huxley and Humphry Osmond* (2018); and *A Culture's Catalyst: Historical Encounters with Peyote* (2016). Dyck is the co-editor of the *Canadian Bulletin for Medical History/Bulletin canadien d'histoire de la medicine*, the co-editor of the *Intoxicating Histories* book series, and guest editor for the Chacruna Institute for Psychedelic Plant Medicines.

DAVID FARBER is the Roy A. Roberts Distinguished Professor at the University of Kansas. His most recent book is *Crack: Rock Cocaine, Street Capitalism, and the Decade of Greed* (2019).

KATHLEEN J. FRYDL holds a PhD in history and specializes in American political development in the twentieth century. Her published work includes two books: the award-winning *The GI Bill* (2009), and *The Drug Wars in America, 1940–1973* (2013), named one of *Vox's* "Best Books We Read in 2014." Her interest in government response to "disorder" goes beyond illicit drugs, addressing kindred subjects like kidnapping (published in *Studies in American Political Development*) and foundlings (published in the *Journal of Policy History*). Writing for a general audience, her work has appeared in *Vox, Dissent,* and *Washington Monthly*.

DAVID HERZBERG (University at Buffalo-SUNY) is a historian of drugs with a focus on the legal kind—psychoactive pharmaceuticals. His work has appeared in numerous scholarly and medical journals, in popular media, and in two books: *Happy Pills in America: From Miltown to Prozac* (2009) and *White Market Drugs: Big Pharma and the Hidden History of Addiction in America* (2020). He is also Coordinator of Addiction Studies at the University at Buffalo and co-editor of the journal *Social History of Alcohol and Drugs*.

PETER C. PIHOS is an assistant professor of history at Western Washington University. He earned a BA at Harvard, a JD at New York University, and his PhD at the University of Pennsylvania. A scholar of African American history, criminal justice, and legal history, he is completing a book on Black police officers in the post–Second World War period.

MICHAEL POLSON is a Visiting Assistant Professor in anthropology at Davidson College. A founding member of UC–Berkeley's Cannabis Research Center, he investigates prohibition, legalization and their ramifications for political economy and ecology. He has published in journals from multiple disciplines and is currently working on a book manuscript that draws on a decade of qualitative research on cannabis cultivation.

LUCAS RICHERT is George Urdang Chair in the History of Pharmacy at the University of Wisconsin-Madison. Richert is the author of *A Prescription for Scandal* (2014), which won the Arthur Miller Centre First Book Prize in 2015. He is also author or editor of *Strange Trips* (2019), *Break On Through* (2019), and Cannabis: Global Histories (2021). Richert serves as an editor for the journals *The Social History of Alcohol and Drugs* and *History of Pharmacy and Pharmaceuticals*. He is the Historical Director of the American Institute of the History of Pharmacy.

AILEEN TEAGUE is an Assistant Professor of International Affairs at Texas A&M's Bush School of Government and Public Service. She previously held a postdoctoral fellowship at Brown University's Watson Institute for International and Public Affairs. Teague earned her PhD in History from Vanderbilt University in 2018 and served in the US Marine Corps from 2006 to 2014. Her work has been published in academic journals including *Diplomatic History* and the *Social History of Alcohol and Drugs*. She is currently drafting a book manuscript that examines the effects of United States drug policies and policing efforts on Mexican politics and society in the 1970s and 1980s.

ALEXIS TURNER is completing their dissertation, "Lost Souls Delivered: LSD, Technopolitics, and the Battle for the Soul of a Nation, 1949–1980," at Harvard University in the Department of the History of Science. Their awards include the Herbert Dissertation Fellowship in the History of Science, Harvard University.

INDEX

Angola, 97

Anslinger, Harry J., 26–28, 34n30, 98–99, 164–165, 182–183; and marijuana as "Assassin of Youth," 27, 161–162, 164. *See also* Federal Bureau of Narcotics

Anti-Drug Abuse Act of 1986, 52, 54–55, 232–233

Anti-Drug Abuse Act of 1988, 12n4, 326–327

anti-smuggling units (ASUs), 255–256, 260

Antonoff, Michael, 172–173

Appalachia, 325. *See also* opioid crisis

Arellano Félix, Enendina, 77

Armando Villela, Luis, 83

Armenteras, Dolors 119

aspirin, 24, 286. *See also* Bayer

"Assassin of Youth," marijuana as. *See* Anslinger, Harry

Astorga, Luis, 229

AstraZeneca, 319

Atlanta, Georgia, 165, 169–171

Aurora, Illinois, 65, 73

Australia, 259; export of concentrated poppy straw (CPS), 326–329

Automation of Reports and Consolidated Order Systems (ARCOS), 281, 285

Avilés Pérez, Pedro, 75–76, 81; in *Narcos: Mexico*, 75

azidothymidine (AZT), 312–313

Azzam, Abraham L., 67

Back-to-the-Land movement, 106–107, 110–111, 116. *See also* counterculture

Badakhshan, Afghanistan, 244, 248–249, 265n33

Bail Reform Act, 80

Baltimore, Maryland, 56–57

barbiturates, 29, 276–277, 279, 283, 289, 291, 298n37, 310–311. *See also* Controlled Substances Act of 1970; prescription drugs

Bari, Judi, 113

Barrie, Michael, 197

Barron, Frank, 198

Baucus, Max, 319

Bauer, William, 134

Bayer, 24. *See also* aspirin; heroin; pharmaceutical industry

Bayh, Birch, 279

Bearman, Joshua, 44

Belgium, 110

Belize, 103

Bennett, William, 62n66

Bensinger, Peter, 225–226

benzodiazepines, 291, 323. *See also* Valium

Beveridge Report, 308

Bias, Len, 54

Biden, Joe, 1–3, 20–21, 55, 62n68

Biphetamine-20, 285

birth control, 279

Black Gangster Disciples. *See* organized crime

Black Panther Party, 49

Board Briefs (newsletter), 289

Bolivia, 119

border patrol (US Border Patrol), 159, 220, 254, 261

Bourne, Peter, 171–173

Brazil, 97, 104

Brazille, Leo, 47

Brotherhood of Eternal Love. *See* organized crime; surfer culture

Brown, Pat, 18

Brownell, Herbert Jr., 18

Buckley, William, 13n9

Buendía, Miguel, 229–230

Bureau of Alcohol and Other Drug Abuse, 284

Bureau of Alcohol, Tobacco, and Firearms, 82

Bureau of Chemistry. *See* Food and Drug Administration

Bureau of Drug Abuse Control, 278, 296n20. *See also* Bureau of Narcotics